GEORGE GASCOIGNE'S

A Hundreth Sundrie Flowres

Edited, with an Introduction and Notes
by C. T. Prouty

Volume XVII   University of Missouri Studies   Number 2

University of Missouri Press
Columbia

HOUSTON PUBLIC LIBRARY

78-159194-b

R01 0814 1850

Copyright © 1970 by
The Curators of the
University of Missouri
University of Missouri Press, Columbia, Missouri 65201
ISBN 0-8262-0591-7
Library of Congress Card Number 43-52910
Printed and bound in the United States of America
Originally printed by the University of Missouri
as Volume XVII, Number 2
of the University of Missouri Studies, 1942
Reprinted 1970 by the University of Missouri Press
All rights reserved

PREFACE

The reasons for this edition of George Gascoigne's *A Hundreth Sundrie Flowres* will, I trust, be made apparent in the ensuing Introduction. That the edition has appeared is due to the kind efforts of several individuals and institutions and to them I wish to acknowledge my indebtedness.

The Librarian of Emmanuel College, Cambridge, has kindly consented to the use of the College's copy of the *Flowres* as the basis of the present text. The Research Council of the University of Missouri has generously granted funds for the purchase of photostats and for clerical assistance.

During my tenure of a Research Fellowship at the Folger Shakespeare Library I was afforded not only the time to collate the text with the two Folger copies of the *Flowres,* but as well the invaluable advice and counsel of the Director, Dr. J. Q. Adams; his Assistant, Dr. James G. McManaway; the Reference Librarian, Dr. Giles Dawson; and the Chief Bibliographer, Dr. Edwin E. Willoughby.

My colleagues at the University of Missouri have been indeed generous in giving of their time and advice. Dr. A. H. R. Fairchild, in particular, has given me the benefit of his wide Elizabethan scholarship. Dr. H. M. Belden, editor of the *Studies,* has been extremely helpful by reason of his considerable knowledge of Elizabethan and Stuart textual problems.

My wife has once again devoted herself untiringly to the problems attendant upon an interest in George Gascoigne. In this instance she has not only checked the text against all the copies collated, but, as well, she has checked all the references.

There remain two explanations of my bibliographical procedure. Throughout I refer by the short title *George Gascoigne* to my recent biographical and critical study *George Gascoigne, Elizabethan Courtier, Soldier, and Poet,* Columbia University Press, New York, 1942. The short title, *Works,* refers to J. W. Cunliffe's *The Complete Works of George Gascoigne,* 2 vols., Cambridge, 1907-10.

Since my purpose is, as will appear in the Introduction, to present as nearly as may be *A Hundreth Sundrie Flowres* as originally planned by Gascoigne, I have not reproduced the two plays which made up the first part of the 1573 volume. The numbering of the poems and the numbering of the lines of both prose and verse do not appear in the original. They are my additions designed for greater ease of reference.

C. T. PROUTY

Larrabee's Point
Shoreham, Vermont
September 26, 1942

To
H. S. BENNETT

CONTENTS

PUBLISHER'S FOREWORD

C. T. Prouty's edition of George Gascoigne's *A Hundreth Sundrie Flowres* first appeared in 1942 and has long been recognized as the standard edition of Gascoigne's work. Because copies of that paperbound, limited edition have become quite scarce in recent years, interested scholars have been forced to work from microfilm.

The present reprinting is intended to make accessible to a new generation of scholars the work of Gascoigne, an important figure in Renaissance English literature, and the historical and textual criticism of Professor Prouty, for the work of both men has proved to be most durable.

T.H.L.

Columbia, Missouri
September, 1970

INTRODUCTION

FOREWORD

When George Gascoigne proceeded with his plans to publish his accumulated works in the winter of 1572-73,[1] he not only created a volume of verse and prose that stands in the forefront of early Elizabethan literature, but as well, through his consistent desire for mystery, posed a series of technical problems which have been largely responsible for the comparative disregard that has hitherto been accorded *A Hundreth Sundrie Flowres*. In the first place, the book itself presents a number of bibliographical questions which, in my judgment, can only be answered by relating the printing to events which occurred in Gascoigne's affairs during this winter. Secondly, the lack of an author's name has recently led to the unwarrantable assumption that *A Hundreth Sundrie Flowres* is an anthology.[2] In addition to these technical matters, there are certain literary and social aspects of the volume which were concealed by the poet's attempts to evade censorship in his revised and expanded second edition entitled *The Posies of George Gascoigne*. In this he altered the original order of the poems and quite successfully persuaded the world to accept his autobiographical prose tale, "The Adventures of Master F.J.," as a translation from the Italian of a nonexistent Bartello. An examination of these several problems is a complicated matter that is best understood by the sectional presentation which ensues.

BIBLIOGRAPHICAL PROBLEMS

At the present time ten copies[3] of *A Hundreth Sundrie Flowres* are known, and I list them herewith.

1. Emmanuel College (Cambridge) Library
2. Cambridge University Library
3. British Museum (George III)
4. British Museum (Grenville)
5. Bodleian
6. Folger Library (Folger)
7. Folger Library (Harmsworth)
8. Huntington Library
9. White
10. Pforzheimer[4]

The first four, as well as the two Folger copies and the Huntington Library

---

1 For the details of this period in the poet's life *vide infra* pp. 13-17.

2 *A Hundreth Sundrie Flowres*, ed. by B. M. Ward, London, 1926, pp. vii-xi.

3 Mr. Ward (*A Hundreth Sundrie Flowres, op. cit.*, p. viii) noted the British Museum and Bodleian copies. Miss Ambrose, in her review of Ward's book (*M. L. R.*, XXII, p. 214), noted the other copies in England.

4 The compilers of the catalogue, *The Carl H. Pforzheimer Library* (3 vols., N. Y. 1940), discuss the *Flowres* at length. They conclude that the title *A Hundreth Sundrie Flowres* belongs only to the second section of the work, *i.e.*, pp. 201-245. Their theory that Richard Smith was responsible for the appearance of the work ignores Gascoigne's presence in England during the printing. Secondly, their explanation of the two sections of the book as resulting from the publisher's sudden acquisition of the prose and verse seems at variance with the facts which I record below. Finally, they seem to accept Ward's theory of multiple authorship—a theory which is refuted in the section of this Introduction dealing with the authorship.

copy, have been collated for the present text and I give a bibliographical description which applies to copies 1-4 and 6-8, those which I have been able to examine.

1. Title: [Within a rule; within a border] A Hundreth sun-/drie Flowres bounde/vp in one small Poesie./*Gathered partely* (*by transla-*/tion) in the fyne outlandish Gardins/of Euripides, Ouid, Petrarke, Ariosto,/and others: and partly by inuention,/out of our owne fruitefull Or-/chardes in Englande:/Yelding sundrie svveete sauours of Tra-/gical, Comical, and Morall Discour-/ses, bothe pleasaunt and profitable to the/well smellyng noses of lear-/ned Readers./*Meritum petere, graue.*/AT LONDON,/Imprinted for Richarde Smith./

2. Colophons: [page 164, Xiiij^v] [Ornament] Printed by Henrie Bynneman/ for Richarde Smith./
   [page 445, I1iij^r/] IMPRINTED AT LON/don for Richard Smith./

3. Format: Quarto in fours

4. Collation: A^4, B^4 [1 and 2 cancelled], C-X^4, A-Y^4, Aa-Hh^4, I1^4, [I14 missing].

5. Contents before pagination:

Ai^r	Title
Ai^v	"The contents of this Booke"
Aij^r	(signature) "Printer to Reader"
Aij^v	"Printer to Reader"
Aiij^r	"Printer to Reader"
Aiij^v	"Faultes escaped"
Aiiij^r	*Supposes* title
Aiiij^v	"Prologue"
Bj$^{r \& v}$	Missing
Bij$^{r \& v}$	Missing
Biij^r	Text of *Supposes* begins.

6. Pagination: 1(Biij^r)-36Fiiij^v), 45(Gi^r)-164(Xiiij^v), 201(Ai^r)-445(I1iij^r) [Pagination of 82 and 83 is reversed and the page numbers are printed on the inside corners of the pages. There is no pagination on I1iij^r.]

7. Special notes on the Cambridge University Library copy: A few pages which were torn or lost are supplied by a modern MS., and I list these.
   1. Entirely in MS. pp. 223, 224, 307, 308, 309, 310, 331, 332, 333, 334, 353, 354, 445.
   2. Partially in MS. p. 321, lines 9-34, p. 322, lines 8-30.
   3. Thus the following signatures are missing: 307: Oii; 309: Oiii; 331: Rij; 333: Riij; 353: Uj.

From this description it appears that there are several errors and omissions which require explanation. Why are Bj and Bij missing? In the George III and Grenville copies, one can see two cut edges between Biiij^v and Cj^r and from this fact it is clear that these two pages were reversed in the folding and were cancelled. The explanation seems to be that the printing of the text of the *Supposes* began originally on Biiij with Bj, Bij, and all of A left for introductory material or else Bj and Bij contained introductory material which had to be altered.

Iiiij may have been originally an end leaf or may have been used for printing material not necessarily connected with the volume.

Errors in Pagination. The most curious features, however, are the errors in pagination. The break from 36 to 45 is obviously a printer's error since the signatures follow and the text reveals no excisions. The reversing of pages 82 and 83 is again a common typographical error. However, these errors do have a positive value in showing that all the copies which I have examined were printed from the same setting of type. The textual notes of this reprint offer further proof of this single setting of type and will thus, I trust, end any question of there having been two editions.

The pagination error which is most puzzling is the break from 164 to 201. At first glance one would be tempted to say that the intervening leaves were cancelled. There are, however, certain objections to such a theory. First, the colophon on 164 indicates an end of at least a section of the book, a fact which finds partial confirmation in that pages 1-164 contain the text of the two plays *Supposes* and *Jocasta* and nothing else. Secondly, if the system of signatures had been followed through those leaves which we might suppose to have been cancelled, page 201 would be signed Ddiij. Further, none of the copies which I have examined reveals any trace of cancellation. Therefore, the only possible conclusion seems to be that the book was printed in two sections.

Introductory Letters. A feature of the volume which supports this theory seems to have been overlooked. The letters which explain how the book came to be printed are to be found not at the beginning, as one would expect, but on page 201. On this page begins *H.W.*'s letter explaining how he got possession of the manuscript from his friend G.T., and how, realizing its intrinsic worth, he entreated his friend *A.B.* to have it imprinted. *G.T.*'s letter describes the manuscript and mentions the tale of "F.J." and "a number of *Sonets,* layes, letters, Ballades, Rondlets, verlayes and verses," but contains not a single reference to the plays, *Supposes* and *Jocasta.* After *G.T.*'s letter comes his introduction to "The Adventures of Master F.J.," which serves as the beginning of that story.

As far as I can determine, there can be only one explanation for the position of these letters and the lack of any mention of the plays. If we assume, in view of evidence which I shall submit below, that these letters were the work of Gascoigne, it follows that originally Gascoigne had no intention of publishing the plays. If he had planned to include them it would have been an easy matter to place the letters at the beginning of the book and at that point develop the character of *G.T.* as editor. Surely *G.T.* could have been the mouthpiece for considerable editorial information regarding the plays, but such a procedure was not followed.

The lack of any introductory material at the beginning of the whole volume apparently inspired the printer to write his letter to the reader which, although

placed directly after the "contents," assumes knowledge of those far removed
letters of *H.W.* and *G.T.*:

> Master .H.W. in the beginning of this worke, hath in his letter (written to the
> Readers) cunningly discharged himselfe of any such misliking, as the graver
> sort of greyheared judgers mighte (perhaps) conceive in the publication of these
> pleasant Pamphlets.[5]

Thereupon the printer excuses himself of any liability in connection with
the work and mentions "the Tragedie translated out of Euripides" and "the
comedie translated out of Ariosto." Obviously the printer is not going to explain
how "the beginning of this worke" is to be found on page 201; rather he is trying
to pass over this strange phenomenon by a casual mention of the plays which
intervene, leaving the reader to puzzle over the mystery if he so desires.

The Printer. The colophon on page 164 gives Henry Bynneman as the printer
of the first 164 pages, but this cannot be accepted as complete proof that the same
man printed the rest of the book. Evidence for such a conclusion, however, does
exist in the fact that the ornamental border of the title page is identical with the
ornament on the title page of *Historia Brevis Thomae Walsingham* which appeared
in 1574 with Bynneman's name[6] as printer. If, then, Bynneman printed the title
page of the *Flowres,* he must also have printed the other pages of sheet A which
includes the "contents." Since this contains page references for the entire volume,
Bynneman must have had the printed pages at hand and the assumption is that
he had printed the second part as well. Further confirmation of this is found in
the watermark of the paper, which is the same throughout this volume and is
identical with that used by Bynneman when, in 1576, he printed for Richard
Smith George Gascoigne's *The Steele Glas* and *The Complaynt of Phylomene.*[7]
In addition, the type used appears, to me at least, to be the same throughout the
volume. The cumulation of evidence certainly points to Bynneman as the sole
printer. A glance at the list of this printer's work as listed in *The Stationers'
Register* relieves us of any doubt as to the extent of his publications. He certainly
had sufficient presses to enable him to carry on the simultaneous printing of both
parts of the *Flowres.*

The Edition. Although Dr. Greg has shown that Miss Ambrose's theory of
two editions was based on a misapprehension,[8] I have been careful to note those
typographical peculiarities which prove that all seven collated copies were printed
from the same setting of type. Actually, the errors noted in the bibliographical

5 *Infra,* p. 47.
6 R. B. McKerrow, *Printers and Publishers Devices,* Bibliographical Society,
London, 1913, Item No. 168.
7 Examples are to be found in Charles Briquet's *Les Filigraines* (4 vols., Paris,
1907), items Nos. 11377-11382, 11384.
8 Miss Ambrose (*M. L. R.,* XXII, 214) used Arber's Bibliographical Summary
(the fifth volume of *The Stationers' Register*) to argue two editions of the *Flowres* and
the date 1572 as the year of publication. Dr. Greg (*M. L. R.,* XXII, 441-442) pointed
out that the Summary was not evidence but merely Arber's guess as to the probable
dates of publication of volumes printed in the years for which the actual *Register* is
missing.

description seem sufficient to prove such a contention; however, an examination of the "Textual Notes" will show many examples of such errors as mis-spaced words and omitted hyphens that would have been corrected in a second edition, but which appear in all copies examined. The minor variants are not of sufficient importance to be considered as more than corrections during the printing.

THE DATE OF PUBLICATION OF
A Hundreth Sundrie Flowres

It has been observed that no date of publication is given in any part of *A Hundreth Sundrie Flowres*. Two poems, however, are dated and one of these gives us a backward time limit for the publication of the volume. Poem No. 74 has the following introductory comment:

> Gascoignes voyage into *Hollande, An.* 1572. written to the ryghte honourable the Lorde Grey of *Wilton.*

The table of contents (Ai[v]) lists this same poem under the heading, "Gascoines last voyage into Holland in Marche," and the poem itself gives the 19th of March as the day of departure. Elsewhere I have shown that internal references to the siege of Haarlem and to the newly opened port of Brill date this "last voyage" as March 19, 1572/3, which thus serves as a backward limit of publication.[9] A less exact forward limit is found in Gascoigne's remarks in the introductory letters to *The Posies,* where we read:

> It is verie neare two yeares past, since (I beeing in Hollande in service with the vertuous Prince of Orenge) the most parte of these Posies were imprinted. . . .[10]

This letter bears the date, "this last day of Januarie. 1574" which must be Jan. 31, 1574/5, because the backward limit already established precludes the possibility of 1574 being two years after March 19, 1572/3, and because I have shown elsewhere that Gascoigne returned to England in the autumn of 1574, after being absent continuously since March 19, 1572/3.[11] The evidence thus is that the end of January was "verie neare" the date of publication. Since we know that this was subsequent to March 19th, I suggest April as the probable month of publication.

Other evidence found in the text itself confirms such an hypothesis. The verse narrative "Dan Bartholmew of Bathe" is incomplete in *A Hundreth Sundrie Flowres.* This rather loose narrative of separate poems, written as it were by Dan Bartholmew, is held together by the narrative links of the Reporter. One of these links is misplaced and we find it appearing, quite out of any context,

9 C. T. Prouty, "Gascoigne in the Low Countries and the Publication of *A Hundreth Sundrie Flowres," R. E. S.,* XII (1936), 139-146.
10 *Works,* I, 3.
11 *George Gascoigne,* p. 77. Dr. Greg, though unaware of the backward limit, established the spring of 1573 as the time of publication (*The Library,* 4th Series, VII, 272-73). Dr. Greg used the introductory letters to *The Posies* and Gascoigne's use of both the calendar and legal systems of dating.

between "His Farewell" and "The Reporters conclusion unfinished," with this heading:

> This should have bin placed in the dolorous discourse, before the Supplication to Care in Folio. 430.[12]

The folio reference correctly places the link between "Dan Bartholmew his Triumphe" and "Dan Bartholmews Dolorous discourses," where it explains the seemingly abrupt transition from the joy of the former to the sorrow of the latter.

The misplacing of this link when considered together with the fact that "Dan Bartholmew" is unfinished suggests not only that the printing of the volume was being carried on after Gascoigne left England, but that publication was achieved within a comparatively short time after this departure. Reference to another poem may clarify this problem in chronology. The poem which directly precedes "Dan Bartholmew" is No. 74, "Gascoignes voyage into *Hollande*." Since this was obviously written after the poet arrived in the Low Countries, and since we know that he did not return to England until the autumn of 1574, it becomes apparent that the manuscript of this poem must have been sent from Holland to the printer in London. If then we know that Gascoigne was sending copy from Holland to England, it seems reasonable to conclude that the misplaced link was a part of such copy which arrived too late for inclusion in its proper place in the text. The need for rapid publication was evidently such that Bynneman not only proceeded apace with that portion of the text in his possession without waiting to receive copy from Gascoigne, but that he finally allowed the volume to be published with the story of Dan Bartholmew still unfinished.

A suggestion as to the reason for this haste will be found in the next section, but for the present we may confine our considerations to another item of evidence which inforces my hypothesis as to the rapid printing. In the George III copy in the British Museum the table of contents appears without page references for "Gascoignes voyage" and "Dan Bartholmew." In all other copies which I have examined the page references for these two items are to be found. Therefore, it would seem that the exception noted contains the contents in the first state—a state which indicates that Bynneman was beginning the printing of the prefatory material before the compositors had set the type for the last two items in the book.

The accumulation of evidence—the misplaced Reporter's link, the unfinished nature of "Dan Bartholmew," and the omission of two page references on the first state "contents" page—all these point to a date of publication within at most a month after Gascoigne left Queenborough on March 19, 1572/3.

THE CIRCUMSTANCES OF PUBLICATION OF
A Hundreth Sundrie Flowres

The manifest haste of the printing of *A Hundreth Sundrie Flowres* with which we have been concerned in the preceding section, as well as certain of the bibliographical peculiarities of the volume, are, in my judgment, closely connected with Gascoigne's personal affairs during the winter of 1572-73.

12   *A Hundreth Sundrie Flowres*, London, [1573], p. 441.

At the end of May 1572 George Gascoigne set out with a group of professional soldiers, ardent enemies of Catholic Spain, and fortune seekers, in an attempt to remedy his decayed state. He had lost large sums of money, and, after a number of law suits, found himself locked up in Bedford gaol. To a man on whom Fortune had scowled so harshly, the rebellion of the Dutch against their Spanish overlords was a Heaven-sent opportunity to re-establish himself. The wars, however, failed to open an easy highway to success, since the Dutch were suspicious of the English volunteers and Sir Humphrey Gilbert proved a cowardly, as well as stupid, leader. Thoroughly disillusioned with his martial experiences, Gascoigne returned to England in October 1572.[13]

The need to refurbish his impoverished state was perhaps the principal impulse that led him to utilize his pen in search of a patron. An acquaintance with certain members of the family of Anthony Browne, Viscount Montague, led to the poet's writing a masque for the double wedding of Lord Montague's son and daughter with the daughter and son of Sir William Dormer.[14] As a seeming reward for this service Gascoigne gained election as Burgess to Parliament from Midhurst in Sussex, a seat under the control of Lord Montague, whose famous country home of Cowdray was near the village.[15]

Another powerful nobleman whose patronage Gascoigne sought was Arthur, Lord Grey of Wilton. An invitation to join a party hunting the winter deer was one of the first marks of favor which the poet received from this future friend and patron of Edmund Spenser. Failure as a marksman during this hunt gave Gascoigne a welcome opportunity to recite the full measure of failure which he had consistently experienced and to appeal for the patronage of Lord Grey.[16] Matters in this realm proceeding in the right direction, as we judge by the rather easy tone of "Gascoignes voyage"[17] addressed to Lord Grey, Gascoigne decided to publish his writings. That this decision to publish was motivated by a desire for patronage is attested by Gascoigne himself, who, in his letter "To the reverende Divines" which prefaced the revised and expurgated *Posies,* says of his reason for publishing *A Hundreth Sundrie Flowres:*

> Thirdly, as I seeke advauncement by vertue, so was I desirous that there might remaine in publike recorde, some pledge or token of those giftes wherwith it hath pleased the Almightie to endue me: To the ende that thereby the vertuous might bee incouraged to employ my penne in some exercise which might tende both to my preferment, and to the profite of my Countrey.[18]

If Lord Montague and Lord Grey had been grateful for his individual works, what might not a volume of verse entail?

---

13 For a complete account of these years in the poet's life see *George Gascoigne,* ch. iii.
14 No. 69. For a detailed examination of this masque see *George Gascoigne,* pp. 173-77.
15 *George Gascoigne,* pp. 61-3.
16 No. 70.
17 No. 74.
18 *Works,* I, 5.

Unhappily, Fortune had not yet finished with Gascoigne. His creditors, a large group with extensive unsatisfied claims, if the various bonds and notes signed by the poet are trustworthy evidence, had found themselves prevented from taking action against their debtor by reason of the parliamentary immunity which he had gained by becoming a Burgess for Midhurst. Angered by this, the tradesmen prepared and sent to the Privy Council a document bearing the title:

Against Georg Gascoyne y^t he ought not to be Burgess.

The first charge in this document is that the accused is avoiding his creditors on the grounds of parliamentary immunity, and then the full arsenal is brought forth. The poet is charged with being "a defamed person," "a murderer," "a common Rymer," a "deviser of slaunderous Pasquelles againste divers personnes of greate callinge," "a notorious Ruffianne," "a spie," an "Atheist, and [a] godlesse personne."[19]

Such a formidable document was not to be taken lightly, particularly by a man who had been involved in as much litigation as had George Gascoigne. The threat of investigation and perhaps of prosecution implicit in this petition was, in my judgment, the cause both of his precipitate flight to Holland and his desire to publish his works with all speed.

In the first place, Gascoigne had, on his return from Holland, categorically stated that he had seen and had known enough of warfare; he was determined not to become embroiled again.[20] Obviously, something of great moment was required to lead him to journey once more to Holland within five months of his return. Likewise, something of importance led him to conceal the fact that he had been in England during the winter of 1572-73. In his verse account of his experiences in the Dutch wars, Gascoigne says of his adventures between the siege of Tergoes (raised Oct. 21, 1572) and the siege of Ramykins (August, 1573) that he roamed over "Zeeland, Holland, Waterland, and all," wherever "good *Guyllam* of *Nassau* bade [him] go," but says nothing about his return to England.[21] Indeed, Gascoigne so successfully concealed the fact of his presence in England that only recently has the truth been made known.[22]

His sudden return to Holland is perfectly understandable if we consider the threat of possible investigation by the Privy Council on the basis of the creditors' complaint. Even though he had no desire to return to the Low Countries, it was far safer to be out of England if an investigation was imminent. In fact, what little we know of Gascoigne's activities in Holland in the spring of 1572/3 reveals that he was not connected with any English volunteers until May 25.[23] His departure, then, was not made in connection with any expedition, and the unpremeditated nature of his journey seems apparent.

The relation of the creditors' complaint and the speedy publication of *A Hundreth Sundrie Flowres* is not as easily perceived. We know that, having

19 This document is printed and discussed in *George Gascoigne*, pp. 61-63.
20 No. 70.
21 *Works*, I, 160.
22 C. T. Prouty, "Gascoigne in the Low Countries," *R. E. S.*, XII, 139-46.
23 *George Gascoigne*, pp. 65-66.

decided to publish, Gascoigne was, during the winter of 1572-73, engaged in preparing his copy for the printer. That he had not finished his preparations is revealed by the incomplete nature of "Dan Bartholmew." Thus when he was faced with the complaint he found himself in a difficult situation. The *Flowres* was designed to secure a patron, but the book was not printed and if ever he needed a patron it was at this very time when he feared a Privy Council investigation. Confronted with such a dilemma, Gascoigne evidently decided to leave England but to have the printer proceed with the publication of the volume so that any good resulting from it would rapidly accrue to the author. With this idea and hope in mind, he departed but sent back to London the remaining sections of his manuscript.

The Original Contents of
A Hundreth Sundrie Flowres

The bibliographical and biographical evidence thus far presented leads to the next problem, namely, just what material did Gascoigne originally plan to publish under the title of *A Hundreth Sundrie Flowres*, and what material, therefore, should an editor reprint if he desires to reproduce the intention of the author. The main question is whether or no Gascoigne originally planned to include the two plays, *Supposes* and *Jocasta*. It will be remembered that the evidence cited above indicated the simultaneous printing of the two parts of the volume which Richard Smith published under the title *A Hundreth Sundrie Flowres*. Gascoigne's evident desire for haste in the publication of his book may explain the simultaneous printing of the two parts and the break in pagination from 164, on which page *Jocasta* is concluded, to page 201, where begins the letter of *H.W.* But even a desire for haste does not reveal why the letter of *H.W.* and that of *G.T.*, which follows, claim to explain how the book came to be printed. Surely one would expect to find such an explanation at the beginning of the whole work, not at the beginning of a second section. As has been observed, a letter from "The Printer to the Reader," on Aij^r, further confuses the matter with its casual reference to the letter of *H.W.* "in the beginning of this worke." Clearly we are faced with a problem which must be decided if a correct reprint of *A Hundreth Sundrie Flowres* is to be produced.

A very real indication of what was meant by the title, *A Hundreth Sundrie Flowres*, has been pointed out by Mr. B. M. Ward, who has emphasized the fact that in the second section there are one hundred poems.[24] Each separate poem thus becomes one of the *Hundreth Sundrie Flowres*. Such a correlation between titles and contents can be pointed out in the works of both Tusser[25] and Watson,[26]

24 B. M. Ward, "Letter to the Editor," *The Library*, 4th Series, VIII (1928), 126-27. Although Dr. Greg (*ibid.*, pp. 128-29) objected to this theory that *"Hundreth"* in the title signified the number of poems in the volume, I think that the presence of that number of poems and the evidence of Watson and Tusser prove the point.
25 Thomas Tusser, *A Hundreth Good Pointes of Husbandrie*, London, 1557.
26 Thomas Watson, *The EKATOMΠAΘIA or Passionate Centurie of Love*, London, 1582.

where the number found in the title indicates the number of poems in the text. There seems, therefore, to be no reason to doubt that Gascoigne devised his title to describe only the second section of the volume which ultimately appeared under that title.

Certainly this hypothesis is borne out by the facts. The letters explaining how the volume came to be printed appear in the proper place prefacing the one hundred poems. These letters, which do not mention the two plays, were obviously never designed to preface the entire volume as published. A letter prefacing the whole volume is present, but it is the letter of "The Printer to the Reader"—a fact that suggests how the two plays came to be included.

The printer must, almost inevitably, be the responsible party. His motive was probably the very obvious one of profit. The inclusion of the plays must have made the volume more attractive to possible buyers, since we know that the number of plays either entered or printed before 1570 was ten times as great as the number of original books of verse.[27] With published drama far more in demand than poetry, Bynneman's profit motive in adding the plays becomes apparent.

It cannot be said with assurance that Gascoigne was unaware of the printer's intention to include the plays, since he was in England until a comparatively short time before publication. If the poet at this time was in the printing house to supervise the daily proof, as we know he was some years later,[28] he must have known of the plan to bind the two sections together. The important fact is that Gascoigne's original purpose in composing the title *A Hundreth Sundrie Flowres* was to describe the contents of his writings in verse and prose which he intended to publish and that the second section of the volume which was printed by Bynneman and published by Richard Smith represents the poet's original intention.

A minor point argued by Mr. Ward remains for consideration. Mr. Ward felt that, since each poem, and only the poem, represented a "flowre" according to the title, an editor should delete the prose portion of "F.J."[29] Such an excision seems unwarranted. In the first place, *G.T.* says that his prose links fully describe how each poem in "F.J." came to be written. In this respect the prose then fulfills the same function as does the introductory material which prefaces each poem in the remainder of the volume. To be consistent, Mr. Ward should have omitted each of these introductory passages. The manifest absurdity of such excision leaves no justification for the omission of the prose passages in "F.J."

27 E. K. Chambers (*The Elizabethan Stage*, Oxford, 1923, IV, 380-81) lists 45 plays entered and 43 printed before 1570. Original verse printed before 1570 was composed of the work of Googe, Turbervile, and Howell.
28 An "advertisement of the Prynter to the Reader" which prefaces *The Droomme of Doomes day (Works*, II, 215) says: "Understand (gentle Reader) that whiles this worke was in the presse, it pleased God to visit the translatour thereof with sicknesse. So that being unable himselfe to attend the dayly proofes, he apoynted a servaunt of his to oversee the same."
29 *A Hundreth Sundrie Flowres*, ed. by Ward, p. viii.

More important than such metaphysical reasoning is the fact that the letters of *H.W.* and *G.T.* are obviously a part of that second section to which the title applies. Therefore, since any excision of their words defeats the editorial principle of reprinting what Gascoigne clearly intended to be printed under the title of *A Hundreth Sundrie Flowres,* the present reprint contains everything in the original two-sectioned volume with the exception of *Supposes* and *Jocasta.*

AUTHORSHIP OF

A Hundreth Sundrie Flowres

In the introduction to his partial reprint of *A Hundreth Sundrie Flowres,*[30] Mr. B. M. Ward put forward the theory that the volume was an early Elizabethan anthology. Although Dr. Greg[31] pointed out the impossibility of such a theory, both Miss Ambrose[32] and Dr. McKerrow[33] in their reviews seemed, at least tentatively, to accept the hypothesis. Since that time the idea of multiple authorship of the *Flowres* has received some approval. Drs. Hebel and Hudson printed two poems from the *Flowres* in the section of their anthology[34] devoted to Elizabethan Miscellanies, and in the notes[35] they endorsed Ward's theory. Miss L. C. John[36] recently found it impossible to make a categorical statement regarding Gascoigne's authorship. In view of the seeming acceptance of such a theory it has seemed advisable to examine the problem anew.

The title page and introductory letters of the present edition give no clue to the author. All we can learn is that an anonymous *G.T.* possessed in manuscript certain prose writings and poems which he loaned to an anonymous *H.W.* who, in turn, entreated his friend *A.B.* to have the work printed. The printer in his letter to the reader confirms these details. In 1575, there appeared *The Posies of George Gascoigne,* also printed by Bynneman for Richard Smith, which contained, with four exceptions, all the poems and prose passages contained in *A Hundreth Sundrie Flowres.* Although few poems were omitted, the order of all poems was greatly altered by grouping them under three main headings: "Flowres," "Herbes," and "Weedes." Additions consisted of: the conclusion of "Dan Bartholmew," by means of "The Reporters conclusion," which appears for the first time in its complete state; three poems dealing with the greene Knight (Gascoigne's pseudonym used in Holland after 1573); a series of complimentary prefatory verses and an epilogue by Gascoigne; and, most important, three introductory epistles. In these letters Gascoigne does not make a positive claim to the authorship of the *Flowres,* rather he accepts the authorship, as if the fact were

---

30 *A Hundreth Sundrie Flowres,* ed. by Ward, London, 1926.
31 W. W. Greg, *"A Hundreth Sundrie Flowres,"* *The Library,* VII (1927), 269-282.
32 Genevieve Ambrose, *"A Hundreth Sundrie Flowres,"* *M. L. R.,* XXII (1927), 214-220.
33 R. B. McKerrow, *"A Hundreth Sundrie Flowres,"* *R. E. S.,* III (1927), 111-114.
34 Hebel, J. W. and H. H. Hudson, *The Poetry of the English Renaissance, 1509-1660,* New York, 1929, pp. 187-88.
35 *Ibid.,* p. 928.
36 L. C. John, *Elizabethan Sonnet Sequences,* New York, 1938, pp. 12-13.

well known.[37] Nothing whatsoever is said that would indicate any claim by any other poet to the authorship of any part of the volume. The main reason for the letters is thus stated by Gascoigne:

> It is verie neare two yeares past, since (I beeing in Hollande in service with the vertuous Prince of Orenge) the most parte of these Posies were imprinted, and now at my returne, I find that some of them have not onely bene offensive for sundrie wanton speeches and lascivious phrases, but further I heare that the same have beene doubtfully construed, and (therefore) scandalous.

The matter of doubtful construction is subsequently clarified in these words:

> I understande that sundrie well disposed mindes have taken offence at certaine wanton wordes and sentences passed in the fable of *Ferdinando Jeronimi,* and the *Ladie Elinora de Valasco,* the which in the first edition was termed The adventures of master F.J. And that also therwith some busie conjectures have presumed to thinke that the same was indeed written to the scandalizing of some worthie personages, whom they woulde seeme therby to know.[38]

From 1575 until comparatively recent times, the *Flowres* rested in oblivion. Hazlitt printed the *Posies* and thought that the *Flowres* was an unauthorized edition.[39] Dr. Cunliffe considered the *Flowres* as a first edition.[40] However, Mr. Ward has given an entirely new interpretation to the *Flowres.* Since he has listed his conclusions[41] in tabular form, I have thought it well to use this summary as a basis for discussion:

(a) The *Flowres* was an anthology in part written by Gascoigne.
(b) Sir Christopher Hatton was the largest anonymous contributor, his pseudonym or "posy" being "Fortunatus Infoelix" or "Master F.J."
(c) Both Gascoigne and Hatton being abroad at the time it came out—the former certainly, the latter probably—the Earl of Oxford was the editor who arranged the publication, he himself contributing sixteen lyrics signed with the posy "Meritum petere, grave."

First, it will be well to consider how Mr. Ward came to his original conclusion, that the *Flowres* was an anthology. *H.W.* in his letter to the reader says:

> IN *August last* passed my familiar friend Master *G.T.* bestowed upon me ye reading of a written Booke, wherein he had collected divers discourses & verses, invented uppon sundrie occasions, by sundrie gentlemen (in mine opinion) right commendable for their capacitie.

G.T. in his letter to *H.W.* further describes the volume.

> . . . a number of *Sonets,* layes, letters, Ballades, Rondlets, verlayes and verses, the workes of your friend and myne Master *F.J.* and divers others. . . .

37 *Works,* I, 3, 4. "To the reverende Divines."
38 *Ibid.,* I, 3, 7.
39 *The Complete Poems of George Gascoigne,* ed. by W. C. Hazlitt, 2 vols., London, 1868-70. "Introduction."
40 J. W. Cunliffe, "George Gascoigne," *Cambridge History of English Literature,* III, 203-204. Mr. Ward's statement that Dr. Cunliffe seemed to regard *The Posies* as the definitive text is hardly fair, for Dr. Cunliffe collated *The Posies* with one copy of the *Flowres* and noted the variant readings.
41 B. M. Ward, "Further Research on *A Hundreth Sundrie Flowres,*" *R. E. S.,* IV (1928), 35. This is a more concise statement than is found in the Introduction to his reprint, and I have thought best to use Mr. Ward's words rather than to attempt my own summary.

This letter ended, *G.T.* begins the story of "F.J." at the end of which is found the following:

> Now henceforwardes I will trouble you no more with such a barbarous style in prose, but will onely recite unto you sundry verses written by sundry gentlemen. . . . Neyther can I declare unto you who wrote the greatest part of them, for they are unto me but a posie presented out of sundry gardens. . . .

Hereupon the poems follow in certain groupings: the first twenty-one are signed with the posy, "Si fortunatus infoelix," numbers 22 through 28 are signed "Spreta tamen vivunt," 29 through 31 are signed "Ferenda Natura," 32 through 47 are signed "Meritum petere, grave," while number 48, signed "Ever or Never," has this introduction:

> I will now deliver unto you so many more of Master Gascoignes Poems as have come to my hands, who hath never been dayntie of his doings, and therfore I conceale not his name: but his word or posie he hath often changed and therefore I will deliver his verses with such sundrie posies as I received them.

This comment at once provokes our interest with its "so many more of Master Gascoignes Poems." Surely it means that at least some of the preceding poems are also by Gascoigne, but if that be so, what can be the meaning of the remarks of *G.T.* and *H.W.* about sundry authors? As we have noted, Mr. Ward claims that these letters were written by the Earl of Oxford. Why this noble lord should have sought such concealment of his identity is explained by Mr. Ward as part of a plot to bring Hatton into disfavor with the Queen. It is assumed that "The Adventures of Master F.J." is a recital of the amorous intrigues of Sir Christopher, and that Oxford, having secured the poems therein contained, wrote the prose narrative to elaborate Hatton's lascivious conduct.[42]

Such a theory rests upon a variety of assumptions, inventions, and misapprehensions. First, it will be well to examine the use of anonymous letters as a means of explaining the publication of the works of Gascoigne's contemporaries and other sixteenth century writers. If we find that it was conventional for a gentleman to conceal his authorship of a published book, the introductory letters will then lose their value as evidence of the concealing both of a noxious plot and of multiple authorship. Secondly, I shall show that the identification of Sir Christopher Hatton by the posy "Si fortunatus infoelix" is based on a misunderstanding, and that the identification of Edward de Vere with "Meritum petere, grave" is achieved solely by means of a cipher invented by Mr. Ward.

The Arte of English Poesie is prefaced by a letter in which the printer explains that the book came into his hands "without any Authors name."[43] In general, this lack of an author's name presented no problem to Elizabethan readers, at least not to the author's intimates or to members of the literary world. Sir John Harington did not consider the authorship of *The Arte* to be a matter of argument, nor did Bolton in his *Hypercritica*.[44] Mr. Ward, however, has here put forward the

---

42 *A Hundreth Sundrie Flowres,* ed. by Ward, pp. xiii-xiv.
43 *The Arte of English Poesie,* ed. by G. D. Willcock and A. Walker, Cambridge, 1936, p. 2.
44 *Ibid.,* pp. xi-xii.

theory that Lord Lumley was the author. Such an hypothesis requires, in the words of the recent editors of *The Arte,*

> . . . that Lumley's desire for anonymity was so strong that he arranged, with Field's [the printer's] connivance, a Puttenham camouflage which Harrington knew of and respected. . . .[45]

The erroneous nature of such a complicated hypothesis has been shown by Miss Willcock and Miss Walker.[46]

The Arte's anonymous publication well illustrates the literary convention which required either anonymity or an explanation as to why the author allowed publication. For example, Barnabe Googe found it necessary to write a dedicatory letter for his *Eglogs, Epytaphes, & Sonettes* which carefully explained that he was not responsible for the publication of his work.[47] Many persons had urged him to publish, but he had always refused. Finally, during his absence abroad, a friend gave the poems to the printer and the book was nearly finished when Googe returned to England. At this point, consideration for the printer moved the poet to allow the edition to proceed. Directly after Googe's letter, we find that of the friend, Lord Blundeston, who, in language very close to that of *H.W.,* explains that the merit of the volume induced him to seek its publication.[48]

A petite Pallace of Pettie his pleasure is introduced by three letters.[49] The author of the first, R.B., explains that he had received the manuscript from G[eorge]. P[ettie]., who loaned it only on the condition that it be kept secret. However, R.B. thought the volume too valuable to remain unpublished. Therefore he caused it to be printed. The second letter is that of G[eorge]. P[ettie]. which accompanied the original loan, and in the third the printer excuses himself for printing a manuscript which the author seemingly did not want published.

As Professor Schelling has noted,[50] Gascoigne figured in a similar device for the publication of Sir Humphrey Gilbert's *A Discourse of a Discoverie for a New Passage to Cataia.* In a prefatory letter to this work, Gascoigne relates that the pamphlet was originally written to persuade Sir Humphrey's brother to permit the voyage in search of the northwest passage. Some seven years later, at a most opportune time when Frobisher was planning a similar voyage, Gascoigne *happened* to be at Gilbert's home, and *happened* to find the pamphlet in the study. Gilbert kindly "loaned" the manuscript to Gascoigne who, realizing its great value, caused it to be printed.

If, as we see in the case of *The Arte,* a book could be anonymously published, without implying some mystery, then there is no reason to believe that the lack

---

45 *Ibid.,* p. xv.
46 *Ibid.,* pp. xi-xliv.
47 Barnabe Googe, *Eglogs, Epytaphes, & Sonettes,* ed. by Edward Arber, London, 1871, pp. 24-25.
48 *Ibid.,* pp. 26-27.
49 *A petite Pallace of Pettie his pleasure,* ed. by Sir Israel Gollancz, 2 vols., London, 1908, I, 1-9.
50 F. E. Schelling, *The Life and Writings of George Gascoigne,* University of Pennsylvania Publications, Series in Philology Literature and Archaeology, II, No. 4, 89-95. Gascoigne's introductory letter can be found in *Works,* II, 562-66.

of Gascoigne's name on the title page of the *Flowres* indicated a dark secret. The sonnets which Spenser had anonymously written for *A Theatre for Voluptuous Worldlings* were reprinted in an acknowledged collection of the poet's minor work and, as far as I know, there was no particular reason for the original anonymity nor was there any attempt to claim authorship. Most Elizabethan men of letters knew that the sonnets were Spenser's exactly as Harington knew that Puttenham was the author of *The Arte,* and as probably it was known that George Gascoigne was the author of the *Flowres.*

Googe's introductory letter may offer an explanation as to why anonymous letters should appear in the *Flowres,* and why, at the same time, certain poems are noted as Gascoigne's. Googe says:

> For I both consydered and wayed with my selfe, the grosenes of my Style: whiche thus commytted to the gasynge shewe of every eye shuld forth with disclose ye manifest foly of the Writer, and also I feared and mistrusted the disdaynfull myndes of a nombre both scornefull and carpynge Correctours, whose Heades are ever busyed in tauntyng Judgementes. Least they shuld otherwyse interprete my doyings than in deade I meant them.[51]

Thus there are two main reasons why it was well to avoid publication, and it seems fair to conclude that those same reasons would be good cause to conceal the author's share in having his work published. First, there is the question of modesty. Should an author allow his writings to come to public view? Googe does not think so, but the fact remains that, having a good excuse, he allows his work to be published. In like manner, is it reasonable to think that George Pettie and Sir Humphrey Gilbert did not want their books printed? Surely these two men only wanted a reasonable defence which would exonerate them of any censure arising from such publication. Therefore, I suggest that one purpose of the anonymous letters of the *Flowres* was to provide Gascoigne with a defence against the charge of vain and ungentlemanly conduct in having his work printed. What other reason than this can there be for Gascoigne's protestations that he had never received money from the printer,[52] or his fulsome explanation of his reasons for publishing *A Hundreth Sundrie Flowres?*

The second point made by Googe will, I think, show why Gascoigne wanted some of the poems, as well as "F.J.," attributed to other men. Googe feared the possibile misinterpretation of his poems. Similarly, Pettie feared the interpreta-

---

51 Googe, *op. cit.,* p. 24. On this question of the author's connection with the printing of his work the case of Donne a few decades later is instructive. Probably no poet was so highly esteemed, at least in cultivated circles, in the period 1600-1630 as Donne. His verses circulated, 'among his private friends,' in a score or more of manuscripts. They would have made a good venture for a bookseller. But with the exception of the *Anniversaries,* which we may be sure were published to feed the vanity of his patron Drury, they did not appear in print till after his death. Why? The answer must be, because Donne—not, in this case, from modesty, but because he thought they might interfere with his prospects as a seeker of court appointment under James or, later, with his standing in the church—did not wish them published. And might we not assume, by parallel reasoning in reverse, that Shakespeare was privy to the publication of his sonnets in 1609?
52 *Works,* I, 4. "To the reverende Divines."

tion of his tales which "touch nearly divers of my near friends." That Gascoigne feared the same thing is proved by the introductory letters to *The Posies,* the revised, expurgated, and enlarged second edition, in which he says:

> . . . some busie conjectures have presumed to thinke that the same ["The Adventures of Master F.J."] was indeed written to the scandalizing of some worthie personages whom they woulde seeme thereby to know.[53]

Now it is most strange that in view of such suppositions Gascoigne did not, in *The Posies,* disclaim authorship of this dangerous prose tale as he well could, by the evidence of *H.W.* and *G.T.* Instead, he devised the further fiction that "F.J." was a translation from a feigned Bartello. The reason that the poet followed this course rather than the former lies in the fact that his poems had been known in manuscript to a number of people. This custom of passing his manuscript poems among friends is twice alluded to. *G.T.,* speaking of two poems which he has not seen, says:

> . . . as that contrary to his wonted use, he hath hitherto withhelde it from sight of any his familiers. . . .

Of poem No. 8 in "F.J.," the editor says:

> . . . for this and divers other of his most notable Poems, have come to view of ye world. . . .

Obviously it was impossible to deny authorship, for too many people knew that Gascoigne was the author. So too, I feel, we may conclude with regard to those poems signed "Si fortunatus infoelix," "Meritum petere, grave," "Spreta tamen vivunt," and "Ferenda Natura." Ostensibly these were not to be connected with Gascoigne, but they would be known as his by his friends and by the members of the court circle who had seen them in manuscript.

If, then, we see that other writers concealed their responsibility for publication under the veil of anonymous letters and if we see that Gascoigne had good reason for following such a convention, it is reasonable to conclude that the letters which prefaced the *Flowres* are a device and are therefore untruthful and that Gascoigne either caused them to be written or wrote them himself.[54]

One misapprehension under which Mr. Ward labors and which he uses as evidence that Gascoigne had nothing to do with the publication of the volume is the supposition that Gascoigne was in Holland from March 19, 1571/2 until November 1574.[55] In the preceding sections of this Introduction and elsewhere

53 *Ibid.,* I, 7.
54 Since I shall show that Gascoigne wrote all the poems and since I have shown there is good reason to think that Gascoigne wrote the letters, it seems both tedious and futile to embark on a discussion of Mr. Ward's latest theory (*R. E. S.,* IV (1928), 35-48) that *G. T.* was a real person. This hinges on a supposed friendship between Hatton ("Si fortunatus infoelix") and *G. T.* Dr. Bowers' contention (*Harvard Studies and Notes in Philology and Literature,* XVI, 13-35) that *H. W.* was a real person seems beside the point, which is, as Dr. Bowers says, that Gascoigne either caused to be written or himself wrote the introductory letters. It is reasonable to assume that it would be wise to choose initials which were possible of identification, even though Gascoigne was the author. The use of the initials E. K. for the editor of *The Shepherd's Calendar* is a case in point. The editor may or may not have been Edward Kirk.
55 *A Hundreth Sundrie Flowres,* ed. by Ward, pp. xvii ff.

I have shown that Gascoigne was in England from October or November 1572 until March 19, 1572/3. Furthermore, I have shown that the printing of the volume began before the poet left for the Low Countries and that even after his departure he sent back to England copy which was included in the printed book.

Thus it becomes impossible to argue that Gascoigne had nothing to do with the printing of *A Hundreth Sundrie Flowres*. He obviously planned the publication and set the printing underway for reasons that I have indicated above. This fact of his close connection with the printing when considered together with the common use of anonymous or initialed prefatory letters, pretty clearly shows that Gascoigne was the sole author of *A Hundreth Sundrie Flowres* and that he was either the author or deliberate instigator of the letters of *H.W.* and *G.T.*

Further proof, not only of Gascoigne's sole authorship but of the erroneous nature of Mr. Ward's hypothesis, may be found by examining Mr. Ward's supposed identification of Hatton and Oxford by means of the posies which are signed to every poem in the book. Mr. Ward, in commenting on *G.T.*'s concluding remarks in "F.J.," says:

> It is obvious from these notes that the several authors can be distinguished by the Latin "posy" or motto which serves as a signature at the end of each one.[56]

A brief reference to the passage in question, which is found on pages 105-6 of the present work, will show the reader that the supposed clues are to be found in "such short notes as the aucthors themselves have delivered," and that these notes, which are the introductory comments to the various poems, in no way suggest Mr. Ward's conclusion.

However, Mr. Ward is convinced that "Si fortunatus infoelix" represents Sir Christopher Hatton. The evidence[57] upon which he bases this conclusion is contained in two statements by Gabriel Harvey. In his copy of *The Posies*, Harvey made a marginal notation beside "Fortunatus Infoelix" which is signed to the verses that give "the argument of the Tragedie" of *Jocasta*. This note reads "lately the posie of Sir Christopher Hatton." One of the poems in Harvey's *Gratulationes Valdinensis* is addressed to Hatton "de suo Symbolo, Foelix Infortunatus." In the first place, "Fortunatus Infoelix" and "Foelix Infortunatus" are two different posies and neither of them is "Si fortunatus infoelix." Secondly, as Dr. Greg has said,[58] there is no reason to believe that because Hatton used either of these at one time or other, no other person could have used "Si fortunatus infoelix." An examination of the subject of emblems shows that such an assumption is based on a misunderstanding of contemporary usage. Finally, there is positive proof in the introductory remarks to Poem No. 16 which identifies the author as G[eorge]. G[ascoigne]. This poem is signed with the posy "Si fortunatus infoelix," which thus clearly applies to Gascoigne.

56 *A Hundreth Sundrie Flowres*, ed. by Ward, pp. viii-ix.
57 *A Hundreth Sundrie Flowres*, ed. by Ward, pp. xi-xii.
58 W. W. Greg, *"A Hundreth Sundrie Flowres,"* *op. cit.*, p. 277.

Mr. Ward next attempts to prove that "Meritum petere, grave" represents the Earl of Oxford by means of poem No. 47 which has the following introduction,

> The absent lover (in ciphers) disciphering his name, doth
> crave some spedie relief as followeth,

and which is signed "Meritum petere, grave." Mr. Ward at once assumes that the poem contains a cipher or an acrostic which, if known, will spell out the name of the author. Let us examine Mr. Ward's acrostic,[59] which is supposed to have the sanction of Francis Bacon, but which, as Dr. Bowers[60] has shown, is not mentioned by Bacon, nor by any other Elizabethan or Jacobean. I list Mr. Ward's rules in tabular form.

1. Make a string of letters composed of the initial letter of every word.
2. Make this string by reading the first line from left to right, the second from right to left and so on in a swinging chain.
3. Guess at the name.
4. See if the name fits without disarranging the order of the letters.
5. Eliminate "non-significants" (non-significants are letters not required to spell the name guessed at).
6. At this point, Mr. Ward anticipates the reader's scepticism and proceeds: "Therefore, the rule is that the correct name must be so 'keyed' into the string as to eliminate all possibility of chance. For a name to key into an acrostic poem it should—
   a. Commence on some prominent letter in the first line;
   b. Finish exactly on a letter in the last line;
   c. Read backwards through the poem, beginning and ending exactly on the same two letters."
7. Thus we have the name, *Edward de Vere*.

Dr. Bowers has discussed this acrostic at some length, and has shown that these rules for keying a name into an acrostic poem have no authority in Francis Bacon's writings nor in those of any other writer on ciphers. Indeed, Dr. Bowers says that this system is Mr. Ward's own invention. It will be noted that Mr. Ward's system precludes any name which does not begin and end with the same letter, and since the only restrictive rule is this reading backwards beginning and ending on the same two letters, the elimination of that rule would allow of the insertion of practically any name.

But if Mr. Ward's explanation of the poem is erroneous, what is the name of the absent lover? The crux of the matter seems to lie in the word "disciphering" which means "explaining," most certainly not "concealing." There is a name which is explained and that is "Scudamore" which derived from the French "L'Escu d'amour" which in turn derived from the motto of the family, Scuto amoris divini.[61] The whole poem is a play upon the literal English equivalent

59 *A Hundreth Sundrie Flowres*, ed. by Ward, pp. xxv-xxviii.
60 F. T. Bowers, "Gascoigne and the Oxford Cipher," *M. L. N.*, LII (1937), 183-86.
61 Matthew Gibson (*A View of the Ancient and Present State of the Churches of Door, Home-Lacy and Hempsted*, London, 1727, p. 55) gives a list of names from the Roll Book of "Battail-Abbey" and of the last, Seint Scudamore, says "The last a surname derived from their *bearing Scutum amoris divini*, the Shield of divine love. . . ."
Sir Richard Colt Hoare (*The Modern History of South Wiltshire*, London, 1825, II, 54) says "This Seint Scudame seems to have derived his name from bearing some

of this name, and in the light of this fact the introduction becomes understandable. The absent lover is explaining his name but he does so by symbolic means, *i.e.*, in ciphers.

Dr. Gregg,[62] in his objection to Mr. Ward's cipher, said that the name to be found in the poem was not necessarily that of the author, and in the prefatory letter "To the Readers" in *The Posies*, Gascoigne said:

> I thought good to advertise thee, that the most part of them [the Posies] were written for other men.

And so we see that at least one poem was written for Sir John Scudamore, the father of the Sir James who figures in Higford's *Institutions of a Gentleman*. (Sir James was born in 1568 and so could not be concerned with the present poem.) Sir John was a student of the Middle Temple, gentleman usher to Queen Elizabeth, standard-bearer to the honorable band of Gentlemen Pensioners, one of Her Highness Council for the Marches of Wales, and a good friend, as well as benefactor, of Sir Thomas Bodley.[63]

If, then, the ubiquitous Earl of Oxford is not the author of this poem, Mr. Ward's whole theory of Oxford's editing the manuscript falls to the ground, for it was by this poem that Mr. Ward identified Edward de Vere as "Meritum petere, grave" and as author of all the other poems so signed, and, finally, as the editor of the volume. As a matter of fact, Gascoigne can be identified with "Meritum petere, grave" by the evidence of poem No. 38, which is signed with that posy. The whole poem is concerned with the respective merits of G[ascoigne]. and B[oyes]. and definite proof of the author's identity is found in the fourth line where the anagram A.O.G.N.C.S. may be arranged to read "Gascon."[64]

Thus the two posies which Mr. Ward had seemingly identified have been shown to belong to Gascoigne. Of "Ferenda Natura" and "Spreta tamen vivunt," the only other posies that are not directly attributed to Gascoigne by the introductory remarks of the several poems, Mr. Ward has been less certain. "Ferenda Natura," he thought, might represent Elizabeth Bacon Gascoigne. The falsity of this theory has been demonstrated by Dr. Bowers[65] by means of a reference in "Gascoignes Recantation" (No. 56) to one of the "Ferenda Natura" poems. Line 24 of No. 56, reading "That once I soong, I *Bathe in Blisse*, amidde my wearie *Bale*," obviously refers to No. 29 whose first line is "Amid my Bale I bath in blisse."

sacred shield in defence of his love to the faith of Christ, and conformably to this we find that their most ancient bearing was, *Gules*, a cross patee fitchee *Or*, to which their motto in after ages very properly applied, Scuto Amoris Divini. . . . It should be observed that this family name is found written Saint Scudamore, Escutamore, Escudemor, de Scudamore, Skidemore, Skydmore, etc. according to the very uncertain orthography of proper names in early times."

62   W. W. Greg, *"A Hundreth Sundrie Flowres," op. cit.*, p. 280.
63   D. N. B., "Sir John Scudamore." Matthew Gibson, *op. cit.*, p. 61.
64   Mr. Ward is obviously in difficulty when he maintains that Edward de Vere wrote this poem and that the "B" discussed is Elizabeth Bacon Gascoigne. Dr. Greg (*"A Hundreth Sundrie Flowres," op. cit.*, p. 280) pointed out the absurdity of such a theory.
65   F. T. Bowers, *op. cit.*, p. 16.

Since poem No. 56 is Gascoigne's by reason of the title, then it is clear that poem No. 29 is also his and that the posy "Ferenda Natura," signed to this latter poem, is also Gascoigne's.

I have observed a similar proof for "Spreta tamen vivunt." The last line of the first stanza of poem No. 4 in "Dan Bartholmew" reads, "I cannot weepe, nor wayle my fill," and line 1 of poem No. 25, signed "Spreta tamen vivunt" reads: "Now have I found the way, to weepe & wayle my fill." Since no one has yet denied Gascoigne's authorship of "Dan Bartholmew" it would seem that the posy, "Spreta tamen vivunt"[66] signed to No. 25 is Gascoigne's.

Since all the other posies are signed to poems which bear Gascoigne's name, and since I have shown that "Si fortunatus infoelix," "Spreta tamen vivunt," "Ferenda Natura," and "Meritum petere, grave" are Gascoigne's, it is safe to conclude that on the ground of the identification of the author by the posy, Gascoigne wrote the entire volume. This fact being established, the evidence produced to explain the anonymous introductory letters becomes almost inevitable. Finally, when we realize that no credence can be placed in Mr. Ward's identification of the Earl of Oxford, and that the Hatton identification is unsupportable on the basis of the Elizabethan use of posies, the whole of Mr. Ward's theory regarding the multiple authorship of *A Hundreth Sundrie Flowres* vanishes into thin air.

"POSIES" AND THE SEQUENTIAL NATURE OF
A Hundreth Sundrie Flowres

Two distinctive features of *A Hundreth Sundrie Flowres* have been omitted from consideration not only by students of Gascoigne but as well by critics of Elizabethan literature. The first of these features is the fact that every poem in the volume is signed with what Gascoigne calls a "posy." The second, based on this, is the fact that all poems signed with the same posy are in a group in *A Hundreth Sundrie Flowres* whereas in *The Posies* this seemingly organic relationship has been disrupted.

While *A Hundreth Sundrie Flowres* is, as far as I know, unique among Elizabethan books in having a posy signed to every poem,[67] the use of posies was a distinctive feature of the fashionable world. Puttenham well describes this custom which so greatly appealed to the Elizabethan fondness for the vaguely concealed allusion:

> And besides all the remembered points of Metricall proportion, ye have yet two other sorts of some affinitie with them, which also first issued out of the Poets head, and whereof the Courtly maker was the principall artificer, having many high conceites and curious imaginations, with leasure inough to attend his idle inventions: and these be the short, quicke and sententious propositions, such as be at these dayes all your devices of armes and other amorous inscriptions

----

66 Mr. Ward (*The Library,* VIII, 124-25) uses the discovery that "Spreta tamen vivunt" is found as the motto on a portrait of Sir Gervase Holles (R. W. Goulding, "Letter to Editor," *T. L. S.,* July 1926, p. 448) to prove that this knight was one of the authors!

67 In the notes to the two or three poems which do not have posies I discuss the probable reason for such omission.

which courtiers use to give and also to weare in liverie for the honour of their ladies, and commonly containe but two or three words of wittie sentence or secrete conceit till they be unfolded or explaned by some interpretation. For which cause they be commonly accompanied with a figure or purtraict of ocular representation, the words so aptly corresponding to the subtiltie of the figure, that aswel the eye is therwith recreated as the eare or minde. The Greekes call it *Emblema,* the Italiens *Impresa,* and we, a Device, such as a man may put into letters of gold and sende to his mistresses for a token, or cause to be embrodered in scutchions of armes, or in any bordure of a rich garment to give by his noveltie marvell to the beholder.[68]

Historically the emblem may be traced to ancient Egypt but its use really flourished during the sixteenth century when scholars and courtiers followed, almost as a Bible, the Aldine edition of Horapollo, a re-issue of a Graeco-Egyptian treatise on hieroglyphics and emblems. In 1522, Andrea Alciat's *Emblemata Libellus* was published at Milan and by 1600 over one hundred and fifty editions of this book were published including translations into French, German, Spanish, Italian, and possibly English. By 1564 twenty more books on and of emblems were published on the Continent and many found their way to England. The making of emblems became a form of recreation similar perhaps to crossword puzzles and anagrams which appear in the daily press.[69] Theodore Beza found such pleasure in this pastime that he published a book of emblems of his own devising, albeit they were all of a religious turn. In 1585 Samuel Daniel, then a young gallant just down from Oxford, published a translation of Paolo Giovio's *Dialogo dell' Imprese.*[70] The learned Bishop of Nocera had, in 1552, published the first regular treatise on the subject of emblems. In 1586 Geoffrey Whitney published at the Plantin Press in Leyden the first English book of emblems. In London in 1591 Parradin's *Devises Héroiques* was translated and published together with a translation of Symeoni's *Emblems.* Translations and new collections continued well into the seventeenth century, but by the nineteenth century the tradition degenerated into a series of books designed to lead the young to a good and holy life.

The strict emblem consists of a design either in metal or cloth, but more popularly of a woodcut. This pictorial representation is pointed by a Latin or vernacular motto. Then certain verses are appended which explain the picture and the motto. Examples of the strict traditional form of the emblem are to be found among the pages of Gascoigne's *Hemetes the Heremyte,* where woodcuts and

68 George Puttenham, *The Arte of English Poesie,* ed. by G. D. Willcock and Alice Walker, Cambridge, 1936, p. 102.

69 This brief summary and the ensuing details concerning emblems are, in the main, derived from H. R. Green's *Shakespeare and the Emblem Writers,* London, 1870. I am not unaware of the modern interest in emblems, but most of the recent work deals with the seventeenth century and with the cataloging of emblems, and therefore has no immediate connection with my purpose.

70 *The Worthy tract of Paulus Iovius, contayning a Discourse of rare inuentions, both Militarie and Amorous called Imprese. Whereunto is added a Preface contayning the Arte of composing them, with many other notable devises by Samuel Daniell late Student in Oxenforde at London Printed for Simon Waterson 1585*

their verses illustrate the traditional subjects of the emblem devisers. A foot emerging from a cloud crushes a snake, while appended is the posy, "Spretaq[ue] sic vivunt sic conculcata resurgunt."[71] Again, a man holds a huge bundle of staves and the verse points out that anyone who tries to embrace too much holds nothing.[72] Or again, a walnut tree is being hit by two men with staves. A verse explains that the trees, though beaten by men for the nuts, reclothe themselves but that the author beaten by the world is sterile and yields worthless fruit.[73]

The first and last are not quite in the traditional vein but the other could have come straight from the pages of Whitney or any of the emblem books. Similarly, when Gascoigne returned to Gray's Inn, five of his friends gave him themes on which he should write. The first, put forward by Francis Kinwelmarshe, was "Audaces fortuna iuvat," and Gascoigne wrote a sonnet giving classic examples proving that Fortune favors the brave.[74] The same posy appears in Whitney's *Choice of Emblems* with a woodcut and explanatory verses; the verses, however, celebrate Marcus Scaevas.[75] This particular motto or posy thus allows of variation, as in fact do many others. The other themes[76] given to Gascoigne by his friends I have not been able to find in Whitney nor in the 1552 edition of Alciat, but that does not alter the fact that these themes are typical emblem material.

These exercises in the traditional vein, while they are the source of the motto or posy do not reveal how the latter came to be used independently of the accompanying woodcut and explanatory verses. That this custom was widespread is shown by two of Gascoigne's contemporaries, Whetstone and Turbervile. On the title page of Whetstone's *The Rocke of Regard* appears the posy, "Formae nulla fides."[77] "Cressids complaint" in the same volume is signed, "Sive bonum, sive malum, fama est."[78] Similarly, the story of Roberto Rinaldo and Giletta is signed, "El fine fa el tutto."[79] An epitaph on Robert Wingfield is signed quite appropriately, "Vivit post funera virtus.[80] Another epitaph, this time on his friend Thomas Cornelius who was killed in the Dutch wars, has the final posy, "Mors honesta ignominiosae vitae praeferenda."[81] This habit of co-ordinating the posy and the subject matter of the poem to which it is appended is repeated in other instances.

71   *Works*, II, 485.
72   *Ibid.*, II, 494.
73   *Ibid.*, II, 502. This is, of course, an imitation of the pseudo-Ovidian *Nux*.
74   No. 57.
75   *Geoffrey Whitney's "Choice of Emblems,"* A Fac-Simile Reprint ed. by Henry Green, London, 1866, p. 117.
76   No. 59, on the theme "Magnum vectigal parcimonia," bears some resemblance to the "Magnum vectigal" emblem in *The Heroicall Devises of M. Claudius Paradin Canon of Beauieu Whereunto are added the Lord Gabriel Symeons and others. Translated out of Latin into English by P. S. London Imprinted by William Kearney dwelling in Adlingstreete 1591*, p. 5.
77   *The Rocke of Regard, diuided into foure parts . . . being all the inuention, collection and translation of George Whetstone Gent.* [Colophon] *Imprinted at London for Robert Waley. Anno.* 1576.
78   *Ibid.*, I, 22.
79   *Ibid.*, I, 45.
80   *Ibid.*, II, 46.
81   *Ibid.*, II, 49.

A recital of criminal life in London has the final message, "Quod nocet, docet;"[82] while both a selection of fifty aphorisms on the avoidance of evil and the epilogue of the volume conclude with "Quod cavere possis, stultum est admittere."[83]

Somewhat more sophisticated is George Turbervile's use of posies in his *Tragical Tales*.[84] He has his own posy on the title page as does Whetstone. In this instance it is, "Nocet empta dol[o]re volupt[a]s." His first "history," that of Nastagio and Euphymia, not only has the final posy, "Amo chi t[']ama" which points Nastagio's foolish love for one who cared not for him, but as well a couplet to the same purpose:

> Minor paena Tantall nil inferno
> Pate, che chi di donna sta al governo.[85]

Each of the other histories is concluded with a similar posy and set of verses which emphasize and sum up the moral of the narrative.

Another example of the usage of emblems in the first half of Elizabeth's reign is to be found in *The Shepherd's Calendar*, where each eclogue ends with an emblem or, strictly speaking, a posy for the principal characters, and where each gloss concludes with a discussion of the significance of the emblem or posy. It is readily seen that Colin, for example, has a different posy for each eclogue. In January his posy, "Anchora speme," is explained by E.K. as "that notwithstande his extreme passion and lucklesse love, yet leaning on hope, he is somewhat recomforted."[86] Such a posy is suitable for the lovelorn shepherd who has recited the story of his unrequited love. When, however, in the June eclogue we realize that his love for Rosalind is now hopeless, we are not surprised to find "Gia speme spenta" as the posy with this explanation by E.K.:

> You remember, that in the fyrst Æglogue, Colins Poesie was Anchora speme: for that as then there was hope of favour to be found in tyme. But nowe being cleane forlorne and rejected of her, as whose hope, that was, is cleane extinguished and turned into despeyre, he renounceth all comfort and hope of goodnesse to come. Which is all the meaning of thys Embleme.[87]

A change in the relation between poet and posy is found in the November eclogue. Here Colin is not concerned with his private affairs; instead he is singing a dirge for "some mayden of greate bloud, whom he calleth Dido."[88] The posy, "La mort ny mord,"[89] which is explained by E.K. as "death biteth not,"[90] clearly applies to the subject matter of the dirge and has no connection whatsoever with Colin's

---

82   *Ibid.*, II, 66.
83   *Ibid.*, II.
84   *Tragical Tales translated by Tvrbervile . . . Imprinted at London by Abell Ieffs . . . Anno. Dom. 1587.*
85   *Ibid.*, fol. 34ᵛ.
86   *The Poetical Works of Edmund Spenser*, ed. by J. C. Smith and E. de Selincourt, Oxford, 1926, pp. 422, 423.
87   *Ibid.*, pp. 442, 443.
88   *Ibid.*, p. 460.
89   *Ibid.*, p. 462.
90   *Ibid.*, p. 463.

love for Rosalind. In other words the posy depends on the circumstances of the poem. With the December posy we return to Colin the lover; but now we find that he has resolved his unhappy love in favor of poetry which will endure, or as he says, "Vivitur ingenio: caetera martis erunt,"[91] which E.K. explains thus:

> The meaning wherof is that all thinges perish and come to theyr last end, but workes of learned wits and monuments of Poetry abide for ever.[92]

If we look back over Colin's four posies, we see in the three dealing with his love a development: at first he hopes, then he becomes desolate, finally he attempts to reconcile himself. Thus, to anyone who has read the *Calendar* these three posies tell the story, at least in outline, of Colin's reactions to his love affair. The November posy obviously deals with another phase of Colin's interests and so does not apply to the love affairs, but it does stand as an example of the change of posy according to the circumstances and subject matter involved.

A final example of the Elizabethan usage of posies is found in the introductory letter of an anonymous N.W. which prefaced Samuel Daniel's translation of Paolo Giovio.

> They [emblems] are differed by sondrie Cognisances, established by reason and conformed by reading, and may be authorized by experience. The mot of an *Impresa* may not exceed three words. *Emblemes* are interpreted by many verses. An *Impresa* is not garnished with many different images, *Emblemes* are not limited. . . . In *Devises* it is enacted that the figure without the mot or the mot without the figure should not interprete the Authors meaning. In *Emblems* is more libertie and fewer lawes. *Impreses* manifest the special purpose of Gentlemen in warlike combats or chamber tornaments. [Here follow examples of ancient imprese.] . . . Have not our Printers also of late honored this profession? Have they not bene at emulation for ingenious *Devises? Stephen* glorieth in his tree, and moderateth those (that love to mount by loftie witts) with this Posie: *Noli altum sapere. Plantin* beareth a compasse in a hande stretched out of the cloudes which measureth all, *Constantia & labore.* I will omit *Griphius Episcopus*: I will forget all artificers, who commonly buy such inventions at the second hand. I will not meddle with Courtiers, I will passe over the knowen *Impreses* of *Moore* and *Cromwell,* a payre royall of nobles. . . . Tell me how you like this *Heroycall Impresa* of *Curtius Gonzaga.* An Egle flying on high against the Sunne, with this word purche, a parte of that verse of *Petrarche. Pur che ne godan gli occhi, ardan le piume.* For that which delighteth my eyes burneth my fethers. A frend of mine, whom you know, M.P. climing for an *Egles* nest, but defeated by the mallalent of fortune limmed in his studie a *Pine* tree striken with lightning carying this mot. Il mio sperar which was borrowed also from *Petrarch. Allor che fulmirato e morto giacque il mio sperar che tropp'alto mintana* [montava?]. Yet in despight of fortune he devised also a Pinnace or small Barke, tossed with tempestious stormes, and in the saile was written *expectanda dies,* hoping as I thinke for one Sunne shine day to recompence so many glomy and winter monethes. . . .[93]

These extensive references to the use of posies in the work of Gascoigne, his contemporaries, and immediate successors have been adduced so that we might

91 *Ibid.,* p. 656.
92 *Ibid.,* p. 467.
93 *The Worthy tract of Paulus Iovius, op. cit.,* Introductory Letter of N. W.

have a fairly complete understanding of the way in which posies were employed in the fashionable world, since it was as a member of that world that Gascoigne wrote his poems and signed them with posies. It is obvious from the examples cited that a posy could sum up the poem or story to which it was appended. On the other hand it is impossible to understand on this basis why Whetstone used as his personal posy, "Formae nullae fides;" Turbervile, "Nocet empta dol[o]re volupt[a]s;" and Gascoigne, the eight different posies employed in *A Hundreth Sundrie Flowres.*

This latter usage finds an explanation in the examples of *The Shepherd's Calendar* and in the comments of N.W. where we see that the posies describe the emotional or intellectual attitude of the person involved. Thus "Anchora speme" describes the state of mind of Colin at the time of the January eclogue, and "Gia speme spenta" describes his attitude after Menalcas has won Rosalind. If the posy merely summed up the subject matter, any one of a great variety of posies could have been employed, but when we read E.K.'s explanations, we see that here is another use of the posy, namely, to describe the state of mind of Colin.

Similarly, in N.W.'s account of his friend M.P. who, in despair over his ruined hopes, wrote "il mio sperar," and yet, reviving from such pessimism, wrote "expectanda dies," we see another instance of the use of different posies to indicate the individual's state of mind.

That Gascoigne used his posies in exactly this same way is demonstrated by the poet's own statement:

> I have also sundrie tymes chaunged mine owne worde or devise. And no mervaile: For he that wandereth much in those wildernesses, shall seldome continue long in one minde.[94]

To this statement of his own usage of posies, the poet adds another which at once recalls the impersonal posy used by Colin in the November eclogue.

> And by that it proceedeth, that I have so often chaunged my Posie or worde. For when I did compile anything at the request of other men, if I had subscribed the same with mine owne usual mot or devise, it might have bewrayed the same to have beene of my doing.[95]

From this last statement it would seem that Gascoigne carefully differentiated between the posies that referred to him and those which applied to poems written for other men. Since we know that No. 47 was written for Sir John Scudamore we might conclude that its posy, "Meritum petere, grave," should be the hallmark of a poem written for another man. Such is not the case, for No. 38, so signed, is concerned with a matter very near to the affections and fortunes of George Gascoigne—his merits in comparison with those of Edward Boyes, his hated rival in the quest for the love and wordly goods of Elizabeth Bacon Bretton. How many other poems of this group concern Gascoigne I do not know, but there is evidence that a number were written for other persons. In any case this particular posy is

94 *Works,* I, 17.
95 *Ibid.,* I, 17.

of such a general nature that it could suit equally well poems written for other men and those which dealt with the poet's own affairs.

A clue to Gascoigne's method of using his various posies is found by examining his most famous, "Tam Marti Quam Mercurio." Beginning with *The Posies*, which was published in 1575, and continuing to his death in 1577, Gascoigne used this posy exclusively. Clearly the posy would have had no significance until after the poet had taken part in the wars in the Low Countries. Thus, I think it is evident that this posy, by being signed to all works of the last two years of the poet's life, indicates a general method, namely, that all the posies, beginning with "Si fortunatus infoelix" and ending with "Tam Marti Quam Mercurio," represent successive stages in Gascoigne's life.[96]

Proceeding to *A Hundreth Sundrie Flowres*, we see that the order of the poems from No. 67 on to the end is chronological: No. 67 bears the date 1572; No. 68 refers to the death of Captain Bourcher which occurred in the summer of 1572; No. 69 was composed in the autumn of 1572; No. 70 deals with events of the winter of 1572-73; Nos. 71-73, though not datable by external evidence, certainly suit the poet's general attitude during this same winter; No. 74 tells of Gascoigne's departure for Holland on March 19, 1572/3; and we know by its unfinished nature that "Dan Bartholmew" was being written during the spring of 1572/3.[97]

All of these poems are signed "Haud ictus sapio," a posy which well describes Gascoigne's state of mind not only during this year of 1572-73 but for some time before. Indeed, he had been struck down but he had not learned wisdom. Financially ruined, he knew not how to recoup his fortunes. In search of gain he went to Holland, but that venture was a failure and this same theme is echoed in No. 70 where he says:

> And sure I feare, unlesse your lordship deigne
> To traine him yet into some better trade
> It will be long before he hit the veine
> Whereby he may a richer man be made.

The posy, when compared with the facts known about this stage of the poet's life, reveals his attitude exactly as do Colin Clout's posies and those of M.P., the friend of the anonymous N.W. And thus we have seen that at least two of Gascoigne's posies are signed to poems written when that particular posy described his general intellectual or emotional attitude toward himself and the world.

Thus far we have proceeded on the basis of external evidence which confirmed the applicability of the posy. With one exception, none of the other posies can be dated by external means, but this one, the "Sic tuli" signed to the poems

96 Weight is given this hypothesis by Pollard's discovery of the erroneous date on the title page of Hollyband's *The Frenche Littleton* (*Bibliographical Soc. Transactions*, XIII (1916), 253-72). A commendatory verse in this volume was contributed by Gascoigne and was signed "Tam Marti Quam Mercurio." The date, 1566, which Pollard has shown to be an error for 1576, would establish the usage of the posy before any martial experiences. One could have predicted Pollard's discovery on the basis of the use of posy.

97 See the individual poems and the critical notes on them for verification of these dates.

written on his return to Gray's Inn in 1564 or 1565, further establishes his general method of using a particular posy for all poems written during a specific time period. By 1564 Gascoigne had been involved in a number of difficulties but he was not yet completely beaten. His marriage to Elizabeth Bacon Bretton Boyes had taken him into involved litigation; he had tried to defraud John Gostwick; and he had squandered a large share of his inheritance. Still hopeful, he returned to Gray's Inn to resume his study of the law. With these facts in mind we may look at "Sic tuli" and poems 57-60 and see that there is a very real significance to the posy. He has learned that the world is not what he thought it was; his disappointments have been manifold and in a rather self-conscious fashion he can say, "Thus I bear my many burdens." The posy has very real meaning for that period of his life when he still had hope of achieving success.

With the other posies, as has been said, there is no external evidence by which they may be dated and thus related to a specific period in Gascoigne's life, and it is at this point that we must proceed to a conclusion relying only on what we do know about Gascoigne's custom in respect to the three posies which have been discussed. The first group of poems following "F.J." is that signed "Si fortunatus infoelix." In my opinion, this posy is a general one used by Gascoigne to describe himself as a young courtier first adventuring into courtly intrigue and affairs of love. "If I am fortunate, then I am unhappy"—how well this echoes the romantic melancholia of the adolescent who is overwhelmed by *weltschmerz!* How well does it also catch that essential antithesis of the Petrarchan love jargon where frost and fire, love and disdain, bale and bliss, must always be mentioned together. All of the poems in this group deal with unrequited love, and all, abounding with trite figures, are quite unlike those sections of "Dan Bartholmew" which represent his later work. On every score these poems are youthful compositions.

Of "Meritum petere, grave" much the same sort of generalization may be made. We know that a number of these were written for other persons and obviously such writing was not done gratuitously but for a reward. In other words, this posy represents a time period when Gascoigne was seeking preferment at court. The majority of the poems were probably written to further this end, but there is no reason to conclude that the poet wrote nothing during this time which concerned him personally. Gabriel Harvey's annotation on this posy in his copy of *The Posies* points clearly to such a general significance.

Meritum petere, vile: capere generosum. In hoc mundo, non loquendum de merito, sed reverâ merendum.[98]

In thus upbraiding the poet for seeking a reward rather than doing something to deserve a reward, Harvey shows that for him, at least, the posy described a general attitude on the part of Gascoigne. Finally, the use of this posy on the title page of *A Hundreth Sundrie Flowres* reveals Gascoigne's purpose in publication. As I have noted, he hoped to gain a patron and preferment from the publica-

98 *Gabriel Harvey's Marginalia,* ed. by G. C. Moore Smith, Stratford, 1913, p. 290.

tion of his work. I would qualify this use of the posy by noting that as used on the title page the posy does not properly belong to a time period; it is used because of its obvious significance in relation to the book itself.

Of the other posies, some are easily understood and others are quite baffling. "Spreta tamen vivunt" is explained by Gascoigne in poem No. 28 where he says, "Despysed things may live, altho' they pyne in pain." A love affair has turned out badly with the lady preferring the rival. Unlike a similar situation in the "Si fortunatus infoelix" group, for example No. 14, this affair has caused a bitter reaction in the poet's heart and so for a time he is a despised thing that yet lives.

"Ferenda Natura" is also explained by Gascoigne in connection with this lady in "Dan Bartholmew" where we read:

> I can appoint hir well no better name,
> Than this, wherein dame *Nature* beares the blame.

Thus I would conclude that, viewing his harsh treatment as the result of the lady's instinctive nature rather than her duplicity, he used this posy to represent his reaction.

"Ever or Never" seems to be a more general posy like "Si fortunatus infoelix" or "Meritum petere, grave." We find no specific application of the posy, and the poems so signed are on a variety of subjects.

Finally, "Fato non fortuna," used in "Dan Bartholmew," is explained in "The Subscription and seale" to Dan Bartholmew's will, "I *Fato*: non *Fortuna* hight, lo nowe you know my name." In other words, all the dire events in this affair came to Dan Bartholmew as a result of his fate not his fortune. The events of the verse narrative are indeed best explained on such a basis!

It now remains to gather all the evidence so that a final judgment may be reached as to Gascoigne's use of posies and the reason why he broke down the arrangement of his poems by posy groups in his revised and enlarged *Posies*. First, let us consider the sequence of the material found in *A Hundreth Sundrie Flowres*. G.T. says that the first poem in "F.J." was "the first verses that ever he [Gascoigne] wrote uppon like occasion." Since the occasion was falling in love, the poet was presumably a comparatively young man. From this and from the details in the story as well as from the other poems in "F.J." I conclude that these poems represent his earliest work. If, then, we see that not only is his earliest work at the beginning of the volume but that the last eight poems and "Dan Bartholmew" are arranged in chronological order, and that the other poems which can be dated (Nos. 57-60) are also in an approximately chronological position, we are making no unwarranted assumption in concluding that the entire order of the book is very nearly chronological.

If the poems are so arranged, then the various posies represent successive periods in Gascoigne's life and the reason for disturbing this organic relationship in his revised edition becomes discernible. As they stand in *A Hundreth Sundrie Flowres* the posies tell a story much as do Colin Clout's posies in *The Shepherd's Calendar*. First of all, we have our young lover of "The Adventures of Master F.J." Next we see him as the young courtier ("Si fortunatus infoelix") entering upon his life in the fashionable world. Unfortunately, he falls seriously in love with a lady who treats him shabbily ("Spreta tamen vivunt"). Either she excuses herself or he does, on the grounds that she is not duplicitous, rather she is but a weak woman given to vacillation by her very nature ("Ferenda Natura"). Having recovered from this affair he devotes himself to seeking preferment ("Meritum petere, grave"). Already he is beginning to realize with bitterness that he has ruined his opportunities and so we have an early appearance of "Haud ictus sapio." For some time there is a vacillation among the two posies, "Ever or Never" and "Haud ictus sapio," while all poems signed "Sic tuli," representing not only a sense of burden but also a sense of purpose, appear in a group in the midst of this mingling of the other two. The period of instability indicated by this mingling of posies is followed by the emergence of "Haud ictus sapio" as his general attitude in those years before he went to Holland for the second time.

If we now look at *The Posies* to note the alteration in order of the poems we shall, I think, see why Gascoigne altered the original chronological arrangement which roughly approximated the course of his life. First of all, we find that of the five poems of *A Hundreth Sundrie Flowres* which are omitted in the revised *Posies* only one, "F.J." No. 10, is easily discernible as excised on moral grounds, those grounds on which objection was made to the original volume. Of the other four omitted poems one furnishes us with a clue to its disappearance. This, No. 38, with its obvious reference to Gascoigne and Boyes is the only poem ever written by the poet which mentioned specifically his marriage and its attendant circumstances. Such specific reference must have been the cause of its deletion in *The Posies*, exactly as "The Adventures of Master F.J." was altered so that its specific references to the English scene and English persons might be concealed. Such a reason is the only one which I can suggest for the omission of such poems as Nos. 1 and 20, (the other "omitted" poem, No. 34, appears in *The Posies* as Dan Bartholmew's second "Triumph"). These two poems are seemingly innocuous: the first is a translation of Ariosto with an original six line envoie applying the subject matter of Ariosto to the poet and his lady; the second tells of the poet's departure from London, a departure enforced by friendship, but there are very specific references to the "Popler walles" which enclosed the lady, to his picture which she possesses, to his habit of walking by the shore of the Thames, and finally to his custom of visiting her at such times by means of his "sayling boate." These references must have been sufficiently definite for the average courtier to have guessed the identity of the lady and the friend.[99] Again, it was the poet's desire to conceal that of which he had too tangibly spoken that led to the deletion of this poem. A similar reason must be behind the omission of

99 As a matter of fact, one of Gascoigne's contemporaries has left us proof of this very point. George Puttenham (*op. cit.*, p. 258) in discussing No. 24, which deals with this custom of crossing the river in his own boat, says, "His intent was to declare how upon the tenth day of March he crossed the river Thames, to walke in Saint *Georges* field, the matter was not great as ye may suppose." Nothing in the poem indicates the destination as St. George's Field. Therefore it seems that Puttenham knew something about Gascoigne's journeys across the Thames.

No. 1, although in this case we would need the knowledge of gossip of a courtier to ascertain the exact references.

Those posy groups whose order Gascoigne altered most radically reveal similar references which a courtier might easily have understood. For example, the "Spreta tamen vivunt" poems are completely separated in *The Posies* and we have only to look at these to see that, read in their original order by one familiar with court gossip, the lady would probably have been identified.[100] Similarly, there must have been some connection between poems 8 and 9 so that if the two were read together an identity might have been revealed. Both contain quite specific references and for that very reason I think that Gascoigne separated them by some hundreds of pages in *The Posies*. Even though they are still signed by the same posy in the revised edition, a reader would not know, unless he had the *Flowres*, that the one followed the other.

In the same "Si fortunatus infoelix" group are two poems whose introductory comments seem to link them so that their subsequent separation is again a part of the pattern of concealment. Poems 10, 11, and 12 all deal with one lady but nothing of a particularly scandalous nature is revealed. Poem No. 13, however, has this introduction:

> Enough of this Dame. And let us peruse his other doings which have come to my hands, in such disordered order, as I can best set them down. I will now then present you with a Sonet written in prayse of the brown beautie, which he compyled for the love of Mistresse E.P. as foloweth.

This poem is a trite working over of familiar conceits ending with praise for "a lovely nutbrowne face." The next poem, however, is a bitter attack on presumably this same lady. By separating the two poems no one will realize that Mistresse E.P. is the lady of the second poem. That the two poems dealt with the same lady may be concluded from the fact that just before this we find three poems dealing with one person and that directly after there is a sequence of six poems concerned with one person. Clearly Gascoigne was writing his poems in sequences even within the posy group, and these sequences must have revealed much to any well-informed courtier.

The reverse of this process of concealment may be seen in those poems that preserve in *The Posies* their original order. For example, all the "Sic tuli" poems, which deal with his return to Gray's Inn, appear in their original sequence. There was no reason for changing them; they concealed nothing, and so they remained as they were. Similarly, those poems of "Si fortunatus infoelix" which have not been mentioned preserve their original order with Nos. 2-7 appearing together, and 15-19 also together. No. 21, left alone by the omission of No. 20, is quite rightly placed in the "Weedes" section of *The Posies*.

It is this division of *The Posies* into three sections: "Flowres," "Hearbes," and "Weedes" which may account for the placing of a group of similarly signed

---

100 In *The Posies* not only is No. 23 separated from the other poems of the "Spreta tamen vivunt" group, but its posy is altered to "Si fortunatus infoelix."

poems in one category and another group in another.[101] The reasons for this
rather arbitrary allocation of the groups I find difficult to understand. If the curi-
ous reader cares to examine those poems which Gascoigne chose to place among
"Flowres" and to compare them with those which were evidently considered
"Weedes," he will, I fear, find that there is no even remotely consistent principle
at work. Why the sequence of Nos. 15-19 is among the "Flowres" and not the
"Weedes" is a question that I cannot attempt. One must be content to let Gas-
coigne preserve yet "another misterie that is to be understood by the aucthor
alone."[102]

As far as the general reason for grouping the poems of *A Hundreth Sundrie
Flowres* goes, I think we may safely arrive at a conclusion. The use of posies
was a very real part of the social pattern of the courtly world and George Gas-
coigne was both proud of and true to the conventions. Every courtier should have
a posy denoting the current state of his affairs. Only George Gascoigne, however,
signed his posy to all his poems and thus revealed not only his connection with the
ladies and events of which he wrote but as well gave the scandal mongers a holi-
day by giving them the means to know the approximate time relationship of the
various affairs. His mistake was, of course, his decision to publish so many poems
that dealt with ladies and gentlemen of high station. Having published, he did his
best to remedy his liability to further censorship by concealing, through the
alteration of the original order, as much as he could.

Thus an examination of what appears, at least on the surface, to be a matter
of slight importance, the mere alteration of the order of poems, has led us through
the by-ways of the ephemeral social conventions of the courtly world at a time
when Elizabeth still deserved the compliments of Sir Christopher Hatton, my
Lord of Leicester, and the submissive homage of George Gascoigne.

After a sudden frenzied whirl in this courtly world, posies and emblems
lost their youthful freshness. The rules for their use became strict; they fell into
the hands of systematic exploiters; and ultimately the Puritans wrenched what
had once been part of the evanescent language of love into the symbols of a harsh
morality that clipped the golden wires and destroyed the Maypole. And so
George Gascoigne by preserving for us in print the poetry of the court has once
again demonstrated his unique quality of seeing first and telling us what he saw.

The Social and Literary Significance of
A Hundreth Sundrie Flowres

The widespread use of posies by the members of the court circle which has
been noted in the preceding section suggests the essential nature of *A Hundreth
Sundrie Flowres*. This volume was the work of an amateur poet who was also
a gentleman, and it was concerned with those topics upon which a gentleman was

101 Gascoigne offers an explanation of his arrangement in these words, "I pray
thee to smell unto these Posies, as *Floures to comfort, Herbes to cure,* and *Weedes to
be avoyded."* (*Works*, I, 17.)
102 This phrase is used frequently in *The Posies* as a marginal notation to obscure
passages involving unknown persons.

expected to comment in verse, upon a moment's notice. In this respect the *Flowres* is close to *Songes and Sonettes,* but whereas the latter is an anthology, the former is the work of one man. Only Turbervile, and perhaps Whetstone, among Gascoigne's contemporaries, published books of a similar nature. The work of other gentlemen poets sometimes appeared in the anthologies, but the majority of their compositions have disappeared. After Gascoigne, the labors of courtier-poets met with a similar fate, with the exception of a few sonnet cycles, and the writings of Sidney. The reason, of course, lies in the fact that the writing of poetry came, beginning, perhaps, with *The Shepherd's Calendar* in 1579, into the hands of "professional" poets who regarded themselves as poets first and foremost, and dilettante courtiers either secondarily or not at all, and through such professionals Elizabethan poetry came of age.

Tudor poetry, before the publication of *The Shepherd's Calendar,* had been merely one of the handmaidens in the train of a Renaissance gentleman and had been treated as one among many, not as the first lady. Wyatt's diplomatic career was obviously the most important aspect of that courtier's life. He was, of course, interested in his verses, but they were not paramount. Lord Buckhurst's abandonment of literature after *Gorboduc* and *The Induction* is another instance of the relative unimportance of literary activity in the life of a man bent on a career. Examples of a similar attitude toward poetry and, in fact, all literature could be multiplied, but the career of George Gascoigne well represents in microcosm the point of view of the fashionable world.

As I have pointed out elsewhere,[103] Gascoigne and his contemporaries were primarily interested in establishing themselves in the new world which the Tudors, as well as economic and political forces, were bringing into being. Unwilling to pursue a country existence as had his father, he set out to become a lawyer. Soon attracted by the fashionable life in London he sought to become a courtier in imitation of men like Leicester, Sir Christopher Hatton, and the others who found fame and fortune by dancing attendance on the Queen. The prodigal expenditure of such a venture ruined him in short order and he seems to have tried in vain to live in the country. Grasping at straws, he embarked as a soldier of fortune in the Dutch wars, but here again he was a failure. Finally, he turned to his pen, not as a means of making money, but as a means of securing a patron. For a time he enjoyed the good offices of the Viscount Montague and Arthur, Lord Grey of Wilton, and ultimately he was favored by the Queen, or the government, to the extent of a mission to the Low Countries.

In neither his life nor his works does Gascoigne give any indication of that serious attitude toward literature and particularly poetry which is so significant in the utterances of the "newe poet" of *The Shepherd's Calendar.* While it is not until Milton, and even then in a limited degree, that the English man of letters came to occupy the important position that was accorded a Petrarch, an Ariosto, or a Tasso, it is true that in Spenser we find not only a sincere devotion to poetry

103   *George Gascoigne,* pp. 5 ff., 22 ff.

but as well a sense of the importance of poetry. To Gascoigne literature was never an end itself, it was always the means to an end.

Such, too, was the attitude of the fashionable dabblers in verse. A sonnet packed with trite figures might mollify a stony heart, a rhetorical compliment in verse might bring the reversion of an office, and a poem written for a powerful friend might also bring a reward. And it is as a record of such a view of literature that we should regard *A Hundreth Sundrie Flowres*. This volume is not only one of the few written by a single court poet, but is, as well, the best of that *genre*.

By looking backward and viewing the work of Gascoigne's predecessors, we may understand more clearly the social significance of *A Hundreth Sundrie Flowres*, since Gascoigne was obviously continuing and developing, and not breaking with, the tradition of literature. The earliest extant volume of English Renaissance poetry, *Songes and Sonettes*, was, of course, an anthology; perhaps the commonplace book of some member of the court circle. Whatever the immediate source, it is evident that the principal contributors, Wyatt and Surrey, had had no thought of doing more than circulating their poems in manuscript. It is well to remember that by the date of publication both Wyatt and Surrey were dead and that the majority of the other contributors belonged to the time of Henry VIII. In other words, *Songes and Sonettes* represented not contemporary poetry but that of a previous generation.

After the death of Henry VIII in 1547, the times were not propitious for the muse of English verse. The strenuous days of the protectorate, the religious struggles of bloody Mary, and the uncertainty of the early years of Elizabeth's reign—all these turned men's minds from songs and sonnets to the reality of existence. It is, perhaps, too easy to see in the subject matter of *A Mirror for Magistrates*, the first important work by contemporary authors in Elizabeth's reign, a very real indication of the thoughts with which the men of the middle years of the century had been concerned. The vagaries of fortune which had in generations past raised men to high station only to hurl them down were well understood by those who had seen the pathetic death of Lady Jane Grey, the exiles departing for the Low Countries, Germany, and Switzerland, and the fires burning in Smithfield. Even though the *Mirror* might superficially echo the words of Chaucer's monk and even though men might easily see how low the mighty had fallen, the philosophical pattern which underlay the *Mirror* was, however, something new. As Miss Campbell has pointed out in her recent edition,[104] the tragedies in the *Mirror* were chosen to illustrate the Tudor doctrine that history was a glass wherein men might find lessons for current guidance and that, furthermore, history taught the obedience of subjects to the Magistrate as God's regent on earth, and the obedience of such regents to God. An age that could produce such a concept was looking forward to a period of relative stability when the thoughts of men could be directed toward intellectual matters. It is little wonder then that we expectantly look for parallel intellectual developments in poetry.

104 *The Mirror for Magistrates,* ed. by Lily B. Campbell, Cambridge, 1938, pp. 48-55.

The first volume of lyric poetry after *Songes and Sonettes* is, however, hardly encouraging to such a view. Barnabe Googe's *Eglogs, Epytaphes, & Sonettes*, published in 1563, is of little interest even for a student of the development of Elizabethan poetry. The majority of the poems are short ephemeral pieces written to a friend or in reply to a similar piece by a friend. A few interesting eclogues are overwhelmed by dull, prosaic obituary laments in the vein which George Whetstone was later to exploit to exhaustion. The one longish poem in the volume is "Cupido Conquered," a strange survival of the mediaeval dream allegory. Of even less merit is *The Arbor of Amitie* by Thomas Howell. This volume, printed in 1567, contains little that is more than doggerel, but an antiquarian interest may find pleasure in the following lines which utter haltingly a thought so well expressed only a few years later:

> As Player playes on stage till parte be done
> So man alike his race on earth doth runne
> To day alyve in silkes and fine aray
> To morrow dead and cladde with clot of clay,
> Of earthly things, loe here the slipper stay.[105]

One year before, however, George Turbervile's *Epigrams, Songs and Sonnets* had appeared in its first extant edition, although a previous edition seems implicit in the words on the title page, "newly corrected with additions." Here for the first time in the reign of Elizabeth, we encounter a volume of verse by one poet who can claim our attention on the grounds of the intrinsic rather than the antiquarian value of his writings. True it is that there are many ephemeral, occasional verses, heavy-handed obituaries, and sententious moral animadversions, but the fact remains that a certain respectable fluency of expression is coupled with a true Renaissance interest in the classic past. Of all the early poets Turbervile seems to have had the best knowledge of Latin literature. He had, in 1567, published translations of Ovid's *Heroycall Epistles*, and *The Eglogs of Mantuan*. Some years later, in 1587, another of Turbervile's translations appeared under the title, *Tragical Tales*. These tales from the *Decameron* and Renaissance collections of novelle were undertaken after the poet realized his own inability to translate Lucan. The breadth of intellectual interest demonstrated by these translations is also in evidence in his original works and this it is that gives Turbervile a claim to recognition which he would not deserve on a basis of the technical merits of his verse. Painter, Pettie, and Golding, the translators of Seneca, enriched the vernacular by their work, but none of them carried forward original work based in any way on their knowledge of Italian or Latin. It is in contrast with these men that we see Turbervile's importance.

It remained, however, for George Gascoigne to produce a volume of verse and prose that established the Renaissance tradition in the vernacular. The subject matter of *A Hundreth Sundrie Flowres* covers all the themes of the Italian poets. Love conceits are, of course, paramount, but, as well, we find

---

105 Thomas Howell, *The Arbor of Amitie . . . Imprinted at London by Henry Denham . . . Anno. 1568*, ed. by A. B. Grosart, London, 1879, p. 60.

satire blending the native tradition of Piers Plowman with the conventional Renaissance attack on the busy, worldly life. Moral reflections embellished in the manner of Petrarch and his imitators stand alongside pieces whose delightful jesting strikes a new and sophisticated note in English Renaissance poetry, and recalls Chaucer. Labored verses of compliment and ephemeral pieces written for friends in need of a poetic appeal to a disdainful lady or to jealous enemies round out the full measure of the activities of a court poet, and thus gathered together in the work of one man we have a synthesis of poetic interests of the courtly world during the early years of Queen Elizabeth's reign.

Almost as soon as it was published, however, *A Hundreth Sundrie Flowres* became representative of an age that was passing. In 1578 *Euphues* appeared and established a new vogue for the courtiers. Ordinary conversation reached the heights, or depths, of artificiality, and soon the creation of sonnet sequences embalmed the love conceits of Petrarch. The cleavage between professional and amateur poetry that became apparent with the publication of *The Shepherd's Calendar,* grew even more pronounced as the Sidney-Pembroke group tried to oppose the development of the popular drama. In other words, literature came of age soon after the amateurs had carried its development as far as they could.

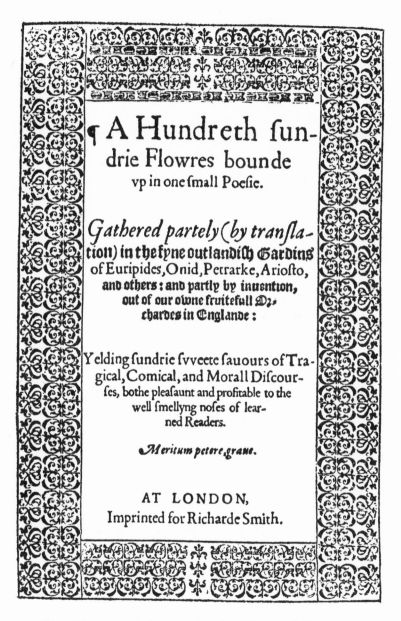

¶ A Hundreth sun-
drie Flowres bounde
vp in one small Poesie.

Gathered partely (by transla-
tion) in the fyne outlandish Gardins
of Euripides, Onid, Petrarke, Ariosto,
and others : and partly by inuention,
out of our owne fruitefull Or-
chardes in Englande :

Yelding sundrie svveete sauours of Tra-
gical, Comical, and Morall Discour-
ses, bothe pleasaunt and profitable to the
well smellyng noses of lear-
ned Readers.

Meritum petere, graue.

AT LONDON,
Imprinted for Richarde Smith.

*The title page of the copy in the Library of Emmanuel
College, Cambridge. Reproduced by the kind permission
of the Librarian.*

The contents[1] of this Booke

The Printer to the Reader

IT hath bin an old saying, that whiles two doggs do strive for a bone, the thirde may come and carie it away. And this proverbe may (as I feare) be wel verefied in me which take in hand the imprinting of this poeticall Poesie. For the case seemeth doubtful, and I will disclose my con- 5
jecture. Master .H.W. in the beginning of this worke, hath in his letter (written to the Readers) cunningly discharged himselfe of any such misliking, as the graver sort of greyheared[1] judgers mighte (perhaps) conceive in the publication of these pleasant Pamphlets. And nexte unto that learned preamble, the letter of .G.T. (by whome as seemeth, the first 10
coppie hereof was unto the same .H.W. delivered,)[2] doth with no lesse clerkly cunning seeke to perswade the readers, that he (also) woulde by no meanes have it published. Now I feare very muche (all these words notwithstanding) that these two gentlemen were of one assent compact to have it imprinted: And yet, finding by experience that nothing is so wel 15
handled now adayes, but that some malicious minds may either take occasion to mislike it themselves, or else finde meanes to make it odious unto others: They have therefore (each of them) politiquely prevented the daunger of misreport, and suffered me the poore Printer to runne away with the palme of so perillous a victorie. Notwithstanding, having 20
wel perused the worke, I find nothing therein amisse (to my judgemente) unless it be two or three wanton places passed over in the discourse of an amorous enterprise: The which for as much as the words are cleanly (al-though the thing ment be somewhat naturall) I have thought good also to let them passe as they came to me, and the rather bicause (as master .H.W. 25
hath well alleadged in his letter to the Reader) the well minded man may reape some commoditie out of the most frivolous works that are written. And as the venemous spider will sucke poison out of the most holesome herbe, and the industrious Bee can gather hony out of the most stinking weede: Even so the discrete reader may take a happie example by the 30
most lascivious histories, although the captious and harebraind heads can neither be encoraged by the good, nor forewarned by the bad. And thus muche I have thought good to say in excuse of some savours, which may perchance smell unpleasantly to some noses, in some part of this poeticall poesie. Now it hath with this fault a greater commoditie than common 35
poesies have ben accustomed to present, and that is this, you shall not be constreined to smell of the floures therein conteined all at once, neither yet to take them up in such order as they are sorted: But you may take any one flowre by itselfe, and if that smell not so pleasantly as you wold wish, I doubt not yet but you may find some other which may supplie the 40
defects thereof. As thus, he which wold have good morall lessons clerkly handled, let him smell to the Tragedie translated out of Euripides. He that wold laugh at a prety conceit closely conveyed, let him peruse the comedie translated out of Ariosto. He that would take example by the unlawfull affections of a lover bestowed uppon an unconstant dame, let them reade 45

the report in verse, made by Dan Bartholmew of Bathe, or the discourse in
prose of the adventures passed by master F.J. whome the reader may name
Freeman Jones, for the better understanding of the same: he that
would see any particuler pang of love lively displayed, may here
approve every Pamphlet by the title, and so remaine con-   5
tented. As also divers godly himnes and Psalmes may in
like manner be founde in this recorde. To conclude,
the worke is so universall, as either in one place
or other, any mans mind may therewith be
satisfied. The which I adventure (un-   10
der pretext of this promise) to
present unto all indifferent
eyes as followeth.
(·.·)

A discourse of the adventures
passed by Master F.J.
H. W. to the Reader.

N *August Last* passed my familiar friend Master *G.T.* be-
stowed upon me yᵉ reading of a written Booke, wherin 5
he had collected divers discourses & verses, invented uppon
sundrie occasions, by sundrie gentlemen (in mine opinion)
right commendable for their capacitie. And herewithal my
said friend charged me, that I should use them onely for
mine owne particuler commoditie, and eftsones safely deliver the originall 10
copie to him againe, wherein I must confesse my selfe but halfe a marchant,
for the copie unto him I have safely redelivered. But the worke (for I
thought it worthy to be published) I have entreated my friend *A.B.* to em-
print: as one that thought better to please a number by common commoditie
then to feede the humor of any private parson by nedelesse singularitie. 15
This I have adventured, for thy contentation (learned Reader.) And
further have presumed of my selfe to christen it by the name of *A hun-
dreth sundrie Flowers*: In which poeticall posie are setforth manie trifling
fantasies, humorall passions, and straunge affects of a Lover. And therin
(although the wiser sort wold turne over the leafe as a thing altogether 20
fruitlesse) yet I my selfe have reaped this commoditie, to sit and smile
at the fond devises of such as have enchayned them selves in the golden
fetters of fantasie, and having bewrayed themselves to the whole world, do
yet conjecture yᵗ they walke unseene in a net. Some other things you may
also finde in this Booke, which are as voyde of vanitie, as the first are lame 25
for government. And I must confesse that (what to laugh at the one, &
what to learne by the other) I have contrary to the chardge of my said
friend *G.T.* procured for these trifles this day of publication. Wherat if the
aucthors onely repyne, and the number of other learned mindes be thank-
full: I may then boast to have gained a bushell of good will, in exchange for 30
one pynt of peevish choler. But if it fal out contrary to expectation that
the readers judgements agree not with myne opinion in their commenda-
cions, I may then (unless their curtesies supplie my want of discretion)
with losse of some labour, accompt also the losse of my familier friendes,
in doubt whereof, I cover all our names, and referre you to the well written 35
letter of my friende *G.T.* next following, whereby you may more at large
consider of these occasions. And so I commend the praise of other mens
travailes together with the pardon of mine owne rashnes, unto the well
willing minds of discrete readers. From my lodging nere the Strande
the xx. of January. *1572.* 40

H.W.

The letter of G.T. to his very friend
H.W. concerning this worke.

Emembring the late conference passed betwene us in my
lodging, and how you seemed to esteeme some Pamphlets,
which I did there shew unto you farre above their worth   5
in skill, I did straightwaye conclude the same your judg-
ment to procede of two especiall causes, one (and princi-
pall) the stedfast good will, which you have ever hitherto
sithens our first familiaritie borne towardes mee. An other (of no lesse
weight) the exceding zeale and favour that you beare to good letters. The   10
which (I agree with you) do no lesse bloome and appeare in pleasaunt
ditties or compendious Sonets, devised by green youthful capacities, than
they do fruitefully florish unto perfection in the ryper workes of grave
and grayheared writers. For as in the last, the yonger sort maye make
a mirror of perfecte life: so in the first, the most frosty bearded Philosopher,   15
maye take just occasion of honest recreation, not altogether without hol-
some lessons, tending to the reformation of manners. For who doubteth
but that Poets in their most feyned fables and imaginations, have meta-
phorically set forth unto us the right rewardes of vertues, and the due pun-
nishments for vices? Marie in deede I may not compare Pamphlets unto   20
Poems, neither yet may justly advant for our native countrimen, that they
have in their verses hitherto (translations excepted) delivered unto us any
such notable volume, as have bene by Poets of antiquitie, left unto the pos-
teritie. And the more pitie, that amongst so many toward wittes no one
hath bene hitherto encouraged to followe the trace of that worthy and   25
famous Knight *Sir Geffrey Chaucer,* and after many pretie devises spent
in youth, for the obtayning a worthles victorie, might consume and consum-
mate his age in discribing the right pathway to perfect felicitie, with the
due preservation of the same. The which although some may judge over
grave a subject to be handled in stile metrical, yet for that I have found   30
in the verses of eloquent Latinists, learned Greeks, & pleasant *Italians,*
sundrie directions, whereby a man may be guided toward thattayning of
of that unspeakeable treasure, I have thus farre lamented, that our coun-
treymen, have chosen rather to winne a passover praise by the wanton pen-
ning of a few loving layes, than to gayne immortall fame, by the Clarkely   35
handlinge of so profitable a Theame. For if quicknes of invencion, proper
vocables, apt Epythetes, and store of monasillables may help a pleasant
brayne to be crowned with Lawrell,[1] I doubt not but both our countrey-
men & countrie language might be entronised amonge the olde foreleaders
unto the mount *Helicon.* But nowe let mee returne to my first pur-   40
pose, for I have wandred somwhat beside the path, and yet not
cleane out of the way. I have thought good (I say) to present you with
this written booke, wherein you shall find a number of *Sonets,* layes, letters,
Ballades, Rondlets, verlayes and verses, the workes of your friend and myne
Master *F.J.* and divers others, the which when I had with long travayle   45

confusedly gathered together, I thought it then *Opere precium,* to reduce
them into some good order. The which I have done according to my bar-
reyne skill in this written Booke, commending it unto you to read and to
peruse, and desiring you as I onely do adventure thus to participate the
sight therof unto your former good will, even so that you will by no meanes   5
make the same common: but after your owne recreation taken therin y^t
you wil safely redeliver unto me the originall copie. For otherwise I shall
not onely provoke all the aucthors to be offended with mee, but further
shall leese the opertunitie of a greater matter, halfe and more graunted
unto mee alreadie, by the willing consent of one of them. And to be playne   10
(with you my friend) he hath written (which as farre as I can learne)
did never yet come to the reading or perusinge of any man but himselfe:
two notable workes. The one called, the *Sundry lots of love.* The other of
his owne invencion entituled. *The clyming of an Eagles neast.* These
thinges (and especially the later) doth seeme by the name to be a work   15
worthy the reading. And the rather I judge so because his fantasie is so
occupied in the same, as that contrary to his wonted use, he hath hitherto
withhelde it from sight of any of his familiers, untill it be finished, you may
gesse him by his *Nature.* And therefore I requier your secresie herein,
least if he hear the contrary, we shall not be able by any meanes to   20
procure these other at his handes. So fare you wel, from my Chamber
this tenth of August. *1572.*

Youres or not his owne.

G.T.

W Hen I had with no small entreatie obteyned of Master *F.J.* and   25
sundry other toward young gentlemen, the sundry copies of these sun-
dry matters, then aswell for that the number of them was great, as also for
that I found none of them, so barreyne, but that (in my judgment) had in it
Aliquid Salis, and especially being considered by the very proper occasion
whereuppon it was written (as they them selves did alwayes with the verse   30
reherse unto me the cause y^t then moved them to write) I did with more
labour gather them into some order, and so placed them in this register.
Wherein as neare as I could gesse, I have set in the first places those which
Master *F.J.* did compyle. And to begin with this his history that ensueth, it
was (as he declared unto me) written uppon this occasion. The said *F.J.*   35
chaunced once in the north partes of this Realme to fall in company of a
very fayre gentlewoman whose name was Mistresse *Elinor,* unto whom bear-
inge a hotte affection, he first adventured to write this letter following.

G.T.

M Istresse I pray you understand that being altogether a straunger   40
in these parties, my good hap hath bene to behold you to my
(no small) contentation, and my evill happ accompanies the same,
with such imperfection of my deserts, as that I finde alwayes a readie
repulse in mine owne forwardnes.[1] *So that consideringe the naturall*
clymate of the countrie, I must say that I have found fire in frost. And yet   45

comparing the inequalitie of my deserts, with the least part of your worthi-
nes, I feele a continuall frost, in my most fervent fire. Such is then thextremi-
tie of my passions, the which I could never have bene content to committe
unto this telltale paper, weare it not that I am destitute of all other helpe.
Accept therefore I beseeke you, the earnest good will of a more trustie   5
(than worthy) servaunt, who being thereby encouraged, may supplie the
defects of his abilities with readie triall of duetifull loyalty. And let this
poore paper (besprent with salt teares, and blowen over with skalding
sighes) be saved of you as a safe garde for your sampler, or a bottome to
wind your sowing silke, that when your last nedelfull is wrought, you maye   10
returne to readinge therof and consider the care of hym who is

More youres than his owne.

F. J.

THis letter by hir received (as I have hard him say) hir answere was
this: She toke occasion one daye, at his request to daunce with him,   15
the which doinge, she bashfully began to declare unto him, that she
had read over the writinge, which he delivered unto hir, with like protes-
tation, that (as at deliverie therof, she understode not for what cause he
thrust the same into hir bosome,) so now she coulde not perceyve therby
any part of his meaning, neverthelesse at last semed to take uppon hir   20
the matter, and though she disabled hir selfe, yet gave him thankes as &c.
Wheruppon he brake the braule, and walkinge abrode devised immediatly
these fewe verses followinge.

G.T.

[1]

FAyre Bersabe the bright once bathing in a Well,   25
With deawe bedimmd King Davids eyes that ruled Israell.
And Salomon him selfe, the source of sapience,
Against the force of such assaultes could make but small defence:
To it the stoutest yeeld, and strongest feele like woo,
Bold Hercules and Sampson both, did prove it to be so.   30
What wonder seemeth then? when starres stand thicke in skies,
If such a blasing starre have power to dim my dazled eyes?

Lenvoie.

To you these fewe suffise, your wittes be quicke and good,
You can conject by chaunge of hew, what humors feede my blood.   35

F.J.

I Have heard the Aucthor saye, that these were the first verses that
ever he wrote uppon like occasion. The which considering ye matter
precedent, may in my judgement be well allowed, and to judge his
doings by the effectes he declared unto me, that before he coulde put the   40
same in legible writinge, it pleased the sayd Mystresse *Elinor* of hir
curtesie thus to deale with him. Walking in a garden among divers other
gentlemen & gentlewomen, with a little frowning smyle in passing by him,
she delivered unto him a paper, with these words. *For that I understand*
not (quoth shee) th'intent of your letters, I pray you take them here   45

againe, and bestow them at your pleasure. The which done and sayde, shee passed by without change either of pace or countenaunce. *F.J.* somewhat troubled with her angrie looke, did sodenly leave the companie, & walking into a parke neare adjoyning, in great rage began to wreake his mallice on this poore paper, and the same did rend and teare in peeces. When sodenly at a glaunce he perceaved it was not of his owne hande writing, and therewithall abashed, uppon better regard he perceyved in one peece therof written (*in Romaine*) these letters *SHE:* wherefore placing all the peeces therof, as orderly as he could, he found therin written, these fewe lynes hereafter followinge.

G.T.

Y Our sodeyn departure, from our pastime yesterday, did enforce me for lacke of chosen company to return unto my worke,[1] wherein I did so long continew, till at the last the bare bottome did drawe unto my remembraunce your straunge request.[2] And although I founde therin no just cause to credite your coulored woordes, yet have I thought good hereby to requite you with like curtesie, so that at least you shall not condemne me for ungratefull. But as to the matter therin conteyned, if I could perswade my selfe, that there were in mee any coales to kyndle such sparkes of fire, I might yet peradventure bee drawen to beleve that your minde were frosen with like feare. But as no smoke ariseth, where no cole is kindled, so without cause of affection the passion is easie to be cured. This is all that I understand of your darke letters. And as much as I meane to aunsweare.

SHE.

M Y friend *F.J.* hath tolde me divers times, that imediatly uppon receit hereof, he grew in jelosy, that the same was not her owne devise. And therin I have no lesse allowed his judgment, than commended his invention of the verses, and letters before rehersed. For as by the stile this letter of hirs bewrayeth that it was not penned by a womans capacitie, so the sequell of hir doings may discipher, that she had mo ready clearkes then trustie servants in store. Well yet as the perfect hound, when he hath chased the hurt deere, amidde the whole heard, will never give over till he have singled it againe. Even so *F.J.* though somewhat abashed with this doubtfull shewe, yet still constant in his former intention, ceased not by all possible meanes, to bringe this Deere yet once agayne to the Bowes, wherby she might be the more surely stryken: and so in the end enforced to yeeld. Wherfore he thought not best to commit the sayde verses willingly into hir custodie, but privily lost them in hir chamber, written in counterfeit. And after on the next day thought better to replie, either upon hir, or uppon hir Secretary in this wyse as here followeth.

G. T.

T*He much that you have answered is very much, and much more than
I am able to replye unto: neverthelesse in myne owne defence, thus
much I alleage: that if my sodein departure pleased not you, I cannot
my selfe therwith be pleased, as one that seeketh not to please many, and
more disirous to please you then any. The cause of myne affection, I sup-
pose you behold dayly. For (self love avoyded) every wight may judge of
themselves as much as reason perswadeth: the which if it be in your good
nature suppressed with bashfulnes, then mighty Jove graunt, you may once
behold my wan cheeks wasshed in woe, that therein my salt teares may be
a myrrour to represent your owne shadow, and that like unto Narcissus
you may bee constrayned to kisse the cold waves, wherein your counter-
fait is so lively portrayed.[1] For if aboundance of other matters fayled to
drawe my gazing eyes in contemplacion of so rare excellency, yet might
these your letters both frame in me an admiration of such divine esprit, and
a confusion to my dull understanding, which so rashly presumed to wander
in this endles Laberinthe. Such I esteeme you, and thereby am become such,
and Even*

HE.   F.J.

THis letter finished and fayre written over, his chaunce was to meete
hir alone in a Gallery of the same house: where (as I have heard
him declare) his manhood in this kind of combat was first tryed, and
therein I can compare him to a valiant Prince, who distressed with power of
enemies had committed the safeguard of his person to treaty of Ambassade,
and sodenly (surprised with a *Camnassado* in his own trenches) was
enforced to yeeld as prisoner. Even so my friend *F.J.* lately overcome by y^e
beautifull beames of this Dame *Elynor,* and having now committed his
most secrete intent to these late rehearsed letters, was at unwares en-
countred with his friendly foe, and constrayned either to prepare some
new defence, or else like a recreant[2] to yeeld himself as already van-
quished. Wherfore (as in a traunce) he lifted up his dazled eyes, & so con-
tinued in a certen kind of admiration, not unlike the Astronomer, who
(having after a whole nights travayle, in the grey morning found his desired
starre) hath fixed his hungry eies to behold the *Comete* long looked for:
wherat this gracious Dame (as one that could discerne ye sun before
hir chamber windowes were wide[3] open) did deign to embolden the
feinting Knight w^t these or like words.

I perceive now (quod she) how mishap doth follow me, that having
chosen this walke for a simple solace, I am here disquieted by the man that
meaneth my distruction: & therwithal, as half angry, began to turne hir
back, when as my friend *F.J.,* now awaked, gan thus salute hir.

Mystres (quod he) and I perceive now, y^t good hap haunts me, for
being by lack of oportunitie constreined to commit my welfare unto these
blabbing leaves of bewraying paper (shewing y^t in his hand) I am here
recomforted w^t happy view of my desired joye, & therewithall reverently
kissing his hand, did softly distreine hir slender arme & so stayed hir de-

parture. The first blow thus profered & defended, they walked & talked traversing divers wayes, wherein I doubt not but y^t my friend *F.J.* could quit himself resonably well. And though it stood not with duty of a friend that I should therin require to know his secrets, yet of him selfe he declared thus much, that after long talke shee was contented to accept his proferd service, but yet still disabling hir self, and seeming to marvell what cause had moved him to subject his libertie so wilfully, or at least in a prison (as she termed it) so unworthy. Whereunto I neede not rehearse his answere, but suppose now, y^t thus they departed: saving I had forgotten this, shee required of him the last rehearsed letter, saying that his first was lost, & now she lacked a new bottome for hir silke, the which I warrant you, he graunted: and so profering to take an humble *congé* by *Bezo las manos,* shee graciously gave him the *zuccado dez labros*: and so for then departed. And therupon recompting hir words, he compyled these following, which he termed *Terza sequenza,* to sweet Mystres *SHE.*

G.T.

[2]   O F thee deare Dame, three lessons would I learne,
     What reason first persuades the foolish Fly
    (As soone as shee a candle can discerne)
    To play with flame, till shee bee burnt thereby?
    Or what may move the Mouse to byte the bayte
    Which strykes the trappe, that stops hir hungry breth?
    What calles the Byrd, where snares of deepe deceit
    Are closely coucht[1] to draw hir to hir death?
    Consider well, what is the cause of this,
    And though percase thou wilt not so confesse,
    Yet deepe desire, to gayne a heavenly blisse,
    May drowne the mynd in dole and darke distresse:
    Oft is it seene (whereat my hart may bleede)
    Fooles playe so long till they be caught in deed.
            And then
    It is a heaven to see them hop and skip,
    And seeke all shiftes to shake their shackles of:
    It is a world, to see them hang the lip,[2]
    Who (earst) at love, were wont to skorne and skof.
    But as the Mouse, once caught in crafty trap,
    May bounce and beate, agaynst the boorden wall,
    Till shee have brought hir head in such mishape,
    That doune to death hir fainting lymbes must fall:
    And as the Flye once singed in the flame,
    Cannot commaund hir wings to wave away:
    But by the heele, shee hangeth in the same
    Till cruell death hir hasty journey stay.[3]
    So they that seeke to breake the linkes of love
    Stryve with the streame, and this by payne I prove.

For when

I first beheld that heavenly hewe of thyne,
Thy stately stature, and thy comly grace,
I must confesse these dazled eyes of myne
Did wincke for feare, when I first viewd thy face: 5
But bold desire, did open them agayne,
And bad mee looke till I had lookt to long,
I pitied them that did procure my payne,
And lov'd the lookes that wrought me all the wrong:
And as the Byrd once caught (but woorks her woe)   10
That stryves to leave the lymed twigges¹ behind:
Even so the more I strave to parte thee fro,
The greater grief did growe within my minde:
Remediles then must I yeeld to thee,
And crave no more, thy servaunt but to bee   15
     Tyll² then and ever. HE. F.J.*

W Hen he had wel sorted this sequence, he sought oportunitie to leave
it where she might finde it before it were lost. And now the coles
began to kindle, wherof (but ere whyle) she feigned hir self altogither ig-
norant. The flames began to break out on every syde: & she to quench   20
them, shut up hir self in hir chamber solitarely. But as the smithie gathers
greater heat by casting on of water, even so the more she absented hir self
from company, the fresher was the grief which galded hir remembrance:
so that at last the report was spred thorough the house, that Mystres
Elinor was sicke. At which newes *F.J.* tooke small comfort: neverthelesse   25
Dame *Venus* with good aspect dyd yet thus much furder his enterprise.
The Dame (whether it were by sodain chaunge, or of wonted custome)
fell one day into a great bleeding at the nose. For which accident the said
F.J. amongst other prety conceits, hath a present remedy, wherby he tooke
occasion (when they of the house had all in vayne sought many ways to   30
stop hir bleeding) to worke his feate in this wyse: First he pleaded ig-
norance, as though he knewe not hir name, and therefore demaunded the
same of one other Gentlewoman in the house, whose name was Mistres
Frances,³ who when shee had to him declared that hir name was *Elinor*,
hee said these wordes or very lyke in effect: If I thought I should not   35
offend Mystres *Elynor*, I would not doubt to stop hir bleeding, without
eyther payne or difficulty. This gentlewoman somewhat tyckled wyth hys
words, did incontinent make relacion thereof to the sayd Mystres *Elynor*,
who immediately (declaring that *F.J.* was hir late receyved servaunt) re-
turned the sayd messanger unto him with especiall charge, that hee shoulde   40
employ his devoyre towards the recovery of hir health, with whom the same
F.J. repayred to the chamber of his desired: and finding hir sette in a
chayre, leaning on the one side over a silver bason: After his due rever-
ence,⁴ hee layd his hand on hir temples, and privily rounding hir in hir eare,
desired hir to commaund a Hazell sticke and a knyfe: the which being   45

brought, hee delivered unto hir, saying on this wyse. Mystres I wil speak certen words in secret to my selfe, and doe require no more: but when you heare me saie openly this word *Amen,* that you with this knyfe will make a nycke uppon this hasell stycke: and when you have made fyve nickes, commaunde mee also to cease. The Dame partly of good wil to the knight,   5 and partly to be stenched of hir bleeding, commaunded hir mayd, and required the other gentils, somewhat to stand asyde, which done, he began his oraisons, wherein he had not long muttered before he pronounced *Amen,* wherewith the Lady made a nyck on the stick with hir knyfe. The said *F.J.* continued to an other *Amen,* when the Lady having made an   10 other nyck felt hir bleeding[1] began to steynch: and so by the third *Amen* throughly steinched. *F.J.* then chaunging his prayers into private talk, said softly unto hir. Mystres, I am glad that I am hereby enabled to do you some service, and as the staunching of your own bloud may some way recomfort you, so if ye shedding of my bloud may any way content you, I   15 beseech you commaund it, for it shalbe evermore readily employed in your service, and therwithal with a loud voyce pronounced *Amen*: wherwith the good Lady making a nyck did secretly answere thus. Good servaunt (quod shee) I must needs think my self right happy to have gained your service and good will, and be you sure, that although ther be in me no such desert   20 as may draw you into this depth of affection, yet such as I am, I shalbe alwayes glad to shewe my self thankfull unto you, and now, if you think your self assured, that I shall bleede no more, doe then pronounce your fifth *Amen,* the which pronounced, shee made also hir fifth nicke, and held up hir head, calling the company unto hir, and declaring unto them, that   25 hir bleeding was throughly steinched. Well, it were long to tell, what sundry opinions were pronounced upon this acte, and I doe dwell overlong in the discourses of this *F.J.* especially having taken in hand only to copie out his verses, but for the circumstance doth better declare the effect, I will returne to my former tale. *F.J.* tarying a while in the chamber found oportunitie   30 to loose his sequence neere to his desired Mistres: And after *congé* taken departed. After whose departure the Lady arose out of hir chayre, & hir mayd going about to remove the same, espied, & tooke up the writing: the which hir mistres perceiving, gan sodenly conjecture that ye same had in it some like matter to the verses once before left in like maner, & made   35 semblant to mistrust that the same shuld be some words of conjuration: and taking it from hir mayd, did peruse it, & immediatly said to the company, that she would not forgo the same for a great treasure. But to be plain, I think that (*F.J.* excepted) she was glad to be rid of all company untill shee had with sufficient leasure turned over & retossed every card in   40 this sequence. And not long after being now tickled thorough all the vaines with an unknown humour, adventured of hir self to commit unto a like Ambassadour the discyphring of that which hitherto she had kept more secret, & therupon wrot with hir own hand & head in this wyse.

G. T.   45

G *Ood servant, I am out of al doubt much beholding unto you, and I have great comfort by your meanes in the steinching of my bloud, and I take great comfort to reade your letters, and I have found in my chamber divers songs which I think to be of your making, and I promise you, they are excellently made, and I assure you that I wilbe ready to doe for you any pleasure that I can, during my lyfe: wherefore I pray you come to my chamber once in a day, till I come abroad again, and I wilbe glad of your company, and for because that you have promised to bee my HE: I will take upon me this name, your SHE.*

T His letter I have seene, of hir own hand writing: and as therin the
Reader may finde great difference of Style, from hir former letter, so may you nowe understand the cause. Shee had in the same house a friend, a servaunt, a Secretary: what should I name him? such one as shee esteemed in time past more than was cause in tyme present, and to make my tale good, I will (by report of my very good friend *F.J.*) discribe him unto you. Hee was in height, the proportion of twoo *Pigmeys,* in bredth the thicknesse of two bacon hogges, of presumption a *Gyant,* of power a Gnat, Apishly wytted, Knavishly mannerd, & crabbedly favord, what was there in him then to drawe a fayre Ladies liking? Marry sir even all in all, a well lyned pursse, wherwith he could at every call, provide such pretie conceytes as pleased hir peevish fantasie, and by that meanes he had throughly (long before) insinuated him selfe with this amorous dame. This manling, this minion, this slave, this secretary, was nowe by occasion rydden to London forsothe: and though his absence were unto hir a disfurnishing of eloquence: it was yet unto *F.J.* an opertunitie of good advauntage, for when he perceived the change of hir stile, and therby grew in some suspicion that the same proceded by absence of hir chiefe Chauncellor, he thought good now to smyte while the yron was hotte, and to lend his Mistresse suche a penne in hir Secretaries absence, as he should never be able at his returne to amende the well writing thereof, wherfore according to hir commaund he repayred once every daye to hir chamber, at the least, whereas he guided him selfe so wel, and could devise such store of sundry pleasures and pastymes, that he grew in favour not onely with his desired, but also with the rest of the gentlewomen. And one daye passing the time amongst them, their playe grew to this end, that his Mistresse, being Queene, demaunded of him these three questions. Servaunt (quod she) I charge you, aswell uppon your allegiance being nowe my subject, as also uppon your fidelitie, having vowed your service unto mee that you aunswere me these three questions, by the very truth of your secret thought. First, what thing in this universall world doth most rejoyce and comforte you? *F.J.* abasing his eyes towardes the ground, toke good advisement in his aunswere, when a fayre gentlewoman of the company clapped him on the shoulder, saying, how now sir, is your hand on your halfpeny? To whom he aunswered, no fayre Lady, my hand is on my harte, and yet my hart is not in myne owne handes: wherewithall abashed, turning towardes dame *Elinor* he sayed. My

sovereigne & Mistresse, according to the charge of your commaund, and the
dutie that I owe you, my tongue shal bewraye unto you the truth of myne
intent. At this present a rewarde given me without desert, doth so rejoyce
mee with continuall remembraunce therof, that though my mind be so
occupied to thinke thereon, as that daye nor night I can be quiet from that   5
thought, yet the joye and pleasure which I conceive in the same is such,
that I can neither be cloyed with continuaunce therof, nor yet afrayde,
that any mishap can countervayle so great a treasure. This is to me such
a heaven to dwell in, as that I feede by day, and repose by night, upon the
fresh record of this reward, this (as he sayeth) he ment by the kysse that   10
she lent him in the Gallery, and by the profession of hir last letters and
wordes. Well, though this aunswere be somewhat mistie, yet let my friendes
excuse be: that taken uppon the sodeyne, he thought better to aunswere
darkely, than to be mistrusted openly. Hir second question was, what
thing in this life did moste greve his harte, and disquiet his mind, where-   15
unto he answered. That although his late rehersed joye were incomparable,
yet the greatest enimie that disturbed the same, was the privie worme of
his owne giltie conscience, which accused him evermore with great un-
worthinesse: and that this was his greatest grief. The Lady byting uppon
the bit at his cunning answeres made unto these two questions, gan thus   20
replie. Servant, I had thought to have touched you yet nearer with my
third question, but I will refrayne to attempt your pacience: and now for
my third demaund aunswere me directly in what manner this passion doth
handle you? and howe these contraries maye hang together by any possi-
bilitie of concorde? for your wordes are straunge.[1] *F.J.* now rowsing him   25
selfe boldly, toke occasion thus to handle his aunswere. Mistresse (quod
he) my wordes in dede are straunge, but yet my passion is[2] much straunger,
and theruppon this other day to content mine owne fantasie I devised a
Sonet, which although it be a peece of Cocklorells musicke, and such as I
might be ashamed to publish in this company, yet because my truth in   30
this aunswere may the better appeare unto you, I pray you vouchsafe to
receive the same in writing: and drawing a paper out of his pocket[3] pre-
sented it unto hir, wherin was written this *Sonet*.

G.   T.

[3]   L Ove, hope, and death, do stirre in me such strife,   35
     As never man but I led such a life.
  First burning love doth wound my hart to death,
  And when death comes at call of inward griefe
  Colde lingering hope, doth feede my fainting breath
  Against my will, and yeeldes my wound reliefe: 40
  So that I live, but yet my life is such,
  As death would never greve me halfe so much.
  No comfort then but only this I tast,
  To salve such sore, such hope will never want,
  And with such hope, such life will ever last,   45

And with such life, such sorrowes are not skant.
Oh straunge desire, O life with torments tost
Through too much hope, mine onely hope is lost.
                    Even HE   F. J.

THis Sonet was highly commended, and in my judgement it deserveth   5
no lesse, I have heard *F.J.* saye, that he borrowed th'inventiun of an
Italian: but were it a translation or invention (if I be Judge) it is both
prety and pithy. His dutie thus perfourmed, their pastimes ended, and at
their departure for a watch worde hee counselled his Mistresse by little
and little to walke abrode, sayinge that the Gallery neare adjoyning was   10
so pleasaunt, as if he were halfe dead hee thought that by walking therin
he might bee halfe and more revived. Thinke you so servaunt (quod she?)
and the last tyme that I walked there I suppose I toke the cause of my mal-
lady, but by your advise (and for you so clerkly steynched my bleeding) I
will assaye to walke there to morow. Mistres quod he, and in more ful   15
accomplishment of my duetie towards you, and in sure hope that you wil
use ye same onelie to your owne private commoditie, I^1 wil there awaite
uppon you, & betwene you & me wil teach you the ful order how to steynch
the bleeding of any creature, wherby you shall be as cuning as my selfe.
Gramercy good servaunt, qd. she, I thinke you lost the same in writing here   20
yesterday, but I cannot understand it, and therfore to morrowe (if I feele
my selfe any thing amended) I wil send for you thither to enstruct me
throughly: thus they departed. And at supper time, the Knight of the
Castel finding fault that his gestes stomacke served him no better, began to
accuse the grosenes of his vyands, to whom one of the gentlewomen which   25
had passed the afternoone in his company, aunswered. Nay sir, qd. she,
this gentleman hath a passion, the which once^2 in a daye at the least doth
kill his appetite. Are you so well acquainted with the disposition of his body
qd. the Lord of the house? by his owne saying, qd. she, and not otherwise.
Fayre Ladie qd. *F.J.* you either mistoke me or overheard me then, for I   30
told of a comfortable humor which so fed me with continual remembrance
of joye, as y^t my stomack being ful therof doth desire in maner none other
vittayles. Why sir, qd. ye host, do you then live by love? God forbid Sir
quod *F.J.* for then my cheekes wold be much thinner then they be, but
there are divers other greater causes of joy, then ye doubtful lottes of love,   35
and for myne owne part, to be playne, I cannot love, and I dare not hate.
I would I thought so, quod the gentlewoman. And thus with pretty nyppes,
they passed over their supper: which ended, the Lord of the house required
F.J. to daunce and passe the tyme with the gentlewoman, which he refused
not to doe. But sodenly, before the musicke was well tuned, came out Dame   40
Elynor in hir night attyre, and said to the Lord, that (supposing the soli-
tarinesse of hir chamber had encreased hir maladie) she came out for hir
better recreation to see them daunce. Wel done daughter (quod the Lord.)
And I Mistres (quod *F.J.*) would gladly bestowe the leading of you about
this great chamber, to dryve away the fayntnesse of your fever. No good   45

servaunt, quod the Lady, but in my steede, I pray you daunce with this
fayre Gentlewoman, pointing him to the Lady that had so taken him up
at supper. *F.J.* to avoyde mistrust, did agree to hir request without furder
entreaty. The daunce begon, this Knight marched on with the Image of
S. *Fraunces* in his hand, and S. *Elynor* in his hart. The violands at ende   5
of the pavion staied a whyle: in which time this Dame sayde to *F.J.* on
this wyse. I am right sorry for you in two respects, although the familiarity
have hytherto had no great continuance betwene us: and as I do lament
your case, so doo I rejoyce (for myne own contentation) that I shall now
see a due triall of the experiment which I have long desired. This sayd, she   10
kept silence. When *F.J.* (somewhat astonied with hir straunge speeche)
thus aunswered: Mystres although I cannot conceyve the meaning of your
wordes, yet by curtesy I am constrayned to yeelde you thankes for your
good will, the which appeareth no lesse in lamenting of mishaps, than in
rejoycing at good fortune. What experiment you meane to trye by mee, I   15
know not, but I dare assure you, that my skill in experiments is very simple.
Herewith the Instruments sounded a new Measure, and they passed forth-
wardes, leaving to talke, untill the noyse ceassed: which done, the gentle-
woman replied. I am sory sir, that you did erewhile, denie love and all his
lawes, and that in so open audience. Not so quod *F.J.* but as the word   20
was roundly taken, so can I readely aunswere it by good reason. Wel quod
she, how if the hearers will admit no reasonable aunswere? My reason shall
yet be neverthelesse (quod he) in reasonable judgement. Herewith she
smyled, and he cast a glance towardes dame *Elinor* askances art thou
pleased? Againe the vyols called them forthwardes, and againe at the end   25
of the braule sayd *F.J.* to this gentlewoman: I pray you Mistres, and what
may be the second cause of your sorow sustained in my behalfe? Nay soft
quod she, percase I have not yet told you the first, but content your selfe,
for the second cause you shall never know at my handes, untill I see due
trial of the experiment which I have long desired. Why then (quod he[1]) I   30
can but wish a present occasion to bring ye same to effect, to ye end that I
might also understand ye mistery of your meaning. And so might you fail
of your purpose (quod she) for I meane to be better assured of him that
shall know the depth of mine intent in such a secrete, than I do suppose that
any creature (one except) may be of you. Gentlewoman (quod he) you   35
speak *Greeke,* the which I have now forgotten, and myne instructers are
to farre from mee at this present to expound your words. Or els to neare
(quod she) and so smiling stayed hir talke, when the musick called them to
another daunce. Which ended, *F.J.* halfe afrayd of false suspect, and more
amazed at this straunge talke, gave over, and bringing Mistresse *Fraunces*   40
to hir place was thus saluted by his Mistresse. Servaunt (quod she) I hadde
done you great wrong to have daunced with you, considering that this
gentlewoman and you had former occasion of so waighty conference. Mis-
tresse sayd *F.J.* you had done mee great pleasure, for by our conference I
have but brought my braynes in a busie conjecture. I doubt not (sayd   45

his Mistresse) but you wil end that busines easely. It is hard said *F.J.* to
end the thing, wherof yet I have founde no beginning. His Mistresse with
change of countenaunce kept silence, whereat dame *Fraunces* rejoycing,
cast out this bone to gnawe on. I perceyve (quod she) it is evill to halt
before a Creple. *F.J.* perceyving now that his Mistresse waxed angry,   5
thought good on hir behalfe thus to aunswere: and it is evill to hop before
them that runne for the Bell: his Mistresse replied, and it is evill to hang
the Bell at their heeles which are always running. The L. of the[1] Castle
overhearing these proper quippes, rose out of his chayre, and comming
towards *F.J.* required him to daunce a Gallyard. Sir sayd *F.J.* I have   10
hitherto at your apoyntment but walked about the house, now if you be
desirous to see one tomble a turne or twayne, it is like ynough that I might
provoke you to laugh at mee, but in good faith my dauncing dayes are
almost done, and therfore sir (quod he) I pray you speake to them that are
more nymble at tripping on the toe. Whilest hee was thus saying dame   15
Elynor had made hir *Congey,* and was now entring the doore of hir cham-
ber: when *F.J.* all amazed at hir sodeyne departure followed to take leave
of his Mistresse: but she more then angrie, refused to heare his good night,
and entring hir chamber caused hir mayde to clappe to[2] the doore. *F.J.*
with heavie cheare returned to his company, and Mistresse *Fraunces* to   20
toutch his sore with a corosive sayd to him softly in this wise. Sir you may
now perceyve that this our countrie cannot allowe the French maner of
dauncing, for they (as I have heard tell) do more commonly daunce to
talke, then entreate to daunce. *F.J.* hoping to drive out one nayle with
another, and thinking this a meane most convenient to suppresse all   25
jelous supposes, toke Mistresse *Fraunces* by the hande and with a heavie
smyle aunswered. Mistresse and I (because I have seene the french
maner of dauncing) will eftsones entreat you to daunce a Bargynet: what
meane you by this quod Mistresse *Fraunces*. If it please you to followe
(quod he) you shall see that I can jest without joye, and laugh without   30
lust, and calling[3] the musitions, caused them softly to sound the *Tyntarnell,*
when he clearing his voyce did *Alla Napolitana* applie these verses follow-
ing, unto the measure.

G.T.

[4]   I*N prime of lustie yeares, when Cupid caught me in*   35
     And nature taught the way to love, how I might best begin:
  To please my wandring eye, in beauties tickle trade,
  To gaze on eche that passed by, a carelesse sporte I made.

  With sweete entising bayte, I fisht for many a dame,
  And warmed me by many a fire, yet felt I not the flame: 40
  But when at last I spied, the face that pleasde[4] me most,
  The coales were quicke, the woode was drie, & I began to toste.

And smyling yet full oft, I have beheld that face,
When in my hart I might bewayle mine owne unluckie case:
And oft againe with lokes that might bewray my griefe,
I pleaded hard for just reward, and sought to find reliefe.

What will you more? so oft, my gazing eyes did seeke   5
To see the Rose and Lilly strive uppon that lively cheeke:
Till at the last I spied, and by good profe I found,
That in that face was paynted playne, the pearcer of my wound.

Then (all to late) agast, I did my foote retire,[1]
And sought with secrete sighes to quench my greedy skalding fire: 10
But lo, I did prevayle asmuch to guide my will,
As he that seekes with halting heele, to hop against the hill.

Or as the feeble sight, would serche the sunny beame,
Even so I found but labour lost, to strive against the streame.
Then gan I thus resolve, since liking forced love,   15
Should I mislike my happie choyce, before I did it prove?

And since none other joye I had but hir to see,
Should I retire my deep desire? no no it would not bee:
Though great the duetie were, that she did well deserve,
And I poore man, unworthy am so worthy a wight to serve.   20

Yet hope my comfort stayd, that she would have regard
To my good will, that nothing crav'd, but like for just reward:
I see the Faucon gent sometimes will take delight,
To seeke the sollace of hir wing, and dally with a kite.

The fayrest Woulf will chuse the foulest for hir make,   25
And why ? because he doth endure most sorrowe for hir sake,
Even so had I like hope, when dolefull dayes were spent
When weary wordes were wasted well, to open true entent.

When fluddes of flowing teares, had washt my weeping eyes,
When trembling tongue had troubled hir, with loude lamenting cries: 30
At last hir worthy wil would pitie this my playnt,
And comfort me hir owne poore slave, whom feare had made so faint.

    Wherfore I made a vow, the stonie rocke should start,
    Ere I presume, to let her slippe out of my faithfull hart.

Lenvoie   35
And when she sawe by proofe, the pith of my good will,
She tooke in worth this simple song, for want of better skill:
And as my just deserts, hir gentle hart did move,
She was content to answere thus: I am content to love.
F. J.   40

T Hese verses are more in number than do stand with contentation of
some judgements, and yit the occasion throughly considered, I can
commend them with the rest, for it is (as may be well termed) *continua
oratio*, declaring a full discourse of his first love: wherin (over and besides
that the Eypthetes are aptly applied, & the verse of it self pleasant   5
enough) I note that by it he ment in cloudes to discipher unto Mistres
Fraunces such matter as she wold snatch at, and yit could take no good
hold of the same. Furthermore, it aunswered very aptly to the note which
the musike sounded, as the skilfull reader by due triall may approve. This
singing daunce, or daunsing song ended, Mistres *Fraunces* giving due   10
thanks, seemed weary also of the company, and profering to departe, gave
yit this farewell to *F.J.* not vexed by choller, but pleased with contentation,
and called away by heavy sleepe: I am constreyned (quod she) to bid you
good night, and so turning to the rest of the company, tooke hir leave. Then
the Maister of the house commaunded a torch to light *F.J.* to his lodging,   15
where (as I have heard him saye) the sodeyn chaunge of his Mistres coun-
tenance, togither with the straungenes of Mistresse *Fraunces* talke, made
such an encounter in his mynde, that he could take no reste that night:
wherefore in the morning rysing very earely (although it were farre before
his Mistres hower) he cooled his choller by walking in the Gallery neare   20
to hir lodging, and there in this passion compyled these verses following.

G.T.

[5]   *A cloud of care hath covred all my coste,*
        And stormes of stryfe doo threaten to appeare:
        The waves of woo, which I mistrusted moste,   25
        Have broke the bankes wherein my lyfe lay cleere:
        Chippes of ill chaunce, are fallen amyd my choyce,
        To marre the mynd, that ment for to rejoyce.

        Before I sought, I found the haven of hap,
        Wherein (once found) I sought to shrowd my ship,   30
        But lowring love hath[1] lift me from hir lap,
        And crabbed lot beginnes to hang the lip:
        The droppes of dark mistrust do fall so thick,
        They pearce my coate, and touch my skin at quick.

        What may be sayd, where truth cannot prevayle?   35
        What plea may serve, where will it selfe is Judge?
        What reason rules, where right and reason fayle?
        Remediles then must the giltlesse trudge:
        And seeke out care, to be the carving knyfe
        To cut the thred, that lingreth such a lyfe.   40

F.J.

This is but a rough meeter, and reason, for it was devised in great disquiet of mynd, and written in rage, yet have I seene much worse passe the musters, yea and where both the Lieutenant and Provost Marshall were men of rype judgement: and as it is, I pray you let it passe here, for the truth is that *F.J.* himselfe had so slender liking thereof, or at least of one worde escaped therin, that he never presented it, but to ye matter. When he had long (and all in vayn) looked for the coming of his Mistres into hir appointed walk: he wandred into ye park neere adjoyning to the Castle wall, where his chaunce was to meete Mistresse *Fraunces,* accompanied with one other Gentlewoman, by whom he passed with a reverence of curtesie: and so walking on, came into the side of a thicket, where he sat down under a tree to allay his sadnesse with solitarines. Mistres *Fraunces,* partly of curtesie and affection, and partly to content hir mind by continuance of such talk as thei had commenced over night, entreated hir companion to goe with hir unto this tree of reformacion, whereas they found the Knight with his armes foulded[1] in a heavy kind of contemplation, unto whom Mistres *Fraunces* stepped apace, (right softly) & at unwares gave this salutation. I little thought Syr Knight (quod she) by your evensong yesternight, to have found you presently at such a morrow masse, but I perceive you serve your Saint with double devotion: and I pray God graunt you treble meede for your true intent. *F.J.* taken thus upon the sodeine, could none otherwise answer but thus: I told you Mistresse (quod he) that I could laughe without lust, and jest without joye: and there withall starting up, with a more bolde countenance came towardes the Dames, profering unto them his service, to wayte upon them homewards. I have heard say oft times (qd. Mistres *Fraunces*) that it is hard to serve two Maisters at one time, but we wilbe right glad of your company. I thank you (quod *F.J.*) and so walking on with them, fell into sundry discourses, still refusing to touch any part of their former communicacion, untill Mistresse *Fraunces*[2] sayd unto him: by my troth (quod shee) I would bee your debtour these two dayes, to aunswer me truely but unto one question that I will propound: fayre Gentlewoman (quod hee) you shall not neede to becomme my debtour, but if it please you to quit question by question, I wil be more ready to gratifie you in this request, than either reason requireth, or than you would be willing to worke my contentation. Maister *F.J.* (qd. she, & y^t sadly) peradventur you know but a little how willing I would be to procure your contentation, but you know that hitherto familiaritie hath taken no deepe roote betwixt us twayne. And though I find in you no maner of cause whereby I might doubt to commit this or greater matter unto you, yit have I stayed hitherto so to doe, in doubt least you might thereby justly condempne mee both of arrogancy and lack of discretion, wherwith I must yit foolishly affirm, that I have with great payne brydeled my tonge from disclosing the same unto you. Such is then the good will that I beare towards you, the which if you rather judge to bee impudencie, than a friendly meaning, I may then curse the hower that

I first concluded thus to deale with you: herewithall being now red for
chaste bashefulnesse, shee abased hir eyes, and stayed hir talke, to
whom *F.J.* thus aunswered. Mistresse *Fraunces,* if I should with so exceed-
ing villanie requite such and so exceeding courtesie, I might not onely
seeme to digenerate from all gentry, but also to differ in behaviour from all   5
the rest of my lyfe spent: wherefore to be playne with you in few wordes,
I thinke my self so much bound unto you for divers respects, as if abilitie
doe not fayle mee, you shall fynde mee myndfull in requitall of the same:
and for disclosing your mind to mee, you may if so please you adventure
it with out adventure, for by this Sunne, quod hee, I will not deceyve such   10
trust as you shall lay uppon mee, and furthermore, so farre foorth as I may,
I wilbe yours in any respect: wherfore I beseech you accept me for your
faithfull friend, and so shall you surely find mee. Not so, quod shee, but
you shalbe my *Trust,* if you vouchsafe the name, and I wilbe to you as you
shall please to terme mee: my *Hope* (quod hee) if you so be pleased: and[1]   15
thus agreed, they two walked a parte from the other Gentlewoman, and
fell into sad talke, wherein Mistresse *Fraunces* dyd very curteousely de-
clare unto him, that in deed, one cause of hir sorrow susteyned in his be-
halfe, was that he had sayd so openly over night, that hee could not love,
for shee perceyved very well the affection betweene him and Madame   20
Elynor, and she was also advertised that Dame *Elynor* stood in the portall
of hir chamber, harkening to the talke that they had at supper that night,
wherefore she seemed to be sory that such a woord (rashely escaped) might
become great hinderaunce unto his desire: but a greater cause of hir grief
was (as she declared) that hys hap was to bestowe his lyking so un-   25
worthely, for shee seemed to accuse Dame *Elynor,* for the most unconstant
woman lyving: In full profe whereof, she bewrayed unto *F.J.* how she the
same Dame *Elynor,* had of long time ben yeelded to the Mynion *Secretary,*
whom I have before described: in whom though there bee (quod shee) no
one point of worthynesse, yit shameth she not to use him as hir dearest   30
friend, or rather hir holyest Idoll, and that this not withstanding Dame
Elynor had bene also sundry tymes woone to choyce of chaunge, as she
named unto *F.J.* two Gentlemen whereof the one was named *H.D.* and that
other *H.K.* by whom shee was during sundry tymes of their severall aboad
in those parties, entreated to like curteousie, for these causes the Dame   35
Fraunces seemed to mislike *F.J.* choice, and to lament that she doubted in
processe of time to see him abused. The experiment she ment was this, for
that she thought *F.J.* (I use hir wordes) a man in every respect very
woorthy to have the severall use of a more commodious common, she
hoped nowe to see if his enclosure thereof might be defensible against hir   40
sayd Secretary, and such like. These things and divers other of great
importance, this courteouse Lady *Fraunces* did friendly disclose unto
F.J. and furthermore, did both instruct and advise him how to proceede in
his enterprise. Now to make my talke good, and least the Reader might
bee drawen in a jelouse suppose of this Lady *Fraunces,* I must let you un-   45

derstand that she was unto *F.J.* a kinswoman, a virgin of rare chastitie, singular capacitie, notable modestie, and excellent beauty: and though *F.J.* had cast his affection on the other (being a married woman) yit was ther in their beauties no great difference: but in all other good giftes a wonderfull diversitie, as much as might be betwene constancie & flitting fantasie, betwene womanly countenance & girlish garishnes, betwene hot dissimulacion & temperate fidelitie. Now if any man will curiously aske the question why *F.J.* should chuse the one and leave the other, over and besides the common proverbe? (So *many men, so many minds*) thus may be answered: we see by common experience, y^t the highest flying faucon, doth more commonly pray upon the corn fed crow, & the simple shiftles dove, then on the mounting kyte: & why? because the one is overcome with lesse difficultie then that other. Thus much in defence of this Lady *Fraunces,* & to excuse the choice of my friend *F.J.* who thought himself now no lesse beholding to good fortune, to have found such a trusty friend, then bounden to Dame *Venus,* to have wonne such a Mistres. And to returne unto my pretence, understand you, y^t *F.J.* (being now with these two fair Ladies come very neer the castel) grewe in some jelouse doubt (as on his own behalf) whether he were best to break company or not. When his assured *Hope,* perceiving the same, gan thus recomfort him: Good sir (qd. she) if you trusted your trusty friends,[1] you should not neede thus cowardly to stand in dread of your friendly enimies. Well said in faith (quod *F.J.*)[2] and I must confesse, you were in my bosome before I wist, but yit I have heard said often, that in *Trust* is treason. Wel spoken for your self quod his *Hope.* *F.J.* now remembring that he had but erewhile taken upon him ye name of hir *Trust,* came home *per misericordiam,* when his *Hope* entring the Castle gate, caught hold of his lap, and half by force led him by the gallery unto his Mistres chamber: wheras after a little dissembling disdain, he was at last by the good helpe of his *Hope,* right thankfully receyved: and for his Mistres was now ready to dyne, he was therfore for that time arrested there, & a *supersedias* sent into the great chamber unto the Lord of the house, who expected his comming out of the parke. The dinner ended, & he throughly contented both w^t welfare & welcome, they fell into sundry devices of pastime: at last *F.J.* taking into his hand a Lute that lay on his Mistres bed, did unto the note of y^e *Venetian* galliard applie the *Italian* dittie written by the woorthy *Bradamant* unto the noble *Rugier,* as *Ariosto* hath it. *Rugier qual semper fui,* &c. but his Mistres could not be quiet until shee heard him repeat the *Tyntarnell* which he used over night, the which *F.J.* refused not, at end wherof his Mistres thinking now she had shewed hir self to earnest to use any further dissimulation, especially perceiving the toward enclination of hir servaunts *Hope,* fell to flat playn dealing, and walking to the window, called hir servaunt apart unto hir, of whom she demaunded secretly & in sad earnest, who devised this *Tyntarnell?* My Fathers Sisters brothers sonne (quod *F.J.*) His Mistresse laughing right hartely, demaunded yit again, by whom the

same was figured: by a niece to an Aunt of yours, Mistres (quod he).
Well then servaunt (quod she) I sweare unto you here by my Fathers
soule, y^t my mothers youngest daughter, doth love your fathers eldest son,
above any creature living. *F.J.* hereby recomforted, gan thus reply. Mis-
tres, though my fathers eldest son be far unworthy of so noble a match,   5
yit since it pleseth hir so well to accept him, I would thus much say
behind his back, y^t your mothers daughter hath done him some[1] wrong:
& wherin servaunt (qd. she) by my troth Mistres (qd. he) it is not yit
xx. houres, since without touch of brest she gave him such a nip by the hart,
as did altogither bereave him his nights reste, with the bruse thereof.   10
Well, servaunt (quod she) content your selfe, and for your sake, I will
speake to hir to provide him a playster, the which I my selfe will applye
to his hurt: And to the ende it may woorke the better with him, I will pur-
vey a lodging for him, where hereafter he may sleepe at more quiet. This
sayd the rosie hewe, distained hir sickly cheekes, and she returned to the   15
company, leaving *F.J.* ravished betwene hope and dread, as one that could
neyther conjecture the meaning of hir misticall wordes, nor assuredly trust
unto the knot of hir slyding affections. When the Lady *Fraunces* comming
to him, demaunded, what? dreame you sir? Yea mary do I fayre Lady
(quod he). And what was your dream, sir (quod she?) I drempt (quod   20
F.J.) that walking in a pleasaunt garden garnished with sundrie delights,
my hap was to espie hanging in the ayre, a hope wherin I might well behold
the aspectes and face of the heavens, and calling to remembrance the day
and hower of my nativitie, I did therby (accordyng to my small skill in
Astronomy) trie the conclusions of myne adventures. And what found you   25
therin (quod Dame *Fraunces?*) you awaked me out of my dreame (quod
he) or ells paradventure you should not have knowne. I beleve you well
(quod the Ladie[2] *Fraunces*) and laughing at his quicke aunswere brought
him by the hand unto the rest of his companie: where he taried not long
before his gracious Mistresse bad him to farewell, and to kepe his hower   30
there againe, when he should by hir be sommoned. Hereby, *F.J.* passed the
rest of that daye in hope awayting the happy time when his Mistresse
shoulde sende for him. Supper time came and passed over, and not long
after came the handmayd of the Lady *Elynor* into the great chamber,
desiring *F.J.* to repayre unto their Mistresse, the which hee willingly ac-   35
complished: and being now entred into hir chamber, he might perceyve his
Mistresse in hir nightes attyre, preparinge hir selfe towardes bed, to whom
F.J. sayed: Why howe now Mistresse? I had thought this night to have sene
you daunce (at least or at last) amongst us? By my troth good servaunt
(qd. she) I[3] adventured so soone unto the great chamber yesternight, that   40
I find my selfe somewhat sickly disposed, and therfore do streyne curtesie
(as you see) to go the soner to my bed this night: but before I slepe (quod
she) I am to charge you with a matter of waight, and taking him apart from
the rest, declared that (as that present night) she would talke with him
more at large in the gallery neere ajoyning to hir chamber. Here uppon   45

F.J. discretely dissimuling his joye, toke his leave and returned into the great chamber, where he had not long continued before the Lord of the Castell commaunded a torch to light him unto his lodging, whereas he prepared himselfe and went to bed, commaunding his servant also to go to his rest. And when he thought aswell his servaunt, as the rest of the houshold to be safe, he arose again, & taking his night gowne, did under the same convey his naked sword, and so walked to the gallerie, where he found his good Mistresse walking in hir night gowne and attending his comming. The Moone was now at the full, the skies cleare, and the weather temperate, by reason wherof he might the more playnely and with the greater contentation behold his long desired joyes, and spreding his armes abrode to embrace his loving Mistresse, he sayd: oh my deare Lady when shall I be able with any desert to countervayle the least parte of this your bountifull goodnesse? The dame (whether it were of feare in deede, or that the wylynes of womanhode had taught hir to cover hir conceites with some fyne[1] dissimulation) stert backe from the Knight, and shriching (but softly) sayd unto him. Alas servaunt what have I deserved, that you come against me with naked sword as against an open enimie. *F.J.* perceyving hir entent excused himselfe, declaring that he brought the same for their defence, & not to offend hir in any wise. The Ladie being therwith somwhat apeased, they began w^t more comfortable gesture to expell the dread of the said late affright, and sithens to become bolder of behaviour, more familier in speech, & most kind in accomplishing of comon comfort. But why hold I so long discourse in discribing the joyes which (for lacke of like experience) I cannot set out to ye ful? Were it not that I knowe to whom I write, I would the more beware what I write. *F.J.* was a man, and neither of us are sencelesse, and therfore I shold slaunder him, (over and besides a greater obloquie to the whole genealogie of *Enaeas*) if I should imagine that of tender hart he would forbeare to expresse hir more tender limbes against the hard floore. Suffised that of hir curteouse nature she was content to accept bords for a bead of downe, mattes for Camerike sheetes, and the night gowne of *F.J.* for a counterpoynt to cover them, and thus with calme content, in steede of quiet sleepe, they beguiled the night, untill the proudest sterre began to abandon the fyrmament, when *F.J.* and his Mistresse, were constrayned also to abandon their delightes, and with ten thousand sweet kisses and straight embracings, did frame themselves to play loth to depart. Wel, remedie was there none, but dame *Elynor* must returne unto hir chamber, and *F.J.* must also convey himselfe (as closely as might be) into his chamber, the which was hard to do, the day being so farre sprong, and hee having a large base court to passe over before he could recover his staire foote doore. And though he were not much perceyved, yet the Ladie *Fraunces* being no lesse desirous to see an issue of these enterprises, then *F.J.* was willing to cover them in secresy, did watch, & even at the entring of his chamber doore, perceyved the poynt of his naked sworde glistring under the skyrt of his night gowne: wherat

she smyled & said to hir selfe, this geare goeth well about. Well, *F.J.* hav-
ing now recovered his chamber, he went to bedde, & there let him sleepe, as
his Mistresse did on that otherside. Although the Lady *Fraunces* being
throughly tickled now in all the vaynes, could not enjoye such quiet rest,
but arising, toke another gentlewoman of the house with hir, and walked   5
into the parke to take the freshe ayre of the morning. They had not long
walked there, but they retorned, and though *F.J.* had not yet slept suf-
ficiently, for one which had so farre travayled in the night past, yet they
went into his chamber to rayse him, and comming to his beds side, found
him fast on sleepe. Alas quod that other gentlewoman, it were pitie to   10
awake him: even so it were quod dame *Fraunces,* but we will take awaye
somewhat of his, wherby he may perceyve that we were here, and loking
about the chamber, his naked sworde presented it selfe to the handes of
dame *Fraunces,* who toke it with hir, and softly shutting his chamber doore
againe, went downe the stayres and recovered hir owne lodging, in good   15
order and unperceyved of any body, saving onely that other gentlewoman
which accompanied hir. At the last *F.J.* awaked, and apparreling himselfe,
walked out also to take the ayre, and being throughly recomforted aswell
with remembraunce of his joyes forepassed, as also with the pleasaunt
hermony which the Byrdes made on every side, and the fragrant smel of the   20
redolent flowers and blossomes which budded on every braunche: hee did in
these delightes compyle these verses following.

¶The occasion (as I have heard him rehearse) was by encounter that
he had with his Lady by light of the moone: and forasmuch, as the moone
in middes of their delights did vanish away, or was overspred with a cloud,   25
thereupon he toke the subject of his theame. And thus it ensueth, called
a mooneshine Banquet.

G. T.

[6]   D *Ame Cinthia hir selfe (that shines so bright,*
           And deyneth not to leave hir loftie place: 30
        But only then, when Phoebus shewes his face
        Which is hir brother borne and lends hir light,)
        Disdaynd not yet to do my Lady right:
        To prove that in such heavenly wightes as she,
        It sitteth best that right and reason be.   35
        For when she spied my Ladies golden rayes,
        Into the cloudes,
        Hir head she shrouds,
        And shamed to shine where she hir beames displayes.

        Good reason yet, that to my simple skill,   40
        I should the name of Cynthia adore:
        By whose high helpe, I might behold the more
        My Ladies lovely lookes at mine owne wil,
        With deepe content, to gaze,[1] and gaze my fil:
        Of curteousie and not of darke disdaine,   45

Dame Cinthia disclosd my Lady playne.
She did but lend hir light (as for a lyte)
With friendly grace,
To shewe hir face,
That els would shew and shine in hir dispight.   5

Dan Phoebus he with many a lowring loke,
Had hir beheld of yore in angry wise:
And when he could none other meane devise
To stayne hir name, this deepe deceipt he toke
To be the bayte that best might hide his hoke: 10
Into hir eyes his parching beames he cast,
To skorche their skinnes, that gaz'd on hir full fast:
Whereby when many a man was sonne burnt so
They thought my Queene,[1]
The sonne had been   15
With skalding flames, which wrought them all that wo.

And thus when many a looke had lookt so long,
As that their eyes were dimme and dazled both:
Some fainting hartes that were both leude and loth
To loke againe from whence the error sprong,   20
Gan close their eye for feare of further wrong:
And some againe once drawne into the maze,
Gan leudly blame the beames of beauties blaze:
But I with deepe foresight did sone espie,
How Phoebus ment,   25
By false entent,
To slaunder so hir name with crueltie.

Wherfore at better leasure thought I best,
To trie the treason of his trecherie:
And to exalt my Ladies dignitie   30
When Phoebus fled and drew him downe to rest
Amid the waves that walter in the west.
I gan behold this lovely Ladies face,
Whereon dame nature spent hir gifts of grace:
And found therin no parching heat at all,   35
But such bright hew,
As might renew,
An Angels joyes in reigne celestiall.

The curteouse Moone that wisht to do me good,
Did shine to shew my dame more perfectly,   40
But when she sawe hir passing jollitie,
The Moone for shame, did blush as red as blood,
And shronke a side and kept hir hornes in hood:
So that now when Dame Cynthia was gone,
I might enjoye my Ladies lokes alone,   45

Yet honored still the Moone with true intent:
Who taught us skill,
To worke our will,
And gave us place, till all the night was spent.

                           F. J.   5

T His Ballade, or howsoever I shall terme it, percase you will not like, and yet in my judgement it hath great good store of deepe invention, and for the order of the verse, it is not common, I have not heard many of like proporcion, some will accompt it but a dyddeldome: but who so had heard *F.J.* sing it to the lute, by a note of his own devise, I suppose he   10 would esteme it to bee a pleasaunt diddeldome, and for my part, if I were not parciall, I woulde saye more in commendacion of it than nowe I meane to do, leaving it to your and like judgementes. And nowe to returne to my tale, by that time, that *F.J.* retorned out of the parke, it was dynner time, and at dynner they all met, I meane both dame *Elynor,* dame *Fraunces,* and   15 *F.J.* I leave to discribe that the Lady *Fraunces* was gorgeously attired, and set forth with very brave apparell, and *Madame Elynor* onely in hir night gowne gyrt to hir, with a coyfe trymmed *Alla Piedmonteze,* on the which she ware a little cap crossed over the crowne with two bends of yellowe Sarcenet or Cipresse, in the middest whereof she had placed (of hir owne hand   20 writing) in paper this word, *Contented.* This attyre pleased hir then to use, and could not have displeased Mistresse *Fraunces,* had she not bene more privy to the cause, than to the thing it selfe: at least the Lord of the Castle of ignoraunce, and dame *Fraunces* of great temporance, let it passe without offence. At dynner, bicause the one was pleased with all former   25 reconninges, and the other made privie to the accompt, there passed no word of taunt or grudge, but *omnia bene.* After dynner dame *Elinor* being no lesse desirouse to have *F.J.* company, then dame *Fraunces* was to take him in some pretie trippe, they began to question how they might best passe the day: the Lady *Elynor* seemed desirous to kepe her chamber,   30 but Mistresse *Fraunces* for another purpose seemed desirous to ryde abrode thereby to take the open ayre: they agreed to ryde a myle or twayne for sollace, and requested *F.J.* to accompany them, the which willingly graunted. Eche one parted from other, to prepare themselves, and now began the sporte, for when *F.J.* was booted, his horses sadled, and he ready   35 to ryde, he gan mysse his Rapier, wherat al astonied he began to blame his man, but blame whom he would, found it could not be. At last the Ladies going towardes horsebacke called for him in the base Court, and demaunded if he were readie: to whom *F.J.* aunswered. Madames I am more than readie, and yet not so ready as I would be, and immediatly taking him selfe in trip,   40 he thought best to utter no more of his conceipt, but in hast more than good speede mounted his horse, & comming toward ye dames presented him self, turning, bounding, & taking up his courser to the uttermost of his power in bravery: after suffering his horse to breath him selfe, he gan also allay his owne choller, & to the dames he sayd. Fayre Ladies I am ready when it   45

pleaseth you to ryde where so you commaund. How ready soever you be
servaunt, quod dame *Elinor,* it seemeth your horse is readier at your com-
maunde then at oures. If he bee at my commaund Mistresse (quod hee,)
he shalbe at yours. Gramercy good servaunt (quod shee) but my meaning
is, that I feare he be to stirring for our company. If he prove so Mistres   5
qd. *F.J.* I have here a soberer palfrey to serve you on. The Dames being
mounted they rode forthwardes by the space of a myle or very neare, &
F.J. (whether it were of his horses corage or his own choler) came not so
neare them as they wished, at last the Lady *Fraunces* said unto him:
Maister *J.* you said that you had a soberer horse, which if it be so, we wold   10
be glad of your company, but I beleve by your countinance, your horse
& you are agreed. *F.J.* alighting called his servaunt, chaunged horses with
him, and overtaking the Dames, said to Mistres *Fraunces*: And why doe
you thinke faire Lady that my horse and I are agreed? Bicause by your   15
countenance (quod she) it seemeth your pacience is stirred. In good faith,
quod *F.J.* you have gessed a right, but not with any of you. Then we care
the lesse servaunt, quod Dame *Elinor.* By my troth Mistres, qd. *F.J.*
(looking well about him that none might heare but they two) it is with my
servaunt, who hath lost my sword out of my chamber. Dame *Elinor* little   20
remembring the occasion, replied it is no matter servaunt, quod shee, you
shall heare of it againe, I warrant you, and presently wee ryde in Gods
peace, and I trust[1] shall have no neede of it: yet Mistresse quod he, a
weapon serveth both uses, aswell to defend, as to offend. Now by my troth,
quod Dame *Fraunces,* I have now my dream, for I dreamt this night that   25
I was in a pleasaunt meadow alone, where I met with a tall Gentleman, ap-
parelled in a night gowne of silke all embroadered about with a gard of
naked swords, and when he came towardes me I seemed to be afraide of
him, but he recomforted me saying, be not afrayd fayre Lady, for I use this
garment onely for myne own defence: and in this sort went that warlicke   30
God *Mars* what time hee taught Dame *Venus* to make *Vulcan* a hamer of
the newe fashion. Notwithstanding these comfortable wordes the fright of
the dreame awaked me, and sithens unto this hower I have not slept at al.
And what tyme of the night dreamt you this quod *F.J?* In the grey morn-
ing about dawning of ye day, but why aske you quod Dame[2] *Fraunces?*[3]   35
F.J. with a great sigh answered, because that dreames are to be marked
more at some hower of the night, then at some other, why are you so
cunning at the interpretation of dreames servaunt (quod the Lady *Ely-*
nor?) not very cunning Mistresse quod *F.J.* but gesse, like a young schol-
ler. The dames continued in these and like pleasant talkes: but *F.J.*   40
could not be mery, as one that estemed the preservation of his Mistresse
honor no lesse then the obtayning of his owne delightes: and yet to avoyde
further suspicion, he repressed his passions, asmuch as hee could. The
Lady *Elynor* more carelesse then considerative of hir owne case, pricking
forwardes said softly to *F.J.* I had thought you had received small cause   45

servaunt to bee thus dumpish, when I would be mery. Alas deere Mistresse
quod *F.J.* it is altogether for your sake, that I am pensife: Dame[1] *Fraunces*
with curtesie withdrewe hir selfe and gave them leave when as *F.J.* de-
clared unto his Mistresse, that his sword was taken out of his chamber, and
that he dreaded much by the wordes of the Lady *Fraunces,* that she had   5
some understanding of the matter. Dame *Elynor* now calling to remem-
braunce what had passed the same night, at the first was abashed, but
immediatly (for these women be redely wytted) chered hir servaunt, and
willed him to commit unto hir the salving of that sore. Thus they passed
the rest of the waye in pleasaunt talke with dame *Fraunces,* and so re-   10
turned towards the Castle where *F.J.* suffered the two dames to go to-
gether, and he alone unto his chamber to bewayle his owne misgovernement.
But dame *Elynor* (whether it wer according to olde custome, or by wylie
pollicie) found meane that night, y^t the sword was conveyed out of Mistres
Fraunces chamber and brought unto hirs: and after redeliverie of it unto   15
F.J. she warned him to be more wary from that time forthwards: well I
dwell too long uppon these particular poynts in discoursing this trifling
history, but that the same is the more apte meane of introduction to y^e
verses, which I meane to reherse unto you, and I think you wil not disdaine
to read my conceipt with his invention about declaration of his commedie.   20
The next that ever *F.J.* wrote then, upon any adventure hapned betwene
him and this fayre Lady, was this as I have heard him say, and uppon this
occasion. After he grew more bold & better acquaynted with his Mistresse
disposition, he adventured one Fryday in the morning to go unto hir
chamber, and theruppon wrote as followeth: which he termed a Frydayes   25
Breakefast.

G.T.

[7]   T*Hat*[2] *selfe same day, and of that day that hower,*
        When she doth raigne, that mockt Vulcane the Smith:
      And thought it meete to harbor in hir bower,   30
      Some gallant gest for hir to dally with.
      That blessed hower, that blist and happie daye,
      I thought it meete, with hastie steppes to go[3]
      Unto the lodge, wherein my Lady laye,
      To laugh for joye, or ells to weepe for wo.   35
      And lo, my Lady of hir wonted grace,
      First lent hir lippes to me (as for a kisse:)
      And after that hir body to embrace,
      Wherein dame nature wrought nothing amisse.
      What followed next, gesse you that knowe the trade,   40
      For in this sort, my Frydayes feast I made.

F.J.

T His Sonet is short and sweete, reasonably well, according to the occa-
sion &c. Many dayes passed these two lovers with great delight, their af-
fayres being no lesse politikely governed, then happely atchived. And
surely I have heard *F.J.* affirme in sad earnest, that hee did not onely love
hir, but was furthermore so ravished in Extasies with continual remem-   5
brance of his delights, that he made an Idoll of hir in his inward conceypte.
So seemeth it by this challenge to beautie, which he wrote in hir prayse
and uppon hir name.   *G.T.*

[8]

B *Eautie shut up thy shop, and trusse up all thy trash,*
  My Nell hath stolen thy fynest stuff, & left thee in the lash: 10
Thy market now is marred, thy gaynes are gone god wot,
Thou hast no ware, that may compare, with this that I have got.
As for thy paynted pale, and wrinckles surfled up:
Are deare inough, for such as lust to drinke of ev'ry cup:
Thy bodies bolstred out, with bumbast and with bagges,   15
Thy rowles, thy Ruffes, thy caules, thy coyfes, thy Jerkins & thy jagges.
Thy curling and thy cost, thy frisling & thy fare,
To Court to court with al those toyes, & there set forth¹ such ware
Before their hungry eyes, that gaze on every gest:
And chuse the cheapest chaffayre still, to please their fansie best.   20
But I whose stedfast eyes, could never cast a glance,
With wandring loke, amid the prease, to take my choice by chaunce
Have wonne by due desert, a piece that hath no peere,
And left the rest as refuse all, to serve the market there:
There let him chuse that list, there catch the best who can: 25
A paynted blazing bayte may serve, to choke a gazing man.
But I have slipt thy flower, that freshest is of hewe,
I have thy corne, go sell thy chaff, I list to seeke no new:
The wyndowes of myne eyes, are glaz'd with such delight,
As eche new face seemes full of faultes, that blaseth in my sight: 30
And not without just cause, I can compare hir so,
Lo here my glove I challenge him, that can, or dare say no.
Let Theseus come with clubbe, or Paris bragge with brand,
To prove how fayre their Hellen was, that skourg'd the Grecian land:
Let mighty Mars him selfe, come armed to the field: 35
And vaunt dame Venus to defend, with helmet speare & shield.²
This hand that had good hap, my Hellen to embrace,
Shal have like lucke to foyl hir foes, & daunt them with disgrace.
And cause them to confesse by verdict and by othe,
How farre hir lovely lookes do steyne the beauties of them both.   40
And that my Hellen is more fayre then Paris wife,
And doth deserve more famous praise, then Venus for hir life.
Which if I not perfourme, my life then let me leese,
Or elles be bound in chaines of change, to begge for beauties fees.
                                    F. J.   45

B Y this challenge I gesse, that either hee was than in an extasie or els sure I am nowe in a lunacie, for it is a proud challenge made to *Beautie* hir selfe, and all hir companyons: and ymagining that *Beautie* having a shop where she uttred hir wares of all sundry sortes, his Ladie had stollen the fynest away, leaving none behind hir, but paynting, 5 bolstring, forcing and such like, the which in his rage he judgeth good ynough to serve the Courte: and theruppon grew a great quarrell. When these verses were by the negligence of his Mistresse dispersed into sundry hands, and so at last to the reading of a Courtier. Well *F.J.* had his desire if his[1] Mistresse lyked them, but as I have heard him declare, she grew in 10 jeolosie, that the same were not written by hir, because hir name was *Elynor* and not *Hellen*. And about this poynt have bene divers and sundry opinions, for this and divers[2] other of his most notable Poems, have come to view of ye world, althogh altogether w^{t}out his consent. And some have attributed this prayse unto a *Hellen*, who deserved not so well as this dame 15 *Elynor* should seeme to deserve by the relation of *F.J.* and yet never a barell of good herring betwene them both: But that other *Hellen*, bycause she was and is of so base condicion, as may deserve no maner commenda-cion in any honest judgement, therfore I will excuse my friend *F.J.* and adventure my penne in his behalfe, that he would never bestow verse of 20 so meane a subject. And yet some of his acquayntance, being also ac-quainted (better then I) that *F.J.* was sometimes acquaynted with *Hellene*, have stoode in argument with mee, that it was written by *Hellene*, and not by *Elynor*. Well *F.J.* tolde me himselfe that it was written by this Dame *Elynor*, and that unto hir he thus alleged, that he toke it all for one name, 25 or at least he never red of any *Elinor* such matter as might sound worthy like commendation for beautie. And in deede, considering that it was in the first beginning of his writings, as then he was no writer of any long continuaunce, comparing also the time that such reportes do spread of his acquayntaunce with *Hellene*, it cannot be written lesse then sixe or 30 seven yeres before he knewe *Hellene*: mary paradventure if there were any acquayntance betwene *F.J.* and that *Hellene* afterwardes, (the which I dare not confesse) he might adapt it to hir name, and so make it serve both their turnes, as elder lovers have done before and still do and will do worlde without end. *Amen* Well by whom he wrote it I know not, but once I am 35 sure that he wrote it, for he is no borrower of inventions, and this is al that I meane to prove, as one that sende you his verses by stealth, and do him double wrong, to disclose unto any man the secrete causes why they were devised, but this for your delight I do adventure and to returne to the purpose, he sought more certaynely to please his Mistress *Elynor* with this 40 Sonet written in hir prayse as followeth.

G.T.

[9]   T He stately Dames of Rome, their Pearles did weare,
         About their neckes to beautifie their name:
But she (whom I do serve) hir pearles[1] doth beare,
Close in hir mouth, and smiling shewes the same.
No wonder then, though ev'ry word she speakes,   5
A Jewell seeme in judgment of the wise,
Since that hir sugred tongue the passage breakes,
Betwene two rockes, bedeckt with pearles of price.
Hir haire of gold, hir front of Ivory,
(A bloudy hart within so white a brest)   10
Hir teeth of Pearle, lippes Rubie, christall eye,
Needes must I honour hir above the rest:
Since she is fourmed of none other moulde,
But Rubie, Christall, Ivory, Pearle, and Golde.
                                    F.J.   15

O F this Sonet I am assured that it is but a translation, for I my selfe
     have seene the invention of an Italian, and Master J. hath a little
dylated the same, but not much besides the sence of the first, and the addi-
cion very aptly applied: wherfore I cannot condempne his doing therin,
and for the Sonet, were it not a little to much prayse (as the Italians   20
do most commonly offend in the superlative) I could the more commend
it: but I hope the partie to whom it was dedicated, had rather it were much
more, than any thing lesse. Well, thus these two Lovers passed many dayes
in exceding contentation, & more than speakeable pleasures, in which time
F.J. did compyle very many verses according to sundries occasions proffred,   25
whereof I have not obteyned the most at his handes, and the reason that he
denied me the same, was that (as he alleged) they were for the most part
sauced with a taste of glory, as you know that in such cases a lover being
charged with inexprimable[2] joyes, and therewith enjoyned both by dutie
and discretion to kepe the same covert, can by no meanes devise a greater   30
consolation, than to commit it into some cyphred wordes and figured
speeches in verse, whereby he feeleth his harte halfe (or more than halfe)
eased of swelling. For as sighes are some present ease to the pensife mind,
even so we find by experience, that such secrete entre comoning of joyes
doth encrease delight. I would not have you conster my wordes to this   35
effecte, that I thinke a man cannot sufficiently rejoyce in the luckie lottes of
love, unlesse he empart the same to others: God forbid that ever I should
enter into such an heresie, for I have alwayes bene of this opinion, that as
to be fortunate in love, is one of the most inward contentations[3] to mans
mynde of all earthly joyes: even so if hee do but once bewray y[e] same to   40
any living creature, immediatlye[4] eyther dread of discovering doth bruse
his brest with an intollerable burden, or els he leeseth the principall vertue
which gave effecte to his gladnes, not unlike to a Potycaries pot which being
filled with sweete oyntmentes or parfumes, doth reteyne in it selfe some sent
of the same, and being powred out doth returne to the former state, hard,   45

harshe, and of small savour: So the minde being fraught with delightes, as long as it can kepe them secretly enclosed, may continually feede uppon the pleasaunt record thereof as the well willing and readie horse byteth on the brydle, but having once disclosed them to any other, strayghtway we loose the hidden treasure of the same, and are oppressed with sundry doubt-full opinions and dreadfull conceipts. And yet for a man to record unto him selfe in the inward contemplation of his mynde the often remembrance of his late received joyes, doth as it were ease the hart of burden, and ad unto the mynd a fresh supplie of delight, yea and in verse principally (as I conceyve) a man may best contrive this way of comforte in him selfe. Therfore as I have sayde *F.J.* swymming now in delightes did nothing but write such verse as might accumilate his joyes, to the extremitie of pleasure, the which for that purpose he kept from mee, as one more desirous to seeme obscure and defective, than overmuch to glory in his adventures, especially for that in the end his hap was as heavie, as hitherto he had bene fortunate, amongst other I remembred one hapned uppon this occasion. The husband of the Lady *Elynor* being[1] all this while absent from hir, gan now retorne, & kept Cut at home, with whom *F.J.* found meanes so to ensignuate him-selfe, that familiaritie tooke deepe roote betwene them, and seldome but by stelth you could finde the one out of the others company. On a tyme the knight ryding on hunting desired *F.J.* to accompany him, the which he could not refuse to do, but like a lusty younker, readie at all assayes, appar-relled him selfe in greene, and about his neck a Bugle, pricking & gallowping amongst the formost, according to the mannor of that countrie. And it chaunced that the maried Knight thus gallowping lost his horn, which some devines might have interpreted to be but moulting, & that by Gods grace, he might have a newe come up againe shortly in steede of that. Wel, he came to *F.J.* requiring him to lend him his Beugle, for (sayd the Knight) I hard you not blowe this daye, and I would fayne encourage the houndes, if I had a horne. Quod *F.J.* although I have not ben over lavishe of my comming hitherto, I woulde you shoulde not doubt but that I can tell howe to use a horne well enough, and yet I may little do if I maye not lende you a horne, and therewithall tooke his Beugle from his necke, and lent it to the Knight, who making in unto the houndes, gan assaye to rechate: but the horne was to hard for him to wynde, whereat *F.J.* tooke pleasure, and sayde to him selfe, blowe tyll thou breake that: I made thee one with in these fewe dayes, that thou wilt never cracke whiles thou livest. And hereupon (before the fal of the Buck) devised this Sonet following, which at his home comming he presented unto his mis-tresse.

                                        G.T.

[10]   *As some men say there is a kind of seed*
            Will grow to hornes if it be sowed thick:
            Wherwith I thought to trye if I could breed
            A brood of buddes, well sharped on the prick:

And by good proofe of learned skill I found,
(As on some speciall soyle all seedes best frame)
So jelouse braynes doe breed the battle ground,
That best of all might serve to beare the same.
Then sought I foorth to find such supple soyle, 5
And cald to mynd thy husband had a brayne,
So that percase, by travayll and by toyle,
His fruitfull front might turne my seed to gayne:
And as I groped in that ground to sowe it,
Start up a horne, thy husband could not blow it. 10
F.J.

This Sonet treateth of a straung seede, but it tasteth most of *Rye,* which is more common amongst men nowadays: wel let it passe amongst ye rest, & he that liketh it not, turn over ye leaf to another, I dout not but in this register he may find some to content him, unlesse he 15 be to curious: and here I will surcease to rehearse any more of his verses, untill I have expressed how that his joyes being now exalted to the highest degree, began to bend towardes declination. For now the unhappy *Secretary* whom I have before remembred, was returned from *London,* on whom *F.J.* had no sooner cast his eyes, but immediatly he fel into a great passion of 20 mynd, which might be compared unto a feaver. This fruit grew of the good instructions that his *Hope* had planted in his mind, whereby I might take just occasion to forwarn every lover, how they suffer this venemous serpent jelousie to creepe into their conceipts: for surely, of all other diseases in love, I suppose that to be uncurable, and would hold longer discourse ther- 25 in, were it not that both this tale and the verses of *F.J.* himselfe hereafter to be recited, shalbe sufficient to speak for me in this behalf. The lover (as I say upon the sodein) was droven into such a malladie, as no meate might nourish his body, no delights please his minde, no remembrance of joyes forepassed content him, nor any hope of the lyke to come might recomfort 30 him: hereat (some unto whom I have imparted this tale) have taken occa- sion to discommend his faynting hart, yit surely the cause inwardly & depely considered, I cannot so lightly condempne him, for an old saying is, that every man can give councell better than follow it: and needs must the conflicts of his thoughts be straunge, betwene the remembraunce of his 35 forepassed pleasure, and the present sight of this monster whom before (for lack of like instruction) he had not so throughly marked and beheld. Well, such was the grief unto him, that he became sickly and kept his cham- ber. The Ladies having receyved the newes therof, gan al at once lament his misfortun, and of common consent agreed to visit him: they marched 40 thither in good equipage, I warrant you, and found *F.J.* lying upon his bed languishing, whom they all saluted generally, and sought to recomforte, but especially his Mistresse, having in hir hand a braunch of willow, wherewith shee defended hir from the whot ayre, gan thus say unto him: Servaunt (quod she) for that I suppose your mallady to proceede of none other cause 45 but only slouthfulnesse, I have brought this preaty rod to beate you a little: nothing doubting, but when you feele the smart of a twig or twayne, you will like a tractable yong scholler, pluck up your quickned spirits, & cast this drowsines apart. *F.J.* with a great sighe answered: Alas good Mistres (quod he) if any like chastisement might quicken me, how much more 5 might the presence of all you lovely Dames? recomfort my dulled mynd whom to behold, were sufficient[1] to revive an eye now dazled with the dread of death, and that not onely for the heavenly aspectes which you represent, but also much the more for your exceeding curtesie, in that you have deigned to visit mee so unworthy a servaunt: But good Mistres (quod 10 he) as it were shame for me to confesse that ever my hart could yeelde for feare, so I assure you that my minde cannot be content to induce infirmitie by sluggish conceyt: But in trueth Mistresse I am sicke (quod he), and there withall the trembling of his hart had sent up such throbbing into his throte, as that his voyce (now deprived of breath) commaunded the 15 tong to be still. When Dame *Elynor* for compassion distilled into teares, and drew towards the window, leaving the other Gentlewomen about his bed, who beinge no lesse sory for his grief, yit for that they were none of them so touched in their secrete thoughtes, they had bolder sprits and freeer speech to recomfort him: amongest the rest the Lady *Fraunces,* 20 (who in deede loved him deepely, and could best conjecture the cause of his conceipts) said unto him: Good *Trust* (quod shee) if any helpe of Phisick may cure your maladie, I would not have you hurt your selfe with these doubts which you seeme to retayne: If choice of Dyet may helpe, behold us here (your cookes) ready to minister all things needfull: if com- 25 pany may drive away your anoye, wee meane not to leave you solitary: if grief of mynde be cause of your infirmitie, wee all here will offer our devoyre to turne it into joye: if mishap have given you cause to feare or dreade any thing, remember *Hope,* which never fayleth to recomfort an afflicted mind. And good *Trust* (quod she) ([2]distreining his hand right 30 hartely) let this simple profe of our poore good willes be so accepted of you, as that it may work therby the effect of our desires. *F.J.* (as one in a traunce) had marked very litle of hir curteouse talke, and yet gave hir thanks, and so held his peace: whereat the Ladies (being all amazed) there became a silence in the chamber on all sides. Dame *Elynor* fearing thereby 35 that she might the more easely be espyed, and having nowe dryed up hir teares, returned to *F.J.* recomforting him by al possible meanes of common curtesie, promising that since in hir sicknes he had not only staunched hir bleeding, but also by his gentle company and sundry devices of honest pastime had dryven away the pensivenes of hir mind, she thought hir selfe 40 bound with like willingnes to do hir best in any thing that might restore his health,[3] and taking him by the hand sayd further: Good servaunt, if thou beare in deed any true affection to thy poore Mistres, start upon thy feet agayn, and let hir enjoye thyne accustomed service to hir comfort, for sure (quod shee) I will never leave to visit this chamber once in a day, 45

untill I may have thee down with mee. *F.J.* hearing the harty words of
his Mistres, and perceyving the earnest maner of hir pronunciation, began
to receyve unspeakable comfort in the same, and sayde. Mistres, your
exceeding curtesie were able to revive a man half dead, and to me it
is both great comfort, and it doth also gald my remembraunce with a con-   5
tinuall smart of myn own unworthinesse: but as I would desire no longer
lyfe, than til I might be able to deserve some part of your bounty, so I
will endevour my selfe to live, were it but onely unto that ende, that I might
merit some part of your favour with acceptable service, and requite some
deale the courtesie of all these other faire Ladies, who have so farre (above   10
my desertes) deigned to do me good. Thus said, the Ladies tarried not long
before they were called to Evensong, when his Mistres taking his hand,
kissed it saying: Farewell good servaunt, and I pray thee suffer not the
malice of thy sicknesse to overcome the gentlenes of thy good hart. *F.J.*
ravished with joy, suffered them all to depart, and was not able to pro-   15
nounce one word. After their departure, hee gan cast in his mind the
exceeding curtesie used towards him by them all: but above all other the
bounty of his Mistresse, and therewithall tooke a sounde and firme opinion,
that it was not possible for hir to counterfeit so deeply (as in deed I beleeve
that she then did not) whereby he sodenly felt his hart greatly eased, and   20
began in himselfe thus to reason. Was ever man of so wretched a harte? I
am the most bounden to love (quod he) of all them that ever professed
his service, I enjoy one the fayrest that ever was found, and I find hir
the kindest that ever was heard of: yit in myne owne wicked hart I could
villaynously conceive that of hir, which being compared with the rest of   25
hir vertues is not possible to harbour in so noble a mind. Hereby I have
brought my self without cause into this feeblenes, and good reason that
for so high an offence I should be punished with great infirmitie: what shall
I then doe? yeeld to the same? no, but according to my late protestation
I will recomfort this languishing mind of myne, to the end I may live but   30
onely to doe penaunce for this so notable a crime so rashly committed: and
thus saying, he start from his bed, and gan to walke towards the window:
but the venimous serpent which (as before I rehearsed) had stong him,
could not bee content that these medicines applied by the mouth of his
gentle Mistresse, should so soone restore him to guerison. And although in   35
deed they were such *Mythrydate* to *F.J.* as that they had nowe expelled
the rancour of the poyson, yit that ougly hellish monster had left behinde
hir in the most secret of his bosome, (even betwene the mynd and the man)
one of hir familiars named *Suspect,* which gan work in the weake sprites of
F.J. efects of no lesse perill than before he had conceyved: his head swelling   40
with these troublesome toyes, and his hart swimming in the tempests
of tossing fantasie: he felt his legges so feeble, that he was constrained to lye
down on his bed again, and repeating in his own remembraunce every woord
that his Mistres had spoken unto him, he gan to dreade, that she had
brought the willow braunce to beate him with, in token that he was of hir   45

forsaken: for so lovers doe most commonly expound the willowe garland, and this to think, did cut his hart in twayne. A wonderfull chaunge: and here a little to stay you, I will discribe (for I think you have not red it in *Ariosto*) the beginning, the fall, the retourne, and the bying of this hellish byrd, who in deed may well be counted a very limbe of the Divill. Many   5
yeares since, one of the most dreadfull dastards in the world, and one of them that first devised to weare his beard at length, least the barbor might do him a good turne sooner than he looked for it, and yit not so soone as he deserved, had builded for his securitie a pile on the hyghest and most inaccessible mount of all his Territories: the which being fortified   10
with strong walles, and environed with deepe ditches, had no place of entrie, but one onely doore so streight and narrow, as might by any possibility receive the body of one living man, from which he ascended up a ladder, & so creeping thorough a marvelous strayt hole, attained to his lodging, yᵉ which was so dark & obscure, as scarcely either sunne or ayre could   15
enter into it: thus hee devised to lodge in safetie, and for the more suertie gan trust none other letting downe this ladder but only his wife, and at the foote therof kept alwaies by day light, a firce mastif close enkeneled which never sawe nor heard the face or voyce of any other creature but onely of them two, him by night he trusted with the scout of this pretty passage,   20
having neverthelesse betwene him and this dogge, a double doore with treble locks, quadriple barres: and before all a port coulez of Iron: neyther yit could he be so hardy as to sleep until he had caused a gard of servauntes (whome hee kept abroade for that purpose) to searche all the corners adjoyning to his fortresse, and then betwene fearfull sweate and chyvering   25
cold, with one eye open and the other closed, he stole somtimes a broken sleepe, devided with many terrible dreames. In this sort the wretch lived all to long, untill at last his wife being not able any longer to supporte this hellish life, grew so hardy, as with his owne knife to dispatch his carkas out of this earthly purgatory: the which being done, his soule (and good reason)   30
was quickly conveyed by *Carone* unto hell: there *Radamanthus* Judge of that benche, commaunded him quickly to be thrust into a boyling poole: and being therein plonged very often, he never shriked or cryed, I skalde,[1] as his other companions there cried, but seemed so lightly to esteeme it, that the Judge thought meete to condempne him unto the most terrible place,   35
where are such torments, as neyther penne can write, tongue expresse, or thought conceyve: but the myser (even there) seemed to smyle and to make small accompt of his punishment. *Radamanthus* hereof enformed, sent for him, and demaunded the cause why he made so light of his durance? he aunswered that whyles he lived on earth, he was so continually af-   40
flicted and oppressed with suspicion, as that now (only to thinke that he was out of those meditacions) was sufficient armour to defend him from all other torments. *Radamanthus* astonied hereat, gan call togither the Senators of that kingdome, and propounded this question, how & by what punishment they might devise to touche him according to his deserts?   45

and herupon fell great disputation, at last being considered that he had
already bin plonged in the most unspeakable torments, & therat litle or
nothing had chaunged countenance, therwithal y^t no soule was sent unto
them to be relieved of his smart, but rather to be punished for his former
delights: it was concluded by ye general councel, y^t he shold be eftsones sent 5
into ye world & restored to the same body wherein he first had his resiance,
so to remain for perpetuity, and never to depart nor to perish. Thus this
body and soule being once againe united, and now eftsones with the same
pestilence infected, hee became of a suspicious man *Suspicion* it selfe: and
now the wretch remembring the treason of his wyfe, who had so willingly 10
dispatched him once before, gan utterly abhor hir and fled hir company,
searching in all countries some place of better assurance: and when hee
had in vayn trode on the most part of the earth, he embarked himself to find
some unknowen Iland wherein hee might frame some new habitacion,
and finding none so commodious as hee desired, he fortuned (sayling 15
along by the shoare) to espie a rock, more than sixe hundreth Cubits high,
which hong so suspiciously over the seas, as though it would threaten to fall
at every little blast: this did Suspicion Imagine to be a fit foundacion
whereon he might buyld his second Bower: hee forsooke his boate, and
travayled by land to espie what entrie or accesse might be made unto ye 20
same, and found from land no maner of entrie or accesse, unlesse it were
that some curteouse Byrd of the ayre would be Ambassadour, or convey
some Engins, as whilom the Eagle did carrie *Ganymedes* into heaven. He
then returned to Seas, and approching neere to his rock, founde a small
streame of fresh water issuing out of the same into the Seas: the which, 25
although it were so little and so straight, as might unethes receive a boate
of bignes to carry one living creature at once, yit in his conceipt hee thought
it more large and spacious than that broad way called of our forefathers
Via appia, or than that other named *Flaminia*: hee abandoned his bark, and
putting of hys clothes, adventured (for he was now assured not to drown) 30
to wade and swim against the streame of this unknown brooke, the which
(a wondrous thing to tell, and skarcely to be beleeved) came down from
the very top and height of this rock: and by the way he found six straight
& dangerous places, wher the water seemed to stay his course, passing under
sixe straight and lowe bridges, and hard by every of those places, a pyle 35
raysed up in manner of a Bulworke, the which were hollow, in such sort
as lodginges and other places necessary might in them commodiously be
devised, by such one as coulde endure the hellishnes of the place. Passing
by these hee attayned with much payne unto the toppe of the Rocke, the
which hee found hollowed as the rest, and farre more fit for his securitie, 40
than otherwise apt for any commoditie. There gan suspicion determyne to
nestle him selfe, and having now placed six chosen porters, to wit,
(Dread, Mistrust, Wrath, Desperation, Frensie, and Fury:) at these six
straunge Bulworks, he lodged him self in ye vij. al alone, for he trusted no
companye, but ever mistrustinge that his wyfe should eftsones find him 45

out, therein he shrieketh continually like to a shrich owle to keepe the
watch waking, never content to sleepe by day or by night. But to be sure
that he shoulde not oversleepe him selfe, gan stuffe his couch with Porpen-
tines quilles, to the ende that when heavy sleepe overcame him, and he
therby should be constrayned to charge his pallad with more heavie burden,   5
those plumes might then pricke through and so awake him. His garments
were steele upon Iron, and that Iron uppon Iron, and Iron againe, and the
more he was armed, the lesse he trusted to be out of daunger. He chopped
and changed continually now this, now that, new keyes, new lockes, ditches
newe skowred, and walles newly fortified, and thus alwayes uncontented   10
liveth this wretched helhound *Suspicion* in this hellish dungeon of habita-
tion, from whence he never removeth his foote, but only in the dead & silent
nights, when he may be assured that all creatures (but him selfe) are
whelmed in sound sleepe. And then with stealing steps he stalketh about
the earth, enfecting, tormenting, and vexing al kinds of people with some   15
paſt of his afflictions, but especially such as either do sit in chayre of
greatest dignitie and estimation, or els such as have atchived some deere
and rare emprise: Those above al others he contynually galdeth with fresh
wounds of dread, least they might loose and forgo the roomes wher unto
with such long travayle and good happes they had atteyned, and by this   20
means percase he had crept into the bosome of *F.J.* who (as is before
declared) did earst swimme in the deepest seas of earthly delightes. Nowe
then I must thinke it high time to retorne unto him, who being now
through feeblenes eftsones cast downe uppon his bed, gan cast in his inward
meditations all thinges passed, and as one throughly puffed up and filled   25
with one peevishe conceipt, could thinke uppon nothing elles, and yet
accusing his owne giltie conscience to be infected with jelosie, dyd com-
pyle this translation of *Ariostoes* xxxi. song as followeth.

[11]   W Hat state to man, so sweete and pleasaunt were,
             As to be tyed, in lincks of worthy love?   30
         What life so blist and happie might appere,
         As for to serve Cupid that God above?
         If that our mindes were not sometimes infect,
         With dread, with feare, with care, with cold suspect:
         With deepe dispayre, with furious frensie,   35
         Handmaydes to hir, whome we call jellosie.

         For ev'ry other sop of sower chaunce,
         Which lovers tast amid their sweete delight:
         Encreaseth joye, and doth their love advaunce,
         In pleasures place, to have more perfect plight.   40
         The thirstie mouth thinkes water hath good taste,
         The hungrie jawes, are pleas'd, with ech repaste:
         Who hath not prov'd what dearth by warres doth growe,
         Cannot of peace the pleasaunt plenties knowe.

And though with eye, we see not ev'ry joye,
Yet may the mind, full well support the same,
An absent life long led in great anoye,
When presence comes, doth turne from griefe to game,
To serve without reward is thought great payne,   5
But if dispayre do not therewith remayne,
It may be borne, for right rewardes at last,
Followe true service, though they come not fast.

Disdaynes, repulses, finally eche yll,
Eche smart, eche payne, of love eche bitter tast,   10
To thinke on them gan frame the lovers will,
To like eche joye, the more that comes at last:
But this infernall plague if once it toutche,
Or venome once the lovers mind with grutch,
All feastes and joyes that afterwardes befall,   15
The lover compts them light or nought at all.

This is that sore, this is that poysoned wound,
The which to heale, nor salve, nor oyntments serve,
Nor charme of wordes, nor Image can be found,
Nor observaunce of starres can it preserve,   20
Nor all the art of Magicke can prevayle,
Which Zoroastes found for our avayle.
Oh cruell plague, above all sorrowes smart,
With desperate death thou sleast the lovers hart.

And me even now, thy gall hath so enfect,   25
As all the joyes which ever lover found,
And all good haps, that ever Troylus sect,
Atchived yet above the luckles ground:
Can never sweeten once my mouth with mell,
Nor bring my thoughts, againe in rest to dwell.   30
Of thy mad moodes, and of naught elles I thinke,
In such like seas, fayre Bradamant did sincke.
                                   F.J.

T His is the translation of Ariosto his xxxi. song, all but the last staffe,
which seemeth as an allegory applied to the rest. It will please none   35
but learned eares, hee was tyed to the invention, troubled in mynd &c. So
I leave it to your judgment, and returne to F.J. who continued on his bed,
untill his bountifull Mistresse with the companie of the other curteous
dames retorned after supper to his chamber, at their first entrie: Why how
now servant (quod dame Elynor) we hoped to have found you on foote?   40
Mistresse quod F.J. I have assayed my feete since your departure, but
I find them yet unable to suporte my heavy body, and therfore am con-
strayned as you see, to acquaint my selfe with these pyllowes. Servaunt

sayd she I am right sory therof, but since it is of necessitie to beare sick-
nesse, I will employ my devoyre to allaye some part of your paynes, and to
refreshe your weary limbes with some comfortable matter: and therwithall
calling hir handmayde, delivered unto hir a bounche of pretie little keyes,
and whispering in hir eare, dispatched hir towards hir chamber. The   5
mayde taried not long, but returned with a little Casket, the which hir Mis-
tresse toke, opened and drew out of the same much fyne lynnen, amongst
the which she toke a pillowbere very fyne and sweete, which although it
were of it selfe as sweete as might be, being of long time kept in that odori-
ferous chest, yet did shee with damaske water (and that the best that might   10
bee I warrant you) all to sprinckle it with hir owne handes, which in my
conceipt might much amende the matter. Then calling for a fresh pyllowe,
sent hir mayde to ayre the same, and at hir returne put on this, thus per-
fumed pillowbeare. In meane time also she had with hir owne hands attyred
hir servaunts head in a fayre wrought kerchif taken out of the same Casket,   15
then layde him down uppon this fresh and pleasaunt place, and pretely
as it were in sporte, bedewed his temples with swete water which she had
ready in a casting bottle of Gold, kissing his cheeke and saying: Good serv-
aunt be whole, for I might not longe endure thus to attende thee, and yit
the love that I beare towards thee, cannot be content to see thee languish: 20
Mistres sayd *F.J.* (and that with a trembling voyce) assure your self,
that if there remayn in mee any sparke of lyfe or possibilitie of recovery,
then may this excellent bountie of yours be sufficient to revive me without
any further travayle or payn unto your persone, for whom I am highly to
blame, in that I do not spare to put you unto this trouble: and better it   25
were that such a wretch as I had dyed unknowen, than that by your
exceding curtesie you should fall into any mallady, eyther by resorting unto
me, or by these your paynes taken about me. Servaunt (quod she) all
pleasures seeme paynefull to them that take no delight therin, and likewise
all toyle seemeth pleasaunt to such as set their felicitie in the same, but for   30
mee be you sure, I do it with so good a wyll that I can take no hurt therby,
unlesse I shall perceyve that it be rejected or neglected, as unprofitable or
uncomfortable unto you. To me Mistresse quod *F.J.* it is such pleasure, as
neither my feeble tongue can expresse, nor my troubled mind conceyve.
Why? are you troubled in mynd, then servaunt quod dame *Elynor? F.J.*   35
now blushing answered, but even as all sicke men be Mistresse. Herewith
they staid their talke a while, and the first that brake silence was the Lady
Fraunces, who sayde: and to drive away the troubles of your mynd good
Trust, I wold be glad if we could devise some pastime amongst us to kepe
you company, for I remember that with such devises you did greatly re-   40
comfort this fayre Lady when shee languished in like sorte. She languished in
deede gentle *Hope,* quod *F.J.* but God forbid that she had languished
in like sort. Every body thinketh their griefe greatest qd. dame *Elynor,*
but in deede whether my griefe were the more or the lesse, I am right
sorie that youres is such as it is: And to assay whither our passions   45

proceded of like cause or not, I would we could (according to this Ladies saying) devise some like pastimes to trie if your malladie would be cured with like medicines. A gentlewoman of the company whom I have not hitherto named, and that for good respects, least hir name might altogether disclose the rest, gan thus propound. We have accustomed (quod she) here- 5
tofore in most of our games to chuse a Kyng or Queene, and he or she during their governement have charged every of us eyther with commaunde- mentes or questions as best seemed to their majestie: wherein to speake mine opinion we have given over large a skope, neyther seemeth it rea- sonable that one shoulde have the power to discover the thoughts, or at least 10
to brydle the affects of all the rest. And though in deede in questioning (which doth of the twayne more nerely touche the mind) every one is at free libertie to aunswere what they list: yet oft have I heard a question demaunded in such sorte, and uppon such sodayne, that it hath bene hardly answered without moving matter of contention. And in commaundes also, 15
sometimes it happeneth one to bee commaunded unto such service, as eyther they are unfit to accomplish (and then the parties weakenes is therby detected) or els to do something that they would not, wherof ensueth more grutch then game. Wherefore in myne opinion, we shall do well to chuse by lot amongst us a governour, who for that it shalbe sufficient pre- 20
heminence to use the chayre of majestie, shalbe bound to give sentence uppon all such arguments and questions as we shall orderly propound unto them, and from him or hir (as from an oracle) we will receive aunswere, and decyding of our lytigious causes. This dame had stuffe in hir, an old courtier, and a wylie wench, whome for this discourse I will name *Pergo*, 25
least hir name natural were to brode before, and might not drinke of all waters. Wel this proportion of *Pergo* pleased them wel, and by lot it happened that *F.J.* must be moderator of these matters, and collector of these causes: the which being so constituted, the Lady *Elynor* said unto this dame *Pergo*. You have devised this pastime (qd. she) & because we 30
thinke you to be most expert in the handling therof, do you propound the first question, & we shalbe both the more readye and able to followe your example: the Lady *Pergo* refused not, but began on this wise. Noble governor (qd. she) amongst the adventures that have befallen me, I remem- ber especially this one, that in youth it was my chaunce to be beloved of 35
a very courtlike young gentleman, who abode neare the place wherin my parents had their resiaunce. This gentleman whether it were for beauty, or for any other respect that he sawe in me, I know not, but he was en- amored of me, & that with an exceding vehement passion, & of such force were his affects, that notwithstanding many repulses which he had received 40
at my hands, he seemed dayly to growe in the renewing of his desires. I on the otherside, although I could by no meanes mislike of him by any good reason, considering that hee was of byrth no waye inferior unto me, of possessions not to bee disdeyned, of parson right comely, of behavyour Courtly, of manners modest, of mynde lyberall, and of verteous disposition: 45

yet such was the gaitie of my mynd, as that I coulde not be content to lend
him over large thongs of my love, but alwayes daungerously behaved my
selfe towardes him, and in such sorte, as hee coulde neyther take comforte
of myne aunsweres, nor yet once finde him selfe requited with one good
looke for all his travayle. This notwithstanding, the worthy Knight con-   5
tinued his sute wyth no lesse vehement affection than earst hee hadde
begon it, even by the space of seven yeares. At the last, whether dis-
comfited by my dealinges, or tyred by long travayle, or that he had percase
light uppon the lake that is in the forrest of *Ardena,* and so in haste and all
thristie, had dronke some droppes of disdayne, wherby his hot flames   10
were quenched, or that he had undertaken to serve no longer but his just
terme of apprenticehode, or that the teeth of time had gnawen and tyred
his dulled sprites in such sorte, as that all beenommed hee was constrayned
to use some other artificiall balme for the quickning of his sences, or by
what cause moved I know not, he did not onely leave his long continued sute,   15
but (as I have since perceyved) grew to hate me more deadly than before
I had disdayned him. At the first beginning of his retyre I perceived not
his hatred, but imagined that being over wearied he had withdrawen him
self for a time. And considring his worthynes, therwithall his constancie
of long time proved, I thought that I could not in the whole world find   20
out a fitter match to bestowe my selfe, than on so worthy a person, where-
fore I did by all possible meanes procure that he might eftsones use his
accustomed repayre unto my parents: And further, in all places where I
happened to meete him, I used all the curtesies towardes him that might bee
contayned within the bondes of modestie, but al was in vayne, for he was   25
now become more daungerous to be wonne, than the haggard Faulcon.
Our lottes being thus unluckely chaunged, I grewe to burne in desire, and
the more daungerous that he shewed him selfe unto me, the more earnest I
was by all meanes to procure his consent of love. At the last I might perceive
that not onely he disdayned me, but as me thought boyled in hatred   30
against me: and the time that I thus continued tormented with these
thoughts, was also just the space of seven yeares. Finally when I perceived
no remedie for my parplexities, I assayed by absence to weare away
this malladie, and therfore utterly refused to come in his presence, yea or
almost in any other company, whereby I have consumed in lost time the   35
flower of my youth, and am become as you see (what with yeares, and
what with the tormenting passions of love) pale, wan, and full of
wrinkles, neverthelesse, I have therby gayned thus much, that at last
I have wond my self cleere out of *Cupids* cheines, and remain carelesse at
libertie. Now marke to what end I tell you this: first vii. yeares passed in   40
the which I could never be content to yeeld unto his just desires: next other
vii. yeares I spent in seeking to recover his lost love: and sithens both
those vii. yeares, there are even now on saint *Valentines* day last, other
vii. yeares passed, in the which (neither I have desired to see him) nor he
hath coveted to heare of me. My parents now perceiving how the crowes   45

foot is crept under myne eye, and remembring the long sute that this
gentleman had in youth spent on me, considering therewithall that greene
youth is well mellowed in us both, have of late sought to perswade a
marriage betwene us, the which the Knight hath not refused to heare of,
and I have not disdained to thinke on: by their mediation we have bin   5
eftsoones brought to *Parlee,* wherein over and besides the ripping up of many
old griefes, this hath ben chiefly rehearsed & objected betwene us, what
wrong and injury eche of us hath done to other, and hereabouts wee have
fallen to sharpe contention: he alledged, that much greater is the wrong
which I have done unto him, than that repulse which hee hath sithens   10
used to me: and I have affirmed the contrary, the matter yit hangeth in
variance. Nowe, of you worthy Governour I would be most glad to heare
this question decided, remembring that ther was no difference in the times
betwene us: and surely, unles your judgement helpe me, I am afraide my
marriage wilbe marred, and I may goe lead Apes in hell. *F.J.* aunswered,   15
good *Pergo,* I am sory to heare so lamentable a discourse of your luckles
love, and much the sorier, in that I must needes give sentence against you:
for surely great was the wrong that either of you have done to other, and
greater was the needelesse grief which causelesse eche of you hath con-
ceived in this long time, but greatest in my judgement hath ben both the   20
wrong and the grief of the Knight, in that notwithstanding his deserts
(which your self confesse) he never enjoyed any guerdone of love at your
handes: And you (as you alledge) did enjoy his love of long time togither,
so that by the reckoning, it will fall out (although being blinded in your
owne conceypt) you see it not, that of the one & twenty yeares you en-   25
joyed his love vii. at the least, but that ever he enjoyed yours wee cannot
perceive. And much greater is the wrong that rewardeth evill for good, than
that which requireth tip for tap: further, it seemed that where as you went
about in time to trie him, you did altogither loose time which can never be
recovered: and not onely lost your owne time, whereof you would seeme   30
now to lament, but also compelled him to leese his time, which he might
(be it spoken without offence to you) have bestowed in some other worthy
place: and therefore, as that grief is much greater which hath no kind of
comfort to allay it, so much more is that wrong which altogither without
cause is offered. And I (said *Pergo*) must needes think, that much easier   35
is it for them to endure grief which never tasted of joy, and much lesse is
that wrong which is so willingly profered to be by recompence restored: for
if this Knight will confesse that he never had cause to rejoyce in all the
time of his service, then with better contentation might he abyde grief
than I, who having tasted of the delight which I did secretly conceive of his 40
deserts, do think ech grief a present death by the remembrance of those
forepassed thoughts: & lesse wrong seemeth it to be destitut of ye thing
which was never obteyned, than to be deprived of a jewell whereof we have
bin already possessed: so y^t under your correction I might conclude, that
greater hath bin my grief & injury susteined, than that of the Knight.   45

To whom *F.J.* replied, as touching delight, it may not be denied but that
every lover doth take delight in the inward contemplacion of his mind, to
think of the worthiness of his beloved, & therfore you may not alledge that
the Knight had never cause to rejoyce, unlesse you will altogither con-
dempne your self of unworthiness: Mary if you will say that he tasted not   5
the delights that lovers seeke, then mark, who was the cause but your self?
And if you would accuse him of like ingratitude, for that he disdained you
in the latter vii. yeres, when as he might by accepting your love, have re-
compenced him self of all former wrongs: you must remember therwithal,
that the crueltie by you shewed towards him was such, y^t he could by no   10
meanes perceive y^t your chaunge proceeded of good will, but rather eft-
sones to hold him enchained in unknown links of subtil dealings, & ther-
fore not without cause he douted you: & yit without cause you rejected him.
He had often sought occasion, but by your refusals he could never find him:
you having occasion fast by the foretop did dally with him so long, til at   15
last he slipped his head from you, & then catching at the bald noddle, you
found your self ye cause, & yit you would accuse another. To conclude,
greater is the grief that is susteined without desert, and much more is the
wrong that is offred without cause. Thus *F.J.* decided the question pro-
pounded by *Pergo,* & expected that some other dame should propound   20
another: but his mistres (having hir hand on another halfpeny) gan thus
say unto him. Servant this pastime is good, and such as I must needs
like of, to drive away your pensive thoughts: but sleeping time approcheth,
& I feare we disquiet you, wherefore the rest of this time we will (if so like
you) bestowe in trimming up your bed, and to morrow we shall meete here   25
and renew[1] this new begon game with Madame *Pergo.* Mistres (qd. *F.J.*)
I must obey your will, and most humbly thanke you of your great good-
nesse, and all these Ladies for their curtesie: Even so, requiring you that
you will no further trouble your selves about me, but let my servaunt alone
with conducting me to bed. Yes servaunt (quod she) I wil see if you can   30
sleepe any better in my sheetes: and therewith commaunded hir handmayd
to fetch a paire of cleane sheetes, the which beeing brought (marvailous fine
and sweete) the Ladies *Fraunces* and *Elynor* did curteously unfold them,
and layd them on the bed, which done, they also entreated *F.J.* to uncloth
him and go to bed: being layd, his Mistres dressed and couched the clothes   35
about him, sithens moistened his temples with rosewater, gave him hand-
kerchewes and other fresh linnen about him, in dooing wherof, she whis-
pered in his eare, saying: Servaunt, this night I will bee with thee, and after
with the rest of the Dames gave him good night and departed, leaving *F.J.*
in a traunce betwene hope and dispayre, trust and mistrust. Thus he lay   40
ravished, commaunding his servaunt to goe to bed, and fayning that
himself would assay if he could sleepe. About ten or eleven of the clock
came his Mistresse in hir night gowne, who knowing all privy wayes in that
house very perfectly, had conveied hir self into *F.J.* chamber, unseene and
unperceyved, and being nowe come unto his beds side kneeled down, and   45

laying hir arme over him sayed these or like wordes: My good Servaunt,
if thou knewest what perplexiteis I suffer in beholding of thine infirmities,
it might then suffise, eyther utterly to dryve away thy mallady, or much
more to augment thy griefs: for I know thou lovest me, and I think also
that thou hast had sufficient profe of myne unfained good will, in remem-   5
brance whereof, I fall into sundry passions: First, I compt the happy lots of
our first acquaintance, and therin I call to mynde the equalitie of our
affections, for I think that there were never two lovers conjoyned with freeer
consent on both parties: and if my overhasty delivery of yeelding words
be not wrested hereafter to my condempnacion, I can then assure my self   10
to escape for ever without desert of any reprofe: herewithall I can not
forget the sundry adventures happened since we became one hart devided
in two bodies, all which have ben both happily atchieved, and delectably
enjoyed: what resteth then to consider but this thy present state? The
first corosive that I have felt, and the last cordiall that I looke for, the end   15
of my joyes, and the beginning of my torments, and hereat hir salt teares
gan bathe the dying lips of hir servaunt: who hearing these wordes, and
well considering hir demeanor, began now to accuse him selfe of such and so
haynous treason, as that his gilty harte was constreined to yeelde unto a
just scourge for the same. Hee swooned under hir arme: the which when   20
she perceyved, it were hard to tel what feares did most affright hir. But
I have heard my friend *F.J.* confesse, that he was in a happy traunce, and
thought himself for divers causes unhappely revived. For surely I have
heard him affirme, that to dye in such a passion, had ben rather pleasant,
than like to panges of death. It were hard now to rehearse how hee was   25
revived, since there wer none present, but he dying, (who could not declare)
& she living, who wold[1] not disclose so much as I meane to bewray. For my
friend *F.J.* hath to me emported, that returning to life, the first thing
which he felt, was that his good mistres lay pressing his brest w^t the
whole weight of hir body, and biting his lips with hir friendly teeth: and   30
peradventure shee refrayned (either of curtesie towards him, or for
womanish feare, to hurt hir tender hand) to strik him on the cheekes in
such sorte, as they doe that strive to call agayne a dying creature: and
therefore thought this the aptest meane to reduce him unto remembrance.
F.J. now awaked, could no lesse do, than of his curteous nature receyve   35
his Mistresse into his bed: Who, as one that knew that waye better, than
how to help his swooning, gan gently strip of hir clothes, and lovingly
embracing him, gan demaund of him in this sorte. Alas good Servaunt
(quod she) what kinde of maladie is this that so extreemely doth torment
thee ? *F.J.* with faynting speech aunswered: Mistresse, as for my maladie,   40
it hath ben easely cured by your bountifull medicines applied: But I must
confesse, that in receiving that guerison at your handes, I have ben con-
streined to fall into an Extasie, through the galding remembrance of myne
own unworthines: Neverthelesse good Mistresse, since I perceive such
fidelitie remayning betwene us, as that fewe wordes will perswade such   45

trust as lovers ought to embrace, let these fewe wordes suffise to crave your
pardon, and doe eftsones powre upon me (your unworthy servaunt) the
haboundant waves of your accustomed clemency: for I must confesse, that
I have so highly offended you, as (but your goodnesse surpasse the malice
of my conceipts) I must remayne (and that right woorthely) to the severe   5
punishment of my desertes: and so should you but loose him who hath
cast away him self, and neither can accuse you, nor dare excuse him selfe
of the crime. Dame *Elynor,* who had rather have found hir servaunt per-
fectly revived, than thus with straunge conceipts encombred: and musing
much at his darke speech, became importunat to know ye certainty of   10
his thoughts. And *F.J.* as one not maister of him selfe, gan at the last
playnly confesse howe he had mistrusted the chaunge of hir vowed affec-
tions: Yea and (that more was) he playnly expressed with whom, of whom,
by whom, and too whom shee bent hir better liking.

Now, here I would demaund of you and such other as are expert: Is   15
there any greater impediment to the fruition of a Lovers delights, than to
be mistrusted? or rather, is it not the ready way to race all love and former
good will out of remembrance, to tell a gilty mynd that you doe mistrust
it? It should seeme yes, by Dame *Elynor,* who began nowe to take the
the matter whottely, and of such vehemency were hir fancies, that shee nowe   20
fell into flat defiance with *F.J.* who although hee sought by many faire
wordes to temper hir chollerike passions, and by yeelding him selfe to get
the conquest of an other, yet could hee by no meanes determine the quar-
rell. The softe pillowes being present at these whot wordes,[1] put forth
themselves as mediatours for a truce betwene these enemies, and desired   25
that (if they would needes fight) it might be in their presence but onely
one pusshe of the pike, and so from thenceforth to become friends again for
ever. But the Dame denied flatly, alleadging that shee found no cause
at all to use such curtesie unto such a recreant, adding further many wordes
of great reproche: the which did so enrage[2] *F.J.* as that having now for-   30
gotten all former curtesies, he drewe uppon his new professed enimie, and
bare hir up with such a violence against the bolster, that before shee could
prepare the warde, he thrust hir through both hands, and &c. wher by the
Dame swoning for feare, was constreyned (for a time) to abandon hir
body to the enemies curtesie. At last when shee came to hir selfe, shee rose   35
sodeinly and determined to save hir selfe by flight, leaving *F.J.* with many
dispytefull wordes, and swearing that hee should never (eftsoones) take
hir at the like advantage, the which othe she kept better than hir former
professed good will: and having nowe recovered hir chamber (bicause shee
founde hir hurt to be nothing daungerous) I doubt not, but shee slept   40
quietly the rest of the night: As *F.J.* also perswading himselfe that hee
should with convenient leysure recover hir from this hagger conceipt, tooke
some better rest towardes the morning, than hee had done in many nights
forepast. So let them both sleepe whyles I turne my penne unto the before
named *Secretary,* who being (as I sayd) come lately from London, had   45

made many proffers to renew his accustomed consultations: but the sorrow
which his Mistresse had conceyved in *F.J.* his sicknesse, togither with hir
continuall repayre to him during the same, had ben such lettes unto his
attempts, as it was long time before he could obtayne audience. At the
last these newe accidentes fell so favourably for the furtherance of his   5
cause, that he came to his Mistresse presence, and there pleaded for him-
selfe. Nowe, if I should at large write his allegations, togither with hir
subtile aunsweres, I should but comber your eares with unpleasaunt re-
hearsall of feminine frayeltie. To be short, the late disdaynefull moode which
she had conceyved against *F.J.* togither with a scrupule which lay in hir   10
conscience, touching the xi. article of hir beleeve, moved hir presently with
better will to consult with this *Secretary,* aswel upon a speedy reveng
of hir late received wrongs as also upon the reformation of hir religion. And
in very deed, it fell out that the *Secretary* having bin of long time absent,
& therby his quils & pennes not worn so neer as they were wont to be, did   15
now prick such faire large notes, y^t his Mistres liked better to sing faburden
under him, than to descant any longer uppon *F.J.* playne song: and thus
they continued in good accorde, untill it fortuned that Dame *Fraunces*
came into hir chamber uppon such sodeyn as shee had like to have marred
all the musick. Wel thei conveied their clifs as closely as they could, but   20
yit not altogither w^{t}out some suspicion given to ye said dame *Fraunces,*
who although shee could have bin content to take any payn in *F.J.* behalf,
yit otherwise she would never have bestowed the watching about so
wortheles a prise. After womanly salutacions they fel into sundry dis-
courses, y^e *Secretary*[1] stil abyding in ye chamber with them. At last two   25
or three other gentlewomen of the Castle came into Madam *Elynors*
chamber, who after their *Bon jour* did all (*una voce*) seeme to lament the
sicknes of *F.J.* and called upon the Dames *Elinor* and *Fraunces,* to go visite
him againe. The Lady *Fraunces* curteously consented, but Madame *Elinor*
first alledged that she hir selfe was also sickly, the which she attributed to   30
hir late paynes taken about *F.J.* and sayd that onely for that cause she was
constrayned to kepe hir bed longer than hir accustomed hower. The Dames
(but especially the Lady *Fraunces*) gan streight waies conjecture some
great cause of sodaine change, and so leaving dame *Elynor,* walked altoe-
gether into the parke to take the ayre of the morning: And as they thus   35
walked it chaunced that Dame *Pergo* heard a Cuckoe chaunt, who (because
the pride of the spring was now past) cried Cuck cuck Cuckoe in hir stam-
eringe voyce. A ha (quod *Pergo*) this foule byrd begines to flye the coun-
trie, and yet before hir departure, see how spitefully she can devise to
salute us. Not us (quod Dame *Fraunces*) but some other whom she hath   40
espyed: wherewith Dame *Pergo* looking round about hir, and espying none
other company sayd. Why here is no body but we few women qd. she.
Thanks be to God the house is not farre[2] from us (quod Dame *Fraunces.*)
Here at the wylie *Pergo* partely perceyving Dame *Fraunces* meaning replyed
on this sort: I understand you not (quod she) but to leape out of this mat-   45

ter, shall we go visite Maister *F.J.* and see how he doth this morning? Why
quod dame *Fraunces,* do you suppose that the Cuckoe called unto him?
Nay marry quod Pergo, for (as farre as I know) he is not maried. As
who should say (quod Dame *Fraunces,*) that the Cuckoe envieth none but
maryed folkes. I take it so, sayd *Pergo:* the Lady *Fraunces*[1] aunswered.   5
Yes sure I have noted as evill lucke in love (after the cuckoes call) to have
happened unto divers unmaried folkes, as ever I did unto the maried: but
I can be well content that we go unto Master *J.* for I promised on the
behalfe of us al, that we wold use our best devoyre to recomfort him untill
he had recovered health, and I do much mervayle that ye Lady *Elinor*   10
is now become so unwilling to take any travayle in his behalfe, especially
remembring that but yesternight she was so diligent to bring him to bed,
but I perceyve that all earthly thinges are subject unto change. Even so
they be quod *Pergo,* for you may behold the trees which but even this other
daye were clad in gladsome greene, and now their leaves begin to fade and   15
change colour. Thus they passed talking and walking untill they returned
unto the Castle, whereas they went straight unto *F.J.* chamber, & found
him in bed: why how now *Trust* (quod Dame *Fraunces,*) will it be no
better? Yes shortly I hope quod *F.J.* The Ladies all saluted him: & he gave
them the gramercy: at the last *Pergo* popped this question unto him. And   20
howe have you slept in your Mistres sheetes Master *F.J.* quod she? reason-
ably[2] well quod *F.J.* but I pray you where is my Mistresse this morning?
Mary sayd *Pergo,* wee left hir in bed scarce well at ease. I am the more
sorye quod *F.J.* Why *Trust* (sayd Mistresse *Fraunces*) be of good com-
forte, and assure your selfe that here are others who would be as glad of   25
your wel doing, as your Mistresse in any respect. I ought not to doubt
therof (quod *F.J.*) having the proofe that I have had of your great cur-
tesies, but I thought it my dutie to aske for my Mistresse being absent.
Thus they passed some time with him untill they were called away unto
prayers, and that being finished they went to dinner, where they met   30
Dame[3] *Elynor* attired in a night kerchief after the soolenest (the solemp-
nest fashion I should have sayed) who loked very drowsely upon all folkes,
unlesse it were hir secretary, unto whom she deigned sometime to lend a
freendly glaunce. The Lord of the Castle demaunded of hir howe *F.J.* did
this morning. She answered that she knew not, for she had not seene him   35
that day. You may do wel then daughter (qd. the Lord) to go now unto
him, & to assay if he wil eate any thing, & if here be no meates that like him,
I pray you commaund (for him) any thing that is in my house. You must
pardon me sir (quod she,) I am sickly disposed, and would be loth to take
the ayre: why then go you Mistres *Fraunces* (quod he) and take somebody   40
with you: and I charge you see that he lacke nothing. Mistresse *Fraunces*
was glad of the ambassade, & arysing from the table with one other gentle-
woman, toke with hir a dishe of chickins boyled in white broth, saying to
hir father: I thinke this meate meetest for Master *J.* of any that is here.
It is so (quod he) daughter, and if he like not that, cause somewhat els   45

to be dressed for him according to his apetite. Thus she departed and
came to *F.J.* who being plonged in sundry woes and thrilled with restlesse
thoughtes, was now beginning to aryse: but seing the Dames, couched
downe againe, and sayd unto them. Alas fayre Ladies you put your
selves to more paynes than eyther I do desire, or can deserve. Good *Trust*   5
quod dame *Fraunces,* our paines are no greater than dutie requireth, nor
yet so great as we could vouchsafe in your behalfe, and presently my father
hath sent us unto you (quod she) with this pittaunce, and if your apetite
desire any one thing more than other, wee are to desire likewise that you
will not refrayne to call for it. Oh my good *Hope* (quod hee) I perceive   10
that I shall not dye as longe as you maye make mee live. And being nowe
somedeale recomforted with the remembraunce of his Mistres words which
shee hadde used over night at hir first comming, and also thinkinge that
although shee parted in choller, it was but justly provoked by him selfe,
and that at leasure hee shoulde fynde some salve for that soore also: hee   15
determyned to take the comforte of his assured *Hope,* and so to expell
all venomnes of mistrust before receyved: wherfore raysing him selfe in his
bed, he cast a night gowne about his shoulders saying: It shall never be
sayd that my faynting hart can reject the comfortable Cordialles of so
freendly phisitions. Nowe by my troth well sayed gentle *Trust* quod Dame   20
Fraunces, and in so doing assure your selfe of guerison with speed. This
thus sayed, the curteous Dame became his kerver, & hee with a bold
spirite gan tast of hir cookery, but the late conflicts of his conceipts had
so disaquainted his stomack from repastes, that he could not wel away
with meate: and yet neverthelesse by little & little receyved some noury-   25
ture. When his *Hope* had crammed him as long as she coulde make him
feede, they delivered the rest to the other gentlewoman, who having not
dyned, fell to hir provander. In which meane while the Lady *Fraunces*
had much comfortable speech with *F.J.* and declared that she perceyved
very well the cause of his malladie, but my *Trust* (quod she) be all whole,   30
and remember what I foretold you in the beginning: neverthelesse you
must thinke that there are remedies for all mischiefes, and if you wilbe
ruled by myne advise, we will soone find the meane to ease you of this
mishap. *F.J.* toke comforte in hir discretion, and freendly kissing hir hand,
gave hir a cartlode of thankes for hir great good will, promising to put to   35
his uttermost force, and evermore to be ruled by hir advise. Thus they
passed the dynner while, the Ladie *Fraunces* always refusing to declare
hir conceipt of the late change which she perceyved in his Mistresse, for shee
thought best first to wynne his will unto conformitie by little and little, and
then in the end to persuade him with necessitie. When the other gentle-   40
woman had vytayled hir, they departed, requiring *F.J.* to arise and boldly
to resist the fayntnesse of his fever, the which he promised and so bad
them *a Dio.* The Ladyes at their returne found the courte in Dame *Elynors*
chamber, who had there assembled hir secretary, Dame[1] *Pergo,* and the
rest: there they passed an hower or twayne in sundry discourses, wherin   45

Dame *Pergo* did alwaies cast out some bone for Mistresse *Fraunces* to
gnaw uppon, for that in deede she perceyved hir harty affection towardes
F.J.: whereat Mistresse *Fraunces* changed no countenaunce, but reserved
hir revenge untill a better oportunitie. At last (quod Dame *Fraunces* unto
Mistresse *Elinor*) and when will you go unto your servaunt fayre Lady?   5
When he is sicke and I am whole quod Dame *Elynor*. That is even now
quod the other, for how sicke hee is your self can witnesse: and how well
you are we must beare record. You may aswel be deceived in my dis-
position (quod Dame *Elynor*) as I was overseene in his sodain alteration,
and if he be sicke you are meetest to be his phisition: for you sawe yester-   10
day that my paines did little profite towardes his recomfort. Yes surely
sayd the other, not onely I but all the rest had occasion to judge that your
curtesie was his chiefe comfort. Well quod Dame *Elinor* you know not what
I know. Nor you what I think quod Dame *Fraunces*. Thinke what you
list quod *Elynor*. In deede quod *Fraunces* I may not thinke that you care,   15
neither will I die for your displeasure[1]: and so halfe angry shee departed.
At supper they met againe, and the Maister of the house demaunded of
his daughter *Fraunces* how *F.J.* did? Sir (quod she) he did eate somewhat
at dinner, and sithens I saw him not. The more to blame quod he, and now
I would have al you gentlewomen take of the best meates and go suppe   20
with him: for company driveth away carefulnesse, and leave you me here
with your leavinges alone. Nay sir quod Mistresse *Elynor*, I pray you
give me leave to beare you company, for I dare not adventure thither.
The Lord of the Castle was contented & dispatched away the rest: who
taking with them such vyandes as they thought meetest, went unto *F.J.*   25
chamber, fynding him up, and walking about to recover strength, whereat
Dame *Fraunces* rejoysed, and declared how hir father had sent that com-
pany to attend him at supper. *F.J.* gave great thankes, and missing now
nothing but his Mistresse, thought not good yet to aske for hir, but because
he partly gessed the cause of hir absence, he contented him selfe, hoping   30
that when his lure was newe garnished, he shoulde easely reclayme hir
from those coye conceiptes. They passed over their supper all in quiet,
and sone after Mistresse *Fraunces*, being desirous to requite Dame
Pergoes quippes, requested that they might continue the pastime which
Dame *Pergo* had begon over night: whereunto they all consented, and   35
the lot fell unto Dame *Fraunces* to propounde the second question, who
adressing hir speeche unto *F.J.* sayde in this wyse. Noble governor, I will
reherse unto you a straunge historie, not fayned, neither borowed out of
any olde aucthorritie, but a thing done in deede of late daies, and not
farre distant from this place where wee nowe remayne. It chaunced that a   40
gentleman our neighbor being maried to a very fayre gentlewoman, lived
with hir by the space of fower or five yeares in great contentation, trusting
hir no lesse than he loved hir, and yet loving hir as much as any man coulde
love a woman. On that otherside the gentlewoman hadde woon (unto hir
beautie) a singular commendation for hir chast and modest behaviour.   45

Yet it happened in time that a lustie younge gentleman (who very often resorted to them) obtayned that at hir handes, which never any man coulde before him attayne: and to be playne, he woon so much in hir affections, that forgetting both hir own dutie and hir husbandes kindnes, she yeelded hir body at the commaundement of this lover, in which pastime they passed long time by their polliticke government. At last the friendes of this Lady (and especially three sisters which she had) espied overmuch familiaritie betwene the two lovers, and dreading least it might breake out to their common reproch, toke their sister apart, and declared that the worlde did judge scarce well of the repayre of that gentleman unto hir house: and that if she did not foresee it in time, she shoulde not onely leese the good credite which she hir selfe had hitherto possessed, but furthermore should distayne their whole race with common obloquy and reproch. These and sundry other godly admonitions of these sisters could not sinke in the mind of this gentlewoman, for she did not onely stand in defiaunce what any man coulde thinke of hir, but also seemed to accuse them, that because they saw hir estimation (being their yonger) to growe above their owne, they had therfore devised this meane to set variance betwene hir husbande and hir. The sisters seeing their holesome counsell so rejected, and hir continue still in hir obstinate opinion, adressed their speech unto hir husbande, declaring that the worlde judged not the best, neyther they themselves did very wel like of the familiaritie betwene their sister and that gentleman, and therfore advised him to forecast all perils, and in time to forbid him his house. The husband (on that otherside) had also conceyved such a good opinion of his gest, & had growen into such a stricte famyliaritie with him, y^t you might with more ease have removed a stone wall, than once to make him thinke amisse, eyther of his wyfe, or of hir lover: Yea, and immediately after this conference he would not sticke thus to say unto his wife. *Besse*: (for so in deede was hir name) thou hast three such busie brayned sisters, as I thincke shortly their heads will breake: they would have me to bee jellous of thee, no no *Besse* &c. so that hee was not onely farre from any such beliefe, but furthermore dyd every day encrease his curtesies towardes the lover. The sisters being thus on all sides rejected, and yet perceiving more and more an unseemely behaviour betwene their sister and hir minion, began to melt in their owne grease: and such was their enraged pretence of revenge, that they suborned divers servants in the house to watch so dilligently, as that this treason might be discovered. Amongst the rest, one mayde of subtill spirite had so long watched them, that at last she espied them go into a chamber together, and locke the doore to them: whereuppon she ranne with all hast possible to hir Maister, and tolde him that if he would come with hir, shee woulde shewe him a very straunge sight. The gentleman (suspectinge nothinge) went with hir untill he came into a chamber neare unto that wherin they had shut themselves, and she poynting hir Maister to the keyhole, bad him looke through, where he sawe the thing which most might mislike him to behold. Where at he sodaynely drew his Dagger, and turned

towardes the mayde, who fled from him for feare of mischiefe: but when he
could not overtake hir in the heat of his choller, he commaunded that she
should forthwith trusse up that little which she had and to depart his
service: and before hir departure he found meanes to talke with hir, threat-
ening that if ever she spake any word of this mystery in any place where   5
she should come, it shuld cost hir lyfe. The mayde for feare departed in
silence, and the Master never changed countenance eyther to his wife or
to hir peramour, but feyned unto his wyfe that he had turned away the
mayde uppon that sodaine, for that shee had throwen a Kitchin knife at
him, whyles he went about to correct a fault in hir &c. Thus the good   10
gentleman dranke up his owne swette unseene every day, encreasing
curtesie to the lover, and never chaunging countenaunce to his wyfe in any
thing, but onely that he refrayned to have such knowlege of hir carnally as
he in times past had, and other men have of their wives. In this sort he
continued by the space all most of halfe a yeare, neverthelesse lamenting   15
his mishap in sollitary places. At last (what moved him I know not) he fell
agayn to company with his wife as other men doo, and as I have heard it
saied he used this pollicy: every time that he had knowledge of hir, he
would leave either in the bed, or in hir cushencloth, or by hir looking
glasse, or in some place wher shee must needes find it, a piece of mony   20
which then was fallen to three halfpence: and I remember they called them
Slippes. Thus he dealt with hir continually by the space of foure or five
monethes, using hir neverthelesse very kindly in all other respectes, & pro-
viding for hir al things necessary at the first call: But unto his geast he
still augmented his curtesie, in suche sorte, that you would have thought   25
them to be sworne brothers. Al this notwithstanding his wife much musing
at these three half peny peeces which she founde in this sorte, and further-
more, having sundry times found hir husband[1] in solitarie places making
great lamentation, she grew enquisitive, what should be the secret cause
of these alteracions: unto whom he would none otherwise answere, but   30
that any man shuld finde occasion to be more pensive at one time than at
another. The wife notwithstanding encreasing hir suspect, emported the
same unto hir lover, alledging therwithall that shee doubted very much
least hir husband had some vehement suspicion of their affaires. The lover
encoraged hir, & likewise declared, y[t] if she would be importunate to en-   35
quire the cause, hir husband would not be able to keepe it from hir: and
having now throughly enstructed hir, she dealt with hir husband in this
sorte. One day when shee knew him to be in his study alone, she came in
to him, and having fast locked the dore after hir, and conveyed the key
into hir pocket,[2] she began first with earnest entreaty, and then with   40
teares to crave that he would no longer keepe from hir the cause of his
sodein alteration. The husband dissimuled the matter still:[3] at last she was
so earnest to know for what cause he left money in such sort at sundry
times, that he aunswered on this wise: Wyfe (quod he) thou knowest how
long we have ben maried togither, & how long I made so deare accompt   45

of thee as ever man made of his wife: since which dayes, thou knowest
also how long I refreyned thy company, and how long again I have used thy
company leaving the mony in this sorte, and the cause is this. So long as
thou didst behave thy selfe faithfully towards me, I never lothed thy
company, but sithens I have perceived thee to be a harlot, & therfore did 5
I for a time refreine and forbeare to lie with thee: & now I can no longer
forbeare it, I do give thee every time that I lye with thee a slip, which
is to make thee understande thine owne whordome: and this reward is suf-
ficient for a whore. The wife began stoutly to stand at defiance, but the
husband[1] cut off hir speeche and declared when, where, and how he had 10
seene it: hereat the woman being abashed, and finding hir conscience
gilty of asmuch as he had alledged, fel down on hir knees, & with most bitter
teares craved pardon, confessing hir offence: whereat hir husband (moved
with pitie) & melting likewise in fluds of lamentation, recomforted hir
promising that if from that day forwards she would be true unto him, he 15
wold not only forgive al that was past, but become more tender & loving
unto hir than ever he was. What do I tary so long? they became of
accord: & in full accomplishment therof, the gentlewoman did altogither
eschew the company, the speech, & (as much as in hir lay) the sight of hir
lover, although hir husband did continue his curtesie towards[2] him, and 20
often charged his wife to make him fair semblant. The Lover was now onely
left in perplexitie, who knewe nothing what might be the cause of all these
chaunges, & that most greeved him, he could by no meanes obteyne agayn
the speech of his desired: hee watched all opportunities, hee suborned mes-
sangers, he wrote letters, but all in vayne. In the end shee caused to be 25
declared unto him a time and place where she would meete him and speake
with him. Being mett, she put him in remembrance of all that had passed
betwene them: she[3] layed also before him howe trusty shee had bin unto
him in all professions: she confessed also how faithfully he had discharged
the dutie of a friend in all respects, and therewithall she declared that hir 30
late alteration and pensivenes of mind was not with out great cause, for
that she had of late such a mishap, as might change the disposition of any
living creature: Yea and that the case was such, as unlesse she found
present remedy, hir death must needes ensue and that speedely: for the
preventing whereof, she alledged that she had beaten hir braynes with all 35
devises possible, and that in the end she could think of no redresse but one,
the which lay only in him to accomplishe. Wherfore she besought him for
all the love and good will which passed betwene them, nowe to shew the
fruites of true friendship, and to gratifie hir with a free graunt to this re-
quest. The lover who had always ben desirous to pleasure hir in any thing, 40
but now especially to recover hir woonted kindnesse, gan frankly promise
to accomplish any thing that might be to him possible, yea though it were
to his great detriment: and therewithall did deepely blame hir in that she
would so long torment hir selfe with any grief, considering that it lay in him
to helpe it. The Lady aunswered, that she had so long kept it from his 45

knowledge, bycause she doubted whether he would be contented to per-
forme it or not, althogh it was such a thing as he might easely graunt with-
out any maner of hurt to himself: & yit that now in ye end she was forced
to adventure upon his curtesie, being no longer able to bear ye burden of hir
grief: the lover solicited hir most earnestly to disclose it: and she (as fast)   5
seemed to mistrust y^t he would not accomplish it. In the end she tooke out
a booke (which shee had brought for the nonce) and bound him by oth to
accomplish it. The lover mistrusting nothing lesse than that ensued, tooke
the othe willingly: which don she declared al that had passed betwene hir
& hir husband: his grief, hir repentance, his pardon, hir vow, & in ye ende   10
of hir tale enjoined the lover, that from thenceforthwards, he should never
attempt to break hir constant determination: the lover replied that this
was unpossible: but shee plainly assured him, y^t if he graunted hir that
request, she would be his friend in all honest & godly wise: if not, shee put
him out of doubt that she would eschew his company & flie from his sight as   15
from a scorpion. The lover considering that hir request was but just, ac-
cusing his own gilty conscience, remembring the great curtesies always
used by hir husband, & therwithall seeing the case now brought to such an
issue, as y^t by none other meanes than by this it could be conceiled from
knowledge of the world: but most of all, being urged by his oth, did at last   20
give an unwilling consent, & yit a faithful promise to yeeld unto hir wil in
al things: and thus being become of one assent, he remaineth the dearest
friend & most welcome gest that may be, both to the Lady & hir husband,
and the man & wife so kind (ech to other) as if there never had bin such
a breache betwene them. Now, of you noble Governor I would fayn learn,   25
whether the perplexitie of the husband when he looked in at the key hole, or
of the wife when she knewe the cause why the slippes were so scattered,
or of the lover when he knew what was his Mistres charge, was greater of
the three? I might have put in also the troubled thoughts of the sisters
& the mayd, when they sawe their good will rejected, but let these three   30
suffise. Gentle *Hope* (quod *F.J.*) you have rehearsed (& that right elo-
quently) a notable tale, or rather a notable history, bycause you seeme
to affirme, that it was don in deed of late, & not far hence. Wherein I
note five especiall pointes: that is a marvelous pacience in the husband, no
lesse repentance in the wyfe, no small boldnesse of the mayd, but much   35
more rashnesse in the sisters, and last of all, a rare tractabilitie in the lover.
Neverthelesse to returne unto your question, I think the husbands per-
plexitie greatest, bicause his losses abounded above the rest, & his injuries
were uncomparable. The Lady *Fraunces* did not seeme to contrary him,
but rather smyled in hir sleeve at Dame *Pergo,* who had no lesse patience   40
to heare the tale recited, than the Lady *Fraunces* had pleasure in telling
of it, but I may not rehearse the cause why, unlesse I shuld tell all. By this
time the sleeping houre aproched, & the Ladies prepared their departure,
when as mistres *Fraunces* said unto *F.J.* Although percase I shal not do
it so handsomly as your mistres, yit good *Trust* (quod she) if you vouch-   45

safe it, I can be content to trim up your bed in ye best maner that I may, as one who would be as glad as she to procure your quiet rest. *F.J.*[1] gave hir gret thanks desiring hir not to trouble hirself, but to let his man alone with that charge: thus they departed, and how all parties tooke rest that night I know not: but in the morning *F.J.* began to consider w^t himself that he might lye long enough in his bed before his mistres would be apeased in hir peewish conceipts: wherfor he arose, & being aparelled in his night gown, tooke occasion to walk in the gallery neer adjoyning unto his Mistres chamber: but ther might he walk long enough ere his mistres would come to walk w^t him. When dinner time came he went into the great chamber wheras the Lord of the castle saluted him being joyful of his recovery. *F.J.* giving dewe thanks, declared that his frendly entretainement togither with the great curtesie of the gentlewomen was such, as might revive a man although he were half dead. I would be loth (qd. the hoste) that any gentleman coming to me for good wil, shuld want any curtesie of entertainment y^t lieth in my power. When ye meat was served to the table, the gentlewomen came in all but Dame *Elynor* & mistres *Pergo*, the which *F.J.* marked very well, & it did somewhat abate his apetit. After dinner, his *Hope* came unto him and demaunded of him howe hee would passe the day for his recreation? to whom he aunswered even as it best pleased hir. She devised to walke into the park, & so by little & litle to acquaint himself with the ayre: he agreed, & they walked togither being accompanied with one or two other gentlewomen. Here (least you shuld grow in some wrong conceit of *F.J.*) I must put you out of dout, that although ther were now more cause that he shuld mistrust his mistres than ever he had before received, yit the vehement passions which he saw in hir when she first came to visit him, & moreover, the earnest words which she pronounced in his extremity, were such a refreshing to his mind, as that he determined no more to trouble himself w^t like conceipts:[2] concluding further, y^t if his mistres wer not faulty, then had he committed a foule offence in needlesse jelousie, & that if she were faulty (especially with the *Secretary*) then no persuasion could amend hir, nor any passion help him: and this was the cause y^t enabled him after such passing pangs to abyde the doubtfull conclusion, thus manfully and valiantly to represse feintnesse of his mind: nothing doubting but that he should have wonne his Mistres to pardon his presumption, & lovingly to embrace his service in wonted maner, but he was far deceyved, for she was now in another tewne, the which Mistres *Fraunces* began partly to discover unto him as they walked togither: for shee burdened him that his mallady proceeded only of a disquiet mind. And if it did so my gentle *Hope* (quod he) what remedy? My good *Trust* (quod she) none other but to plant quiet where disquiet began to grow. I have determined so (qd. he) but I must crave the helpe of your assured friendship. Therof you may make accoumpt (qd. she) but wherin? *F.J.* walking apart with hir, began to declare that ther was some contention hapened betwene his mistres & him: the Lady told him that she was not

ignorant therof. Then he desired hir to treat so much in y[e] cause, as they
might eftsones come to *Parlee*: therof I dare assure you (qd. Mistresse
Fraunces,)[1] & at their retorne she led *F.J.* into his Mistres chamber, whom
thei found lying on hir bed, whether galded with any grief, or weary of the
thing (which you wot[2] of) I know not, but there she lay; unto whom *F.J.*   5
gave two or three salutations before she seemed to mark him. At last said
the Lady *Fraunces* unto hir, your servant hearing of your sicknes, hath
adventured thus far into the ayre to see you. I thank him (qd. Dame
Elynor) & so lay still, refusing to give him any countenance. Wherat
F.J. perceyving al the other gentlewomen fal to whispering, thoght good,   10
boldly to plead his own case: & aproching the bed began to enforce his un-
willing mistres unto curtesie, wherin he used such vehemence as she could
not well by any meanes refuse to talke with him: but what their talk was
I may not take upon me to tell you, unlesse you would have me fill up a
whole volume only with his matters, and I have dilated them over largely   15
already. Suffyseth this to be knowne, that in the ende shee pretended to
passe over all old grudges, & thenceforth to pleasure him as occasion[3] might
serve: the which occasion was so long in hapening, that in the end *F.J.*
being now eftsones troubled with unquiet fantasies, & forced to use his pen
again as an Ambassadour betwene them: one daye amongst the rest found   20
oportunitie to thrust a letter into hir bosome, wherin he had earnestly
requested another mooneshyne banquet or frydayes breakfast to recomfort
his dulled spirits wherunto the Dame yeelded this aunswer in writing, but
of whose endyting judge you.

G.T.   25

I can but smyle at your simplicity, who burden your friends with an
impossibility. The case so stood as I could not though I would. Where-
fore from henceforth eyther learne to frame your request more reasonably,
or else stand content with a flat repulse.   *SHE.*

F.J. liked this letter but a little: and being thereby droven into his   30
accustomed vayne, he compiled in verse this answere following, uppon these
woords contened in hir letter, *I could not though I would.*   *G.T.*

[12] *I could not though I would: good Lady say not so,*
  Since one good word of your good wil might soone redresse[4] *my wo*
  Where would is free before, there could can never fayle: 35
  For profe, you see how gallies passe where ships can beare no sayle.
  The weary mariner when skies are overcast,
  By ready will doth guyde his skill and wins the haven at last.
  The prety byrd that sings with pricke against hir brest,
  Doth make a vertue of hir need to watch when others rest.   40
  And true the proverbe is, which you have layed apart,
  There is no hap can seeme to hard unto a willing hart.
  Then lovely Lady myne, you say not as you should,
  In doubtful termes to aunswer thus: I could not thogh I would.
  Yes, yes, full well you know, your can is quicke and good: 45

And wilfull will is eke too swift to shed¹ my giltlesse blood.
But if good will were bent as prest as power is,
Such will would quickly find the skill to mend that is amisse.
Wherfore if you desire to see my true love spilt,
Commaund and I will slea my self, that yours may be the gilt.   5
But if you have no power to say your servaunt nay,
Write thus: I may not as I would, yet must I as I may.

F.J.

Thus *F.J.* replied upon his Mistres aunswer, hoping therby to recover some favour at hir hands, but it wold not be: so that nowe he had bene   10
as likely (as at the first) to have fretted in fantasies, had not the Lady *Fraunces* continually comforted him: and by little & little she drove such reason into his minde, that now he began to subdue his humors with discretion, and to determine that if hee might espie evident profe of his Mistresse frayeltie, hee would then stand content with pacience perforce, &   15
give his Mistres the *Bezo las manos*. And it happened one day amongst others, that he resorted to his Mistresse chamber & found hir *(allo solito)* lying upon hir bed, & the secretary with Dame *Pergo* & hir handmayd keping of hir company. Wherat *F.J.* somwhat repyning, came to hir and fell to dalliance, as one yᵗ had now rather adventure to be thought presump-   20
tious than yeeld to be accompted bashfull, he cast his arme over his Mistresse and began to accuse hir of slogishnes, using some other bold parties, as well to provoke hir, as also to greeve the other. The Lady seemed little to delight in his dallying, but cast a glance at hir secretary and therwith smyled, when as the Secretary & dame *Pergo* burst out into open laughter.   25
The which *F.J.* perceyving, and disdayning hir ingratitude, was forced to depart, and in that fantasie compyled this Sonet.

G.   T.

[13] **W**ith hir in armes that had my hart in hold,
        I stoode of late to plead for pittie so: 30
And as I did hir lovely lookes behold,
She cast a glance uppon my ryvall foe.
His fleering face provoked hir to smyle,
When my salte teares were drowned in disdayne:
He glad, I sad, he laught, (alas the while)   35
I wept for woe: I pyn'd for deadly payne.
And when I sawe none other boote prevayle,
But reasons rule must guide my skilfull minde:
Why then (quod I) olde proverbes never fayle,
For yet was never good Cat out of kinde: 40
Nor woman true but even as stories tell,
Woon with an egge, and lost againe with shell.

F.J.

T His Sonet declareth that he began nowe to accompt of hir as she deserved, for it hath a sharpe conclusion, and it is somewhat too generall. Wel, as it is he lost it where his Mistresse found it, and she immediatly emparted the same unto Dame *Pergo,* and Dame *Pergo* unto others: so that it quickely became common in the house. Amongst others   5
Mistres *Fraunces* having recovered a copie of it, did seeme to pardon the generallitie, and to be well pleased with the perticularitie therof, the which she bewrayed one day unto *F.J.* in this wise. Of all the joyes that ever I had (my good *Trust* quod she) there is none wherein I take more comforte than in your conformitie, and although your present rage is such that you   10
can bee content to condemne a nomber unknowen, for the transgression of one too well knowne: yet I do rather rejoyce that you should judge your pleasure over many, than to be abused by any. My good *Hope* (quod he) it were not reason that after such manifold proofes of your exceding cur-tesies, I should use straunge or contentious speech with so deare a friend,   15
and in deede I must confesse that the opinion which I have conceived of my Mistresse, hath stirred my penne to write very hardly against all the feminine gender, but I pray you pardon me (quod he) & if it please you I wil recant it: as[1] also (percase) I was but cloyed with *Surquedry,* and presumed to think more than may be proved. Yea but how if it were   20
proved quod Dame *Fraunces?* If it were so (which God forbid quod he) then coulde you not blame me to conceive that opinion. Howsoever I might blame you (quod she) I meane not to blame you, but I demaund further, if it be as I thinke & you suspect, what will you then do? Surely (quod *F.J.*) I have determined[2] to drinke up mine owne sorowe secretely, and to   25
bid them both a *Dieu.* I like your farewell better than your fantasie (quod she) and whensoever you can be content to take so much paynes, as the Knight (which had a night gowne garded with naked swordes) dyd take, I thinke you may put your selfe out of doubt of all these thinges. By these wordes and other speech which she uttered unto him, *F.J.* smelt how the   30
world went about, and therfore did one day in ye grey morning adventure to passe through the gallery towards his Mistres chamber, hoping to have found the doore open, but he found the contrary, and there attending in good devocion, heard the parting of his Mistresse and hir Secretary, with many kind words: wherby it appeared that the one was very loth to   35
departe from the other. *F.J.* was enforced to beare this burden, and after he had attended there as long as the light wold give him leave, he departed also to his chamber, and aparaling himselfe, could not be quiet untill he had spoken with his Mistresse, whom he burdened flatly with this despitefull trechery: and as she as fast denied it, untill at last being still urged with   40
such evident tokens as he alleged, she gave him this bone to gnawe uppon. And if I did so (quod she) what than? Whereunto *F.J.* made none answere, but departed with this farewel. *My losse is mine owne, and your gayne is none of yours, and soner can I recover my losse than you enjoy the gaine*

which you gape after. And whan he was in place sollitary, he compyled these following for a fynall end of the matter.

G.T.

[14]
    And if I did what then?
    Are you agreev'd therfore?   5
    The Sea hath fishe for every man,
    And what would you have more?

    Thus did my Mistresse once,
    Amaze my mind with doubt:
    And popt a question for the nonce,   10
    To beate my braynes about.

    Wherto I thus replied,
    Eche fisherman can wishe,
    That all the Sea at every tyde,
    Were his alone to fishe.   15

    And so did I (in vaine,)
    But since it may not be:
    Let such fishe there as find the gaine,
    And leave the losse for me.

    And with such lucke and losse,   20
    I will content my selfe:
    Till tydes of turning time may tosse,
    Such fishers on the shelfe.

    And when they sticke on sands,
    That every man may see: 25
    Then will I laugh and clappe my hands,
    As they do now at mee.[1]

F.J.

IT is time now to make an end of this thriftlesse Historie, wherein although I could wade much further,[2] as to declare his departure, what 30 thankes he gave to his *Hope* &c. Yet I will cease, as one that had rather leave it unperfect than make it to plaine. I have past it over with quod he, and quod she, after my homely manner of writing, using sundry names for one person, as the Dame, the Lady, Mistresse, &c. The Lorde of the Castle, the Master of the house, and the hoste: neverthelesse for that 35 I have seen good aucthors terme every gentlewoman a Lady, and every gentleman *domine*, I have thought it no greater faulte then pettie treason thus to entermyngle them, nothing doubting but you will easely[3] understand my meaning, and that is asmuch as I desire. Now henceforwardes I will trouble you no more with such a barbarous style in prose, but will 40

onely recite unto you sundry verses written by sundry gentlemen, adding
nothing of myne owne, but onely a tytle to every Poeme, wherby
the cause of writinge the same maye the more evidently appeare:
Neyther can I declare unto you who wrote the greatest part
of them, for they are unto me but a posie presented out   5
of sundry gardens, neither have I any other names
of the flowers, but such short notes as the
aucthors themselves have delivered therby
if you can gesse them, it shall no waye
offende mee. I will begin with   10
this translation as fol-
loweth.
G.T.

[1]   *A translation of*
                        Ariosto allegorized.

WHen worthy *Bradamant,* had looked long in vain,
      To see hir absent love and Lord, *Ruggier:* returne againe:
Uppon hir lothed bed hir lustlesse limbes did cast,
And in deceitfull dreames she thought, she saw him come at last.
But when with open armes, she ran him to embrace,   5
With open eyes she found it false, & thus complain'd hir case.
That which me pleased (qd. she) was dreames which fancy drewe,
But that which me torments (alas) by sight I find it true.
My joye was but a dreame, and soone did fade away,
But my tormenting cruell cares, cannot so soone decaye.   10
Why heare I not and see, since now I have my sences?
That which in fained fading dreames, appered by pretences.
Or whereto serve mine eyes, if sights they so mistake,
As seeme to see ech joy in sleepe, and woo when they awake.
The sweete & slumbring sleape, did promise joye & peace,   15
But these unpleasaunt sights do rayse, such warres as never cease.
The sleape I felt was false, and seem'd to ease my grief,
But that I see is all to true, and yeeldes me no relief.
If truth anoy me then, and fayned fancyes please me,
God graunt I never heare nor see, true thing for to disease me.   20
If sleaping yeeld me joy, and waking worke me woe,
God graunt I sleape, & never wake, to ease my torment so.
O happy slumbring soules, whom one dead drowsy sleepe
Six monethes (of yore) in silence shutte, with closed eyes did keepe.
Yet can I not compare, such sleepe to be like death,   25
Nor yet such waking, as I wake, to be like vitall breath.
For why my lot[1] doth fall, contrary to the rest,
I deeme it death when I awake, & life while I do rest.
Yet if such sleepe be like to death in any wise,
O gentle death come quick at call, & close my drery eyes.   30
Thus sayd the worthy dame, whereby I gather this,
No care can be compard to that, where true love parted is.

                        Lenvoie.

Lo Lady if you had but halfe like care for mee,
That worthy *Bradamant* had then hir own *Ruggier* to see: 35
My readie will should be so prest to come at call,
You should have no such sight or dreame to trouble you withall.
Then when you list commaund, & I wil come in hast,
There is no hap shal hold me backe, good will shal roon so fast.
                Si fortunatus infoelix.

[2]   *Written uppon a reconciliation be-*
twene two freendes

T He hatefull man that heapeth in his mynde,
    Cruell revenge of wronges forepast and done,
May not (with ease) the pleasaunt pathway finde,
Of friendly verses which I have now begone,
Unlesse at first his angry brest untwinde,   5
The crooked knot which canckred choller knit,
And then recule with reconciled grace.
Likewise I find it sayed in holy write,
If thou entend to turne thy fearefull face,
To God above: make thyne agrement yet,   10
First with thy Brother whom thou didst abuse,
Confesse thy faultes thy frowardnes and all,
So that the Lord thy prayer not refuse.
When I consider this, and then the brall,
Which raging youth (I will not me excuse)   15
Did whilome breede in mine unmellowed brayne,
I thought it meete before I did assay,
To write in ryme the double golden gayne,
Of amitie: first yet to take away
The grutch of grief, as thou doest me constrayne.   20
By due desert whereto[1] I now must yeeld,
And drowne for aye in depth of *Lethes* lake,
Disdaynefull moodes whom frendship cannot weeld:
Pleading for peace which for my parte I make
Of former strife, and henceforth let us write   25
The pleasant fruites of faythfull friends delight.
                      Si fortunatus infoelix.

[3]   ¶*Two gentlemen did roon three courses at the rynge for one kysse, to be tak-*
en of a fayre gentlewoman being then present, with this condicion: that the
winner shold have the kisse, and the loser be bound to write some verses uppon
the gayne or losse therof. Now it fortuned so that the wynner triumphed
saying, he much lamented that in his youth he had not seene the warres.
Whereuppon the looser compiled these following in discharge of the condicion
above rehearsed.

T His vayne avayle which thou by Mars hast woon,
    Should not allure thy flytting[1] mynd to feeld:
Where sturdie Steedes in depth of daungers roon,
With guts wel gnawen by clappes that Cannons yeeld.
Where faythlesse friends by warfare waxen ware,   5
And roon to him that geveth best rewarde:
No feare of lawes can cause them for to care,
But robbe and reave, and steale without regard

The fathers cote, the brothers steede from stall:
The deere friends purse shall picked be for pence,   10
The native soyle, the parents left and all,
With *Tant tra Tant,* the campe is marching hence.
But when bare beggrie bids them to beware,
And late repentaunce rules them to retyre.
Like hyvelesse Bees they wander here and there,   15
And hang on them (who earst) might dread their yre.
This cutthrote life (me seemes) thou shouldst not like,
And shoon the happie haven of meane estate:
High *Jove* (perdie) may send what thou doest seeke,
And heape up poundes within thy quiet gate.   20
Nor yet I would that thou shouldst spend thy dayes,
In idlenesse to teare a golden time:
Like country loutes which compt none other prayse,
But grease a sheepe and learne to serve the swine.
In vayne were then the giftes which nature lent,   25
If *Pan* so preasse to passe Dame *Pallas* lore:
But my good friend let thus thy youth be spent,
Serve God thy Lord, and prayse him evermore.
Search out the skill which learned bookes do teach,
And serve in feeld when shadowes make thee sure: 30
Hold with the head, and rowe not past thy reach,
But plead for peace which plenty may procure.
And (for my life) if thou canst roon this race,
Thy bagges of coyne will multiply apace.

Si fortunatus infoelix.

[4] ¶*Not long after the writing hereof: he departed from the company of his sayd friend (whom he entirely loved) into the west of England, and feeling himselfe so consumed by womens craft that he doubted of a safe retorne: wrote before his departure as followeth.*

T He feeble thred which *Lachesis* hath spoon,
   To drawe my dayes in short abode with thee,
Hath wrought a webb which now (welneare) is done,
The wale is worne: and (all to late) I see
That lingring life doth dally but in vaine,   5
For *Atropos* will cut the twist in twayne.

I not discerne what life but lothsome were,
When faithfull friends are kept in twayne by want:
Nor yet perceyve what pleasure doth appeere,
To deepe desires where good successe is skant.   10
Such spight yet showes dame fortune (if she frowne,)
The haughty harts in high mishaps to drowne.

Hot be the flames which boyle in friendly mindes,
Cruell the care and dreadfull is the doome:
Slipper the knot which tract of time untwynds,   15
Hatefull the life and welcome were the toome.
Blest were the day which might[1] devower such youth,
And curst the want that seekes to choke such trueth.

This wayling verse I bathe in flowing teares,
And would my life might end with these my lynes: 20
Yet strive I not to force into thine eares,
Such fayned plaintes[2] as fickell fayth resignes.
But high forsight in dreames hath stopt my breath,
And causd the Swanne to sing before his death.

For lo these naked walles do well declare,   25
My latest leave of thee I taken have:
And unknowen coastes which I must seeke with care
Do well divine that there shalbe my grave.
There shall my death make many for to mone,
Skarce knowne to them, well knowne to thee alone.   30

This bowne of thee (as last request) I crave,
When true report shal sounde my death with fame:
Vouchsafe yet then to go unto my grave,
And there first write my byrth and then my name.
And how my life was shortned many yeares,   35
By womens wyles as to the world appeares.

And in reward of graunt to this request,
Permit O God my toung these wordes to tell:
(When as his pen shall write uppon my chest)
With shriking voyce mine owne deare friend farewell.   40
No care on earth did seeme so much to me,
As when my corps was forst to part from thee.

                              Si fortunatus infoelix.

[5]   ¶*He wrote to the same friend from*
                Excester, this Sonet following.

A Hundreth sonnes (in course but not in kind)
   Can witnesse well that I possesse no joye:
The feare of death which fretteth in my mynd
Consumes my hart with dread of darke anoye.
And for eche sonne a thousand broken sleepes,   5
Devide my dreames with fresh recourse of cares:
The youngest sister sharpe hir sheare she kepes,
To cut my thred and thus my life it weares.
Yet let such dayes, such thousand restlesse nightes,

Spit forth their spite, let fates eke showe their force: 10
Deathes daunting dart where so his buffets lights,
Shall shape no change within my friendly corse:
But dead or live, in heaven, in earth, in hell
I wilbe thine where so my carkase dwell.

Si fortunatus infoelix.

[6]   ¶*He wrote to the same friend from Founteine belle eaü in Fraunce, this Sonet
in commendation of the said house of Fountaine bel'eaü.*

N Ot stately *Troy* though *Priam* yet did live,
    Could now compare *Founteine bel'eaü* to passe:
Nor *Syrriane* towers, whose loftie steppes did strive,
To clymbe the throne where angry *Saturne* was.
For outward shew the ports are of such price,   5
As skorne the cost which Cesar spilt in Roome:
Such works within as stayne the rare devise,
Which whillome he *Apelles* wrought on toome.
Swift *Tiber* floud which fed the Romayne pooles,
Puddle to this where Christall melts[1] in streames,   10
The pleasaunt place where *Muses* kept their schooles,
(Not parcht with *Phoebe*, nor banisht from his beames)
Yeeld to those Dames, nor sight, nor fruite, nor smell,
Which may be thought these gardens to excell.

Si fortunatus infoelix.

[7]   ¶*He wrote unto a Skotish Dame whom he chose for his Mistresse in the french
Court, as followeth.*

L Ady receyve, receyve in gracious wise,
    This ragged verse, these rude ill skribled lynes:
Too base an object for your heavenly eyes,
For he that writes his freedome (lo) resignes
Into your handes: and freely yeelds as thrall   5
His sturdy necke (earst subject to no yoke)
But bending now, and headlong prest to fall,
Before your feete, such force hath beauties stroke.
Since then myne eyes (which skorned our English dames[1])
In forrayne courtes have chosen you for fayre,   10
Let be this verse true token of my flames,
And do not drench your owne in deepe dispayre.
Onely I crave (as I nill change for new)
That you vouchsafe to thinke your servaunt trew.

Si fortunatus infoelix.

[8]   ¶*Written to a gentlewoman who had refused him and chosen a husband (as
he thought) much inferior to himself, both in knowledge byrth and parsonage.
Wherin he bewrayeth both their names in cloudes, and how she was woon
from him with sweete gloves and broken ringes.*

I Cannot wish thy griefe, although thou worke my woe
  Since I profest to be thy friend, I cannot be thy foe:
But if thinges done and past, might wel be cald againe,
Then woulde I wishe the wasted wordes, which I have spent in vaine:
Were yet[1] untold to thee, in earnest or in game,   5
And that my doubtfull musing mind, had never thought the same.
For whyles I thee beheld, in carefull[2] thoughts I spent
My liking lust, my lucklesse love which ever truly ment.
And whyles I sought a meane, by pitie to procure,
Too late I found that gorged haukes, do not esteme ye lure.   10
This vauntage hast thou then, thou mayst wel brag & bost
Thou mightst have had a lusty lad, of stature with the most,
And eke of noble mind: his vertues nothing base,
Do well declare that he descends,[3] of auncient worthy race.
Save that I not his name, and though I could it tell,   15
My friendly pen shall let it passe, bycause I love him wel.
And thou hast chosen one of meaner parentage,
Of stature small & therwithall, unequall for thine age.
His thewes unlike the first, yet hast thou hot desire,
To play thee in his flitting flames, God graunt they prove not fyre. 20
Him holdest thou as deare, and he thy Lord shall bee,
(Too late alas) thou lovest him, that never loved thee.
And for just proofe hereof, marke what I tell is true,
Some dismold day shall change his mind, and make him seeke a new.
Then wilt thou much repent thy bargaine made in hast,   25
And much lament those parfumd gloves, which yeeld such sower tast.
And eke the falsed faith, which lurkes in broken ringes,
Though hand in hand say otherwise, yet do I know such thinges.
Then shalt thou sing and say, farewell my trusty Squier,
Wold god my mind had yeelded once, unto to thy just desire.   30
Thus shalt thou waile my want, and I thy great unrest,
Which cruel *Cupid* kindled hath, within thy broken brest.
Thus shalt thou find it griefe, which earst thou thoughtest game,
And I shal hear ye weary newes, by true reporting fame.
Lamenting thy mishap, in source of swelling teares,   35
Harding my hart w^t cruel care, which frosen fancy beares.
And though my just deserte, thy pitie could not move,
Yet[4] wil I wash in wayling words, thy careles childish love
And say as *Troylus* sayd, since that I can no more,
Thy wanton wil did waver once, and wo is me therfore.   40
          Si fortunatus infoelix.

[9]   *In prayse of a gentlewoman who though she were*
not very fayre, yet was she as hard
favored as might be.

I F men may credite give, to true reported fames,
   Who douts but stately Roome had store of lusty loving Dames?
Whose eares have bene so deafe, as never yit heard tell
How farre the fresh *Pompeia*, for beautie did excell.
And golden *Marcus* he, that swayde the Romaine sword,   5
Bare witnesse of *Boemia,* by credite of his word.
What neede I mo reherse? since all the world did know
How high ye flouds of beauties blase, within those walles did flowe.
And yet in all that choyce a worthy Romaine Knight,
Antonius who conquered proude Egypt by his might.   10
Not all to please his eye, but most to ease his minde,
Chose *Cleopatra* for his love, & left the rest behinde.
A wondrous thing to read, in all his victory,
He snapt but hir for his owne share, to please his fantasie.
She was not faire God wot, ye country breeds none bright,   15
Well maye we judge hir skinne the foyle, bycause hir teeth were white.
Percase hir lovely lookes, some prayses did deserve,
But brown I dare be bold she was, for so ye solle did serve.
And could *Antonius* forsake the fayre in *Roome?*
To love this nutbrowne Lady best, was this an equall doome?   20
I dare wel say dames there, did beare him deadly grudge,
His sentence had bene shortly sayed, if *Faustine* had bene judge.
For this I dare avow, (without vaunt be it spoke)
So brave a knight as *Anthony*, held al their necks in yoke
I leave not *Lucrece* out, beleve in hir who list,   25
I thinke she would have lik'd his lure, & stooped to his fist.
What mov'd the chieftain then, to lincke his liking thus?
I wold some Romaine dame were here, the question to discusse.
But I that read hir life, do find therin by fame,
How cleare hir curtisie did shine, in honour of hir name.   30
Hir bountie did excell, hir trueth had never peere,
Hir lovely lookes, hir pleasant speech, hir lusty loving chere.
And all the worthy giftes, that ever yet were found,
Within this good Egiptian Queen, did seeme for to abound.
Wherfore he worthy was, to win the golden fleece,   35
Which scornd the blasing sterres in Roome, to conquere such a peece.
And she to quite his love, in spite of dreadfull death,
Enshrinde with Snakes within his tombe, did yeeld hir parting breath.

Allegoria.

I F fortune favord him, then may that man rejoyce,   40
   And think himself a happy man by hap of happy choice.

Who loves and is belov'd of one as good, as true,
As kind as *Cleopatra* was, and yet more bright of hewe.[1]
Hir eyes as grey as glasse, hir teeth as white as mylke,
A ruddy lippe, a dimpled chyn, a skinne as smoth as silke.   45
A wight what could you more y^t may content mans mind,
And hath supplies for ev'ry want that any man can find.
And may himselfe assure, when hence his life shall passe,
She wilbe stong to death with snakes, as *Cleopatra* was.
                    Si fortunatus infoelix.

[10]   ¶*He began to write by a gentlewoman who passed by him with hir armes set
bragging by hir sides, and left it unfinished as followeth.*

W Ere my hart set on hoygh as thyne is bent,
   Or in my brest so brave and stout a will:
Then (long ere this) I could have bene content,
With sharpe revenge thy carelesse corps to kyll.
For why thou knowest (although thou know not all)   5
What rule, what reigne, what power, what segnory,
Thy melting mind did yeeld to me (as thrall)
When first I pleasd thy wandring fantasie.
What lingring lookes bewray'd thyne inward thought,
What pangs were publisht by perplexitie,   10
Such reakes the rage of love in thee had wrought
And no gramercy for thy curtesie.
I list not vaunt, but yet I dare avowe
(Had bene my harmelesse hart as hard as thyne)
I could have bound thee then for sterting now,   15
In bonds of bale, in pangs of deadly pyne.
For why by proofe the field is eath to win,
Where as the chiefteynes yeeld themselves in chaynes:
The port or passage playne to enter in
Where porters list to leave the key for gaines.   20
But did I then devise with crueltie,
(As tyrants do) to kyll thy yeelding pray?
Or did I bragge and boast triumphantly,
As who should say, the field were myne that day?
Did I retire my self out of thy sight   25
To beate (a fresh[1]) the bulwarks of thy brest?
Or did my mind in choyse of change delight,
And render thee as refusd with the rest?
No Tygre no: the Lion is not lewd,
He showes no force on seely wounded sheepe, &c.   30

[11] *Whiles he sat at the dore of his lodging, devysing these verses above re-*
hearsed, the same Gentlewoman passed by agayne, and cast a longe looke
towards him, wherby he left his former invention and wrote thus.

H Ow long she lookt that lookt at mee of late,
   As who would say, hir lookes were all for love:
When God he knowes they came from deadly hate,
To pinch me yit with pangs which I must prove.
But since my lookes hir liking may not move,   5
Looke where she likes: for lo this looke was cast,
Not for my love, but even to see my last.
                Si fortunatus infoelix.

[12]   *An other Sonet written by the same Gentlewoman*
                uppon the same occasion.

I Lookt of late and saw thee looke askance,
   Upon my dore to see if I satt there,
As who should say: If he be there by chance,
Yet may he think I looke him every where.
No cruell no, thou knowst and I can tell,   5
How for thy love I layd my lookes a side:
Though thou (percase) hast lookt and liked well
Some new found looks amid this world so wide.
But since thy lookes my love have so enchaynd
That in my lookes thy liking now is past: 10
Looke where thou likest, and let thy hands be staynd,
In true loves bloud which thou shalt lack at last.
So looke so lack, for in theis toyes thus tost,
My lookes thy love, thy lookes my life have lost.
                Si fortunatus infoelix.

[13] *Enough of this Dame. And let us peruse his other doings which have come*
to my hands, in such disordred order, as I can best set them down. I will now
then present you with a Sonet written in prayse of the brown beautie, which
he compyled for the love of Mistresse E. P. as foloweth.

T He thriftles thred which pampred beauty spinnes,
   In thraldom binds the foolish gazing eyes:
As cruell Spyders with their crafty ginnes,
In worthlesse webbes doe snare the simple Flies.
The garments gay, the glittring golden gite,   5
The tysing talk which floweth from *Pallas* pooles:
The painted pale, the (too much) red made white,
Are smyling baytes to fishe for loving fooles.
But lo, when eld in toothlesse mouth appeares,
And whoary heares in steed of beauties[1] blaze: 10
Than Had I wist, doth teach repenting yeares,

The tickle track of craftie *Cupides* maze.
Twixt faire and foule therfore, twixt great and small,
A lovely nutbrowne face is best of all.
                    Si fortunatus infoelix.

[14]   *Written by a Gentlewoman in court, who (when shee was
          there placed) seemed to disdain him, contrary
                  to a former profession.*

W Hen daunger kepes the dore, of lady beauties bowre,
      When jelouse toys have chased Trust out of hir strongest towre:
Then faith and troth may flie, then falshod wins the field
Then feeble naked faultlesse harts, for lack of sence must yeld,
And then prevailes as much to hop against the hil,   5
As seeke by suite for to apease a froward Ladies will.
For othes and solemne vowes, are wasted then in vain,
And truth is compted but a toy, when such fond fancies reign.
The sentence sone is said, when will it self is Judge,
And quickly is the quarel pickt when ladies list to grudge.   10
This sing I for my selfe, (which wrote this weary song)
Who justly may complain my case, if ever man had wrong.[1]
A Lady have I serv'd, a Lady have I lov'd,
A Ladies good will once I had, hir ill will late I prov'd.
In country first I knew hir, in countrie first I caught hir,   15
And out of country now in court, to my cost have I sought hir.
In court where Princes reign, hir place is now assignd,
And well were worthy for the roome, if she were not unkind.
There I (in wonted wise) did shew my self of late,
And found y^t as the soile was chang'd, so love was turnd to hate.   20
But why? God knowes, not I: save as I said before,
Pitie is put from porters place, & daunger keepes the dore.
If courting then have skill, to chaunge good Ladies so,
God[2] send ech wilful dame in court, som wound of my like wo
That with a troubled head, she may both turne and tosse,   25
In restlesse bed when she should sleepe & feele of love ye losse.
And I (since porters put me from my wonted place)
And deepe deceit hath wrought a wyle to wrest me out of grace:
Wil[3] home agein to cart, as fitter wer for me,
Then thus in court to serve and starve, wher such proud porters be. 30
                    Si fortunatus infoelix.

[15]   *From this I will skip[1] to certaine verses written to a Gentlewoman whom he
        liked very well, and yit had never any oportunity to discover his affection,
        being always brydled by jelouse lookes, which attended them both, and ther-
        fore gessing by hir looks, that she partly also liked him: he wrot in a booke of
        hirs as foloweth.*

T Hou with thy lookes on whom I looke full ofte,
   And find therin great cause of deepe delight:
Thy face is faire, thy skin is smooth and softe,
Thy lippes are sweet, thine eyes are cleere and bright,
And every part seems pleasant in my sight.   5
Yit wote thou well, those lookes have wrought my wo,
Bicause I love to looke upon them so.

For first those lookes allur'd myne eye to looke,
And streight myne eie stird up my hart to love:
And cruell love with deepe deceitfull hooke,   10
Chokt up my mind whom fancie cannot move,
Nor hope releeve, nor other helpe behove:
But still to looke, and though I looke too much,
Needs must I looke, bicause I see none such.

Thus in thy lookes my love and life have hold,   15
And with such life my death drawes on apace:
And for such death no medcine can be told,
But looking still upon thy lovely face,
Wherein are painted pitie, peace, and grace.
Then though thy lookes should cause me for to dye,   20
Needes must I looke, bicause I live therby.

Since then thy lookes my lyfe have so in thrall,
As I can like none other lookes but thine:
Lo here I yeeld my life, my love, and all
Into thy hands, and all things else resigne,   25
But libertie to gaze upon thyne eyen.
Which when I doe, then think it were thy part,
To looke again, and linke with me in hart.
            Si fortunatus infoelix.

With these verses you shall judge the quick capacity of the Lady: for she wrot
therunder this short aunswer.

    Looke as long as you list, but surely if I take you
    looking, I will looke with you.

[16] *And for a further profe of this Dames quick understanding, you shall now*
understand, that soone after this answer of hirs, the same Author chaunced to
be at a supper in hir company, where were also hir brother, hir husband, and
an old lover of hirs by whom she had bin long suspected. Nowe, although
there wanted no delicate viands to content them, yit their chief repast was
by entreglancing of lookes. For G. G. being stoong with hot affection, could
none otherwise relieve his passion but by gazing. And the Dame of a curteous
enclination deigned (now and then) to requite the same with glancing at
him. Hir old lover occupied his eyes with watching: and hir brother perceyv-
ing all this could not absteyne from winking, wherby he might put his Sister

in remembrance, least she should too much forget hirself. But most of all hir husband beholding the first, and being evill pleased with the second, scarse contented with the third, and misconstruing the fourth, was constreyned to play the fifth part in froward frowninge. This royall banquet thus passed over, G. G.[1] knowing that after supper they should passe the tyme in propounding of Riddles, and making of purposes: contryved all this conceipt in a Riddle as followeth. The which was no sooner pronounced, but she could perfectly perceyve his intent, and drave out one nayle with another, as also enseweth.

His Riddle.

I Cast myne eye and saw ten eies at once,
　All seemely set upon one lovely face:
Two gaz'd, two glanc'd, two watched for the nonce,
Two winked wyles, two fround with froward grace.
Thus every eye was pitched in his place.　　　　　5
And every eye which wrought eche others wo,
Said to itself, alas why lookt I so?
And every eye for jelouse love did pine,
And sigh'd and said, I would that eye were mine.
Si fortunatus infoelix.

[17] *In all this lovely company was none that could and would expound the meaning herof. At last the Dame hirself answered on this wise. Sir, quod she, bicause your dark speech is much too curious for this simple companie, I wilbe so bold as to quit one question with an other. And when you have answered myne, it maye fall out per adventure, that I shall somewhat the better judge of yours.*

Hir Question.

What thing is that which swims in blisse,
And yit consumes in burning grief:
Which being plast where pleasure is,
Can yit recover no relief.
Which sees to sighe, and sighes to see,　　　　　5
All this is one, what may it bee?

[18] *He held himselfe herwith contented: and afterwardes when they were better acquainted, he chaunced once (groping in hir pocket) to find a letter of hir old lovers: and thinking it wer better to wincke than utterly to put out his eyes, seemed not too understand this first offence: but soone after finding a lemman (the which he thought he saw hir old lemman put there) he devised therof thus, and delivered it unto hir in writing.*

I Groped in thy pocket pretty peat,
　And found a Lemman which I looked not:
So found I once (which now I must repeat)
Both leaves and letters which I liked not.
Such hap have I to find and seeke it not,　　　　5
But since I see no faster meanes to bind, then
I will (henceforth) take lemmans as I find them.

[19]   *The Dame within very short space did aunswere it thus.*

A Lymone (but no Lemmane) Sir you found,
  For Lemmans beare their name to broad before:
The which since it hath given you such a wound,
That you seeme now offended very sore:
Content your self you shall find (there) no more.   5
But take your Lemmans henceforth where[1] you lust,
For I will shew my letters where I trust.

[20]   *This Sonet of his shall passe (for me) without any preface.*

WHen stedfast friendship (bound by holy othe)
  Did parte perforce my presence from thy sight.
In dreames I might behold how thou wert loth
With troubled thoughts to parte from thy delight.
When Popler walles enclos'd thy pensive mind,   5
My painted shadow did thy woes revive:
Thine evening walks by Thames in open wind,
Did long to see my sayling boate arive.
But when the dismold day did seeke to part
From London walles thy longing mind for me,   10
The sugred kisses (sent to thy deare hart)
With secret smart in broken sleepes I see.
Wherfore in teares I drenche a thousand fold,
Till these moist eyes thy beauty may behold.
                     Si fortunatus infoelix.

[21]   *He wrote (at his friends request) in prayse of a Gentlewoman,*
           whose name was Phillip, as followeth.

OF all the byrds that I do know,
  Phillip my sparow hath no peare:
For sit shee high or lye shee low,
Be shee far off, or be she neare,
There is no bird so fayre, so fyne,   5
Nor yit so fresh as this of myne.

Come in a morning merely
When Phillip hath ben lately fed,
Or in an evening soberly,
When Phillip[1] list to goe to bed: 10
It is a heaven to heare my phippe,
How she can chirpe with chery lippe.

She never wanders far abrode,
But is at hand when I doe call:
If I commaund she layes on lode,   15
With lips, with teeth, with tonge and all.
She chants, she chirpes, she maks such cheere,
That I beleeve she hath no peere.

And yit besides all this good sport,
My Phillip can both sing and daunce: 20
With newfound[2] toyes of sundry sort,
My Phillip can both prycke and prance:
As if you say but fend cut phippe,
Lord how the peat will turne and skippe.

Hir fethers are so fresh of hew,   25
And so well proyned every day:
She lacks none oyle, I warrant you:
To trimme hir tayle both tryck and gay.
And though hir mouth be somewhat wyde,
Hir tonge is sweet and short beside,   30

And for the rest I dare compare,
She is both tender, sweet and soft:
She never lacketh daynty fare,
But is well fed and feedeth oft:
For if my phip have lust to eate,   35
I warrant you Phip lacks no meat.

And then if that hir meat be good,
And such as like do love alway:
She will lay lips theron by-the-rood,[3]
And see that none be cast away: 40
For when she once hath felt a fitte,
Phillip will crie still, yit, yit, yit.

And to tell trueth he were to blame,[4]
Which had so fyne a Byrde as she,
To make him all this goodly game,   45
Without suspect or jellousie:
He were a churle and knew no good,
Would see hir faynt for lacke of food.

Wherfore I sing and ever shall,
To praise as I have often prov'd,   50
There is no byrd amongst them all,
So worthy for to be belov'd.
Let others prayse what byrd they will,
Sweete Phillip shalbe my byrd still.

                  Si fortunatus infoelix.

[22] *Now to begin with another man, take these verses written to*
be sent with a ryng, wherein were engraved a Patrich
in a Merlines foote.

THe Partridge in the pretie Merlines foote,
  Who feeles hir force supprest with fearefulnesse,
And findes that strength nor strife can do hir boote,
To scape the danger of hir deepe distresse:
These wofull wordes may seeme for to reherse   5
Which I must write in this waymenting verse.

What helpeth now (sayeth she) dame natures skill,
To die my fethers like the dustie ground?
Or what prevayles to lend me winges at will
Which in the ayre can make my bodie bound?   10
Since from the earth the dogges me drave perforce,
And now aloft the Hauke hath caught my corse.

If chaunge of coollors could not me convey,
Yet mought my wings have scapt the dogges despite:
And if my wings did fayle to flie awaye,   15
Yet mought my strength resist the Merlynes might.
But nature made the Merlyne mee to kyll,
And me to yeeld unto the Merlines will.

My lot is like (deere Dame) beleve me well,
The quiet life which I full closely kept: 20
Was not content in happie state to dwell,
But forth in hast to gaze on thee it lept.
Desire the dogge, did spring me up in hast,
Thou wert the Hauke, whose tallents caught me fast.

What should I then, seeke meanes to flie away?   25
Or strive by force, to breake out of thy feete?
No, no perdie, I may no strength assay,
To strive with thee ywis, it were not meete.
Thou art that Hauke, whom nature made to hent me,
And I the Byrd, that must therwith content me.   30

And since Dame nature hath ordayned so,
Hir happie heast I gladly shall embrace:
I yeeld my will, although it were to wo,
I stand content to take, my griefe for grace:
And seale it up within my secrete hart,   35
Which seale receive, as token of my smart.

                Spræta tamen vivunt.

[23]   *To a Dame which challenged the aucthor bycause he*
held his head alwayes downe, and looked
not uppon hir in his wonted wise.

Y Ou must not wonder, though you thinke it straunge,
To see me hold, my lowring head so lowe:
And that mine eyes, take no delight to raunge,
About the gleames, which on your face do growe.
The Mouse which once hath broken out of trappe,   5
Is seldome tysed with the trustlesse bayte:
But lieth aloofe, for feare of more mishappe,
And feedeth still in doubt of deepe disceipt.
The skorched flie, which once hath scapt the flame,
Will hardly come, to play againe with fire: 10
Wherby I learne, that grevous is the game,
Which followes fancie dazled by desire.
So that I wincke, or els hold downe my head,
Bycause your blazing eyes, my bale have bred.
                    Spræta tamen vivunt.

[24]   *A loving Lady being wounded in the spring time, and*
now galded eftsones with the remembrance of
the spring, doth therfore thus bewayle.

T His tenth of March when Aries receyv'd,
Dan¹ *Phoebus* rayes, into his horned head:
And I my selfe, by learned lore perceyv'd,
That *Ver* approcht, and frostie wynter fled.
I crost the *Thames,* to take the cherefull ayre,   5
In open feeldes, the weather was so fayre.

And as I rowed, fast by the further shore,
I heard a voyce, which seemed to lament:
Wherat I stay'd, and by a stately dore,
I left my Boate, and up on land I went.   10
Till at the last by lasting payne I found,
The wofull wight, which made this dolefull sound.

In pleasaunt garden (placed all alone)
I sawe a Dame, who sat in weary wise,
With scalding sighes, she uttred all hir mone,   15
The ruefull teares, downe rayned from hir eyes:
Hir lowring head, full lowe on hand she layed,
On knee hir arme: and thus this Lady sayed.

Alas (quod she) behold eche pleasaunt greene,
Will now renew, his sommers livery,   20
The fragrant flowers, which have not long bene seene,
Will florish now, (ere long) in bravery:
The tender buddes, whom colde hath long kept in,
Will spring and sproute, as they do now begin.

But I (alas) within whose mourning mynde,   25
The graffes of grief, are onely given to growe,
Cannot enjoy the spring which others finde,
But still my will, must wyther all in woe:
The cold of care, so nippes my joyes at roote,
No sunne doth shine, that well can do them boote.   30

The lustie *Ver,* which whillome might exchange
My griefe to joy, and then my joyes encrease,
Springs now elsewhere, and showes to me but strange,
My winters woe, therefore can never cease:
In other coasts, his sunne full clere doth shyne,   35
And comfort lends to ev'ry mould but myne.

What plant can spring, that feeles no force of *Ver?*
What flower can florish, where no sunne doth shyne?
These Bales (quod she)² within my breast I beare,
To breake my barke, and make my pyth to pyne: 40
Needs must I fall, I fade both roote and rynde,
My braunches bowe, at blast of ev'ry wynde.

This sayed: she cast a glance and spied my face,
By sight wherof, Lord how she chaunged hew?
So that for shame, I turned backe a pace   45
And to my home, my selfe in hast I drew:
And as I could hir woofull wordes reherse,
I set them downe in this waymenting verse.

Now Ladies you, that know by whom I sing,
And feele the wynter, of such frozen wylls: 50
Of curtesie, yet cause this noble spring,
To send his sunne, above the highest hilles:
And so to shyne, uppon hir fading sprayes,
Which now in woe, do wyther thus always.

Spreta tamen vivunt.

[25]   *The careful lover combred with pleasure,*
                    thus complayneth.

N Ow have I found the way, to weepe & wayle my fill,
     Now can I end my dolefull dayes, & so content my will.
The way to weepe inough, for such as list to wayle,
Is this: to go abord y⁰ ship, where pleasure beareth sayle.
And there to marke the jests, of every joyfull wight,   5
And with what wynde and wave they fleete, to nourish their delight.
For as the striken Deare, that seeth his fellowes feede
Amid the lustie heard (unhurt,) & feeles him selfe to bleede.

Or as the seely byrd, that with the Bolte is brusd,
And lieth a loofe among the leaves, of al hir peeres refusd,   10
And heares them sing full shrill, yet cannot she rejoyce,
Nor frame one warbling note to passe, out of hir mournfull voyce.
Even so I find by proofe, that pleasure dubleth payne,
Unto a wretched wounded hart, which doth in woe remaine.
I passe where pleasure is, I heare some sing for[1] joye,   15
I see som laugh, some other daunce, in spight of dark anoy.
But out alas my mind, amends not by their myrth,
I deeme al pleasures to be paine, that dwel above ye earth.
Such heavy humors feede, ye bloud that lends me breath,
As mery medcines cannot serve, to kepe my corps from death.   20

Spræta tamen vivunt.

[26] ¶*The lover being disdaynfully abjected by a dame of high calling, who had chosen (in his place) a playe fellowe of baser condicion: doth therfore determine to step a side, and before his departure giveth hir this farewell in verse.*

T Hy byrth, thy beautie, nor thy brave attyre,
(Disdainefull Dame, which doest me double wrong)
Thy high estate, which sets thy hart on fire,
Or new found choyce, which cannot serve thee long,
Shall make me dread, with pen for to reherse,   5
Thy skittish deedes, in this my parting verse.

For why thou knowest, and I my selfe can tell,
By many vowes, how thou to me wert bound:
And how for joye, thy hart did seeme to swell,
And in delight, how thy desires were drownd.   10
When of thy will, the walles I did assayle,
Wherin fond fancie, fought for mine avayle.

And though my mind, have small delight to vaunt,
Yet must I vowe, my hart to thee was true:
My hand was always able for to daunt,   15
Thy slaundrous fooes, and kepe their tongues in mew.
My head (though dull) was yet of such devise,
As might have kept thy name always in price.

And for the rest my body was not brave,
But able yet, of substaunce to allay,   20
The raging lust, where in thy limbes did rave,
And quench the coales, which kindled thee to play.
Such one I was, and such always wilbe,
For worthy Dames, but then I meane not thee.

For thou hast caught a proper paragon,[1]   25
A theefe, a coward, and a Peacocke foole:
An Asse, a mylksop, and a minion,
Which hath none oyle, thy furious flames to coole,
Such one he is, a pheare for thee most fit,
A wandring guest, to please thy wavering wit.   30

A theefe I compt him, for he robbes us both,
Thee of thy name, and me of my delight:
A cowerd is he noted where he goeth,
Since every child, is matcht to him in might.
And for his pride no more, but marke his plumes,   35
The which to princke, he dayes and nights consumes.

The rest thy selfe, in secret sort can judge,
He rydes not me, thou knowest his sadell best:
And[2] thogh these tricks of thine, mought make me grudge
And kyndle wrath, in my revenging brest: 40
Yet of my selfe, and not to please thy mind,
I stand content, my rage in rule to bind.

And farre from thee now must I take my flight,
Where tongues may tell, (and I not see) thy fall:
Where I may drincke these dragges of thy despight,   45
To purge my Melancholicke mind withall.
In secrete so, my stomacke will I sterve,
Wishing thee better than thou doest deserve.

                    Spræta tamen vivunt.

[27]   *An absent Dame thus complayneth.*

MUch like the seely Byrd, which close in Cage is pent,
So sing I now, not notes of joye, but layes of deepe lament.
And as the hooded Hauke, which heares the Partrich spring,
Who though she feele hir self fast tyed, yet beats hir bating wing:
So strive I now to showe, my feeble froward will,   5
Although I know my labour lost, to hop against the Hill.
The droppes of darke disdayne, did never drench my hart,
For well I know I am belov'd, if that might ease my smart.
Ne yet the privy coales, of glowing jellosie,
Could ever kindle needlesse feare, within my fantasie.   10
The rigor of repulse, doth not renew my playnt,
Nor choyce of change doth move my mone, nor force me thus to faynt.
Onely that pang of payne, which passeth all the rest,
And cankerlike doth fret the hart, within the giltlesse brest.
Which is if any bee, most like the panges of death,   15
That present griefe now grypeth me, & strives to stop my breath.

When friendes in mind may meete, and hart in hart embrace,
And absent yet are fayne to playne, for lacke of time and place:
Then may I compt, their love like seede, that soone is sowen,[1]
Yet lacking droppes of heavenly dew, with weedes is overgrowen.   20
The Greyhound is agreev'd, although he see his game,
If still in slippe he must be stayde, when he would chase the same.
So fares it now by me, who know my selfe belov'd
Of one the best, in eche respect, that ever yet was prov'd.
But since my lucklesse lot, forbids me now to taste,   25
The dulcet fruites of my delight, therfor in woes I wast.
And Swallow like I sing, as one enforced so,
Since others reape the gaineful crop, which I with pain did sowe.
Yet you that marke my song, excuse my Swallowes voyce,
And beare with hir unpleasant tunes, which cannot well rejoyce.   30
Had I or lucke in love, or lease of libertie,
Then should you heare some sweeter notes, so cleere my throte would be.
But take it thus in gree, and marke my playnsong well,
No hart feeles, so much hurt as that: which doth in absence dwell.
                    Spreta tamen vivunt.

[28] ¶*This question being propounded by a Dame unto the writer therof, to wit,
      why he should write* Spreta tamen vivunt, *he aunswereth thus.*

D Espysed things may live, although they pyne in payne:
    And things ofte trodden under foote, may once yit rise again.
The stone that lieth full lowe, may clime at last full hye:
And stand aloft on stately tow'rs, in sight of every eye.
The cruell axe which felles the tree that grew full streight: 5
Is worne with rust, when it renewes, and springeth up on height.
The rootes of rotten Reedes in swelling seas are seene:
And when ech tyde hath toste his worst, they grow agein ful greene.
Thus much to please my self, unpleasantly I sing:
And shrich to ease my mourning minde, in spyte of envies sting.   10
I am now set full light, who earst was dearely lov'd:
Som newfound choyce is more esteemd, than y[t] which wel was[1] prov'd.[2]
Some *Diomede* is crept into Dame *Cressydes* hart:
And trustie *Troylus* now is taught in vayne to playne his part.
What resteth then for me? but thus to wade in wo: 15
And hang in hope of better chaunce, when chaunge appointeth so.
I see no sight on earth, but it to Chaunge enclines:
As little clowds oft overcast, the brightest sunne that shines.
No Flower is so fresh, but frost can it deface:
No man so sure in any seate but he may leese his place.   20
So that I stand content (though much against my mind)
To take in worth this lothsome lot, which luck to me assynd,
And trust to see the time, when they that now are up:

May feele the whirle of fortunes wheele, and tast of sorrows cup.
God knoweth I wish it not, it has ben bet for mee: 25
Still to have kept my quiet chayre in hap of high degree.
But since without recure, Dame Chaunge in love must reign:
I now wish chaunge that sought no chaunge, but constant did remain.
And if such chaunge do chaunce, I vow to clap my hands,
And laugh at them which laught at me: lo thus my fancy stands.   30

                Spreta tamen vivunt.

[29]   *A straunge passion of another Author.*

A Mid my Bale I bath in blisse,
   I swim in heaven, I sink in hell:
I find amends for every misse,
And yit my moane no tonge can tell.
I live and love, what would you more?   5
As never loyer liv'd before.

I laugh sometimes with little lust,
So jest I oft and feele no joye:
Myne ease is builded all on trust,
And yit mistrust breedes myne anoye.   10
I live and lack, I lack and have:
I have and misse the thing I crave.

These things seeme straunge, yit ar they trew
Beleeve me (sweete) my state is such:
One pleasure which I would eschew,   15
Both slakes my grief, and breedes¹ my gruch.
So doth one pain which I would shoon
Renew my joyes where grief begoon.

Then like the Larke that past the night
In heavy sleepe with cares opprest: 20
Yit when shee spies the pleasaunt light,
She sends sweete notes from out hir brest.
So sing I now because I think
How joyes approch, when sorrowes shrink.

And as faire *Philomene* ageine   25
Can watch and singe when other sleepe:
And taketh pleasure in hir payne,
To wray the woo that makes hir weepe.
So sing I now for to bewray
The lothsome life I lead alway.   30

The which to thee (deare wench) I write,
That know'st my mirth, but not my moane:
I pray God graunt thee deepe delight,
To live in joyes when I am gone.
I cannot live, it will not bee:　　　　　　　　　　35
I dye to think to part from thee.
                 Ferenda Natura.

[30]　*The Lover leaning onely to his Ladies promises, and finding
them to fayle, doth thus lament.*

THe straightest tree that growes upon one only roote:
  If that roote fayle, will quickly fade, no props can do it boote.
I am that fading plant, which on thy grace did growe.
Thy grace is gone wherefore I mone, and wither all in woe.
The tallest ship that sayles, if shee to Ancors trust:　　　　　5
When ancors slip and cables breake, hir helpe lyes in the dust.
I am the ship my selfe, myne Ancor was thy faith:
Which now is fled, thy promise broke, and I am driven to death.
Who clymeth oft on hie, and trusts the rotten bowe:
If that bowe break may catch a fall such state stand I in now.　　10
Me thought I was aloft, and yit my seate full sure:
Thy hart did seeme to me a rock which ever might endure.
And see, it was but sand, whom seas of subtiltie:
Have soked so with wanton waves, that faith was forst to flye.
The Fluds of ficklenesse have undermyned so,　　　　　　　15
The first foundation of my joy, that myrth is ebb'd to wo.
Yit at lowe water markes, I lye and wayte my time:
To mend the breach, but all in vayn, it cannot passe the prime.
For when the primeflud comes which all this rage begon:
Then waves of will do work so fast, my piles are over ron.　　　20
Dutie and diligence which are my workmen there,
Are glad to take up tooles in haste and run away for feare.
For fancie hath such force, it overfloweth all:
And whispring tales do blow the blasts that make it ryse and fall.
Thus in theis tempests tost, my restles life doth stand:　　　25
Because I builded on thy words, as I was borne in hand.
Thou weart that onely stake, wherby I ment to stay:
Alas, alas, thou stoodst so weake, the hedge is borne away.
By thee I thought to live, by thee now must I dye:
I made thee my Phisicion, thou art my mallady.　　　　　　30
For thee I longd to live, for thee now welcome death:
And welcome be that happie pang, that stops my gasping breath.
Twice happie were that axe, would cut my rootes down right:
And sacred were that swelling sea, which would consume me quight.
Blest were that bowe would break to bring downe clyming youth,　35
Which craks aloft, and quakes full oft, for feare of thine untruth.
             Ferenda Natura.

[31]   *The constancie of a lover hath thus sometymes*
                     ben briefly declared.

T Hat selfe same tonge which first did thee entreat
    To linke thy liking with my lucky love:
That trustie tonge must now these words repeate,
I love the styll, my fancie cannot move.
That dreadlesse hart which durst attempt the thought   5
To win thy will with myne for to consent,
Maintaines that vow which love in me first wrought,
I love thee still and never shall repent.
That happy hand which hardely did touch
Thy tender body, to my deepe delight: 10
Shall serve with sword to prove my passion such
As loves thee still, much more than it can write.
Thus love I still with tonge, hand, hart and all,
And when I chaunge, let vengeance on me fall.
                              Ferenda Natura.

[32] *Now I must desire you with patience to hearken unto the works*
    of another writer, who though he may not compare with the rest
       passed, yit such things as he wrote upon sundrie occa-
             sions, I will rehearse, beginning with this
                     prayse of a Countesse.

D Esire of Fame would force my feeble skill,
    To prayse a Countesse by hir dew desert:
But dread of blame holds back my forward will,
And quencht the coales which kindled in my hart.
Thus am I plongd twene dread and deepe desire,   5
To paye the dew which dutie doth require.

And when I call the mighty Gods in ayd
To further forth some fine invention:
My bashefull spirits be full ill afrayd
To purchase payne by my presumption.   10
Such malice reignes (sometimes) in heavenly mynds,
To punish him that prayseth as he finds.

For *Pallas* first whose filed flowing skill,
Should guyde my pen some pleasant words to write:
With angry mood hath fram'd a froward will,   15
To dashe devise as oft as I endite.
For why? if once my Ladies gifts were knowen,
Pallas should loose the prayses of hir own.

And bloudy *Mars* by chaunge of his delight
Hath made *Joves* daughter now myne enemie: 20
In whose conceipt my Countesse shines so bright,
That *Venus* pynes for burning jelousie.
She may go home to *Vulcane* now agayne:
For *Mars* is sworne to be my Ladies swayne.

Of hir bright beames Dan *Phoebus* stands in dread,   25
And shames to shine within our *Horizon:*
Dame *Cynthia* holds in hir horned head,
For feare to loose by like comparison.
Lo thus shee lives, and laughes them all to skorne:
Countesse on earth, in heaven a Goddesse borne.   30

And I sometimes hir servaunt, now hir friend,
Whom heaven and earth for hir (thus) hate & blame:
Have yit presumed in friendly wise to spend,
This ragged verse in honor of hir name.
A simple gift, compared by the skill: 35
Yit what may seeme so deare as such good will.
Meritum petere, gravè.

[33]   *The Lover declareth his affection, togither*
          with the cause thereof.

WHen first I thee beheld in coulors black and whyt,
     Thy face in forme wel framed w^t favor blooming stil:
My burning brest in cares did choose his chief delight,
With pen to painte thy prayse, contrary to my skill.
Whose worthinesse compar'd with this my rude devise,   5
I blush and am abasht, this work to enterprise.

But when I call to mind thy sundry gifts of grace,
Full fraught with maners meeke in happy quiet mind:
My hasty hand forthwith doth scribble on apace,
Least willing hart might think, it ment to come behind.   10
Thus do both hand and hart these carefull meetres use,
Twixt hope and trembling feare, my deutie to excuse.

Wherfore accept these lines, and banish[1] dark disdayn,
Be sure they come from one that loveth thee in chief:
And guerdon me thy friend in like with love agayne,   15
So shalt thou well be sure to yeeld me such relief,
As onely may redresse my sorrowes and my smart:
For profe whereof I pledge (deare Dame) to thee my hart.
Meritum petere, gravè.

[34]   *Another shorter discourse to the same effecte.*

I f ever man yit found the Bath of perfect blisse,
  Then swim I now amid the Sea where nought but pleasure is.
I love and am beloved (without vaunt be it told)
Of one more fayre than shee of *Grece* for whom proud *Troy* was sold:
As bountifull and good as *Cleopatra* Queene: 5
As constant as *Penelope* unto hir make was seene.
What would you more? my pen unable is to write
The least desart that seemes to shine within this worthy wight.
So that for now I cease, with hands held up on hye,
And crave of God that when I chaunge, I may be forst to dye.   10
                    Meritum petere, gravè.

[35]   *The lover disdaynefully rejected contrary to former promise,*
                    thus complayneth.

THe deadly droppes of darke disdayne,
  Which dayly fall on my desarte.
The lingring suite long spent in vayne,
Wherof I feele no fruit but smart:
Enforce me now theis words to write: 5
Not all for love, but more for spyte.

The which to thee I must[1] rehearce,
Whom I did honor, serve and trust.
And though the musick of my verse
Be plainsong tune both true and just: 10
Content thee yit to heare my song,
For else thou doest me doobble wrong.

I must alledge, and thou canst tell
How faithfull I vowed to serve,
And how thou seemdst to like me well: 15
And how thou saydst I did deserve
To be thy Lord, thy Knight, thy King,
And how much more I list not sing.

And canst thou now (thou cruell one)
Condempne desert to deepe dispayre?   20
Is all thy promise past and gone?
Is faith so fled into the ayre?
If that be so, what rests for mee?
But thus in song to say to thee.

If *Cressides* name were not so knowen,   25
And written wyde on every wall:
If brute of pryd were not so blowen
Upon *Angelica* withall:
For hault disdain thou mightst be she,
Or *Cressyde* for inconstancie.   30

And in reward of thy desart,
I hope at last to see thee payed:
With deepe repentance for thy part,
Which thou hast now so lewdly playd.
Medoro he must be thy make,					35
Since thou *Orlando* doest forsake.

Such is the fruit that groweth always
Uppon the root of rype disdayn:
Such kindly wages *Cupide* payes,
Where constant harts cannot remayne.					40
I hope to see thee in such bands,
When I may laugh and clappe my hands.

But yet for thee I must protest,
That sure the fault is none of thine,
Thou are as true as is the best,					45
That ever came of *Cressedes* lyne:
For constant yet was never none,
But in unconstancie alone.
							Meritum petere, grave.

[36]			*An absent lover (parted from his Lady by Sea)*
					thus complayneth.

BOth deepe and dreadfull were the Seas,
		Which held *Leander* from his love,
Yet could no doubts his mind appease,
Nor save his life for hir behove:
But giltlesse bloud it selfe would spyll,					5
To please the waves and worke his will.

O greedie gulfe, O wretched waves,
O cruell floods, O sinke of shames,
You hold true lovers bound like slaves,
And keepe them from their worthy Dames:					10
Your open mouth gapes evermore,
Till one or both be drownd therfore.

For proofe wherof my selfe may sing,
And shrich to pearce the loftie skies,
Whose Lady left me languishing,					15
Uppon the shore in wooful wise:
And crost the Seas out of my sight,
Wherby I lost my chiefe delight.

She sayd that no such trustlesse flood,
Should keepe our loves (long time) in twayne: 20
She sware no bread should do hir good,
Tyll she might see my selfe againe.
She said and swore these words and mo,
But now I find them nothing so.

What resteth then for me to doo, 25
Thou salt sea foome come say thy mind?
Should I come drowne within thee too,
That am of true *Leanders* kind?
And headlong cast this corps of mine,
Into those greedy guttes of thine? 30

No cruel, but in spite of thee,
I will make Seas where earst were none,
My teares shall flowe in full degree,
Tyll all my myrth may ebbe to mone.
Into such droppes I meane to melt, 35
And in such Seas my selfe to swelt.

Lenvoie.
Yet you deere Dame for whom I fade,
Thus sterving still in wretched state:
Remember once your promise made,
Perfourme it now though all to late. 40
Come home to *Mars* who may you please,
Let *Vulcane* bide beyond the Seas.
Meritum petere, grave.

[37] *A Lady being both wronged[1] by false suspect, and also*
wounded by the durance of hir husband,
doth thus bewray hir grief.

G Ive me my Lute in bed now as I lye,
And lock the doores of mine unluckie bower:
So shall my voyce in mournefull verse descrie,
The secrete smart which causeth me to lower.
Resound you walles an Eccho to my mone, 5
And thou cold bed wherin I lye alone:
Beare witnesse yet what rest thy Lady takes,
When other sleepe which may enjoy their makes.

In prime of youth when *Cupid* kindled fire,
And warmd my wil with flames of fervent love: 10
To further forth the fruite of my desire,
My freends devisd this meane for my behove.
They made a match according to my mind,
And cast a snare my fansie for to bind:
Short tale to make the deed was almost[2] doon, 15
Before I knew which way the worke begoon.

And with this lot I did my selfe content,
I lent a lyking to my parents choyse:
With hand and hart I gave my free consent,
And hung in hope for ever to rejoyce.   20
I liv'd and lov'd long time in greater joy,
Then she which held kyng *Priams* sonne of *Troy:*
But three lewd lots have chang'd my heaven to hel
And those be these, give eare & mark them well.

First slaunder he, which always beareth hate,   25
To happy harts in heavenly state that byde:
Gan play his part to stirre up some debate,
Wherby suspect into my choyse might glyde.
And by his meanes the slime of false suspect,
Did (as I feare) my dearest friend infect.   30
Thus by these twayn long was I plungd in pain,
Yet in good hope my hart did still remaine.

But now (aye me) the greatest grief of all,
(Sound loud my Lute, and tell it out my tongue)
The hardest hap that ever might befall,   35
The onely cause wherfore this song is song,
Is this alas: my love, my Lord, my Roy,
My chosen pheare, my gemme, and all my joye,
Is kept perforce out of my dayly sight,
Wherby I lacke the stay of my delight.   40

In loftie walles, in strong and stately towers,
(With troubled mind in sollitary sorte,)[3]
My lonely[4] Lord doth spend his dayes and howers,
A weary life devoyde of all disport.
And I poore soule must lie here all alone,   45
To tyre my trueth, and wound my will with mone:
Such is my hap to shake my blooming time,
With wynters blastes before it passe the prime.

Now have you heard the summe of all my grief,
Wherof to tell my hart (oh) rends in twayne: 50
Good Ladies yet lend you me some relief,
And beare a parte to ease me of my payne.
My sortes are such, that waying well my trueth,
They might provoke the craggy rocks to rueth,
And move these walles with teares for to lament,   55
The lothsome life wherin my youth is spent.

But thou my Lute, be still now take thy rest,
Repose thy bones uppon this bed of downe:
Thou hast dischargd some burden from my brest,
Wherfore take thou my place, here lie thee downe.   60
And let me walke to tyre my restlesse minde,
Untill I may entreate some curteous wynd:
To blow these wordes unto my noble make,
That he may see I sorowe for his sake.

Meritum petere, grave.

[38]   *Eyther a needelesse or a bootelesse comparison
            betwene two letters.*

O F all the letters in the christs crosse rowe,
   I feare (my sweete) thou lovest *B.* the best,
And though there be good letters many mo,
As *A. O. G. N. C. S.* and the rest,
Yet such a liking bearest thou to *B.*   5
That fewe or none thou thinckest like it to be.

And much I muse what madnesse should thee move,
To set the Cart before the comely horse:
Must *A.* give place, to *B.* for his behove?
Are letters now so changed from their course?   10
Then must I learne (though much unto my paine,)
To read (a new) my christ crosse rowe againe.

When I first learnd, *A.* was in high degree,
A captaine letter, and a vowell too:
Such one as was alwayes a helpe to *B,*   15
And lent him sound and taught him what to doo.
For take away the vowels from their place,
And how can then the consonants have grace?

Yet if thou like a consonant so well,
Why should not *G.* seeme better farre than *B?*   20
G. spelleth God, that high in heaven doth dwell,
So spell we Gold and all good thinges with *G.*
B. serves to spell bald,[1] bawdy, braynsicke, bolde,
Blacke, browne, and bad, yea worse than may be tolde.

In song, the *G.* cliffe keepes the highest place,   25
Where *B.* sounds alwayes (or too sharpe or) flat:
In *G. sol, re, ut:* trebles have trimme grace,
B. serves the base and is content with that.
Beleve me (sweete) *G.* giveth sound full sweete,[2]
When *B.* cries buzze, as is for bases meete.   30

But now percase thou wilt one *G.* permit,
And with that *G.* thou meanest *B.* to joyne:
Alas, alas, me thinkes it were not fit,
(To cloke thy faulte) such fine excuse to coyne.
Take dooble *G.* for thy most loving letter,   35
And cast of *B.* for it deserves no better.

Thus have I played a little with thy *B.*
Wherof the brand is thine, and mine the blame:[3]
The wight which woundes thy wandring will is he,
And I the man that seeke to salve thy name: 40
The which to thinke, doth make me sigh sometime,
Though thus I strive to jest it out in ryme.
Meritum petere, grave.

[39]   *An absent lover doth thus encourage his Lady*
to continew constant.

C Ontent thy selfe with patience perforce,
And quench no love with droppes of darke mistrust:
Let absence have no power to divorce,
Thy faithful freend which meaneth to be just.
Beare but a while thy constance to declare,   5
For when I come one ynch shall breake no square.

I must confesse that promise did me bind,
For to have seene thy seemely selfe ere now:
And if thou knewst what greeves did galde my mynde,
Bycause I could not keepe that faithfull vowe: 10
My just excuse, I can my selfe assure,
With little payne thy pardon might procure.

But call to mind how long *Ulisses* was,
In lingring absence, from his loving make:
And how she deigned then hir dayes to passe,   15
In sollitary silence for his sake.
Be thou a true *Penelope* to me,
And thou shalt soone thine owne *Ulisses* see.

What sayd I? soone? yea soone I say againe,
I will come soone and sooner if I may: 20
Beleve me now it is a pinching payne,
To thinke of love when lovers are away.
Such thoughts I have, and when I thinke on thee,
My thoughts are there, whereas my bones would bee.

The longing lust which *Priames* sonne of *Troy,*   25
Had for to see his *Cressyde* come againe:
Could not exceede the depth of mine anoye,
Nor seeme to passe the patterne of my payne.
I fryse in hope, I thaw in hot desire,
Farre from the flame, and yet I burne like fire.   30

Wherfore deare friend, thinke on the pleasures past,
And let my teares, for both our paynes suffise:
The lingring joyes, when as they come at last,
Are bet then those, which passe in posting wise.
And I my selfe, to prove this tale is true,   35
In hast, post hast, thy comfort will renew.
                    Meritum petere, grave.

[40]   *A letter devised for a young lover.*

R Eceive you worthy Dame this rude & ragged verse,
   Lend willing eare unto ye tale, which I shal now reherse.
And[1] thogh my witles words, might move you for to smile
Yet trust to that which I shal tel, & never mark my stile.
Amongst five hundreth Dames, presented to my view,   5
I find most cause by due desert, to like the best of you.
I see your beautie such, as seemeth to suffise,
To bind my hart in lincks of love, by judgment of mine eyes.
And but your bountie quench, the coales of quicke desire,
I feare y^t face of youres wil set, ten thousand harts on fire.   10
But bountie so aboundes, above all my desert,
As y^t I quake & shrink for fear, to shew you of my smart.
Yet since mine eye made choyce, my hart shal not repent,
But yeeld it selfe unto your will, & therwith stand content.
God knowth I am not great, my power is not much,   15
The greater glory shal you gain, to shew your favor such.
And what I am or have, all that I yeeld to you,
My hand & sword shal serve alwaies, to prove my toung is true.
Then take me for your owne, & so I wilbe still,
Beleve me now, I make this vow, in hope of your good will.   20
Which if I may obtein, God leave me when I change,
This is the tale I ment to tell, good Lady be not strange.
                    Meritum petere, grave.

[41]   *Three Sonets in sequence, written uppon this occasion. The deviser hereof*
   amongst other friends had named a gentlewoman his Berzabe: and she was
   content to call him hir David. The man presented his Lady with a Booke of
   the Golden Asse, written by Lucius Apuleius, and in the beginning of the

Booke wrote this sequence. You must conferre it with the Historie of Apuleius,
for els it will have small grace.

T His *Apuleius* was in Affricke borne,
   And tooke delight to travayle *Thessaly,*
As one that held his native soyle in skorne,
In foraine coastes to feede his fantasie.
And such a gaine as wandring wits find out,   5
This yonker woon by will and weary toyle,
A youth mispent, a doting age in doubt,
A body brusd with many a beastly broyle,
A present pleasure passing on a pace,
And paynting playne the path of penitence,   10
A frollicke favour foyld with foule disgrace,
When hoarie heares should clayme their reverence.
Such is the fruite that growes on gadding trees,
Such kynd of mell most moveth busie Bees.
                    For Lucius he,   15
Esteeming more one ounce of present sporte,
Than elders do a pound of perfect witte:
Fyrst to the bowre of Beautie doth resort,
And there in pleasure passed many a fitte,
His worthy race he (recklesse) doth forget,   20
With small regard in great affayres he reeles,
No counsell grave nor good advice can set,
His braynes in brake that whirled still on wheeles.
For if *Birhena* could have held him backe,
From *Venus* Court where he now nousled was,   25
His lustie limbes had never found the lacke
Of manly shape: the figure of an Asse,
Had not beene blazed on his bloud and bones,
To wound his will with torments all attonce.
                    But Fotys she,   30
Who sawe this Lording whitled with the cuppe,
Of vaine delight wherof he gan to tast:
Pourde out apace and fild the Mazor up,
With dronken dole, yea after that in hast.
She greasd this gest with sauce of Sorcery,   35
And fed his mind with knacks both queynt and strange:
Lo here the treason and the trechery,
Of gadding gyrles when they delight to raunge.
For *Lucius* thinking to become a foule,
Became a foole, yea more then that, an Asse,   40
A bobbing blocke, a beating stocke, an owle,
Well wondred at in place where he did passe:
And spent his time his travayle and his cost,
To purchase paine and all his labour lost.

Yet I poore I,[1]   45
Who make of thee my *Fotys* and my freend,
In like delights my youthfull yeares to spend:
Do hope thou wilt from such sower sauce defend,
                    David thy King.
        Meritum petere grave.

[42]   *A Ryddle.*

A Lady once did aske of me,
  This pretie thing in privetie:
Good sir (quod she) fayne would I crave,
One thing which you your selfe not have:
Nor never had yet in times past,   5
Nor never shall while life doth last.
And if you seeke to find it out,
You loose your labour out of doubt:
Yet if you love me as you say,
Then give it me, for sure you may.   10
        Meritum petere, grave.

[43]   *To a gentlewoman who blamed him for writing his friendly*
        advise in verse unto another lover of hirs.

THe cruell hate which boyles within thy burning brest,
  And seekes to shape a sharpe revenge, on them that love thee best:
May warne all faythfull friendes, in case of jeoperdie,
How they shall put their harmelesse hands, betwene y[e] barck & tree.
And I among the rest, which wrote this weary song,   5
Must needes alledge in my defence, that thou hast done me wrong.
For if in simple verse, I chaunc'd to touch thy name,
And toucht the same without reproch, was I therfore to blame?
And if (of great good will) I gave my best advise,
Then thus to blame w[t]out cause why, me thinkes thou are not wise.   10
Amongst old written tales, this one I beare in mind,
A simple soule much like my selfe, did once a serpent find.
Which (almost dead for colde[1]) lay moyling in the myre
When he for pittie toke it up and brought it to the fyre.
No soner was the Snake, cured of hir grief,   15
But streight she sought to hurt the man, that lent hir such relief.
Such Serpent seemest thou, such simple soule am I,
That for the weight of my good will, am blam'd without cause why.
But as it best beseemes, the harmelesse gentle hart,
Rather to take an open wrong, than for to playne his part: 20
I must and will endure, thy spite without repent,
The blame is myne, the tryumph thine, and I am well content.
        Meritum petere, grave.

[44]   *An uncurteous farewell to an unconstant Dame.*

I F what you want, you (wanton) had at will,
  A stedfast mind, a faythfull loving hart:
If what you speake you would perfourme it still,
If from your word your deede could not revert.
If youthfull yeeres your thoughts did not so rule,   5
As elder dayes may skorne your friendship frayle:
Your doubled fansie would not thus recule,
For peevish pride which now I must bewayle.
For *Cressyde* fayre did *Troylus* never love,
More deare than I esteemd your framed cheare: 10
Whose wavering wayes (since now I do them prove)
By true report this witnesse with me beare:
That if your friendship be not too deare bought,
The price is great, that nothing gives for nought.
                  Meritum petere, grave.

[45]   *A lover often warned, and once againe droven into fantasticall flames by the cheare[1] of company, doth thus bewayle his misfortunes.*

I That my race of youthfull yeares had roon
  Alwayes untyed, and not (but once) in thrall,
Even I which had the fieldes of freedome woon,
And liv'd at large, and playde with pleasures ball:
Lo now at last am tane againe and taught,   5
To tast such sorowes, as I never sought.

I love, I love, alas I love in deede,
I crie alas, but no man pitties me:
My woundes are wyde, yet seeme they not to bleede,
And hidden woundes are hardly heald we see.   10
Such is my lucke to catch a sodeyne clappe,
Of great mischaunce in seeking my good happe.

My mourning mind which dwelt and dyed in dole,
Sought company for sollace of the same:
My cares were cold, and craved comforts coale,   15
To warme my will[2] with flakes of freendly flame.
I sought and found, I crav'd and did obteyne,
I woon my wish, and yet I got no gaine.

For whiles I sought the cheare of company,
Fayre fellowship did woonted woes revive: 20
And craving medcine for my malladie,
Dame pleasures plaster prov'd a corosive.
So that by myrth, I reapt no fruite but mone,
Much worse I feare than when I was alone.

The cause is this, my lot did light too late,   25
The Byrdes were flowen, before I found the nest:
The steede was stollen, before I shut the gate,
The cates consumd, before I smelt the feast.
And I fond foole with emptie hand must call,
The gorged Hauke, which likes no lure at all.   30

Thus still I toyle, to till the barreyne land,
And grope for grapes among the bramble briers:
I strive to sayle and yet I sticke on sand,
I deeme to live, yet drowne in deepe desires.
These lots of love, are fitte for wanton will,   35
Which findes too much, yet must be seeking still.

                            Meritum petere, grave.

[46]   *The lover encouraged by former examples, determineth to*
                    make vertue of necessitie.

W Hen I record within my musing mind,
      The noble names of wightes bewicht in love:
Such sollace for my selfe therin I find,
As nothing may my fixed fansie move:
But paciently I will endure my wo,   5
Because I see the heavens ordayne it so.

For whiles I read and ryfle their estates,
In ev'ry tale I note mine owne anoye:
But whiles I marke the meanings of their mates,
I seeme to swimme in such a sugred joye,   10
As did (percase) entise them to delight,
Though turnd at last, to drugges of sower despite.

Peruse (who list) *Dan Davids* perfect deedes,
There shal he find the blot of *Berzabe*,
Wheron to thinke, my heavie hart it bleedes,   15
When I compare my love like hir to be:
Urias wife, before myne eyes that shynes,
And[1] *David* I, from dutie that declines.

Then *Salomon* this princely Prophets sonne,
Did *Pharaos* daughter make him fall or no?   20
Yes, yes,[2] perdie, his wisedome[3] could not shoone[4]
Hir subtill snares, nor from hir counsell go.
I nam (as he) the wisest wight of all,
But well I wot, a woman holdes me thrall.

So am I like the proude *Assirian* Knight   25
Which blasphem'd God, and all the world defied:
Yet could a woman overcome his might,
And daunt his force in all his pompe and pride.
I *Holyferne,* am dronken brought to bead,
My love like *Judith,* cutting of my head.   30

If I were strong, as some have made accompt,
Whose force is like to that which *Sampson* had?
If I be bold, whose courage can surmount,
The hart of *Hercules,* which nothing dread?
Yet *Dalila,* and *Deyanyraes* love,   35
Did teach them both, such pangs as I must prove.

Well let these passe, and thinke on *Nasoes* name,
Whose skilfull verse did flowe in learned stile:
Did he (thinke you) not dote uppon his Dame?
*Corina*⁵ fayre, did she not him beguile?   40
Yes God he knowes, for verse nor pleasaunt rymes,
Can constant keepe, the key of *Cressides* crimes.

So that to end my tale as I began,
I see the good, the wise, the stoute, the bolde:
The strongest champion and the learnedst man,   45
Have bene and be, by lust of love controld.
Which when I thinke, I hold me well content,
To live in love, and never to repent.

Meritum petere, grave.

[47]   *The absent lover*¹ *(in ciphers) disciphering his name, doth
crave some spedie relief as followeth.*

L 'Escü d'amour,* the shield of perfect love,
    The shield of love, the force of stedfast faith,
The force of fayth which never will remove,
But standeth fast, to byde the broonts of death:
That trustie targe, hath long borne of the blowes,   5
And broke the thrusts, which absence at me throwes.

In dolefull dayes I lead an absent life,
And wound my will with many a weary thought:
I plead for peace, yet sterve in stormes of strife,
I find debate, where quiet rest was sought.   10
These panges with mo, unto my paine I prove,
Yet beare I all uppon my shield of love.

In colder cares are my conceipts consumd,
Than *Dido* felt when false *Enæas* fled:
In farre more heat, than trusty *Troylus* fumd,   15
When craftie *Cressyde* dwelt with *Diomed.*
My hope such frost, my hot desire such flame,
That I both fryse, and smoulder in the same.

So that I live, and dye in one degree,
Healed by hope, and hurt againe with dread: 20
Fast bound by fayth when fansie would be free,
Untyed by trust, though thoughts enthrall my head:
Reviv'd by joyes, when hope doth most abound,
And yet with grief, in depth of dollors drownd.

In these assaultes I feele my feebled force   25
Begins to faint, thus weried still in woes:
And scarcely can my thus consumed corse,
Hold up this Buckler to beare of these blowes.
So that I crave, or presence for relief,
Or some supplie, to ease mine absent grief.   30

Lenvoie.

To you (deare Dame) this dolefull plaint I make,
Whose onely sight may sone redresse my smart:
Then shew your selfe, and for your servauntes sake,
Make hast post hast, to helpe a faythfull harte.   35
Mine owne poore shield hath me defended long,
Now lend me yours, for elles you do me wrong.

Meritum petere, grave.

[48] *I will now deliver unto you so many more of Master Gascoignes Poems as
have come to my hands, who hath never beene dayntie of his[1] doings, and ther-
fore I conceale not his name: but his word or posie he hath often changed
and therfore I will deliver his verses with such sundrie posies as I received
them. And first I will begin with Gascoigns Anatomie.*

TO make a lover knowne, by playne Anatomie,
    You lovers all that list beware, lo here behold you me.
    Who though mine onely lookes, your pittie wel might move,
Yet every part shall play his part to paint the pangs of love.
If first my feeble head, have so much matter left,   5
If fansies raging force have not his feeble skill bereft.
These locks that hang unkempt, these hollowe dazled eyes,
These chattring teeth, this trembling tongue, wel tewed with
        carefull cries.
These wan & wrinckled cheeks, wel washt w^t waves of wo,
May stand for patterne of a ghost, where so this carkasse go.   10

These shoulders they susteyne, the yoke of heavie care,
And on my brused broken backe, the burden must I beare.
These armes are braunfalne now, with beating on my brest,
This right hand weary is to write, this left hand craveth rest:
These sides enclose the forge, where sorow playes the smith,   15
And hot desire, hath kindled fire, to worke his mettall with.
The anvile is my hearte, my thoughtes they strike the stroke,
My lights & lungs like bellows blowe, & sighs ascend for smoke.
My secrete parts are so with secrete sorowe soken,
As for the secrete shame therof, deserves not to be spoken.   20
My thighes, my knees, my legs, and last of all my feete,
To serve a lovers turne, are so unable and unmeete,
That scarce they can beare up this restlesse body well,
Unlesse it be to see the boure, wherin my love doth dwell,
And there by sight eftsoones to feede my gazing eye,   25
And so content my hungrie corps tyll dolours doe me die:
Yet for a just rewarde of love so dearely bought,
I pray you say, lo this was he, whom love had worne to nought.

Ever or never.

[49]   *Gascoignes araignement.*

A T Beauties barre as I did stande,
      When false suspecte accused mee,
George (quod the Judge) holde up thy hande,
Thou art araygnde of Flatterie:
Tell therfore howe thou wylte be tryde?   5
Whose judgement here wilte thou abyde?

My lorde (quod I) this lady here,
Whome I esteeme above the rest,
Dothe knowe my guilte if any were:
Wherefore hir doome shall please mee beste,   10
Let hir be Judge and Jurour bothe,
To trie mee giltlesse by myne othe.

Quod Beautie, no, it sitteth not,
A Prince hir selfe to judge the cause:
Here is oure Justice well you wote,   15
Appointed to discusse our lawes:
If you will guiltlesse seeme to goe,
God and your countrey quitte you so.

Then crafte the cryer call'd a queste,
Of whome was falshode formoste feere,   20
A packe of pickethankes were the rest,

Whiche came false witnesse for to beare,
The Jurie suche, the Judge unjust,
Sentence was sayde I shoulde be trust.

Jealous the Jayler bounde me fast,   25
To heare the verdite of the bill,
George (quod the Judge) now thou art cast,
Thou muste goe hence to heavie hill,
And there be hangde all but the head,
God reste thy soule when thou art dead.   30

Downe fell I then upon my knee,
All flatte before dame beauties face,
And cryed, good Ladie pardon me,
Whiche here appeale unto your grace,
You knowe if I have ben untrue,   35
It was in too muche praysing you.

And though this Judge does make suche haste,
To shead with shame my giltlesse bloud:
Yet lette your pitie firste be plaste,
To save the man that ment you good,   40
So shall you shewe your selfe a Queene,
And I may be your servant seene.

(Quod beautie) well: bicause I guesse
What thou doest meane henceforth to bee,
Although thy faultes deserve no lesse   45
Than Justice here hath judged thee,
Wylte thou be bounde to stint all stryfe,
And be true prisoner all thy lyfe?

Yea madame (quod I) that I shall,
Lo faith and truthe my suerties: 50
Why then (quod she) come when I call,
I aske no better warrantise.
Thus am I Beauties bounden thrall,
At hir commaunde when she doth call.
                                        Ever or Never.[1]

[50]   *Gascoignes prayse of* Bridges, *nowe Ladie* Sandes

IN Court who so demaundes what dame doth most excell,
    For my conceit I must needs say, faire *Bridges* beares ye bel:
Upon whose lively cheeke, to prove my judgement true,
The Rose and Lillie seeme to strive for equall change of hew:
And therwithall so well hir graces all agree,   5
No frouning cheere dare once presume in hir sweet face to bee.

Although some lavishe lippes, which like some other best,
Will say the blemishe on hir browe disgraceth all the rest:
Thereto I thus replie, God wotte they little knowe
The hidden cause of that mishap, nor how the harm did grow.   10
For when dame nature first had framde hir heavenly face,
And thoroughly bedecked it with goodly gleames of grace.
It lyked hir so well: Lo here (quod she) a peece,
For perfect shape that passeth all *Apelles* worke in *Greece*.
This bayt may chaunce to catche the greatest god of love,   15
Or mightie thundring *Jove* himself that rules the rost above:
But out, alas, those wordes were vaunted all in vayne,
And some unseen wer present there (pore *Bridges*) to thy pain,
For *Cupide* craftie boy, close in a corner stoode,
Not blyndfold then, to gaze on hir, I gesse it did him good.   20
Yet when he felte the flame gan kindle in his brest,
And herd dame nature boast by hir, to break him of his rest,
His hot newe chosen love he chaunged into hate,
And sodeynly with myghtie mace, gan rap hir on the pate.
It greeved Nature muche to see the cruell deede: 25
Me seemes I see hir how she wept to see hir dearling bleede.
Wel yet (quod she) this hurt shal have some helpe I trowe,
And quick with skin she coverd it, y^t whiter is than snow.
Wherwith *Dan Cupide* fled, for feare of further flame,
When angell like he saw hir shine, whome he had smit with shame.   30
Lo thus was *Bridges* hurt, in cradel of hir kynd,
The coward *Cupide* brake hir brow to wreke his wounded mynd,
The skar still there remains, no force, there let it be,
There is no cloude that can eclipse so bright a sunne as she.

Ever or Never.

[51]   *Gascoignes prayse of* Zouche *late the Lady*[1] *Greye of Wilton.*

T Hese rustie walles whome cankred yeares deface,
    The comely corps of seemely *Zouche* enclose,
Whose auncient stocke derivde from worthie race,
Procures hir prayse, where so the carkas goes:
Hir angels face declares hir modest mynde,   5
Hir lovely lookes the gazing eyes allure,
Hir deedes deserve some endlesse prayse to fynde,
To blaze suche brute as ever might endure.
Wherfore my penne in trembling feare shall staye,
To write the thing that doth surmounte my skill,   10
And I will wishe of God both night and day,
Some worthier place to guyde hir worthie will.
Where princes peeres hir due desertes maye see,
And I content hir servant there to bee.

Ever or Never.

Gascoignes passion.

I Smile sometimes although my griefe be great,
  To heare and see these lovers paint their paine,
And how they can in pleasaunt rimes repeate,
The passing pangs, which they in fancies faine.
But if I had such skill to frame a verse   5
I could more paine than all their pangs rehearse.

Some say they find nor peace, nor power to fight,
Which seemeth strange: but stranger is my state:
I dwell in dole, yet sojorne with delight,
Reposed in rest, yet weried with debate.   10
For flatte repulse, might well apease my will
But fancie fights, to trie my fortune still.

Some other say they hope, yet live in dread,
They friese, they flame, they flie alofte, they fall,
But I nor hope with happe to raise my hed,   15
Nor feare to stoupe, for why my gate is small.
Nor can I friese, with colde to kill my harte,
Nor yet so flame, as might consume my smarte.

How live I then, which thus drawe foorth my daies?
Or tell me how, I found this fever first?   20
What fits I feele? what distance? what delayes?
What griefe? what ease? what like I best? what worse?
These things they tell, which seeke redresse of paine,
And so will I, although I coumpt it vaine.

I live in love, even so I love to live,   25
(Oh happie state, twice happie he that finds it)
But love to life this cognisance doth give,
This badge this marke, to every man that minds it,
Love lendeth life, which (dying) cannot die,
Nor living live: and such a life lead I.   30

The sunny dayes which gladde the saddest wights,
Yet never shine to cleare my misty Moone,
No quiet sleepe, amidde the mooneshine nights
Can close mine eies, when I am wo by gone.
Into such shades my peevish sorow shrowdes,   35
That Sunne and Moone, are still to me in clowdes.

And feverlike I feede my fancie still,
With such repast, as most empaires my helth,
Which fever first I caught by wanton will,
When coles of kind did stirre my bloud by stelth: 40
And gazing eies, in bewtie put such trust
That love enflamd my liver all with lust.

My fits are like the fever Ectyck fits,
Which one day quakes within and burnes without,
The next day heate within the boosoms sits,   45
And shivring cold the body goes about.
So is my harte most hote when hope is cold,
And quaketh most when I most heate behold.

Tormented thus without delaies I stand,
Alwaies in one and evermore shal be,   50
In greatest griefe when helpe is nearest hand,
And best at ease if death might make me free:
Delighting most in that which hurts my hart,
And hating change which might relieve[1] my smart.

Lenvoie. Yet you dere dame: to whome this cure perteines,   55
Devise betimes some drammes for my disease,
A noble name shall be your greatest gaines,
Whereof be sure, if you will worke mine ease.
And though fond fooles set forth their fitts as fast,
Yet grant with me that *Gascoignes* passion past.   60

Ever or Never.

[53]   *Gascoignes libell of Divorce.*

D Ivorce me now good death, from love and lingring life,
That one hath ben my concubine, that other was my wife.
In youth I lived with love, she had my lusty dayes,
In age I thought with lingering life to stay my wandering ways,
But now abusde by both, I come for to complaine   5
To thee good death, in whome my helpe doth wholly now remain,
My libell loe[1] behold: wherein I do protest,
The processe of my plaint is true, wherein my griefe doth rest.
First love my concubine, whome I have kept so trimme,
Even she for whome I seemd of yore, in seas of joy to swim: 10
To whome I dare avow, that I have served as well,
And played my part as gallantly, as he that beares the bell:
She cast me off long since, and holds me in disdaine,
I cannot pranke to please hir now, my vaunting is but vaine.
My writhled cheekes bewray, that pride of heate is past,   15
My stagring stepps eke tell the truth, that nature fadeth fast.[2]
My quaking crooked joynts, are combred with the crampe,
The boxe of oile is wasted well, which once did feede my lampe.
The greenesse of my yeares, doth wither now so sore,
That lusty love leapes quite away, and liketh me no more.   20
And love my lemman gone, what liking can I take?
In lothsome life that crooked croane, although she be my make?
She cloyes me with the cough, hir comforte is but colde

She bids me give mine age for almes, where first my youth was solde.
No day can passe my head, but she beginnes to brall,   25
No mery thoughts conceived so fast, but she confounds them all.
When I pretend to please, she overthwarts me still,
When I wold faynest part with hir, she overwayes my will.
Be judge then gentle death, and take my cause in hand,
Consider every circumstance, marke how the case doth stande.   30
Percase thou wilte alledge, that cause thou canst none see,
But that I like not of that one, that other likes not me:
Yes gentle judge give eare, and thou shalt see me prove,
My concubine incontinent, a common whore is love.
And in my wife I find, such discord and debate,   35
As no man living can endure the torments of my state.
Wherefore thy sentence say, divorce me from them both,
Since only thou maist right my wrongs, good death now be not loth
But cast thy pearcing dart, into my panting brest,
That I may leave both love & life, & thereby parchase rest.   40
                    Haud ictus sapio.

[54]   *Gascoignes praise of his Mystres.*

THe hap which *Paris* had, as due for his desert,
    Who favorde *Venus* for hir face, & skornde *Menervas* arte:
May serve to warne the wise, y^t they no more esteeme
The glistering glosse of bewties blaze, than reason should it deeme.
Dan[1] *Priams* yonger son, found out ye fairest dame,   5
That ever troade on *Troyane* mold, what followed of the same?
I list not brute hir bale, let others spred it foorth,
But for his part to spek my mind his choice was litle worth.[2]
My meaning is but this, who marks the outward shewe
And never gropes for grafts of grace which in ye mind shuld grow: 10
May chance upon such choise as trusty *Troylus* had
And dwel in dole as *Paris* did, when he wold fayne be glad.
How happie then am I? whose happe hath bin to finde
A mistresse first that doth excell in vertues of the minde,
And yet therewith hath joind, such favoure and such grace,   15
As *Pandars* niece if she wer here wold quickly give hir place,
Within whose worthy brest, dame Bounty seekes to dwel,
And saith to beawty, yeeld to me, since I do thee excell.
Betwene whose hevenly eies, doth right remorce appeare,
And pittie placed by the same, doth much amend hir cheere.   20
Who in my dangers deepe, did deigne to do me good,
Who did releeve my hevie heart, and sought to save my bloud,
Who first encreast my friends, and overthrew my foes,
Who loved all them that wisht me well, and liked none but those.
O Ladies give me leave, I praise hir not so farre,   25

Since she doth passe you all, as much, as *Tytan* staines a starre.
You hold such servants deare, as able are to serve,
She held me deare, when I poore soule, could no good thing deserve.
You set by them that swim in all prosperitie,
She set by me when as I was in great calamitie.   30
You best esteeme the brave, and let the poorest[3] passe,
She best esteemd my poore good will, all naked as it was.
But whether am I went? what humor guides my braine?
I seeke to wey the woolsacke down, with one poore pepper graine.
I seeme to penne hir praise, that doth surpasse my skill,   35
I strive to row against the tide, I hoppe against the hill.
Then let these fewe suffise, she *Helene* staines for hew,
Dydo for grace, *Cressyde* for cheere, and is as *Thisbye* true.
Yet if you furder crave, to have hir name displaide,
Dame *Favor* is my mistres name, dame *Fortune* is hir maid.   40

Attamen ad solitum.

[55]   *Gascoignes Lullabie.*

S Ing lullabie, as women do,
  Wherewith they bring their babes to rest,
And lullabie can I sing to
As womanly as can the best.
With lullabie they still the childe,   5
And if I be not much beguilde,
Full many wanton babes have I
Which must be stilld with lullabie.

First lullaby my youthfull yeares,
It is now time to go to bed,   10
For crooked age and hoarie heares,
Have wonne the haven within my head:
With Lullabye then youth be still,
With Lullabye content thy will,
Since courage quayles, and commes behynde,   15
Goe sleepe, and so beguyle thy mynde.

Next Lullabye my gazing eyes,
Whiche woonted were to glaunce apace:
For every glasse maye nowe suffise,
To shewe the furrowes in my face: 20
With Lullabye then wynke a whyle,
With[1] Lullabye youre lookes beguyle:
Lette no fayre face, nor beautie bryghte
Entice you efte with vayne delyght.

And Lullabye my wanton will,   25
Lette reasons rule nowe reigne thy thought,
Since all too late I fynde by skill,
Howe deare I have thy fansies bought:
With Lullabye nowe take thyne ease,
With Lullabye thy doubtes appease: 30
For trust to this, if thou be still,
My bodie shall obeye thy will.

Eke Lullabye my loving boye,[2]
My little Robyn take thy rest,
Synce Age is colde, and nothyng coye,   35
Keepe close thy coyne, for so is beste:
With Lullabye bee thou content,
With Lullabye thy lustes relente,
Lette others paye whiche have mo pence,
Thou arte to poore for suche expense.   40

Thus Lullabie my youth, myne eyes,
My will, my ware, and all that was,
I can no mo delayes devise,
But welcome payne, lette pleasure passe:
With Lullabye nowe take your leave,   45
With Lullabye youre dreames deceyve,
And when you rise with waking eye,
Remembre *Gascoignes* Lullabye.
                    Ever or Never[3]

[56]   *Gascoignes Recantation.*

NOwe must I needes recant the wordes whiche once I spoke,
Fonde fansie fumes so nye my nose, I needes must smell the smoke:
And better were to beare a faggot from the fire,
Than wilfully to burne and blaze in flames of vayne desire.
You Judges then give eare, you people marke me well   5
I say, bothe heaven and earth record the tale which L shall tell,
And knowe that dreade of death, nor hope of better hap,
Have forced or persuaded me to take my turning cap,
But even that mightie Jove of his great clemencie,
Hath given me grace at last to judge the truth from heresie: 10
I say then and professe, with free and faithfull harte,
That womens vowes are nothing else but snares of secret smart:
Their beauties blaze are baytes which seeme of pleasant taste,
But who devoures the hidden hooke, eates poyson for repast:
Their smyling is deceipt, their faire wordes traynes of treason, 15
Their witte alwayes so full of wyles, it skorneth rules of reason.
Percase some present here, have hearde my selfe of yore,

Both teach and preach the contrary, my fault was then the more:
I graunt my workes were these, first one *Anatomie,*
Wherein I paynted every pang of loves perplexitie: 20
Nexte that I was araignde, with *George* holde up thy hande,
Wherein I yeelded Beauties thrall, at hir commaunde to stande:
Myne eyes so blynded were, (good people marke my tale)
That once I soong, I *Bathe in Blisse,* amidde my wearie *Bale:*
And many a frantike verse, then from my penne did passe,   25
In waves of wicked heresie so deepe I drowned was,
All whiche I nowe recante, and here before you burne
Those trifling bookes, from whose leud lore my tippet here I turne,
And hencefoorth will I write, howe madde is that mans mynde,
Which is entyst by any trayne to trust in womankynde.   30
I spare not wedlocke I, who list that state advaunce,
Aske *Astolfe* king of *Lumbardie,* how trim his dwarf could daunce.
Wherefore faire Ladies you, that heare me what I saye,
If you hereafter see me slippe, or seeme to goe astraye:
Or if my toung revolte from that which nowe it sayth,   35
Then plague me thus, *Beleeve it not,* for this is nowe my fayth.

Haud ictus sapio.

[57]   *I have herde master Gascoignes memorie commended by these verses follow-
ing, the which were written uppon this occasion. He had (in middest of his
youth) determined to abandone all vaine delights and to retourne unto
Greyes Inne, there to undertake againe the study of the common lawes. And
being required by five sundrie gentlemen to wrighte in verse somwhat worthy
to be remembred, before he entred into their felowship, he compiled these
five sundry sortes of metre uppon five sundry theames whiche they delivered
unto him, and the firste was at request of Francis Kinwelmarshe who de-
livered him this theame.* Audaces fortuna juvat. *And thereupon he wrote
thys Sonnet following.*

IF yelding feare, or cancred villanie,
    In *Caesars* haughtie heart had tane the charge,
The walles of *Rome* had not bene rearde so hye,
Nor yet the mightie empire lefte so large.
If *Menelaus* could have rulde his will   5
With fowle reproch to loose his faire delight,
Then had the stately towres of *Troy* stood still,
And *Greekes* with grudge had dronke their owne despight.
If dread of drenching waves or feare of fire,
Had stayde the wandring Prince amidde his race,   10
Ascanius then, the frute of his desire
In *Lavine* lande had not possessed place,
But true it is, where lottes doe light by chaunce,
There Fortune helpes the boldest to advaunce.

Sic tuli.

[58] *The nexte was at request of* Antonie Kynwelmarshe, *who delivered him*
       this theame Satis sufficit, *and thereupon he wrote as followeth.*

THe vaine excesse of flattering Fortunes giftes,
     Envenometh the mind with vanitie,
And beates the restlesse braine with endlesse driftes
To stay the staffe of worldly dignitie:
The begger stands in like extremitie.   5
Wherefore to lacke the most, and leave the least,
I coumpt enough as good as any feast.

By too too much *Dan Croesus* caught his death,
And bought with bloud the price of glittering gold,
By too too litle many one lacks breath   10
And sterves[1] in streetes a mirroure to behold:
So pride for heate, and povert pynes for colde.
Wherefore to lack the moste, and leave the least,
I coumpt enough as good as any feaste.

Store makes no sore, lo this seemes contrarye,   15
And mo the meryer is a Proverbe eke,
But store of sores maye make a maladie,
And one to many maketh some to seeke,
When two be mette that bankette with a leeke:
Wherefore to lacke the moste, and leave the least,   20
I coumpte enough as good as any feast.

The ryche man surfetteth by gluttonie,
Whyche feedeth still, and never standes content,
The poore agayne he pines for penurie,
Whiche lives with lacke, when all and more is spente: 25
So too muche and too little bothe bee shente.
Wherefore to lacke the moste, and leave the least,
I coumpte enough as good as any feast.

The Conquerour with uncontented swaye,
Dothe rayse up rebells by his avarice,   30
The recreaunt dothe yeelde hymselfe a praye,
To forrayne spoyle[2] by slouth and cowardyse:
So too muche and too little, both be vyce.
Wherefore to lacke the moste, and leave the least,
I coumpte enough as good as any feast.   35

If so thy wyfe be too too fayre of face,
It drawes one guest (too manie) to thyne inne:
If she be fowle, and foyled with disgrace,
In other pillowes prickst thou many a pinne:

So fowle prove fooles, and fayrer fall to sinne.   40
Wherefore to lacke the moste, and leave the least,
I coumpte enough as good as any feast.

And of enough, enough, and nowe no more,
Bycause my braynes no better can devise,
When things be badde, a small summe maketh store,   45
So of suche verse a fewe maye soone suffise:
Yet still to this my wearie penne replyes,
That I sayde last, and though you lyke it least,
It is enough, and as good as a feast.
                                    Sic tuli.

[59]   John Vaughan *delivered him this theame.* Magnum vectigal parcimonia,
                    whereuppon he wrote thus.

THe common speech is, spend and God will send,
    But what sends he? a bottell and a bagge,
A staffe, a wallet and a wofull ende,
For such as list in bravery so to bragge.
Then if thou covet coine enough to spend,   5
Learne first to spare thy budget at the brinke,
So shall the bottome be the faster bound:
But he that list with lavish hand to linke,
(In like expence) a pennie with a pound,
May chance at last to sitte aside and shrinke   10
His harbraind head without dame deinties dore.
Hick, Hobbe and Dick with cloutes uppon their knee,
Have many times more goonhole groates in store,
And change of crownes more quicke at call than he,
Which let their lease and tooke their rent before.   15
For he that rappes a royall on 'his cappe,
Before he put one pennie in his pursse,
Had neede turne quicke and broch a better tappe,
Or else his drinke may chance go downe the wursse.
I not denie but some men have good hap,   20
To climbe alofte by scales of courtly grace,
And winne the world with liberalitie:
Yet he that yerks old angells out apace,
And hath no new to purchase dignitie,
When orders fall, may chance to lacke his grace.   25
For haggard hawkes mislike an emptie hand:
So stiffely some sticke to the mercers stall,
Till sutes of silke have swet out all their land.
So ofte thy neighbours banquet in thy hall,
Till Davie *Debet* in thy parlor stande,   30

And bids thee welcome to thine owne decay.
I lyke a Lyons lookes not woorth a leeke
When every Foxe beguyles him of his praye:
What sauce but sorowe serveth him a weeke,
Whiche all his cates consumeth in one daye?   35
Fyrste use thy stomacke to a stonde of ale,
Before thy Malmesey come in Marchantes bookes,
And rather weare (for shifte) thy shirte of male,
Than teare thy silken sleeves with teynter hookes.
Put feathers in thy pillowes greate and small,   40
Lette them bee princkt with plumes that gape for plummes,
Heape up bothe golde and silver safe in hooches,
Catche, snatche, and scratche for scrapings and for crummes,
Before thou decke thy hatte (on highe) with brooches.
Lette first thyne one hande holde fast all that commes,   45
Before that other learne his letting flie:
Remember still that softe fyre makes sweete malte,
No haste but good (who meanes to multiplie:)
Bought wytte is deare, and drest with sowre salte,
Repentaunce commes to late, and then saye I,   50
Who spares the first and keepes the laste unspent,
Shall fynde that Sparing yeldes a goodly rent.

Sic tuli.

[60]   Alexander Nevile *delivered him this theame,* Sat cito, si sat bene, *where-
upon he compiled these seven Sonets in sequence, therin bewraying his owne*
Nimis cito: *and therwith his* Vix bene, *as foloweth.*

I N haste poste haste, when fyrste my wandring mynde,
  Behelde the glistering Courte with gazing eye,
Suche deepe delyghtes I seemde therein to fynde,
As myght beguyle a graver guest than I.
The stately pompe of Princes and their peeres,   5
Did seeme to swimme in floudddes of beaten golde,
The wanton worlde of yong delightfull yeeres,
Was not unlyke a heaven for to beholde,
Wherein did swarme (for every saint) a Dame,
So faire of hue, so freshe of their attire,   10
As might excell dame *Cinthia* for Fame,
Or conquer *Cupide* with his owne desire.
These and suche lyke were baytes that blazed still
Before myne eye to feede my greedie will.

2   Before myne eye to feede my greedie will,   15
Gan muster eke myne olde acquainted mates,
Who helpte the dishe (of vayne delighte) to fill

My emptie mouthe with dayntie delicates:
And foolishe boldenesse tooke the whippe in hande,
To lashe my lyfe into this trustlesse trace,   20
Till all in haste I leapte aloofe from lande,
And hoyste up sayle[1] to catche a Courtly grace:
Eche lingring daye did seeme a worlde of woe,
Tyll in that haplesse haven my head was broughte:
Waves of wanhope so tost mee too and[2] fro,   25
In deepe despaire to drowne my dreadfull thoughte:
Eche houre a daye, eche daye a yeare did seeme,
And every yeare a worlde my wyll did deeme.

    3 And every yeare a worlde my will dyd deeme,
Till lo, at laste, to Courte nowe am I come,   30
A seemely swayne, that myght the place beseeme,
A gladsome guest embraste of all and some:
Not there contente with common dignitie,
My wandring eye in haste, (yea poste post haste)
Behelde the blazing badge of braverie,   35
For wante wherof, I thought my selfe disgraste:
Then peevishe pride pufft up my swelling harte,
To further foorth so hotte an enterpryse:
And comely cost beganne to playe his parte,
In praysing patternes of mine owne devise: 40
Thus all was good that myghte be got in haste,
To prinke me up, and make mee higher plaste.

    4 To prinke mee up and make mee higher plaste,
All came to late that taryed any tyme,
Pilles of provision pleased not my taste,   45
They made my heeles too heavie for to clyme:
Mee thought it beste that boughes of boystrous oke,
Shoulde fyrste be shread to make my feathers gaye,
Tyll at the last a deadly dinting stroke,
Brought downe the bulke with edgetooles of decaye: 50
Of every ferme I then lette flye a lease,
To feede the pursse that payde for peevishnesse,
Till rente and all were falne in suche disease,
As scarse coulde serve to maynteyne cleanlynesse:
The bough, the bodie, fyne, ferme, lease and lande, 55
All were too little for the merchauntes hande.

    5 All were too little for the merchantes hande,
And yet my braverye bigger than his booke:
But when this hotte accompte was coldely scande,
I thoughte highe tyme aboute me for to looke: 60

With heavie cheare I caste my heade abacke,
To see the fountayne of my furious race,
Comparde my losse, my livyng, and my lacke,
In equall balance with my jolye grace,
And sawe expences grating on the grounde   65
Lyke lumpes of leade to presse my pursse full ofte,
When lyghte rewarde and recompence were founde,
Fleeting lyke feathers in the wynde alofte:
These thus comparde, I lefte the Courte at large,
For why? the gaynes doth seldome quitte the charge.   70

   6³ For why? the gaynes doth seldome quitte the charge,
And so saye I, by proofe too dearely boughte,
My haste made waste, my brave and braynsicke barge,
Did floate to faste, to catche a thing of nought:
With leysure, measure, meane, and many mo,   75
I moughte have kepte a chaire of quiet state,
But hastie heades can not bee settled so,
Till crooked Fortune give a crabbed mate:
As busye braynes muste beate on tickle toyes,
As rashe invention breedes a rawe devise,   80
So sodaine falles doe hinder hastie joyes,
And as swifte baytes doe fleetest fyshe entice,
So haste makes waste, and therefore nowe I say,
No haste but good, where wysedome makes the waye.

No haste but good, where wysedome makes the waye   85
For proofe whereof wee see the silly snayle,
Who sees the Souldiers carcasse cast awaye,
With hotte assaulte the Castle to assayle,
By lyne and leysure clymes the loftie wall,
And winnes the turrettes toppe more cunningly,   90
Than doughtie Dicke, who loste his lyfe and all,
With hoysting up his heade too hastily:
The swiftest bitche brings foorth the blyndest whelpes,
The hottest Fevers coldest crampes ensue,
The nakedst neede hathe ever latest helpes: 95
With *Nevyle* then I fynde this proverbe true,
That *Haste makes waste*, and therefore still I saye,
No haste but good, where wysedome makes the waye.
             Sic tuli

[61]   Richard Courtop *(the last of the five) gave him this theame,* Durum
aeneum & miserabile aevum, *and thereupon he wrote in this wyse.*

WHen peerelesse Princes courtes were free from flatterie,
　　The Justice from unequal doome, the queste from perjurie,
The pillers of the state, from proude presumption,
The clearkes from heresie, the Commons from rebellion:
Then righte rewardes were given, by swaye of due deserte,   5
Then vertues dearlings might be plaste aloft to play their parte:
Then might they coumpt it true, that hath ben sayd of olde,
The children of those happie dayes were borne in beds of golde,
And swadled in the same: the Nurse that gave them sucke,
Was wyfe to Liberalitie, and lemman to Good lucke.   10
When *Caesar* woon the fielde, his captains caught the townes,
And every painful souldiors pursse was crammed full of crownes.
Licurgus for good lawes, loste his owne libertie,
And thoughte it better to preferre common commoditie.
But nowe the tymes are turnde, it is not as it was,   15
The golde is gone, the silver sunke, and nothing left but brasse.
To see a king encroache, what wonder should it seeme,
When commons cannot be content, with countrie *Dyadeeme?*
The Prince may dye a babe, trust up by trecherie,
Where vaine ambition doth move trustlesse nobilitie.   20
Errours in pulpit preach, where faith in preesthood failes,
Promotion (not devotion) is cause why cleargie quailes.
Thus is the stage stakt out, where all these partes be plaide,
And I the prologue should pronounce, but that I am afraide.
First *Cayphas* playes the priest, and *Herode* sits as king,   25
Pylate the Judge, *Judas* the Jurour verdicte in doth bring,
Vayne tatling plaies the vice, well cladde in rich aray,
And pore Tom Troth is laught to skorn, w^t garments nothing gay,
The woman wantonnesse, she commes with ticing traine,
Pride in hir pocket playes bo peepe, and bawdrie in hir braine.   30
Hir handmaides be deceipte, daunger, and dalliance,
Riot and Revell follow hir, they be of hir alliance:
Nexte these commes in Simme Swash, to see what sturre they keepe.
Climme of ye Clough then takes his heeles, tis time for him to creep:
To packe the pageaunt up, commes Sorowe with a song,   35
He says these jestes can get no grotes, & al this geare goth wrong:
Fyrst pride without cause why,[1] he sings the treble parte,
The meane he mumbles out of tune, for lack of life and hart:
Cost lost, the counter Tenor chanteth on apace,
Thus all in discords stands the cliffe, and beggrie sings the base.   40
The players loose their paines, where so few pens are sturring,

Their garments weare for lacke of gains, & fret for lack of furring.[2]
When all is done and past, was no part plaide but one,
For every player plaide the foole, till all be spent and gone.
And thus this foolish jest, I put in dogrell rime,   45
Bicause a crosier staffe is best, for such a crooked time.
                        Sic Tuli.

*And thus an end of these five theames, wherein hath bene noted, that as the
theames were sundrie and altogither divers, so Master Gascoigne did accom-
plishe them in five sundrie sortes of metre, yea and that seemeth most strange,
he devised all these admounting to the number of CCLVIII. verses, riding by
the way, writing none of them untill he came at the end of his Journey, the
which was no longer than one day in riding, one day in tarying with his
friend, and the third in returning to Greys Inne: a small time for suche a taske,
neyther wolde I willingly undertake the like. The meetres are but rough in
many places, and yet are they true* (cum licentia poetica) *and I must needes
confesse that he hath more commonly bene over curious in delectation, then
of haughtie stile in his dilatations. And therefore let us passe to the rest of
his works.*

[62]   *Gascoignes gloze uppon this text,*
                   Dominus iis opus habet.

M Y recklesse race is runne, greene youth and pride be past,
      My riper mellowed yeares beginne to follow on as fast.
My glancing lookes are gone, which wonted were to prie
In every gorgeous garish glasse that glistred in mine eie.
My sight is now so dimme, it can behold none such,   5
No mirroure but the merrie meane, can please my fansie muche.
And in that noble glasse, I take delight to view,
The fashions of the wonted worlde, compared by the new.
For marke who list to looke, each man is for him selfe,
And beates his braine to hord & heape this trash & worldly pelfe.   10
Our hands are closed up, great gifts go not abroade,
Few men will lend a locke of heye, but for to gaine a loade.
Give Gave is a good man, what neede we lash it out,
The world is wondrous fearfull now, for danger bids men doubte.
And aske how chanceth this? or what meanes all this meede?   15
Forsooth the common answer is, because *the Lord hath neede.*
A noble jest by gisse, I find it in my glasse,
The same freehold our Savioure Christ, conveyed to his asse.
A text to trie the truth, and for this time full fitte,
For where should we our lessons learne, but out of holy writte?   20
First marke our only God, which ruleth all the rost,
He sets a side all pompe and pride, wherein fond wordlings boast.
He is not fedde with calves, as in the dayes of old,
He cares but litle for their copes, that glister all of gold.

His traine is not so great, as filthy Sathans band,   25
A smaller heard may serve to feede, at our great masters hande.
He likes no numbred prayers, to purchase popish meede,
He askes no more but penitence, thereof *Our Lorde hath neede:*
Next marke the heathens Gods, and by them shall we see,
They be not now so good fellowes, as they were wont to be.   30
Jove, Mars, and *Mercurie,* Dame *Venus* and the rest,
They banquet not as they were wont, they know it were not best:
They shrinke into the cloudes, and there they serve our neede,
As planets and signes moveable, by destenies decreede.
So kings and princes both, have lefte their halles at large,   35
Their privie chambers cost enough, they cut off every charge:
And when an office falles, as chance sometimes may be,
First keepe it close a yere or twayne, then geld it by the fee.
And give it out at last, but yet with this proviso,
(A bridle for a brainsicke Jade) *durante bene placito.*   40
Some think these ladders low, to climbe alofte with speede:
Well let them creepe at leisure then, for sure *the Lord hath neede.*
Dukes Earles and Barons bold, have learnt like lesson nowe,
They breake up house and come to courte, they live not by ye plow.
Percase their roomes be skant, not like their stately boure,   45
A field bed in a corner coucht, a pallad on the floure.
But what for that? no force, they make thereof no boast,
They feede themselves with delycates, and at the princes cost.
And as for all their men, their pages and their swaynes,
They cloke them up with chynes of beefe, to multiply their gaines.   50
Themselves lie neere to looke, when any lease[1] doth fall,
Such croomes were wont to feede poore groomes, but now ye Lords licke al.
And why? oh sir, because, both dukes & lords have neede,
I mock not I, my text is true, beleeve it as your creede.
Our prelates and our priests, can tell this text with me,   55
They can hold fast their fattest fermes, and let no lease go free.
They have both wife and childe, which may not be forgot,
The scriptures say *the Lord hath neede,*[2] & therfore blame them not.
Then come a litle lower, unto the countrey knight,
The squier and the gentleman, they leave the countrey quite,   60
Their halles were all to large, their tables were to long,
The clouted shoes came in so fast, they kepte to great a throng,
And at the porters lodge, where lubbers wont to feede,
The porter learnes to answere now, hence hence *the Lorde hathe neede.*
His gests came in to thicke, their diet was to great,   65
Their horses eate up all the hey, which should have fed his neate:
Their teeth were farre to fine, to feede on porke and souse,
Five flocks of sheepe coulde scarce mainteine good mutton for his house.
And when this count was cast, it was no biding here,

Unto the good towne is he gone, to make his frends good cheere.   70
And welcome there that will, but shall I tell you how?
At his owne dish he feedeth them, that is the fashion now,
Sidebords be laid aside, the tables end is gone,
His cooke shall make you noble cheere, but ostler hath he none.
The chargers now be changde, wherein he wont to eate,   75
An olde frute dish is bigge enough to holde a jointe of meate,
A sallad or a sauce, to tast your cates with all,
Some strange devise to feede mens eies, mens stomacks now be small.
And when the tenauntes come to paye their quarters rent,
They bring some fowle at Midsommer, & a dish of Fish in Lent,   80
At Christmasse a capon, at Mighelmasse a goose:
And somwhat else at Newyeres tide, for feare their lease flie loose.
Good reason by my trouth, when Gentlemen lacke groates,
Let Plowmen pinch it out for pence, and patch their russet coates:
For better Fermers fast, than Manour houses fall,   85
The Lord hath need, then says the text, bring old Asse, colt and all.
Well lowest now at laste, let see the countrey loute,
And marke how he doth swink & sweate to bring this geare about:
His feastings be but fewe, cast whipstockes cloute his shooen,
The wheaten loafe is locked up, as soone as dinners doone: 90
And where he wonte to keepe a lubber, two or three,
Now hath he learnd to keepe no more but Sim his sonne and he,
His wyfe and Mawde his mayde, a boy to pitche the carte,
And turne him up to Hallontyde, to feele the wynters smarte:
Dame Alyson his wyfe doth know the price of meale,   95
Hir bridecakes be not halfe so bigge as she was wont to steale:
She weares no silver hookes, she is content with wursse,
Hir pendants and hir silver pinnes she putteth in hir pursse.
Thus learne I by my glasse, that merrie meane is best,
And he moste wise that fynds the meane to keepe his tackling best.   100
Perchaunce some open mouth will mutter nowe and than,
And at the market tell his mate, our landlords a zore man:
He racketh up our rentes, and keepes the best in hande,
He makes a wondrous deale of good out of his owne measne land:
Yea let suche pelters prate, saint *Needam* be their speede,   105
We neede no text to answer them, but this, *The Lord hath neede.*
                    Ever or never.

[63]   *Gascoignes good morow.*

Y Ou that have spente the silente nighte
       In sleepe and quiet reste,
And joye to see the cheerefull lighte
That ryseth in the East:
Nowe cleere your voyce, nowe cheare your heart,   5

Come helpe me nowe to sing:
Eche wiliyng wight come beare a parte,
To prayse the heavenly King.

And you whome care in prison keepes,[1]
Or sickenesse dothe suppresse,   10
Or secrete sorrowe breakes youre sleepes,
Or dolours doe distresse:
Yet beare a parte in dolefull wyse,
Yea thinke it good accorde,
And acceptable sacrifice,   15
Eche sprite to prayse the Lorde.

The dreadfull night with darksomnesse[2]
Had overspread the lyght,
And sluggishe sleepe with drowsynesse,
Had overpreste our myght: 20
A glasse wherein we maye beholde
Eche storme that stoppes our breath,
Our bedde the grave, oure cloathes lyke molde,
And sleepe lyke dreadfull death.

Yet as this deadly nyghte did laste,   25
But for a little space,
And heavenly daye nowe night is paste,
Doth shewe his pleasant face:
So muste we hope to see Gods face,
At laste in heaven on hie,   30
When wee have chaung'd this mortall place,
For Immortalitie.

And of suche happes and heavenly joyes,
As then wee hope to holde,
All earthly sightes, all worldly toyes,   35
Are tokens to beholde:
The daye is lyke the daye of doome,
The sunne, the Sonne of man,
The skyes the heavens, the earth the toombe
Wherein wee reste till than.   40

The Raynbowe bending in the skye,
Bedeckte with sundrye hewes,
Is lyke the seate of God on hye,
And seemes to telle these newes:
That as thereby he promised   45

To drowne the worlde no more,
So by the bloud whiche Christe hath shead,
He will oure health restore.

The mistie clowdes that fall sometyme,
And overcaste the skyes,   50
Are lyke to troubles of oure tyme,
Whiche doe but dimme oure eyes:
But as suche dewes are dryed up quite,
When *Phoebus* shewes his face,
So are suche fansies put to flighte,   55
Where God dothe guyde by grace.

The carrion Crowe, that lothesome beast,
Whyche cryes agaynst the rayne,
Bothe for hir hew and for the reste,
The Devill resembleth playne: 60
And as with goonnes we kill the Crowe,
For spoylyng oure reliefe,
The Devill so muste wee overthrowe,
With goonshot of beliefe.

The little Byrdes whiche syng so sweete,   65
Are lyke the angels voyce,
Whiche render God his prayses meete,
And teache us to rejoyce:
And as they more esteeme that myrthe,
Than dreade the nightes anoye,   70
So muste wee deeme oure dayes on earthe,
But hell to heavenly joye.

Unto whiche Joyes for to attayne,
God graunte us all his grace,
And sende us after worldly payne,   75
In heaven to have a place.
Where wee may still enjoy that lyght,
Whiche never shall decaye:
Lorde for thy mercie lende us myghte
To see that joyfull daye.   80

                          Haud ictus sapio.

[64]   *Gascoignes good nyghte.*

W Hen thou hast spent the lingring day in pleasure and delight,
    Or after toyle and wearie way, dost seeke to rest at night:
Unto thy paynes or pleasures past, adde this one labour yet,
Ere sleepe close up thyne eye too faste, do not thy God forget,
But searche within thy secret thoughts what deeds did thee befal: 5

And if thou fynde amisse in ought, to God for mercie call:
Yea though thou find nothing amisse, which thou canst cal to mind
Yet evermore remember this, there is the more behynde:
And think howe well soever it be, that thou hast spent the day,
It came of God, and not of thee, so to directe thy waye.   10
Thus if thou trie thy dayly deedes, and pleasure in this payne,
Thy lyfe shal clense thy corne from weeds, & thine shal be ye gaine:
But if thy sinfull sluggishe eye, will venture for to winke,
Before thy wading wyll maye trye, how far thy soule may sink,
Beware and wake, for else thy bed, which soft & smoothe is made,   15
May heap more harm upon thy head, than blows of enmies blade.
Thus if this payne procure thine ease, in bed as thou doste lye,
Perhaps it shall not God displease, to sing thus soberly:
I see that sleepe is lent mee here, to ease my wearie bones,
As death at laste shall eke appeare, to ease my greevous grones.   20
My dayly sports, my paunch full fed, have causde my drousie eye,
As carelesse lyfe in quiet led, might cause my soule to dye:
The streking arms, the yauning breath, which I to bedward use,
Are patternes of the pangs of death, when lyfe will me refuse:
And of my bed eche sundrie parte in shadowes doth resemble   25
The sundry shapes of deth, whose dart shal make my flesh to tremble,
My bed it self is lyke ye grave, my sheetes ye winding sheete,
My clothes the moulde which I must have to cover me most meet:
The hungrie fleas which friske so fresh, to worms I can compare,
Which greedily shal gnaw my flesh, and leave the bones ful bare: 30
The waking Cocke that early crowes to weare the nyght away,
Puts in my mynde the trumpe that blowes before the latter day.
And as I ryse up lustily, when sluggishe sleepe is paste,
So hope I to ryse joyfully, to Judgement at the laste.
Thus will I wake, thus will I sleepe, thus will I hope to ryse,   35
Thus will I neyther wayle nor weepe, but sing in godly wyse.
My bones shall in this bed remayne, my soule in God shall trust,
By whom I hope to ryse agayne from death and earthly dust.
                                        Haud ictus sapio.

These good Morowe and good nyght, together with his Passion, his Libell of divorce, his Lullabye, his Recantation, his De profundis, and his farewell, have verie sweete notes adapted unto them: the which I would you should also enjoy as well as my selfe. For I knowe you will delight to heare them. As also other verie good notes whyche I have for dyvers other Ditties of other mens devyse[1] whiche I have before rehersed.

[65]   *Gascoignes* De profundis.
The occasion of the wrighting hereof (as I have herde Master Gascoigne say) was this, riding alone betwene Chelmisforde and London, his minde mused uppon the dayes past, and therewithall he gan accuse his owne conscience of

*muche time misspent, when a great shoure of rayne did overtake him, and
he beeing unprepared for the same, as in a Jerken without a cloake, the wether
beeing very faire and unlikely to have changed so: he began to accuse him
selfe of his carelessnesse, and thereuppon in his good disposition compiled firste
this sonet, and afterwardes, the translated Psalme of* Deprofundis *as here
followeth.*

T He Skies gan scowle, orecast with mistie cloudes,
   When (as I rode alone by London way,
Clokelesse, unclad) thus did I sing and say:
Behold quoth I, bright *Titan* how he shroudes
His hed abacke, and yelds the raine his reach,   5
Till in his wrath, *Dan Jove* have soust the soile,
And washt me wretch which in his travaile toile.
But holla (here) doth rudenesse me apeach,
Since *Jove* is Lord and king of mightie power,
Which can commande the sunne to shew his face,   10
And (when him list) to give the raine his place.
Why do not I my wery muses frame,
(Although I be well soused in this shoure,)
To wrighte some verse in honor of his name?

[66]   *Gascoignes councell to* Douglasse Dive *written upon this occasion. She had
a booke wherein she had collected sundry good ditties of divers mens
doings, in which booke she would needes entreate him to
write some verses. And thereuppon he wrote
as followeth.*

T O binde a bushe of thornes amongst swete smelling floures,
   May make the posie seeme the worse, and yet the fault is ours:
For throw away the thorne, and marke what will ensew,
The posie then will shew it selfe, sweete, faire, and freshe of hew.
A puttocke set on pearche, fast by a falcons side,   5
Will quickly shew it selfe a kight, as time hath often tride.
And in my musing minde, I feare to finde like fall,
As just reward to recompence my rash attempts withall.
Thou bidst, and I must bowe, thou wilt that I shall write,
Thou canst command my wery muse some verses to endite.   10
And yet perdie, thy booke is fraughte with learned verse,
Such skill as in my musing minde I can none like reherse.
What followes then for me? but if I must needes write,
To set downe by the falcons side, my selfe a sillie kight.
And yet the sillie kight, well weyed in each degree,   15
May serve sometimes (as in his kinde) for mans commoditie.
The kight can weede the worme, from corne and costly seedes,
The kight can kill the mowldiwarpe, in pleasant meads y^t breeds:

Out of the stately streetes, the kight can clense the filth,
As men can clense the worthlesse weedes, from fruteful fallowed tilth.   20
And onely set aside the hennes poore progenie,
I cannot see who can accuse the kight for fellonie.
The falcon, she must feede on partritch, and on quaile,
On[1] pigeon, plover, ducke and drake, hearne, lapwing, teale, & raile,
Hir hungrie throte devours both foode and deintie fare,   25
Whereby I take occasion, thus boldly to compare.
And as a sillie kight, (not falcon like that flie,
Nor yet presume to hover by mount *Hellycon* on hye)
I frendly yet presume, uppon my frends request,
In barreine verse to shew my skill, then take it for the best.   30
And *Doughty*[2] *Douglasse* thou, that arte of faulcons kinde,
Give willing eare yet to the kight, and beare his words in mind.
Serve thou first God thy Lord, and praise him evermore,
Obey thy Prince and love thy make, by him set greatest store.
Thy Parents follow next, for honor and for awe,   35
Thy frends use alwayes faithfully, for so commands the lawe.
Thy seemely selfe at last, thou shalte likewise regard,
And of thy selfe this lesson learne, and take it as reward:
That loke how farre desertes, may seme in thee to shine,
So farre thou maist set out thy selfe, without empeach or crime.   40
For this I dare avow, without selfe love (alight)
It can scarce be that vertue dwell, in any earthly wight.
But if in such selfe love, thou seeme to wade so farre,
As fall to fowle presumption, and judge thy selfe a starre,
Beware betimes and thinke, in our *Etymologie,*   45
Such faults are plainly called pride, and in french *Surquydrye.*
Lo thus can I pore kight, adventure for to teach,
The falcon flie, and yet forewarne, she row not past hir reach.
Thus can I weede the worme, which seeketh to devoure
The seeds of vertue, which might grow within thee every houre.   50
Thus can I kill the mowle, which else would overthrow
The good foundacion of thy fame, with every litle blowe.
And thus can I convey, out of thy comely brest,
The sluttish heapes of peevish pride, which might defile the rest.
Perchance some falcons flie, which will not greatly grutch,   55
To learne thee first to love thy selfe, and then to love to mutch.
But I am none of those, I list not so to range,
I have mans meate enough at home, what need I then seeke change.
I am no peacocke I: my fethers be not gay,
And though they were, I see my feete suche[3] fonde affectes to stay.   60
I list not set to sale a thing so litle worth,
I rather could kepe close my creast,[4] than seeke to set it forth.
Wherefore if in this verse, which thou commands to flowe,

Thou chaunce to fall on construing, whereby some doubtes may grow,
Yet grant this only boone, peruse it twise or thrise,   65
Digest it well eare thou condemne the depth of my devise.
And use it like the nut, first cracke the outward shell,
Then trie the kirnell by the tast, and it may please thee well.
Do not as barbers do, which wash beards curiously,
Then cut them off, then cast them out, in open streetes to lie.   70
Remember therewithall, my muze[5] is tied in chaines,
The goonshot of calamitie hath battred all my braines.
And though this verse scape out, take thou therat no marke,
It is but like a hedlesse flie, that tumbleth in the darke.
It was thine owne request, remember so it was,   75
Wherefore if thou dislike the same, then licence it to passe
Into my brest againe, from whence it flew in hast,
Full like a kight which not deserves by falcons to be plast:
And like a stubbed thorne, which may not seeme to serve,
To stand with such swete smelling floures, like praises to deserve.   80
Yet take this harmelesse thorne, to picke thy teeth withall,
A tooth picke serves some use perdie, although it be but small.
And when thy teeth therewith, be piked faire and cleane,
Then bend thy tong no worse to me, than mine to thee hath bene.
                    Ever or Never.

[67]   *Gascoignes councell given to master* Bartholmew Withipoll, *a litle
                    before his latter journey to Geane. 1572.*

M Ine owne good *Bat,* before thou hoise up saile,
     To make a furrowe in the foming seas,
Content thy selfe to heare for thine availe,
Such harmelesse words, as ought thee not displease.
First in thy jorney, gape not over much,   5
What? laughest thou *Batte,* because I write so plaine?
Bleeve me now it is a friendly touch,
To use few words where frendship doth remaine.
And for I finde, that fault hath runne to fast,
Both in thy flesh, and fancie to sometime,   10
Me thinks plaine dealing biddeth me to cast
This bone at first amid my dogrell rime.
But shall I say, to give thee grave advise?
(Which in my hed is (God he knowes) full geazon)?
Then marke me well, and though I be not wise,   15
Yet in my rime, thou maist perhaps find reason.
First every day, beseech thy God on knee,
So to directe thy staggring steppes alwaye,
That he whiche every secrete thoughte doth see
Maye holde thee in, when thou wouldst goe astray: 20

And that he deigne to sende thee safe retoure,
And quicke dispatche of that whyche is thy due:
Lette this my *Batte* bee bothe thy prime and houre,
Wherein also commende to *Nostre Dieu,*
Thy good Companion and my verie frende,   25
To whome I shoulde (but tyme woulde not permitte)
Have taken payne some ragged ryme to sende
In trustie token, that I not forget
His curtesie: but this is debte to thee,
I promysde it, and nowe I meane to pay: 30
What was I saying? sirra, will you see
Howe soone my wittes were wandering astraye?
I saye, praye thou for thee and for thy mate,
So shipmen sing, and though the note be playne,
Yet sure the musike is in heavenly state,   35
When frendes sing so, and knowe not howe to fayne.
Then nexte to G O D, thy Prince have still in mynde,
Thy countreys honour, and the common wealth:
And flee from them, whiche fled with every wynde
From native soyle, to forraine coastes by stealth: 40
Theyr traynes are trustlesse, tending still to treason,
Theyr smoothed tongues are lyned all with guyle,
Their power slender, scarsly woorthe two peason,
Their malice muche, their wittes are full of wyle:
Eschue them then, and when thou seest them, saye,   45
Da, da, sir *K,* I maye not come at you,
You caste a snare youre countrey to betraye,
And woulde you have me truste you nowe for true?
Remembre *Batte* the foolishe blinkeyed boye
Whiche was at *Rome,* thou knowest whome I meane,   50
Remember eke the preatie beardlesse toye,
Whereby thou foundst a safe returne to *Geane,*
Doe so againe: (God shielde thou shouldst have neede,)
But rather so, than to forsweare thy selfe:
A loyall hearte, (beleeve this as thy Creede)   55
Is evermore more woorth than worldly pelfe.
And for one lesson, take this more of mee,
There are three Ps almoste in every place,
From whiche I counsell thee alwayes to flee,
And take good heede of them in any case,   60
The first is poyson, perillous in deede
To suche as travayle with a heavie pursse:
And thou my *Batte* beware, for thou haste neede,
Thy pursse is lynde wyth paper, whyche is wursse:
Thy billes of credite will not they thinkst thou,   65

Be bayte to sette *Italyan* handes on woorke?
Yes by my faye, and never worsse than nowe,
When every knave hath leysure for to lurke,
And knoweth thou commest for the shelles of Christe:
Beware therefore, where ever that thou go,   70
It maye fall out that thou shalte be entiste
To suppe sometimes with a *Magnifico,*
And have a *fico* foysted in thy dishe,
Bycause thou shouldest digeste thy meate the better:
Beware therefore, and rather feede on fishe,   75
Than learne to spell fyne fleshe with suche a Letter.
Some may presente thee with a pounde or twayne
Of Spanishe soape to washe thy lynnen white:
Beware therefore, and thynke it were small gayne,
To save thy shirte, and caste thy skinne of quite: 80
Some cunning man maye teache thee for to ryde,
And stuffe thy saddle all with Spanishe wooll,
Or in thy stirrops have a toye so tyde,
As bothe thy legges may swell thy buskins full:
Beware therefore, and beare a noble porte,   85
Drynke not for thyrste before an other taste:
Lette none outlandishe Taylour take disporte
To stuffe thy doublet full of suche Bumbaste,
As it maye caste thee in unkindely sweate,
And cause thy haire per companie to glyde,   90
Straungers are fyne in many a propre feate:
Beware therefore, the seconde *P.* is Pryde,
More perillous than was the fyrste by farre,
For that infectes but onely bloud and bones,
This poysons all, and myndes of men dothe marre,   95
It fyndeth nookes to creepe in for the nones:
Fyrste from the mynde it makes the hearte to swell,
From thence the fleshe is pampred every parte,
The skinne is taughte in Dyers shoppes to dwell,
The haire is curlde or frisled up by arte: 100
Beleeve mee *Batte,* oure Countreymen of late
Have caughte suche knackes abroade in forayne lande,
That moste men call them *Devils incarnate,*
So singular in theyr conceiptes they stande:
Nowe sir, if I shall see your maistershippe   105
Come home disguysde and cladde in queynt araye,
As wyth a pyketoothe byting on youre lippe,
Youre brave *Mustachyos* turnde the *Turky* waye,
A Coptanckt hatte made on a Flemmishe blocke,
A nyghtgowne cloake downe trayling to your toes,   110

A slender sloppe close couched to youre docke,
A curtold slipper, and a shorte sylke hose:
Bearyng youre Rapier poynte above the hilte,
And looking bigge lyke *Marquise of al Beefe,*
Then shall I coumpte your toyle and travayle spilte,   115
Bycause my seconde *P,* with you is cheefe.
But forwardes nowe, although I stayde[1] a whyle,
My hindmoste *P,* is worsse than bothe these two,
For it bothe soule and bodie dothe defyle,
With fouler faultes than bothe those other doo.   120
Shorte tale to make, this is a double *P,*
(God shielde my *Batte,* shoulde beare it in his breast)
And with a dashe it spelleth *Papistrie,*
A perlous *P,* and woorsse than bothe the reste:
Nowe though I finde no cause for to suspecte   125
My *Batte* in this, bycause he hath ben tryde,
Yet since the polshorne Prelates can infecte
Kings, Emperours, Princes, and the worlde so wyde.
And since theyr brazen heaven beares suche a glosse,
As moste that travayle come home per *Papist,*   130
Or else muche woorsse (whyche is a heavie losse)
Drowned in errours lyke an *Atheist:*
Therefore I thoughte it meete to warne my frende
Of this foule *P,* and so an ende of *Ps.*
Nowe for thy diet marke my tale to ende,   135
And thanke me then, for that is all my fees.
See thou exceede not in three double *Vs,*
The fyrste is Wyne, whiche maye enflame thy bloud,
The seconde, Women, suche as haunte the stewes,
The thirde is Wilfulnesse, whiche dooth no good.   140
These three eschue, or temper them alwayes:
So shall my *Batte* prolong his youthfull yeeres,
And see long *George* agayne, with happie dayes,
Who if he bee as faythfull to his feeres,
As hee was wonte, wyll dayly praye for *Batte,*   145
And for *Pencoyde:* and if it fall oute so,
That *James a Parrye* doo but make good that,
Whiche he hath sayde: and if he bee (no, no)
The beste companyon that long *George* can fynde,
Then at the *Spawe* I promyse for to bee   150
In *Auguste* nexte, if God turne not my mynde,
Where as I woulde bee glad thy selfe to see:
Tyll then farewell, and thus I ende my song,
Take it in gree, for else thou doest mee wrong.

                Haud ictus sapio.

[68]   *Gascoignes Epitaph uppon capitaine* Bourcher *late slayne in the warres in*
Zelande, *the whiche hath bene termed the tale
of a stone as followeth.*

F Ye Captaines fie, your tongs are tied to close,
    Your souldiers eke by silence purchase shame:
Can no man penne in metre nor in prose,
The life, the death, the valiante acts, the fame,
The birth, behavioure, nor the noble name,   5
Of such a feere as you in fight have lost?
Alas such paines would quickly quite the cost.

    Bourcher[1] is dead, whome each of you did knowe,
Yet no man writes one word to painte his praise,
His sprite on high, his carkasse here belowe,   10
Do both condemne your doting idle dayes:
Yet ceasse they not to sound his worthy wayes,
Who lived to die, and died againe to live,
With death deere bought, he did his death forgive.

    He might for birth have boasted noble race,   15
Yet were his manners meeke and alwayes milde,
Who gave a gesse by gazing on his face,
And judgde thereby, might quickly be beguilde:
In fielde a lion, and in towne a childe,
Fierce to his foe, but courteouse to his friende.   20
Alas the while, his life so soone should end?

    To serve his Prince his life was ever prest,
To serve his God, his death he thought but dew,
In all attempts as frowarde as the best,
And all to forwards whiche we all may rew,   25
His life so shewed, his death eke tried it true:
For where Gods foes in thickest prease did stande,
Bourcher caught bane with bloudy sword in hande.

    And marke the courage of a noble harte,
When he in bedde lay wounded wondrous sore,   30
And heard allarme, he soone forgat his smarte,
And callde for armes to shewe his service more:
I will to fielde (quoth he) and God before.
Which sayde, he sailde into more quiet coast,
Still praysing God, and so gave up the ghost.   35

    Now muze not reader though we stones can speake,
Or write sometimes the deedes of worthy ones,
I could not hold although my harte should breake,

Bycause here by me buried are his bones,
But I must tell this tale thus for the nones.　　　　　　40
When men crie mumme and keepe such silence long,
Then stones must speake, els dead men shall have wrong.

Finis qd. Marmaduke Marblestone.

[69] *Gascoignes devise of a maske for the right honorable Viscount Mountacute,
written (as I have heard Master Gascoigne himselfe declare) upon this occasion,
when the sayde L. had prepared to solemnise two mariages betwene his sonne
and heire and the daughter of sir William Dormer knighte, and betwene the
sonne and heire of sir William Dormer, and the daughter of the saide L.
Mountacute: there were eighte gentlemen (all of bloud or alliance to the saide
L. Mountacute) which had determined to present a maske at the day appoynted
for the sayd mariages, and so farre they had proceeded therin, that they had
alredy bought furniture of silks, &c and had caused their garments to be cut
of the Venetian fashion. Nowe then they began to imagine that (without some
speciall demonstracion) it would seeme somewhat obscure to have Venetians
presented rather than other countrey men. Whereupon they entreated Master
Gascoigne to devise some verses to be uttered by an Actor wherein mighte be
some discourse convenient to render a good cause of the Venetians presence.
Master Gascoigne calling to minde that there is a noble house of the Mountacutes
in Italie, and therewithall that the L. Mountacute here doth quarter the cote
of an ancient english gentleman called Mountherme, and hath the inheritance
of the sayde house, did thereuppon devise to bring in a Boy of the age of twelve
or xiiij. yeres, who shoulde fayne that he was a Mounthermer by the fathers side,
and a Montacute by the mothers side, and that his father being slayne at the
last warres against the Turke, and he there taken, he was recovered by the
Venetians in their last victorie, and with them sayling towardes Venice, they were
driven by tempest uppon these coasts, and so came to the mariage uppon report
as followeth, and the said Boy pronounced the devise in this sorte.*

W Hat wonder you my Lords? why gaze you gentlemen?
　　And wherefore marvaile you *mez Dames,* I pray you tell me then?
Is it so rare a sight, or yet so strange a toy,
Amongst so many noble peeres, to see one *Pouer Boy?*
Why? boyes have bene allowed in every kind of age,　　　　　　5
As *Ganymede* that prety boy, in Heaven is *Jove* his page.
Cupid that mightie God although his force be fearse,
Yet is he but a naked boy, as Poets do rehearse.
And many a pretty boy a mighty man hath proved,
And served his Prince at all assayes deserving to be loved.　　　　　　10
Percase my strange attire my glittering golden gite,
Doth either make you marvell thus, or move you with delite.
Yet wonder not my Lords for if your honors please,
But even to give me eare awhile, I will your doubts apease.

And you shall know the cause, wherefore these robes are worne,   15
And why I go outlandishlike, yet being english borne.
And why I thus presume, to presse into this place,
And why I (simple boy) am bold to looke such men in face.
First then you must perstande, I am no stranger I,
But english boy, in England borne, and bred but even hereby.   20
My father was a knight *Mount Hermer* was his name,
My mother of the *Mountacutes,* a house of worthy fame.
My father from his youth was trained up in field,
And always[1] toke his chiefe delight, in helmet speare and shielde.
Soldado for his life, and in his happie dayes,   25
Soldado like hath lost his life, to his immortall prayse.
The thundering fame which blew about the world so wide,
How that the christian enmie, the Turke that prince of pride,
Addressed had his power, to swarme uppon the seas,
With gallies, foists, and such like ships, wel armde at all assays,   30
And that he made his vaunt, the gredy fishe to glut,
With gobs of chistians carkasses, in cruell peeces cut.
These newes of this report, did pierce my fathers eares,
But never touched his noble harte, with any sparke of feares.
For well he knew the trade of all the *Turkishe* warres,   35
And had amongst them shed his bloud at many cruell jarres.
In *Rhodes* his race begon, a slender tall yong man,
Where he by many martial feats, his spurres of knighthod wan.
Yea though the peece was lost, yet won he honoure still,
And evermore against the *Turkes* he warred by his will.   40
At *Chios* many know, how hardily he fought,
And howe with streames of striving[2] bloud, his honoure deare hee bought.
At length enforst to yeld with many captaines mo,
He bought his libertie with lands and let his goodes ago.
Zechynes of glistering golde, two thousand was his price,   45
The which to pay his lands must leape, for else he were unwise.
Beleeve me now my lords although the losse be mine,
Yet I confesse them better solde, than like a slave to pine.
,, For lands may come againe, but libertie once lost,
,, Can never finde such recompence, as countervailes the cost.   50
My selfe now know the case, who like my fathers lot,
Was like of late for to have lost my libertie god wot.
My father (as I say) enforste to leave his lande
In mortgage to my mothers kinne, for ready coine in hande,
Gan now uppon these newes, which earst I did rehearse,   55
Prepare himselfe to save his pawne or else to leese his pheares.
And first his raunsome paide, with that which did remaine,
He rigged up a proper *Barke,* was called *Leffort Brittayne.*
And like a venturer (besides him seemely selfe)

Determined for to venture me and all his worldly pelfe.   60
Perhaps some hope of gaine perswaded so his minde,
For sure his hauty harte was bent, some great exployte to finde.
How so it were, the winds now hoysted up our sayles,
We furrowing in the foming floudes, to take our best availes.
Now hearken to my words, and marke you well the same,   65
For now I will declare the cause wherefore I hither came.
My father (as I say) had set up all his rest,
And tost on seas both day and night, disdayning idlenesse,
We lefte our forelands end, we past the coast of *France,*
We reacht the cape of *Finestre* our course for to advance.   70
We past *Marrocchus* streights, and at the last descried,
The fertile coasts of *Cyprus* soile, which I my selfe first spied.
My selfe (a forewarde boy) on highest top was plast,
And there I sawe the *Ciprian* shoare, whereto we sailde in hast.
Which when I had declared unto the masters mate,   75
He lepte for joy and thanked God, of that our happie state.
,, But what remaines to man, that can continue long?
,, What sunne can shine so cleare and bright but clouds may rise among?
Which sentence soone was proved, by our unhappie hap,
We thought our selves full nere our frendes, & light in enimies lap.   80
The *Turke* y^t tirant he, with siege had girte the walles,
Of famouse *Famagosta* then and sought to make them thrals.
And as he lay by lande, in stronge and stately trenche,
So was his power prest by sea, his christian foes to drenche.
Uppon the waltring waves, his foistes and gallies fleete,   85
More forrest like than orderly, for such a man most meete.
This heavie sight once seene, we turnd our course a pace,
And set up all our sailes in haste, to give such furie place.
But out alas, our wills, and winds were contrarie,
For raging blasts did blowe us still uppon our enimie.   90
My father seeing then, whereto he needes must go,
And that the mightie hand of God, had it appointed so,
Most like a worthy knight (though certeine of his death)
Gan cleane forget al wailing words as lavish of his breath.
And to his christian crew, this (too shorte) tale he told,   95
To comfort them which seemd to faint, & make the coward bolde,
,, Fellowes in armes, quoth he, although I beare the charge,
,, And take upon me chieftaines name, of this unhappie barge,
,, Yet are you all my pheares, and as one companie,
,, We must like true companions, togither live and die,   100
,, You see quoth he our foes, with furious force at hand,
,, And in whose hands our handfull heare unable is to stand.[3]
,, What resteth then to do, should we unto them yeld?
,, And wilfully receive that yoke,[4] which christians cannot weld.

,, No sure, hereof be sure, our lives were so unsure,   105
,, And though we live, yet so to live, as better death endure.
,, To heare those hellish fends in raging blasphemie,
,, Defye our only saviour, were this no miserie?
,, To see the fowle abuse of boyes in tender yeares,
,, The which I knowe must needes abhor all honest christians eares.   110
,, To see maides ravished, wives, women forst by feare,
,, And much more mischiefe than this time can let me utter here.
,, Alas, quoth he, I tell not all, my tong is tide,
,, But all the slaveries[5] on the earth we should with them abide.
,, How much were better than[6] to die in worthy wise,   115
,, And so to make our carcasses, a willing sacrifice?[7]
,, So shall we pay the debt, which unto God is due,
,, So shall you die in his defence, who deind to die for you.
,, And who with hardy hand most turkish tikes can quell,
,, Let him accompt in conscience, to please his maker well.   120
,, You see quoth he,[8] my sonne, wherewith he lookte[9] on me,
,, Whom but a babe, yet have I brought, my partner here to be,
,, For[10] him I must confesse, my harte is pensive now,
,, To leave him[11] living thus in youth, to die I know not how.
,, But since[12] it pleaseth God, I may not murmure I,   125
,, If God had pleased we both should live, and as god wil we die.
Thus with a braying sigh, his noble tong he staide,
Commaunding all the ordinance, in order to be laide.
And placing all his men[13] in order for to fight,
Fell groveling first uppon his face, before them all in sight.   130
And when in secret so[14] he whispered had a while,[15]
He raisde his hed with cherefull looke, his sorrowes to beguile:
And with the rest he prayde, to God in heaven on hie,
Which ended thus, *Thou only Lord, canst helpe in miserie.*
This said, behold, the Turkes enclosde us round about,   135
And seemd to wonder that we durst[16] resist so great a rout.
Wherat they doubt not long, for though our power was slender,
We sent them signes by Canon shot, that we ment not to render.
Then might we see them chafe, then might we heare them rage,
And all at once they bent their force, about our sillie cage.   140
Our ordinance bestowed, our men them selves defend,
On everie side so thicke beset, they might not long contend.
But as their captaine wild, each man his force did strayne,
To send a Turke (some two or three) unto the hellishe trayne.
And he him selfe which sawe, he might no more abide,   145
Did thrust amid the thickest throng, and so with honour died.
With him there died likewise, his best approved men,
The rest did yeld as men amazd, they had no courage then.
Amongst the which my selfe, was tane by Turks alas,

And with the Turks[17] a turkish life, in *Turkie* must I passe.   150
I was not done to death for so I often cravde,
But like a slave before the Gates, of *Famagosta* savde.
That peece once put to sacke, I thither was conveyed,
And under safegard evermore, I sillie boye was stayed.
There did I see such sights as yet my hart do pricke,   155
I sawe the noble *Bragadine*, when he was fleyd quick.
First like a slave enforst to beare to every breach,
Two baskets laden[18] full with earth *Mustaffa* did him teach.
By whome he might not passe before he kisse the ground,
These cruell torments (yet with mo) that worthy souldier found.   160
His eares cut from his head, they set him in a chaire,
And from a maine yard hoisted him alofte into the aire,[19]
That so he might be shewed with crueltie and spight,
Unto us all, whose weping eies did much abhorre[20] the sight.
Alas why do I thus with wofull words rehearce,   165
These werie newes which all our harts with pittie needes muste pearce?[21]
Well then to tell you foorth, I still a slave remaind,
To one, which *Prelybassa* hight, who held me stil enchaind.
With him I went to Seas into the gulfe of *Pant*,
With many christians captives mo,[22] which did their fredom want.   170
There with the Turkish tirannie we were enforst to stay,
For why? they had avise, that the *Venetian* fleete,
Did flote in *Argostelly* then with whome they hoapt to meete.
And as they waltered thus with tides and billowes tost,
Their hope had hap, for at the last they met them to their cost.   175
As in *October* last upon the seventh day,
They found the force of christian knights addrest in good aray.
And shall I trie my tong to tell the whole discourse,
And how they did encounter first and how they joynd in force?
Then harken now my lords, for sure my memorie,   180
Doth yet record the very plot of all this victorie.
The christian crew came on, in forme of battaile pight,
And like a cressent cast them selves preparing for to fight.
On other side the Turkes, which trusted power to much,
Disorderly did spread their force, the will of God was such.   185
Well, at the last they met, and first with cannons thunder,
Each other sought with furious force to slit their ships in sunder.
The Barkes are battered sore, the gallies gald with shot,
The hulks are hit and every man must stand unto his lot.
The powder sendes his smoke into the cruddy skies,   190
The smoulder stops our nose with stench, the sunne offends our eies,
The pots of lime unsleakt, from highest top are cast,
The parched peas are not forgot to make them slip as fast.
The wilde fire works are wrought and cast in foemens face,

The grappling hooks are stretched foorth, ye pikes are pusht apace.   195
The halberts hew on hed, the browne bills bruze the bones,
The harquebush doth spit his spight, with prety percing stones.
The drummes crie dub a dub, the braying trumpets blow,
The whistling fifes are seldome herd, these sounds do drowne them so.
The voice of warlike wights, to comforte them that faint,   200
The piteous plaints of golden harts, which wer w^t feares attaint.
The groning of such ghosts as gasped now for breath,
The praiers of the better sort, prepared unto death,
And to be short, each griefe which on the earth may growe,
Was eath and easie to be found, uppon these flouds to flowe.   205
If any sight on earth, may unto hell resemble,
Then sure this was a hellishe sight, it makes me yet to tremble:
And in this blouddie fyght, when halfe the day was spent,
It pleazed God to helpe his flocke, which thus in pound was pent.
The generall for *Spayne*, gan galde that Galley sore,   210
Wherin my *Prely Bassa* was, and grievde it more and more:
Upon that other side, with force of swoorde and flame,
The good *Venetian* generall dyd charge upon the same.
At length they came aboorde, and in his raging pride,
Stroke of this Turkish captains hed, which blasphemd as it dide: 215
Oh howe I feele the bloud now tickle in my brest,
To think what joy then pierst my heart, and how I thought me blest
To see that cruell Turke whiche helde me as his slave
By happie hande of Christians his payment thus to have:
His head from shoulders cut, upon a pyke did stande,   220
The whiche *Don John* of *Austrye* helde in his triumphant hand.
The boldest *Bassa* then, that did in lyfe remayne,
Gan tremble at the sight hereof for privy griefe and payne.
Thus when these fierce had fought from morning untill night,
Christe gave his flocke the victorie, and put his foes to flight: 225
And of the Turkish trayne were eight score Galeys tane,
Fifteene soonk, five and twentie burnt, & brought unto their bane,
Of Christians set at large were fourteene thousand soules,
Turks twentie thousande registred in *Beelzebub* his rolles.
Thus have you nowe my Lords, the summe of all their fight,   230
And trust it all for true I tell, for I was still in sight:
But when the seas were calme, and skyes began to cleare,
When foes were all or dead or fled, and victors did appeare,
Then every christian sought amongst us for his frende,
His kinsman or companion some succour them to lende: 235
And as they ransackte so, lo God his will it was,
A noble wyse *Venetian* by me did chaunce to passe:
Who gazing on my face, dyd seeme to like mee well
And what my name, and whence I was, commaunded me to tel:

I nowe whiche waxed bolde, as one that scaped had,
From depest hell to highest heaven, began for to be glad:
And with a lyvely spryte, began to pleade my case,
And hid not from this worthie man, myne auncient worthy race:
And tolde my fathers name, and howe I did descende
From *Mountacutes* by mothers side, nor there my tale did ende:
But furthermore I tolde my fathers late exployte,
And how he lefte landes, goodes and lyfe, to pay *son Dieu son droit.*

The foure torchbearers that came in with the actor.

Nor of my selfe I craved so credited to bee,
For lo ther were remayning yet, *These four whom here you see,*
Whiche all were Englishe borne, and knew I had not lyed,
And were my fathers souldiours eke, and saw him how he dyed.
This grave *Venetian* who hearde the famous name
Of *Mountacutes* rehersed there, which long had ben of fame
In *Italy,* and he of selfe same worthie race,
Gan streight w^t many courteous words in armes me to embrace,
And kissed mee on cheeke, and bad me make good cheere,
And thanke the myghtie hand of[23] God for that whiche hapned there,
Confessing that he was himselfe a *Mountacute,*
And bare the selfe same armes that I did quarter in my scute:
And for a further proofe, he shewed in his hat,

The actor had a token in his cap like to the Mountacutes of Italy.

This token whiche the *Mountacutes* do beare always, for that
They covet to be knowne from *Capels* where they passe,
For ancient grutch which long ago tween those two houses was.
Then tooke me by the hande, and ledde me so aboorde
His galley: where there were yfeere, full many a comely Lorde:
Of whome eight *Montacutes* did sitte in hyghest place,
To whome this first declared first my name, and then my race:
Lo lordings here (quod he) a babe of our owne bloods,
Whom *Turks* had tane, his father slain, w^t losse of lands and goods:
See how God favours us, that I should fynde hym nowe,
I straunge to him, he straunge to mee, wee met I know not how:
But sure when I him sawe, and gazed in his face,
Me thought he was a *Mountacute,* I chose him by his grace:
Herewith he dyd reherse my fathers valyant deede,
For losse of whome each *Mountacute,* did seeme in hart to bleede.
They all embrast me then, and streight as you may see,
In comely garments trimde me up, as brave as brave may bee:
I was in sackcloath I, nowe am I cladde in golde,

The token that he didde weare in his cappe.

And weare suche roabes as I my selfe take pleasure to beholde.
Amongst their other giftes, *this Token they me gave,*
And bad me lyke a *Montacute* my selfe alway behave.
Nowe hearken then my Lordes, I staying on the seas,
In consort of these lovely Lordes, with comfort and with ease,
Determined with them in *Italy* to dwell,

And there by trayne of youthfull yeares in knowledge to excell: 285
That so I might at laste reedifye the walles,
Which my good father had decayde by tossing fortunes balles:
And while they slice the seas to their desired shore,
Beholde a little gale began, encreasing more and more:
At last with raging blast, whiche from Southeast did blowe,   290
Gan send our sayles upon these shores, which I full wel did know:
I spyed the Chalkie Clyves upon the Kentishe coast,
Whereby our lande hight *Albyon,* as *Brutus* once did boast,
Which I no sooner sawe, but to the rest I sayde,
Siate di buona voglia, My lordes be well apayde: 295
I see by certayne signes these tempestes have us caste,
Upon my native countrey coastes with happie hap at laste:
And if your honours please this honour me to doo,
In Englishe havens to harbour you, & see our Cities too:
Lo *London* is not farre, where as my friends woulde be   300
Right glad, with favour to requite your favour shewed to mee:
Vouchsafe my Lordes (quod I) to stay upon this strande,
And whiles your Barks be rigged new, remain with me on land,
Who though I be a boy, my father dead and slayne,
Yet shal you see I have some frendes whiche will you entertaine.   305
These noble men, whiche are the floure of curtesy,
Did not disdayne thys my request, but tooke it thankfully,
And from their battred Barks commaunded to be cast
Some *Gondalaes,* wherin upon[24] our pleasaunt streames they past
Into the mouthe of *Thames,* thus did I them transport,   310
And to *London* at the laste, where as I hearde report,
Even as wee landed first, of this twyse happie day,
To thinke whereon I leapt for joye, as I bothe must and may:
And to these lovely lordes, whiche are *Magnificoes,*
I did declare the whole discourse in order as it rose: 315
That you my Lorde who are our chiefest *Mountacute,*
And he whome Englishe *Mountacutes* their onely stay impute,
Had founde the meanes this day to matche your sonne and heire,
In marriage with a worthie dame which is bothe fresh and faire,
And (as reportes are spread) of goodly qualities,   320
A virgin trayned from hir youth in godly exercise,
Whose brother had lykewise your daughter tane to wyfe,
And so by double lynkes enchaynde themselves in lovers lyfe:
These noble *Mountacutes* whiche were from *Venice* droven,
By tempest (as I tolde before) wherwith they long had stroven   325
Gan nowe give thankes to God whiche so did them convey,
To see suche honours of their kinne in suche a happie day:
And straight they me entreat, whom they might wel commande,
That I should come to you my Lord first them to recommaunde,

And then this boone to crave, that under your protection 330
They mighte be bolde to enter here, devoyde of all suspection,
And so in friendly wyse for to concelebrate,
This happie matche solemnized, according to your state.
Lo this is all they crave, the whiche I can not doubt,
But that youre Lordship soone will graunt, with more, if more ye mought: 335
Yea were it for no more, but for the Curtesye,
Whiche (as I say) they shewed to me in great extremitie:
They are *Venetians,* and though from *Venice* reft,
They come in suche *Venetian* roabes as they on seas had left:
And since they be your frendes, and kinsmen too by blood, 340
I trust your entertainment will be to them right good:
They will not tarrie long, lo nowe I heare their drumme,
Beholde, lo nowe I see them here in order howe they come,
Receyve them well my lorde, so shall I pray alwayes,
That God vouchsafe to blesse this house with many happie days. 345

*After the maske was done, the Actor tooke master Tho. Bro. by the hand and
    brought him to the* Venetians, *with these words:*

G*Uardate Signori,* my lovely Lords behold,
  This is another *Mountacute,* hereof you may be bold.
Of such our patrone here, *The viscount Mountacute,* 350
Hath many comely sequences, well sorted all in sute,
But as I spied him first I could not let him passe,
I tooke the carde that likt me best, in order as it was.
And here to you my lords, I do present the same,
Make much of him, I pray you then, for he is of your name. 355
For whome I dare advance, he may your tronchman be,
Your herald and ambassadour, let him play all for me.

Then the Venetians *embraced and received the same master
    Tho. Browne, and after they had a while whispered
        with him, he tourned to the Bridegroomes and* 360
           Brides, saying thus.

B Rother, these noble men to you now have me sent,
  As for their tronchman to expound theffect of their intent.
They bid me tell you then, they like your worthy choice,
And that they cannot choose therein but triumph and rejoice.
As farre as gesse may give, they seeme to praise it well, 365
They say betwene your ladies eyes doth *Gentilezza* dwell.
I terme it as they do, their englishe is but weake,
And I (God knowes) am all to yong beyond sea speach to speake.
And you my sister eke they seeme for to commend,
With such good words as may be seeme a cosin[25] and a friend. 370
They like your chosen pheare, so pray they for your sake,

That he may alwayes be to you, a faithfull loving make.
This in effect is all, but that they crave a boone,
That you will give them licence yet, to come and see you soone.
Then will they speake them selves, such english as they can,   375
I feare much better than I speake, that am an english man.
Lo now they take their leaves of you and of your dames,
Hereafter shal you see their face and know them by their names.

> *Then when they had taken their leaves the Actor did*
> *make an ende thus.*

And I your *Servidore, vibascio le mani,*   380
These words I learnt amongst them yet, although I learnte not many.

> *Haud ictus sapio.*

[70]   *Gascoignes wodmanship written to the L. Grey of wilton*[1] *uppon this occa-*
sion, the sayde L. Grey delighting (amongst many other good qualities) in
chusing of his winter deare, and killing the same with his bowe, did furnishe
master Gascoigne with a crossebowe cum Pertinencijs, and vouchsafed to
use his company in the said exercise, calling him one of his wodmen. Now
master Gascoigne shooting very often, could never hitte any deare, yea and
often times he let the heard passe by as though he had not seene them.
Whereat when this noble Lord tooke some pastime, and had often put him
in remembrance of his good skill in choosing, and redinesse in killing of a
winter deare, he thought good thus to excuse it in verse.

M Y worthy Lord, I pray you wonder not
   To see your wodman shoote so ofte awrie,
Nor that he stands amased like a sot,
And lets the harmlesse deare (unhurt) go by.
Or if he strike a doe which is but carren,   5
Laugh not good Lord, but favoure such a fault,
Take well in worth, he wold faine hit the barren,
But though his harte be good, his happe is naught:
And therefore now I crave your Lordships leave,
To tell you playne what is the cause of this: 10
First if it please your honour to perceive,
What makes your wodman shoote so ofte amisse,
Beleeve me *L.* the case is nothing strange,
He shootes awrie almost at every marke,
His eyes have bene so used for to raunge,   15
That now God knowes they be both dimme and darke.
For proofe he beares the note of follie nowe,
Who shotte sometimes to hit Philosophie,
And aske you why? forsooth I make avow,
Bycause his wanton wittes went all awrie.   20

Next that, he shot to be a man of lawe,
And spent some time with learned Litleton,
Yet in the end, he proved but a dawe,
For lawe was darke and he had quickly done.
Then could he wish Fitzharbert such a braine,   25
As *Tully* had, to write the law by arte,
So that with pleasure, or with litle paine,
He might perhaps, have caught a trewants parte.
But all to late, he most mislikte the thing,
Which most might helpe to guide his arrow streight,   30
He winked wrong, and so let slippe the string,
Which cast him wide, for all his queint conceit.
From thence he shotte to catch a courtly grace,
And thought even there to wield the world at will,
But out alas he much mistooke the place,   35
And shot awrie at every rover still.
The blasing baits which drawe the gazing eye,
Unfethered there his first affection,
No wonder then although he shot awrie,
Wanting the fethers of discretion.   40
Yet more than them, the marks of dignitie,
He much mistooke and shot the wronger way,
Thinking the purse of prodigalitie,
Had bene best meane to purchase such a pray.
He thought the flattring face which fleareth still,   45
Had bene full fraught with all fidelitie,
And that such words as courtiers use at will,
Could not have varied from the veritie.
But when his bonet buttened[2] with gold,
His comelie cape begarded all with gay,   50
His bumbast hose, with linings manifold,
His knit silke stocks and all his queint aray,
Had pickt his purse of all the Peter pence,
Which might have paide for his promotion,
Then (all to late) he found that light expence,   55
Had quite quencht out the courts devotion.
So that since then the tast of miserie,
Hath bene alwayes full bitter in his bit,
And why? forsooth bicause he shot awrie,
Mistaking still the markes which others hit.   60
But now behold what marke the man doth find,
He shootes to be a souldier in his age,
Mistrusting all the vertues of the minde,
He trusts the power of his personage.
As though long limmes led by a lusty hart,   65

Might yet suffice to make him rich againe,
But flussing fraies have taught him such a parte,
That now he thinks[3] the warres yeld no such gaine.
And sure I feare, unlesse your lordship deigne,
To traine him yet into some better trade,   70
It will be long before he hit the veine,[4]
Whereby he may a richer man be made.
He cannot climbe as other catchers can,
To leade a charge before himselfe be led,
He cannot spoile the simple sakeles man,   75
Which is content[5] to feede him with his bread.
He cannot pinch the painefull souldiers pay,
And sheare him out his share in ragged sheetes,
He cannot stop to take a gredy pray
Upon his fellowes groveling in the streetes.   80
He cannot pull the spoile from such as pill,
And seeme full angrie at such foule offence,
Although the gayne content his greedie will,
Under the cloake of contrarie pretence:
And nowe adayes, the man that shootes not so,   85
Maye shoote amisse, even as your Woodman dothe:
But then you marvell why I lette them go,
And never shoote, but saye farewell forsooth:
Alas my Lorde, whyle I doe muze hereon,
And call to mynde my youthfull yeares myspente,   90
They give mee suche a boane to gnawe upon,
That all my senses are in silence pente.
My mynde is rapte in contemplation,
Wherein my dazeled eyes onely beholde,
The blacke houre of my constellation,   95
Whyche framed mee so lucklesse on the molde:
Yet therewithall I can not but confesse,
That vayne presumption makes my heart to swell,
For thus I thinke, not all the worlde (I guesse,)
Shootes bet than I, nay some shootes not so well.   100
In *Aristotle* somewhat did I learne,
To guyde my manners all by comelynesse,
And *Tullie* taught me somewhat to discerne
Betweene sweete speeche and barbarous rudenesse.
Olde *Parkyns, Rastall,* and *Dan Bractens* bookes,   105
Did lende mee somewhat of the lawlesse Lawe,
The craftie Courtyers with their guylefull lookes,
Muste needes put some experience in my mawe:
Yet can not these with manye maystries[6] mo,

Make me shoote streyght at any gaynfull pricke,[7]   110
Where some that never handled such a bow,
Can hit the white, or touch it neare the quicke,
Who can nor speake, nor write in pleasant wise,
Nor leade their life by *Aristotles* rule,
Nor argue well on questions that arise,[8]   115
Nor pleade a case more than my Lord Maiors mule,
Yet can they hit the marks that I do misse,
And winne the meane which may the man mainteine,
Nowe when my mynde dothe mumble upon this,
No wonder then although I pyne for payne: 120
And whyles myne eyes beholde this mirroure thus,
The hearde goeth by, and farewell gentle does:
So that your lordship quickely may discusse
What blyndes myne eyes so ofte (as I suppose.)
But since my Muse can to my Lorde reherse   125
What makes me misse, and why I doe not shoote,
Let me imagine in this woorthlesse verse:
If right before mee, at my standings foote
There stoode a Doe, and I shoulde strike hir deade,
And then shee prove a carrion carkas too,   130
What figure might I fynde within my head,
To scuse the rage whiche rulde mee so to doo?
Some myghte interprete by playne paraphrase,
That lacke of skill or fortune ledde the chaunce,
But I muste otherwyse expounde the case,   135
I saye *Jehova* did this Doe advaunce,
And made hir bolde to stande before mee so,
Till I had thrust myne arrowe to hir harte,
That by the sodaine of hir overthrowe,
I myght endevour to amende my parte,   140
And turne myne eyes that they no more beholde,
Suche guylefull markes as seeme more than they be:
And though they glister outwardely lyke golde,
Are inwardly but brasse, as men may see:
And when I see the milke hang in hir teate,   145
Me thinkes it sayth, olde babe nowe learne to sucke,
Who in thy youthe couldst never learne the feate
To hitte the whytes whiche live with all good lucke.
Thus have I tolde my Lorde, (God graunt in season)
A tedious tale in rime, but little reason.   150

             Haud ictus sapio.

[71] *Gascoignes gardnings, whereof were written in one end of a close walke*
      which he hath in his Garden, this discourse following.

> THe figure of this world I can compare,
>   To Garden plots, and such like pleasaunt places,
> The world breedes men of sundry shape and share,
> As herbes in gardens, grow of sundry graces:
> Some good, some bad, some amiable faces,   5
> Some foule, some gentle, some of froward mind,
> Subject like bloome, to blast of every wind.
>
> And as you see the floures most fresh[1] of hew,
> That they prove not alwayes the holsomest,
> So fairest men are not alwayes found true: 10
> But even as withred weedes fall from the rest,
> So flatterers fall naked from their neast:
> When truth hath tried, their painting tising tale,
> They loose their glosse, and all their jests seeme stale.
>
> Yet some do present pleasure most esteeme,   15
> Till beames of braverie wither all their welth,
> And some againe there be can rightly deeme,
> Those herbes for best, which may mainteine their helth.
> Considering well, that age drawes on by stelth,
> And when the fairest floure is shronke and gone,   20
> A well growne roote, will stand and shifte for one.
>
> Then thus the restlesse life which men here leade,
> May be resembled to the tender plant,
> In spring it sprouts, as babes in cradle breede,
> Florish in May, like youthes that wisdome want,   25
> In Autumne ripes and rootes, least store waxe skante
> In winter shrinks and shrowdes from every blast,
> Like crooked age when lusty youth is past.
>
> And as the grounde or grasse whereon it grewe,[2]
> Was fatte or leane, even so by it appeares,   30
> If barreyn soyle, why then it chaungeth hewe,
> It fadeth faste, it flits to fumbling yeares,
> But if he gathered roote amongst his feeres,
> And lyght on lande that was well muckte in deede,
> Then standes it still, or leaves increase of seede.   35
>
> As for the reste, fall sundrye wayes (God wote)
> Some faynt lyke froathe at every little puffe,
> Some smarte by swoorde, lyke herbes that serve the pot,

And some be weeded from the fyner stuffe,
Some stande by proppes to maynteyne all their ruffe: 40
And thus under correction (bee it tolde)
Hath *Gascoigne* gathered in his Garden[3] molde.
    Haud ictus sapio.

[72] *In that other ende of his sayde close walke, were written these toyes*
in ryme.

IF any floure that here[1] is growne,
    Or any herbe maye ease youre payne,
Take and accompte it as your owne,
But recompence the lyke agayne:
For some and some is honeste playe,   5
And so my wyfe taughte me to saye.

If here to walke you take delyght,
Why come, and welcome when you will:
If I bidde you suppe here this nyght,
Bidde me an other tyme, and still   10
Thynke some and some is honest playe,
For so my wyfe taughte me to saye.

Thus if you suppe or dine with mee,
If you walke here, or sitte at ease,
If you desire the thing you see,   15
And have the same your mynde to please,
Thinke some and some is honest playe,
And so my wyfe taught me to saye.
    Haud ictus sapio.

[73]   *In a chayre in the same Garden was written this followyng.*

IF thou sitte here to viewe this pleasant garden place,
    Think thus: at last will come a frost, & al these floures deface.
But if thou sitte at ease to rest thy wearie bones,
Remember death brings finall rest to all oure greevous grones.
So whether for delyght, or here thou sitte for ease,   5
Thinke still upon the latter day, so shalt thou God best please.
    Haud ictus sapio.

Upon a stone in the wall of his Garden he had written the yeare wherein he
did the coste of these devises, and therwithall this
poesie in Latine.

Quoniam etiam humiliatos, amoena
delectant.

[74] *Gascoignes voyage into* Hollande, An. *1572. written to the ryghte*
honourable the Lorde Grey of Wilton.

A Straunge conceyte, a vayne of newe delight,
  Twixte weale and woe, twixte joy and bitter griefe,
Hath pricked foorthe my hastie penne to write
This worthlesse verse in hazarde of repreefe:
And to myne *Alderlievest* Lorde I must endite   5
A wofull case, a chippe of sorie chaunce,
A tipe of heaven, a lively hew of hell,
A feare to fall, a hope of high advance,
A life, a death, a drearie tale to tell
But since I know the pith of my pastaunce   10
Shall most consist in telling of a truth,
Vouchsafe my Lord (*en bon gré*) for to take
This trustie tale the storie of my youth,
This Chronicle which of my selfe I make,
To shew my Lord what healplesse happe ensewth,   15
When heddy youth will gad without a guide,
And raunge untide in leas of libertie,
Or when bare neede a starting hole hath spide
To peepe abroade from mother Miserie,
And buildeth Castels in the Welkin wide,   20
In hope thereby to dwell with wealth and ease.
But he the Lord (whome my good Lord doth know)
Can bind or lose, as best to him shall please,
Can save or spill, raise up or overthrowe,
Can gauld with griefe, and yet the payne appease.   25
Which thing to prove if so my L. take time,
(When greater cares his head shall not possesse)
To sitte and reade this raunging ragged rime,
I doubt not then but that he will confesse,
What falles I found when last I leapt to clime.   30
In March it was, that cannot I forget,
In this last March, upon the nintenth day,
When from Gravesend in boate I gan to jette
To boord our shippe in *Quinborough* that lay,
From whence the very twentith day we set   35
Our sayles abrode to slice the Salt sea fome,
And ancors weyde gan trust the trustlesse floud:
That day and night amid the waves we rome
To seeke the coast of *Holland* where it stoode.
And on the next when we were farre from home,   40
And neare the haven whereto we¹ sought to sayle,
A ferly chaunce: (whereon alone to thinke)

My hande nowe quakes, and all my senses fayle)
Gan us befall: the *Pylot* gan to shrinke,
And all agaste his courage seemde to quayle.   45
Whereat amazed, the Maister and his mate
Gan aske the cause of his so sodeyne chaunge.
And from alofte the Stewarde of our state,
(The sounding plumbe) in haste poste hast must raunge,
To trye the depth and goodnesse of oure gate.   50
Mee thinkes (even yet) I heare his heavie voyce,
Fadome three, foure, foote more, foote lesse, that cryde:
Mee thinkes I heare the fearefull whispring noyse,
Of suche as sayde full softely (me besyde)
God graunte this journey cause us to rejoyce.   55
When I poore soule, whiche close in caban laye,
And there had reacht till gaule was welneare burste,
With giddie head, my stumbling steppes must stay
To looke abroade as boldly as I durste.
And whyles I hearken what the Saylers saye,   60
The sonder sings, fadome two full no more.
Aloofe, aloofe, then cryed the maister out,
The Stearesmate strives to sende us from the shore,
And trustes the streame, whereof wee earst had doubt.
Tweene two extremes thus were we tossed sore,   65
And wente to *Hull*: untill we leyzure had
To talke at large, and eke to knowe the cause
What moode had made our *Pylot* looke so sad.
At laste the Dutche with butterbitten jawes,
(For so he was a Dutche, a devill, a swadde,   70
A foole, a drunkarde, or a traytour tone)
Gan aunswere thus: *Ghy zijt te vroegh* here come,
Tis niet goet tijt: and standing all alone,
Gan preache to us, whiche fooles were all and some
To truste him foole, in whome there skill was none.   75
Or what knewe wee if *Albaes* subtill brayne
(So to prevent our enterprise by treazon)
Had him subornde to tice us to this traine
And so him selfe (*per Companye* and seazon)
For spite, for hate, or else for hope of gayne.   80
This must we thinke that *Alba* would not spare
To give out gold for such a sinfull deede:
And glistring gold can oftentimes ensnare,
More perfect witts than *Holland* soyle doth breede.
But let that passe, and let us now compare   85
Our owne fond fact with this his foule offence.
We knew him not, nor where he wond that time,

Nor if he had *Pylots* experience,
Or *Pylats* crafte, to cleare him selfe from cryme.
Yea more than[2] that (how voyde were we of sense)   90
We had small smacke of any tale he tolde,
He powrde out Dutch to drowne us all in drinke,
And we (wise men) uppon his words were bolde,
To runne on head: but let me now bethinke
The masters speech: and let me so unfold   95
The depth of all this folish oversight.
The master spake even like a skilfull man,
And sayde I sayle the Seas both day and night,
I know the tides as well as other can,
From pole to pole I can the courses plight.   100
I know France, Spayne, Greece, Denmarke, Dansk[3] and all,
Frize, Flaunders, Holland, every coast I know,
But truth to tell, it seldome doth befall,
That English merchants ever bend their bowe
To shoote at *Breyll,* where now our flight should fall,   105
They send their shafts farder for greater gayne.
So that this haven is yet (quoth he) unkouth,
And God graunt now that England may attayne
Such gaines by *Breyll,* (a gospell on that mouth)
As is desired: thus spake the master playne.   110
And since (saide he) my selfe knew not the sowne,
How could I well a better *Pylot* fynde,
Than this (which first) dyd saye he dwelt in towne,
And knewe the way where ever sat the wynde?
While we thus talke, all sayles are taken downe,   115
And we to *Hull* (as earst I sayd) gan wend,
Tyll full two houres and somewhat more were past,
Our guyde then spake in Dutch and bad us bend
All sayles againe: for now quod he (at last)
Die tijt is goet, dat heb ick weell bekend.   120
Why staye I long to ende a wofull tale?
We trust his Dutch, and up the foresayle goes,
We fall on knees amyd the happy gale,
(Which by gods wyll full kynd and calmely blowes)
And unto him we there unfolde our bale,   125
Wheron to thinke I wryte and weepe for joye,
That pleasant song the hundreth and seventh psalme,
There dyd we reade to comfort ouer annoye,
Which to my soule (me thought) was sweet as balme,
Yea farre more sweet than any worldly toye.   130
And when we had with prayers praysd the Lord
Our *Edell Bloetts,* gan fall to eate and drynke,

And for their sauce, at takyng up the borde
The shippe so strake (as all we thought to sinke)
Against the grounde, then all with one accorde   135
We fell agayne on knees to pray apace,
And therewithall even at the seconde blowe,
(The number cannot from my mynde outpace)
Our helme strake of, and we must fleete and flowe.
Where winde and waves would guide us by their grace.   140
The winde waxt calme as I have saide before,
(O mightie God so didst thou swage our woes)
The selly shyppe was sowst and smytten sore,
With counter buffetts, blowes and double blowes.
At last the keele which might endure no more,   145
Gan rende in twayne and suckt the water in:
Then might you see pale lookes and wofull cheare,
Then might you heare loude cryes and deadly dinne:
Well noble minds in perils best appeare,
And boldest harts in bale will never blinne.   150
For there were some (of whome I will not say
That I was one) which never changed hew,
But pumpt apace, and labord every way
To save themselves, and all their lovely crew,
Which cast the best fraight overboorde awaye,   155
Both corne and cloth, and all that was of weight,
Which halde and pulde at every helping corde,
Which prayed to God and made their conscience streight.
As for my self: I here protest my Lorde,
My words were these: O God in heaven on height,   160
Behold me not as now a wycked wyght,
A sacke of sinne, a wretch ywrapt in wroth,
Let no fault past (O Lord) offende thy sight,
But weye my will which now those faults doth lothe,
And of thy mercy pittie this our plight.   165
Even thou good God which of thy grace didst saye
That for one good, thou wouldst all *Sodome* save,
Behold us all: thy shyning beames displaye,
Some here (I trust) thy goodnesse shall engrave,
To be chast vessells unto thee alwaye,   170
And so to live in honour of thy name:
Beleve me Lord, thus to the Lord I sayde.
But there were some (alas the more their blame)
Which in the pumpe their onely comforte layde,
And trusted that to turne our griefe to game.   175
Alas (quod I) our pumpe good God must be
Our sayle, our sterne, our tackling, and our trust.

Some other cryed to cleare the shipboate free,
To save the chiefe and leave the rest in dust.
Which word once spoke (a wondrous thing to see)   180
All hast post hast, was made to have it done:
And up it commes in hast much more than speede.
There did I see a woful worke begonne,
Which now (even now) doth make my hart to bleede.
Some made such hast that in the boate they wonne,   185
Before it was above the hatches brought.
Straunge tale to tell, what hast some men shall make
To find their death before the same be sought.
Some twixt the boate and shippe their bane do take,
Both drownd and slayne with braynes for hast crusht out.   190
At last the boate halfe fraighted in the aire
Is hoyst aloft, and on the seas downe set,
When I that yet in God could not despaire,
Still plide the pumpe, and patiently did let
All such take boate as thither made repaire.   195
And herewithall I safely may protest
I might have woonne the boate as well as one,
And had that seemd a safetie for the rest
I should percase even with the first have gone,
But when I saw the boate was over prest   200
And pestred full with moe than it might beare,
And therewithall with cherefull looke might see
My chiefe companions whome I held most deare
(Whose companie had thither trained me)
Abiding still aboord our shippe yfeare: 205
Nay then (quoth I) good God thy will be done,
For with my feeres I will both live and dye.
And eare the boate farre from our sight was gon
The wave so wrought, that they which thought to flee
And so to scape, with waves were overronne.   210
Lo how he strives in vayne that strives with God,
For there we lost the flowre of the band,
And of our crew full twenty soules and odde,
The Sea sucks up, whiles we on hatches stand
In smarting feare to feele that selfe same rodde.   215
Well on (as yet) our battred barke did passe,
And brought the rest within a myle of lande,
Then thought I sure now neede not I to passe,
For I can swymme and so escape this sande.
Thus dyd I deeme all carelesse like an Asse,   220
When sodaynely the wynde our foresayle tooke,
And turned about and brought us eft to Seas.

Then cryed we all cast out the ancor hooke,
And here let byde, such helpe as god may please:
Which ancor cast, we soone the same forsooke,   225
And cut it off, for feare least there upon
Our shippe should bowge, then callde we fast for fire,
And so dischargde our great gunnes everychone,
To warne the towne therby of our desire:
But all in vayne, for succor sent they none.   230
At last a *Hoye* from Sea came flynging fast,
And towards us helde course as streight as lyne.
Then myght you see our hands to heaven up cast
To render thanks unto the power devine,
That so vouchsafte to save us yet at last: 235
But when this *Hoye* gan (welneere) boorde our barke,
And might perceive what peryll we were in,
It turnd away and left us still in carke,
This tale is true (for now to lye were sin)
It lefte us there in dreade and daungers darke.   240
It lefte us so, and that within the sight
And hearing both of all the peare at *Bryll*.
Now ply thee pen, and paint the foule despite
Of drunken Dutchmen standing there even still,
For whome we came in their cause for to fight,   245
For whom we came their state for to defende,
For whom we came as friends to grieve their foes,
They now disdaynd (in this distresse) to lend
One helping boate for to asswage our woes,
They sawe our harmes the which they would not mend,   250
And had not bene that God even then did rayse
Some instruments to succor us at neede,
We had bene sunk and swallowed all in Seas.
But gods will was (in waye of our good spede)
That on the peare (lamenting our mysease)   255
Some englishe were, whose naked swordes did force
The drunken dutch, the cankred churles to come,
And so at last (not moved by remorce,
But forst by[4] feare) they sent us succor some:
Some must I say: and for to tell the course,   260
They sent us succor saust with sowre despyte,
They saved our lives and spoylde us of the rest,
They stale our goods by day and eke by night,
They shewed the worst and closely kept the best.
And in this time (this treason must I wryte)   265
Our *Pylot* fled, but how? not emptie handed:

He fled from us, and with him did conveye
A *Hoy* full fraught (whiles we meane while were landed)
With pouder, shotte, and all our best araye:
This skill he had, for all he set us sanded.   270
And now my Lord, declare your noble mynde,
Was this a *Pylot,* or a *Pilate* judge?
Or rather was he not of *Judas* kynde:
Which left us thus and close away could trudge?
Wel, at the *Bryell* to tell you what we fynde,   275
The Governour was all bedewed with drinke,
His trulls and he were all layde downe to sleepe,
And we must shift, and of our selves must thinke
What meane was best, and how we best might keepe
That yet remaynd: the rest was close in clynke.   280
Wel, on our knees with trickling teares of joye,
We gave God thanks: and as we might, did learne
What might be⁵ founde in every pynke and hoye.
And thus my Lord, your honour may descerne
Our perills past, and how in our anoye   285
God saved me your Lordshippes bound for ever,
Who else should not be able now to tell,
The state wherin this countrey doth persever,
Ne how they seeme in carelesse mindes to dwell,
(So dyd they earst and so they will do ever)   290
And to my Lord for to bewray my mynde
Me thinkes they be a race of Bulbeefe borne,
Whose hartes their *Butter* mollyfyeth by kinde,
And so the force of beefe is cleane outworne:
As eke their braynes with double beere are lynde: 295
So that they march bumbast with butterd beare,
Like soppes of Browesse puffed up with froth,
Where inwardly they be but hollow geare,
As weake as wynde, which with one puffe⁶ up goeth.
And yet they bragge and thinke they have no peare,   300
Bycause *Harlem* hath hetherto helde out.
Although in dede (as they have suffred *Spayne*)
The ende therof even now doth rest in doubt.
Well as for that, let it (for me) remayne
In God his hands, whose hand hath brought me out,   305
To tell my Lord this tale now tane in hand,
As how they traine their treasons all in drinke,
And when themselves for dronk can scarcely stand,
Yet sucke out secretes (as themselves do thinke)
From guests, the best (almost) in all their lande,   310

(I name no man, for that were brode before)
Will (as men say) enure the same sometime,
But surely this (or I mistake him sore)
Or else he can (but let it passe in rime)
Dissemble deepe, and mocke sometimes the more.   315
Well, drunkenesse is here good companye,
And therewithall *per consequence* it falles,
That whoredome is accoumpted Jollytie:
A gentle state, where two such Tenisballes
Are tossed still and better boules let lye.   320
I cannot herewith from my Lord conceale,
How *God* and *Mammon* here do dwell yfeare,
And how the *Masse* is cloked under veale
Of pollicie, till all the coast be cleare:
Ne can I chuse, but I must ring a peale,   325
To tell what hypocrytes the Nunnes here be:
And how the olde Nunnes be content to go,
Before a man in streetes like mother B,
Untill they come whereas there dwells a *Ho,*
(*Re*: ceive that halfe and let the rest go free)   330
There can they poynt with fynger as they passe,
Yea sir sometimes they can come in themselfe,
To strike the bargaine twene a wanton lasse,
And *Edel Bloetts*: now is not this good pelfe?
As for the yong Nunnes, they be bright as glasse,   335
And chast forsothe: *met v*: and *anders niet,*
What sayd I? what? that is a mysterie,
I may no verse of such a theame endyte,
Yong *Rouland Yorke* may tell it bette than I,
Yet to my Lord this litle will I write,   340
That though I have (my selfe) no skill at all,
To take the countnance of a *Colonell,*
Had I a good *Lieuetenant generall,*
As good *John Zuche* wherever that he dwell,
Or else *Ned Dennye,* (faire mought him befall,)   345
I could have brought a noble regiment,
Of smoogskind Nunnes into my countrey soyle,
But farewell they as things impertinent,
Let them (for me) go dwell with master *Moyle*
Who hath behight to place them well in kent.   350
And I shall well my seelly selfe content,
To come alone unto my lovely Lorde,
And unto him (when riming sport is spent)
To tell some sadde and reasonable worde,

Of *Hollands* state, the which I will present,   355
In Cartes, in Mappes, and eke in Modells made,
If God of heaven my purpose not prevent.
And in meane while although my wittes do wade
In rangyng ryme, and flyng some folly forth,
I trust my Lord wyll take it yet in worth.   360
                    Haud Ictus sapio.

*And nowe to recomfort you and to ende this worke, receyve the delectable
historie of sundry adventures passed by Dan Bartholmew
of Bathe, reade it and judge of it.*

[1]   *The Reporter.*

TO tell a tale without authoritye,
    Or fayne a Fable by invention,
That one proceedes of quicke capacitye,
That other proves but small discretion,
Yet have both one and other oft bene done.   5
And if I were a Poet as some be,
You might perhappes heare some such tale of me.

    But for I fynde my feeble skyll to faynte,[1]
To faine in figures as the learned can,
And yet my tongue is tyed by due constrainte,   10
To tell nothing but truth of every man:
I will assaye even as I fyrst began,
To tell you now a tale and that of truth,
Which I my selfe sawe proved in my youth.

    I neede not seeke so farre in coastes abrode,   15
As some men do, which wryte strange historyes,
For whyles at home I made my chiefe[2] abode
And sawe our lovers playe their Tragedyes,
I founde enowe which seemed to suffice,
To set on worke farre finer wits than mine,   20
In painting out the pangs which make them pine.

    Amongst the rest I most remember one
Which was to me a deare familiar friend,
Whose doting dayes since they be past and gone,
And his anoy now come unto an end,   25
Although he seeme his angrie brow to bend,
I will be bold (by his leave) for to tell,
The restlesse state wherein[3] he long did dwell.

    Learned he was, and that became him best,
For though by birth he came of worthy race,   30
Yet beuty, birth, brave personage, and the rest,

In every choyce, must needes give learning place:
And as for him he had so hard a grace,
That by aspect he seemde a simple man,
And yet by learning much renowne he wan.   35

His name I hide, and yet for this discourse,
Let call his name *Dan Bartholmew of Bathe,*
Since in the end he thether had recourse,
And (as he said) did skamble there in skath:
In deede the rage which wroong him ther, was rathe,   40
As by this tale I thinke your selfe will gesse,
And then (with me) his lothsome life confesse.

For though he had in all his learned lore
Both redde good rules to bridle fantasie,
And all good authours taught him evermore,   45
To love the meane, and leave extremitie,
Yet kind had lent him such a qualitie,
That at the last he quite forgat his bookes,
And fastned fansie with the fairest lookes.

For proofe, when greene youth lept out of his eye   50
And left him now a man of middle age,
His happe was yet with wandring lookes to spie
A faire yong impe of proper personage,
Eke borne (as he) of honest parentage:
And truth to tell, my skill it cannot serve,   55
To praise hir bewtie as it did deserve.

First for hir head, the heares were not of gold,
But of some other metall farre more fine,
Whereof each crinet seemed to behold,
Like glistring wiers against the sunne that shine,   60
And therewithall the blazing of hir eyne,
Was like the beames of *Tytan,* truth to tell,
Which glads us all that in this world do dwell.

Uppon hir cheekes the lillie and the rose
Did entremeete, with equall chaunge of hew,   65
And in hir gifts no lacke I can suppose,
But that at last (alas) she was untrue.
Which flinging fault, bycause it is not new,
Nor seldome seene in kits of *Cressides* kind,
I mervaile not, nor beare it much in mind.   70

Dame Natures frutes, wherewith hir face was fraught,
Were so frost bitten with the cold of crafte,
That all (save such as *Cupides* snares had caught)

Might soone espie the fethers of his shafte:
But *Bartholmew* his wits had so bedaft,   75
That all seemd good which might of hir be gotten,
Although it proved no sooner ripe than rotten.

That mouth of hirs which seemde to flowe with mell,
In speech, in voyce, in tender touch, in tast,
That dympled chin wherein delight did dwell,   80
That ruddy lippe wherein was pleasure plast,
Those well shapt hands, fine armes and slender waste,
With all the gifts which gave hir any grace,
Were smiling baites which caught fond fooles apace.

Why strive I then to paint hir name with praise?   85
Since forme and frutes were found so farre unlike,
Since of hir cage Inconstance kept the keyes
And Change had cast hir honoure down in dike:
Since fickle kind in hir the stroke did strike,
I may no praise unto a knife bequeath,   90
With rust yfret, though painted be the sheath.

But since I must a name to hir assigne,
Let call hir now *Ferenda Natura*,
And if thereat she seeme for to repine,
No force at all, for hereof am I sure a,   95
That since hir pranks were for the most unpure a,
I can appoint hir well no better name,
Than this, wherein dame *Nature* beares the blame.

And thus I say, when *Bartholmew* had spent
His pride of youth (untide in links of love)   100
Behold how happe contrary to intent,
(Or destenies ordeined from above)
From which no wight on earth may wel remove)
Presented to his view this fierie dame,
To kindle coles where earst had bin no flame.   105

Whome when he sawe to shine in seemely grace,
And therewithall gan marke hir tender youth,
He thought not like, that under such a face
She could convey the treason of untruth:
Whereby he vowed, (alas the more his ruth)   110
To serve this Saint for terme of all his life,
Lo here both roote and rind of all his strife.

I cannot nowe in loving termes displaye
His suite, his service, nor his sorie fare:
His observaunces, nor his queynt aray,   115

His skalding sighes, nor yet his cooling care,
His wayting still to snatche himselfe in snare,
I can not write what was his sweetest soure,
For I my selfe was never paramoure.

But to conclude, muche worth in little writte,   120
The highest flying hauke will stoupe at laste,
The wyldest beast is drawne with hungrie bitte,
To eate a homely bayte sometymes in haste,
The pricke of kynde can never be unplaste,
And so it seemed by this dayntie dame,   125
Whome he at laste with labour did reclame.

And when he had with mickell payne procured
The calme consente of hir unweldie will,
When he had hir by faithe and trouth assured
To lyke him beste, and ay to love him still,   130
When fansie had of flatterie fedde his fill,
I not discerne to tell my tale aright,
What man but he had ever suche delight?

The lingring dayes he spente in trifling toyes,
To whette the tooles whiche carved his contente,   135
The poasting nightes he past in pleasing joyes,
Wearyng the webbe whiche love to him had lente:
In suche a pinfolde were his pleasures pent
That selde he coulde hir companie eschewe,
Or leave such lookes as might his lacke renewe.   140

But if by force he forced were to parte,
Then mighte you see howe fansie fedde his mynde,
Then all alone he muzed on his marte.
All companie seemd then (but hirs) unkind:
Then sent he tokens true love for to bind,   145
Then wrote he letters, lines and loving layes,
So to begyle his absent dolefull dayes.

And since I know as others eke can tell,
What skill he had, and how he could endite,
Me thinks I cannot better do than well   150
To set downe here, his ditties of delight,
For so at least I may my selfe acquite,
And vaunt to shew some verses yet unknowne,
Well worthy prayse though none of them mine owne.

No force for that, take you them as they be,   155
Since mine emprise is but to make report:
Imagine then before you that you see

A wight bewitcht in manie a subtile sorte,
A lover lodged in pleasures princely port,
Vaunting in verse what joyes he did possesse, 160
His triumpes here I thinke will shewe no lesse.

[2]   *Dan Bartholmew his Triumphes.*

R Esigne king *Pryams* sonnes, that princes were in *Troy,*
Resigne to me your happie dayes, and boast no more of joy:
Sir *Paris* first stand forth, make aunswere for thy pheare,
And if thou canst defend hir cause, whome *Troy* did bye so deare:
What? blush not man, be bold, although thou beare some blame, 5
Tell truth at last, and so be sure to save thy selfe from shame.
Then gentle Shepheard say: what madnesse did thee move
To choose of all the flowres in *Greece,* foule *Helene* for thy love?
Needes must I coumpt hir foule, whose first frutes wer forlorne
Although she solde hir second chaffe, above the price of corne. 10
Alas, she made of thee, a noddye for the nonce,
For *Menelaus* lost her twice, though thou hir foundst but once.
But yet if in thine eye, she seemd a peerelesse peece,
Aske *Theseus* y[t] mighty Duke, what towns she knew in Greece?
Aske him what made hir leave hir wofull aged sire, 15
And steale to *Athens* gyglot like: what? what but foule desire?
Alas pore *Paris* thou didst nothing else but gleane
The partched eares which he cast by, when he had reaped cleane:
He slivde the gentle Slippe, which could both twist and twind,
And growing left the broken braunch, for them that came behind. 20
Yet hast thou filld the worlde with brute, the more thy blame,
And saist, that *Hellens* bewty past each other stately dame.
For proofe thou canst alledge the tast of ten yeares warre,
And how hir blasing beames first brought both *Greece* & *Troy* to jarre:
No no, thou art deceivde, the drugs of foule despite 25
Did worke in *Menelaus* will, not losse of such delighte,
Not love but lothsome hate, not dolour but disdayne,
Did make him seeke a sharpe revenge, til both his foes wer slaine.
Thy brother *Troylus* eke, that gemme of gentle deedes,
To thinke how he abused was, alas my heart it bleedes: 30
He bet about the bush, whiles other caught the birds,
Whome craftie *Cresside* mockt to muche, yet fed him still with words.
And God he knoweth not I, who pluckt hir first sprong rose,
Since *Lollius* and *Chauser* both, make doubt uppon that glose.
But this I know too well, and he to farre it felt, 35
How *Diomede* undid his knots, and caught both brooch and belt,
And how she chose to change, and how she changed still,
And how she died leaper like, against hir lovers will.

Content you then good knights, your triumphe to resigne,
Confesse your starres both dimme and darke, wheras my sunne doth shine: 40
For this I dare avow, without vaunt be it told,
My derling is more faire than she, for whome proud *Troy* was solde.
More constant to conteine, than *Cresside* to be coy,
No *Calcas* can contrive the craft, to traine hir out of *Troy*,
No *Diomede* can draw hir settled hart to change,   45
No madding moode can move hir mind, nor make hir thoughts to range.
For hir alone it is, that *Cupide* blindfold goes,
And dare not looke for feare least he his libertie should loose:
At hir dame *Venus* chafes, and pines in jelowsie,
Least bloudy *Mars* should hir espie, and change his fantasie.   50
Of hir the Queene of Heaven doth stand in dreadfull doubte,
Least *Jove* should melt in drops of gold, if once he find hir out.
Oh that my tong had skill, to tell hir praise aright,
Or that my pen hir due deserts, in worthy verse could write:
Or that my mind could muse, or happie hart conceive,   55
Some words that might resound hir worth, by high *Minervas* leave.
Oh how the blooming joyes, do blossome in my brest,
To thinke within my secret thought, howe farre she steynes the rest.
Me thinks I heare hir speake, me thinks I see hir still,
Me thinks I feele hir feelingly, me thinks I know hir will.   60
Me thinks I see the states, which sue to hir for grace,
Me thinks I see one looke of hirs repulse them all apace.
Me thinks that houre is yet, and evermore shall be,
Wherein my happie happe was first, hir heavenly face to see:
Wherein I spide the writte, which woond betweene hir eyne,   65
And said behold, be bold, *for I, am borne to be but thine.*
Me thinks I feele the joyes, which never yet were[1] felt,
Whome flame before yet never toucht, me thinks I feele them melt.
One word & there an end: me thinks she is the sunne,
Which only shineth now a dayes, she dead, the world wer done.   70
The rest are twinckling starres, or Moones which borrow light
To comfort other carefull soules, which wander in the night.
And night God knowes it is, where other ladies be,
For sure my dame adornes the day, there is no sunne but she.
Then lovers by your leave, and thinke it nothing straunge   75
Although I seeme with calme content, in Seas of joyes to range:
For why, my sailes have found both wind and waves at will,
And depths of all delights in hir, with whome I travell still
And ancors being wayed, I leave you all at large,
To steare this seemely Shippe my selfe, suche is my mistresse charge.   80

Fato non fortuna.

The Reporter.[1]

T Hese vaunting verses with a many mo,
  (To his mishap) have come unto my hands,
Whereof the rest (bycause he sayled so
In braggers boate which set it selfe on sands,
And brought him eke fast bounde in follyes bands)   5
Of curtesye I keepe them from your sight,
Let these suffice which of my selfe I wryte.

The highest tree that ever yet coulde growe,
Although full fayre it florysht for a season,
Founde yet at last some fall to bring it lowe,   10
This olde sayd sawe is (God he knoweth) not geason:[2]
For when things passe the reache and bounds of reason
They fall at last, although they stande a time,
And bruse the more, the higher that they clyme.

So *Bartholmew* unto his payne dyd prove,   15
For when he thought his happe to be most hie,
And that he onely reapt the frutes of love,
And that he swelt in all prosperitie,
His comforte chaunged to calamitie:
And though I do him wrong to tell the same,   20
Yet reade it you, and let me beare the blame.

The Saint he serv'd became a craftie devill,
His goddesse to an Idoll seemed to chaunge,
Thus all his good transformed into evill,
And every joy to raging griefe did raunge: 25
Which *Metamorphosis* was mervells straunge:
Yet shall you seldome otherwyse it prove,
Where wicked Lust doth beare the name of Love.

This sodayne chaunge when he began to spye,
And cold suspect into his mynde had crept,   30
He bounst and bet his head tormentingly,
And from all companye himselfe he kept,
Whereby so farre in stormes of strife he stept,
That nowe he seemed an Image not a man,
His eyes so dead, his colour waxt so wan.   35

And I which alwayes bare him great good will,
(Although I knew the cause of all his griefe,
And what had traynde and tysed him theretyll,
And playne to speake, what moved his myschiefe,
Yet since I sought to ease him with releife:)   40
I did become importunate to knowe,
The secrete cause wheron this grudge shuld growe.

At last with much ado, his trembling tong
Bewrayde theffect of his unwylling will,
Which here to tell since it were all to long,   45
And I therewith too barren am of skyll,
And trouble you with tedyous tydings styll,
Content you nowe to heare himselfe rehearse,
His strange affects in his lamenting verse.

Which verse he wrote at *Bathe* (as earst was sayd)   50
And there I saw him when he wrote the same,
I sawe him there with many moanes dysmayde,
I sawe him there both fryse and flashe in flame,
I saw him greev'd when others made good game:
And so appeareth by his darke discourse,   55
The which to reade I crave your just remorse.

[3]   *Dan Bartholmews Dolorous discourses.*[1]

I Have entreated care to cut the thred
  Which all to long hath held my lingring life,
And here aloofe now have I hid my head,
From companie, thereby to stint my strife.
This solitarie place doth please me best,   5
Where I may weare my willing mind with mone,
And where the sighes which boyle out of my brest,
May skald my heart, and yet the cause unknowne.
All this I do, for thee my sweetest sowre,
For whome (of yore) I counted not of care,   10
For whome with hungrie jawes I did devoure
The secret baite which lurked in the snare:
For whome I thought all forreine pleasures payne,
For whome againe, all paine did pleasure seeme,
But only thine, I found all fansies[2] vayne,   15
But onely thine, I did no dolours deeme.
Such was the rage, that whylome did possesse
The privie corners of my mazed mind:
When hote desire, did coumpt those torments lesse
Which gaind the gaze that did my fredome bind.   20
And now (with care) I can record those dayes,
And call to mind the quiet life I led
Before I first beheld thy golden rayes,
When thine untruth yet troubled not my hed.
Remember thou, as I cannot forget,   25
How I had layd, both love, and lust aside,
And how I had my fixed fancie set,
In constant vow, for ever to abide.

The bitter proofe of pangs in pleasure past,
The costly tast, of hony mixt with gall: 30
The painted heaven, which turnde to hell at last
The freedome faind, which brought me but to thrall.
The lingring sute, well fed with fresh delayes.
The wasted vowes which fled with every winde:
The restlesse nights, to purchase pleasing dayes,   35
The toyling dayes to please my restlesse minde.
All these (with mo) had brused so my brest,
And graft such griefe within my gronyng heart,
That I had left dame fansie and the rest
To greener yeares, which might endure the smart.   40
My wearie bones did beare away the skarres,
Of many a wounde, receyved by disdayne:
So that I founde the fruite of all those warres,
To be naught else but pangs of unknowne payne.
And now myne eyes were shut from such delight,   45
My fansie faynt, my hote desires were colde,
When cruell hap, presented to my sight,
Thy maydens face, in yeares which were not olde.
I thinke the goddesse of revenge devysde,
So to be wreackt on my rebelling will,   50
Bycause I had in youthfull yeares dispysde,
To taste the baytes, which tyste my fansie still.
How so it were, God knowes, I cannot tell:
But if I lye, you heavens, the plague be myne,
I sawe no sooner, how delight did dwell   55
Betweene those lytle infants eyes of thine,
But streight a sparckling cole of quicke desire,
Did kyndle flame within my frozen heart,
And yelding fansie softly blewe the fire,
Which since hath bene the cause of all my smart.   60
What neede I say? thy selfe for me can sweare,
How much I tendred thee in tender yeares:
Thy life was then to me (God knowes) full deare,
My life to thee is light, as nowe appeares.
I loved thee first, and shall do to my laste,   65
Thou flattredst first, and so thou woldst do still:
For love of thee full many paynes I past,
For deadly hate thou seekest me to kyll.
I cannot now, with manly tongue rehearse,
How soone that melting mind of thine did yelde,   70
I shame to write, in this waymenting verse,
With how small fight, I vanquisht thee in fielde:
But *Cesar* he, which all the world subdude,

Was never yet so proude of Victorye,
Nor *Hanyball,* with martiall feates endude,   75
Did so much please himselfe in pollicie,
As I (poore I) did seeme to triumphe then,
When first I got the Bulwarks of thy brest,
With hote Alarmes I comforted my men,
In formost ranke I stoode before the rest,   80
And shooke my flagge, not all to shewe my force,
But that thou mightst thereby perceive my minde:
Askaunces lo, now coulde I kyll thy corce,
And yet my life, is unto thee resinde.
Well let them passe, and think upon the joye,   85
The mutuall love, the confidence, the trust,
Whereby we both abandoned annoye,
And fed our mindes with fruites of lovely lust.
Thinke on the Tythe, of kysses got by stealth,
Of sweete embracings shortened by feare,   90
Remember that which did mainteine our health,
Alas, alas why should I name it here.
And in the mydst of all those happie dayes,
Do not forget the chaunges of my chaunce,
When in the depth of many wayward wayes,   95
I onely sought, what might thy state advaunce.
Thou must confesse, how much I carde for thee,
When of my selfe, I carde not for my selfe,
And when my hap was in mishappes to be,
Esteemd thee more, than all the worldly pelfe.   100
Myne absent thoughts did beate on thee alone,
When thou hadst found a fond and newfound choyce:
For lacke of thee I sunke in endlesse mone,
When thou in chaunge didst tumble and rejoyce.
O mightie goddes needes must I honour you,   105
Needes must I judge your judgements to be just,
Bycause she did forsake him that was true,
And with false love, did cloke a fayned luste.
By high decrees, you ordeyned the chaunge,
To light on such, as she must nedes myslike,   110
A meete reward for suche as seeke to raunge,
When fansies force, their feeble fleshe doth strike.
But did I then give bridle to thy fall,
Thou hedstrong thou, accuse me if thou can?
Did I not hazard love yea life and all,   115
To ward thy will, from that unworthy man?
And when by toyle I travailed to fynde,
The secrete causes of thy madding moode,

I founde naught else but tricks of *Cressides* kynde,
Which plainly provde, that thou weart of hir bloud. 120
I founde that absent *Troylus* was forgot,
When *Dyomede* had got both brooche and belt,
Both glove and hand, yea hart and all god wot,
When absent *Troylus* did in sorrowes swelt.
These tricks (with mo) thou knowest thy self I found, 125
Which now are nedelesse heere for to reherse,
Unlesse it were to touche a tender wound,
With corosives my panting heart to perce.
But as that Hound is counted lytle worthe,
Which giveth over for a losse or twayne, 130
And cannot finde the meanes to single forth,
The stricken Deare which doth in heard remayne:
Or as the kindly Spanyell which hath sprong
The prety partriche, for the Falcons flight,
Doth never spare but thrusts the thornes among, 135
To bring this byrde yet once againe to sight,
And though he knowe by proofe (yea dearely bought)
That, selde or never, for his owne avayle,
This wearie worke of his in vaine is wrought,
Yet spares he not but labors tooth and nayle. 140
So labord I to save thy wandring shippe,
Which recklesse then, was running on the rockes,
And though I saw thee seeme to hang the lyppe.
And set my great good will, as light as flockes:
Yet hauld I in, the mayne sheate of thy mynde, 145
And stayed thy course by ancors of advyce,
I woon thy will into a better wynde,
To save thy ware, which was of precious price.
And when I had so harbored thy Barke,
In happy haven, which saufer was than Dover, 150
The *Admyrall*, which knewe it by the marke,
Streight challengd all, and said thou weart a rover:
Then was I forst in thy behalfe to pleade,
Yea so I did, the judge can say no lesse,
And whyles in toyle, this lothsome life I leade, 155
Camest thou thy selfe the fault for to confesse,
And downe on knee before thy cruell foe,
Didst pardon crave, accusing me for all,
And saydst I was the cause, that thou didst so,
And that I spoon the thred of all thy thrall. 160
Not so content, thou furthermore didst sweare
That of thy selfe thou never ment to swerve,
For proofe wherof thou didst the colours weare,

Which might bewray, what saint y^u ment to serve.
And that thy blood was sacrificed eke,   165
To manyfest thy stedfast martyrd mynde,
Till I perforce, constraynde thee for to seeke,
These raging seas, adventures there to finde.
Alas, alas, and out alas for me,
Who am enforced, thus for to repeate   170
The false reports and cloked guyles of thee,
Whereon (to oft) my restlesse thoughts do beate.
But thus it was, and thus God knowes it is.
Which when I founde by playne and perfect proofe,
My musing minde then thought it not amisse,   175
To shrinke aside, lamenting all aloofe,
And so to beate my simple shiftlesse brayne,
For some device, that might redeeme thy state,
Lo here the cause, for why I take this payne,
Lo how I love the wight which me doth hate: 180
Lo thus I lye, and restlesse rest in Bathe,
Whereas I bathe not now in blisse pardie,
But boyle in Bale and skamble thus in skathe,
Bycause I thinke on thine unconstancie.
And wilt thou know, how here I spend my time,   185
And how I drawe my dayes in dolours still?
Then stay a while: give eare unto my rime,
So shalt thou know the weight of all my will.
When *Titan* is constrayned to forsake,
His lemans couche, and clymeth to his carte,   190
Then I begin to languishe for thy sake,
And with a sigh, which may bewray my smarte,
I cleare mine eyes whom gumme of teares had glewed,
And up on foote I set my ghostlike corse,
And when the stonie walls have oft renewed   195
My pittious plaintes, with *Ecchoes* of remorce,
Then doe I cry and call upon thy name,
And thus I say, thou curst and cruell bothe,
Beholde the man, which taketh griefe for game,
And loveth them, which most his name doth loth.   200
Behold the man which ever truely ment,
And yet accusd as author of thine yll,
Beholde the man, which all his life hath spent,
To serve thy selfe, and aye to worke thy will:
Beholde the man, which onely for thy love,   205
Did love him selfe, whome else he set but light:
Beholde the man, whose blood (for thy behove)
Was ever prest to shed it selfe outright.

And canst thou nowe condemne his loyaltie?
And canst thou crafte to flatter such a friend?   210
And canst thou see him sincke in jeoperdie?
And canst thou seeke to bring his life to ende?
Is this the right reward for suche desart?
Is this the fruite of seede so timely sowne?
Is this the price, appoynted for his part?   215
Shall truth be thus by treason overthrowne?
Then farewell faithe, thou art no womans pheare:
And with that word I stay my tongue in time,
With rolling eyes I looke about eche where,
Least any man should heare my raving ryme.   220
And all in rage, enraged as I am,
I take my sheete, my slyppers and my gowne,
And in the *Bathe* from whence but late I came,
I cast my selfe in dolors there to drowne.
There all alone I can my selfe conveye,   225
Into some corner where I sit unseene,
And to my selfe (there naked) can I saye,
Beholde these braunefalne armes which once have bene[3]
Both large and lustie, able for to fight,
Nowe are they weake, and wearishe God he knowes,   230
Unable now to daunt the foule despight
Which is presented by my cruell foes.
My thighes are thyn, my body lanck and leane,
It hath no bumbast now, but skyn and bones:
And on mine Elbowe as I lye and leane,   235
I see a trustie token for the nones.
I spy a bracelet bounde aboute mine arme,
Which to my shadowe seemeth thus to saye,
Beleve not me: for I was but a Charme,
To make thee sleepe, when others went to playe.   240
And as I gaze thus galded all with griefe,
I finde it fazed almost quite in sunder,
Then thinke I thus: thus wasteth my reliefe,
And though I fade, yet to the world no wonder.
For as this lace, by leysure learnes to weare,   245
So must I fainte, even as the candle wasteth,
These thoughts (deere sweete) within my brest I beare,
And to my long home, thus my life it hasteth.
Herewith I feele the droppes of sweltring sweate,
Which trickle downe my face, enforced so,   250
And in my body feele I likewyse beate,
A burning harte, which tosseth to and fro.
Thus all in flames I sinderlyke consume,

And were it not that wanhope lends me wynde,
Soone might I fret my fancyes⁴ all in fume, 255
And like a Ghost my ghost his grave might finde.
But frysing hope doth blowe full in my face,
And colde of cares becommes my cordiall,
So that I still endure that yrcksome place,
Where sorowe seethes to skald my skynne withall. 260
And when from thence our company me drives,
Or weary woes do make me chaunge my seate,
Then in my bed my restlesse payne revyves,
Untill my fellowes call me downe to meate,
And when I rise, my corpse for to araye, 265
I take the glasse, sometimes (but not for pride,
For God he knowes my minde is not so gaye)
But for I would in comelynesse abyde:
I take the glasse, wherin I seeme to see,
Such wythred wrynckles and so foule disgrace, 270
That little marvell seemeth it to mee,
Though thou so well didst like the noble face.
The noble face was faire and freshe of hewe,
My wrinckled face is foule and fadeth fast:
The noble face was unto thee but newe, 275
My wrinckled face is olde and cleane outcast:
The noble face might move thee with delight,
My wrinckled face could never please thine eye:
Lo thus of crime I covet thee to quite.
And still accuse my selfe of *Surcuydry*: 280
As one that am unworthy to enjoye,
The lasting fruite of such⁵ a love as thine,
Thus am I tyckled still with every toye,
And when my Fellowes call me downe to dyne,
No chaunge of meate provokes mine appetite, 285
Nor sauce can serve to taste my meates withall,
Then I devise the juyce of grapes to dight,
For Suger and for Sinamon I call,
For Ginger, Graines, and for eche other spyce,
Wherewith I mixe the noble wine apace, 290
My fellowes prayse the depth of my devise,
And say it is as good as Ippocrace.
As Ippocrace say I? and then I swelt,
My faynting lymmes streight fall into a sowne,
Before the taste of Ippocrace is felt, 295
The naked name in dolours doth me drowne,
For then I call unto my troubled mynd,
That Ippocrace hath bene thy dayly drincke,

That Ippocrace hath walkt with every winde
In bottells that were fylled to the brincke.   300
With Ipprocrace thou banquetedst full ofte,
With Ippocrace thou madst thy selfe full merry,
Such cheere had set thy new love so alofte,
That olde love now was scarsely worth a cherry.
And then againe I fall into a traunce,   305
But when my breth returnes against my will,
Before my tongue can tell my wofull chaunce,
I heare my fellowes how they whisper still.
One sayth that Ippocrace is contrary,
Unto my nature and complexion,   310
Whereby they judge that all my maladye,
Was long of that by alteration.
An other sayth, no, no this man is weake,
And for such weake, so hote things are not best,
Then at the last I heare no liar speake,   315
But one which knowes the cause of myne unrest,
And saith, this men is (for my life) in love,
He hath received repulse, or dronke disdaine,
Alas crie I: and ere I can remove,
Into a sowne I soone returne againe.   320
Thus drive I foorth, my dolefull dining time,
And trouble others with my troubles still,
But when I here, the bell hath passed prime
Into the Bathe I wallow by my will,
That there my teares (unseene) might ease my griefe,   325
For though I sterve yet have I fed my fill,
In privie pangs I count my best reliefe.
And still I strive in wery woes to drench.
But when I plondge, then wo is at an ebbe,
My glowing coles are all to quicke to quench,   330
And I (to warme) am wrapped in the webbe,
Which makes me swim against the wished wave,
Lo thus (deere wench) I leade a lothsome life,
And greedely I seeke the greedy grave,
To make an end of all these stormes and strife.   335
But death is deafe, and heares not my desire,
So that my dayes continue still in dole,
And in my nights, I feele the secret fire,
Which close in embers, coucheth like a cole,
And in the day hath bin but raked up,   340
With covering ashes of my companie,
Now breaks it out, and boyles the carefull cuppe,
Which in my hart, doth hang full heavily.

I melt in teares, I swelt in chilling sweat,
My swelling heart, breaks with delay of payne   345
I freeze in hope, yet burne in hast of heate,
I wish for death, and yet in life remaine.
And when dead sleepe doth close my dazeled eyes,
Then dreadfull dreames my dolors do encrease,
Me thinks I lie awake in wofull wise,   350
And see thee come, my sorrowes for to cease.
Me seemes thou saist (my good) what meaneth this?
What ayles thee thus to languish and lament?
How can it be that bathing all in blisse,
Such cause unknowne disquiets thy content?   355
Thou doest me wrong to keepe so close from me
The grudge or griefe, which gripeth now thy heart,
For well thou knowest, I must thy partner be
In bale, in blisse, in solace, and in smarte.
Alas, alas, these things I deeme in dreames,   360
But when mine eyes are open and awake,
I see not thee, wherewith the flowing streames,
Of brinish teares their wonted flouds do make,
Thus as thou seest I spend both nights and dayes,
And for I find the world did judge me once   365
A witlesse writer of these lovers layes,
I take my pen and paper for the nonce,
I lay aside this folish riding rime,
And as my troubled head can bring to passe,
I thus bewray the torments of my time: 370
Beare with my Muse, it is not as it was.
                    Fato non fortuna.

[4]   The extremitie of his Passion.

A *Mong the toyes which tosse my brayne,*
        and reave my mind from quiet rest,
This one I find, doth there remayne,
        to breede debate within my brest.
When woe would worke, to wound my will,   5
        I cannot weepe, nor wayle my fill.

My tong hath not the skill to tell,
        the smallest griefe which gripes my heart,
Myne eyes have not the power to swell,
        into such Seas of secret smarte,   10
That will might melt to waves of woe,
        and I might swelt[1] *in sorowes so.*

Yet shed mine eyes no trickling teares,
but fluddes which flowe abundantly,
Whose fountaine first enforst by feares, 15
found out the gappe of jealowsie.
And by that breache,² it soketh so,
that all my face, is still on flowe.

My voyce is like the raging wind,
which roareth still, and never stayes, 20
The thoughts which tomble in my minde,
are like the wheele which whirles alwayes,
Now here, now there, now up, now downe,
in depth of waves, yet cannot drowne.

The sighes which boyle out of my brest, 25
are not like those, which others use,
For lovers sighes, sometimes take rest,
and lend their mindes, a leave to muse,
But mine are like the surging seas,
whome calme nor quiet can appeas. 30

And yet they be but sorrowes smoke,
my brest the fordge where fury playes,
My panting hart, it strikes the stroke,
my fancie blowes the flame alwayes,
The coles are kindled by desire, 35
and Cupide *warmes him by the fire.*

Thus can I neither drowne in dole,
nor burne to ashes, though I wast,
Myne eyes can neither quench the cole,
which warmes my hart in all this hast. 40
Nor yet my fancie make such flame,
that I may smoulder in the same.

Wherefore I come to seeke out care,
beseching him of curtesie,
To cut the thred which cannot weare, 45
by pangs of such perplexitie.
And but he graunt this boone of mine,
thus must I live and ever pine.

Fato non fortuna.

[5]   L O thus (deere hart) I force my frantike Muse,
        To frame a verse in spite of my despighte,
But whiles I do these mirthlesse meeters use
This rash conceite doth reve me from delight.
I call to mind how many loving layes, 5

How manie Sonets, and how many songs
I did devise within those happie dayes,
When yet my will had not received wrongs.
All which were evermore regarded so,
That little frute I seemd thereby to reape,   10
But rather when I had bewrayed my woe
Thy love was light, and lusted still to leape.
The rymes which pleased thee were all in print,
And mine were ragged, hard for to be red,
Lo dere: this dagger dubbes me with this dint,   15
And leaves this wound within my jealouse hed.[1]
But since I have confessed unto care,
That now I stand uppon his curtesie,
And that the bale, which in my brest I bare,
Hath not the skill to kill me cunningly,   20
Therefore with all my whole devotion,
To Care I make this supplication.
                    Fato non fortuna.

[6]   *His libell of request exhibited to Care.*

O Curteous Care, whome others (cruell) call,
  And raile uppon thine honorable name,
O knife that canst cut off the thred of thrall,
O sheare that shredst the semerent sheete of shame,
O happie end of every grevous game: 5
Vouchsafe O Prince, thy vassall to behold,
Who loves thee more, than can with tong be told.
And now vouchsafe to pittie this his plaint,
Whose teares bewray,
His truth alway,   10
Although his feeble tong be forst to faint.

I must confesse O noble king to thee,
That I have bin a Rebell in my youth,
I preast always in pleasures courte to be,
I fled from that, which *Cupide* still eschuth,   15
I fled from Care, lo now I tell the truth,
And in delights, I loved so to dwell,
Thy heavenly house, did seeme to me but hell.
Such was my rage, the which I now repent,
And pardon crave,   20
My soule to save,
Before the webbe of weary life be spent.

But marke what frutes did grow on such a tree,
What crop did rise uppon so rash sowne seede,
For when I thought my selfe in heaven to be,   25

In depth of hell I drowned was in deede:
Whereon to thinke my heavie hart doth bleede:
Me thought I swumme in Seas of all delight,
When as I sunke in puddles of despite.
Alas alas I thought my selfe belov'd,   30
When deadly hate,
Did play check mate,
With my poore pawne, that no such prancks had prov'd.

This when I tryed (ay me) to be to true,
I wept for woe, I pined all for paine,   35
I tare my heare, I often chaunged hewe,
I lefte delight, with dolours to complayne.
I shund each place where pleasure did remaine,
I cride, I calde on every kind of death,
I strove each way to stop my fainting breath.   40
Shorte tale to make, I slept so farre in strife,
That still I sought,
With all my thought,
Some happie helpe to leave my lothed life.

But hope was he that held my hand abacke,   45
From quicke dispatch of all my griping griefe,
When heate of hate had burnt my will to wracke,
Then hope was cold and lent my life reliefe,
In every choyce hope challengde to be chiefe.
When coldest cramps had cleane orecome my harte,   50
Then hope was hotte, and warmde[1] my weary smart,
When hart was hardie, hope was still in dread,
When hart was faint,
With feares attaint,
Then hardie hope held up my fearfull head.   55

Thus when I found that neither flowing teares
Could drowne my hart in waves of wery wo,
Nor hardy hand could overcome my feares,
To cut the sacke of all my sorrow so,
Nor death would come, nor I to death could go.   60
And yet I felt great droppes of secret smart,
Distilling still within my dying harte:
I then perceived that only Care was he,
Which as my frend,
Might make an end,   65
Of all these paines, and set my fancie free.

Wherefore (oh Care) graunt thou my just request,
Oh kill my corps, oh quickly kill me now,
Oh make an end and bring my bones to rest,

Oh cut my thred (good Care) I care not how,   70
Oh Care be kind: and here I make a vowe,
That when my life out of my brest shall parte,
I will present thee with my faithfull harte:
And send it to thee as a Sacrifice,
Bycause thou hast,   75
Vouchsaft at last,
To end my furies in this friendly wise.

Fato non fortuna.

[7]   WHat greater glory can a *Keysar* gaine,
    If madde moode move his subjects to rebell,
Than that at last (when all the traytours traine,
Have trod the path, of deepe repentance well,
And naked neede with *Cold* and *Hunger* both,   5
Hath bitten them abrode in forren land,
Whereby they may their lewde devises loth.
When harebraind hast, with cold advise is scande)
If then at last, they come upon their knee,
And pardon crave with due submission,   10
And for this cause, I thinke that Care of me,
Was moved most, to take compassion.
For now I find, that pittie pricks his mind,
To see me ploonged still in endlesse paine,
And right remorse, his princely hart doth bind,   15
To rule the rage wherein I do remaine.
I feele my teares do now begin to stay,
For Care from them their swelling springs doth soke,
I feele my sighes their labours now allaye,
For care hath quencht the coles that made them smoke.   20
I feele my panting harte begins to rest,
For Care hath staide the hammers of my hed,
I feele the flame which blazed in my brest,
Is¹ now with carefull ashes overspred.
And gentle Care, hath whet his karving knife,   25
To cut in twaine the thred of all my thrall,
Desired death now overcommeth life,
And wo² still works to helpe in hast with all.
But since I feele these pangs approching so,
And lothed life begin to take his leave,   30
Me thinks it meete, to give before I go,³
Such lands, and goodes, as I behind me leave.
So to discharge my troubled conscience,
And eke to set an order for mine heire,
Who might (perhaps) be put to great expence,   35

To sue for that, which I bequeath him here.
Wherefore (deere wench) with all my full intent,
I thus begin to make my Testament.
          Fato non fortuna.

[8]   *His last will and Testament.*

IN *Jove* his mightie name, this eight and twentith day,
Of frosty bearded Januar, the enemie to May:
Since Adam was create, five thousand yeares I gesse,
Five hundreth, forty more and five, as stories do expresse.
I being whole of mind, (immortall Gods have praise)   5
Though in my body languishing with pangs of paine alwayes,
Do thus ordeyne my will which long in woes have wepte,
Beseeching myne executours to see it duely kepte.
Firste I bequeath my soule on *Charons* boate to tende,
Until thy lyfe (my love) at laste may light on luckie ende,   10
That there it may awayte, to wayte upon thy ghost,
When y{u} haste quite & clean forgot what pranks now please thee most.
So shal it wel be seene whose love is lyke to myne:
For so I meane to trie my truth, and there till then to pine.
My bodie be enbalmde, and cloazed up in chest,   15
With oyntments and with spiceries of every sweete the best:
And so preserved still untill the day doe come,
That death devorce my love from life, & trusse hir up in tombe.
Then I bequeath my corps to couche beneath hir bones,
And there to feede the greedie woorms that linger for the nones 20
To frette upon hir fleshe, whiche is too fyne therefore,
This service may it doe hir yet, although it do no more.
My hearte (as heretofore) I must bequeath to Care,
And God he knowes, I thinke the gift to simple for his share,
But that he may perceive, I meane to pay my dew,   25
I will it shall be taken quick, and borne him bleeding new,
As for my funeralls, I leave that toye at large,
To be as mine executors will give thereto in charge.
Yet if my goods will stretch unto my straunge device,
Then let this order be observ'd, mine heire shall pay the price: 30
First let the torche bearers be wrapt in weedes of woe,
Let all their lights be virgin waxe, bicause I lov'd it so.
And care not though the twist be course that lends them light,
If fansie fume, & frewill flame, then must they needs burn bright.
Next them let come the quyer, with psalmes & dolefull song,   35
Recording all my rough repulse and wraying all my wrong,
And when the deskant sings, in treeble tunes above,
Then let fa burden, say (by lowe) *I liv'd and dyde for love*:
About my heavie hearse, some mourners wold I have,

Who might the same accompany, and stand about the grave,　　40
But let them be suche men, as may confesse with me,
Howe contrary the lots of love, to all true lovers be.
Let *Pacience* be the Priest, the Clearke be Close conceit,
The Sexten be *Symplicitie,* which meaneth no disceit.
Let almes of *Love* be delt, even at the Chauncell dore,　　45
And feede them there with fresh delayes, as I have ben of yore:
Then let the yongest sort, be set to ring *Loves* bells,
And pay *Repentance* for their paines, but give them nothing else,
Thus when the Dirge is done, let every man depart,
And learne by me what harme it is to have a faithfull hart.　　50
Those little lands I have, mine heyre must needes possesse,
His name is *Lust,* the lands be losse, few lovers scape with lesse.
The rest[1] of all my goods, which I not here rehearse,
Give learned Poets for their paines, to deck my tomb w^t verse:
And let them wryte these words upon my carefull chest,　　55
Lo here he lyes, that was as true (in love) as is the best.
Alas I had forgot the persons dewe to paye,
And so my soule in *Purgatory,* might remaine alway.
Then for my privie Tythes, as kysses caught by stealth,
Swete collings & such other knacks as multiplyed my wealth:　　60
I give the Vicar here, to please his gredie will,
A deyntie dishe of suger soppes but saust with sorow still:
And twice a weeke at least, let dight them for his dishe,
On frydayes and on wednesdayes, to save expence of fishe.
Now have I much bequeathed and little left behynde,　　65
And others mo must yet be served or else I were unkynde.
Wet eyes and wayling words, Executors I make,
And for their paines ten pounde of teares let either of them take.
Let sorow at the last my Supravisor be,
And stedfastnesse my surest stead, I give him for his fee:　　70
Yet in his pattent place this *Sentence of proviso,*
That he which loveth stedfastly, shall want no sause of sorow.
Thus now I make an ende, of this my wearie will,
And signe it with my simple hand, and set my seale there till.
And you which reade my words, although they be in rime,　　75
Yet reason may perswade you eke, *Thus lovers dote sometime.*

The Subscription[2] and seale.

M Y Mansion house was Mone: from *Dolors* dale I came,
　I *Fato: Non Fortuna,* hight, lo now you know my name:
My seale is sorowes sythe, within a fielde of flame,[3]
Which cuts in twaine a carefull hart, y^t sweltreth in the same.

Fato non Fortuna.

[9]   A Las, lo now I heare the passing Bell,
       Which Care appoynteth carefully to knoule,
       And in my breast, I feele my hart now swell,
       To breake the strings, which joynde it to my soule.
       The Christall yce, which lent mine eyes their light,   5
       Doth now waxe dym, and dazeled all with dread,
       My senses all, will now forsake me quite,
       And hope of health abandoneth my head,
       My weary tongue can talke no longer now,
       My trembling hand now leaves my penne to holde,   10
       My joynts now stretch, my body cannot bowe,
       My skynne lokes pale, my blood now waxeth colde.
       And are not these, the very pangs of death?
       Yes sure (sweete hart) I know them so to be,
       They be the pangs, which strive to stop my breath,   15
       They be the pangs, which part my love from thee.
       What said I? *Love? Nay lyfe:* but not my love,
       My life departes, my love continues still:
       My lothed lyfe may from my corpse remove,
       My loving Love shall always worke thy will.   20
       It was thy will even thus to trye my truth,
       Thou hast thy will, my truth may now be seene,
       It was thy will, that I should dye in youth,
       Thou hast thy will my yeares are yet but grene.
       Thy penance was that I should pyne in paine,   25
       I have performd thy penance all in wo,
       Thy pleasure was that I should here remayne,
       I have bene glad to please thy fansie so.
       Now since I have performed every part
       Of thy commaunde, as neare as tong can tell,   30
       Content thee yet before my Muse departe,
       To take this Sonet for my last farewell.
                         Fato non fortuna.

[10]   *His Farewell.*

       F Arewell deere love whome I have loved and shall,
         Both in this world, and in the world to come,
       For proofe wherof my spryte is *Charons* thrall,
       And yet my corpse attendant on thy toome.
       Farewell deere sweete, whose wanton will to please   5
       Eche taste of trouble seemed mell to me,
       Farewell swete deere, whose doubts for to appease,
       I was contented thus in bale to be.
       Farewell my lyfe, farewell for and my death,
       For thee I lyv'd, for thee nowe must I dye,   10

Farewell from *Bathe,* whereas I feele my breath
Forsake my brest in great perplexitie,
Alas how welcome were this death of mine,
If I had dyde betweene those armes of thine.
                    Fato non Fortuna.

[12]   *The reporters conclusion unfinished.*

WHere might I now find fluddes of flowing teares,
    So to suffise the swelling of mine eyes?
How might my brest unlode the bale it beares?
Alas alas how might my tong devise
To tell this wery tale in wofull wise?   5
To tell I say these tidings now of truth,
Which may provoke the craggy rocks to ruth?

    In depth of dole would God that I were drownde,
Where flattring joyes might never find me out,
Or graved so within the greedy ground,   10
As false delights might never breede my doubt,
Nor guilefull love hir purpose bring about:
Whose trustlesse traines in colours for to paint,
I find by proofe my witts are all to faint.

    I am that man whome destenies ordeine,   15
To beare each griefe that groweth on the mold,
I am that man which prove unto my paine,
More pangs at once than can with tong be told,
I am that man (hereof you may be bold)
Whome heaven and earth did frame to scoffe and scorne,   20
I, I am he which to that end was borne.

    Suffized not myselfe to tast the frute,
Of sugred sowres which growe in gadding yeares,
But that I must with paine of like pursute,
Perceive such pangs by paterne of my peares,   25
And feele how fansies fume could fond my pheares:
Alas I finde all fates against me bent,
For nothing else I live, but to lament.

    The force of frendship bound by holy oth,
Did drawe my will into these croked wayes,   30
For with my frend I went to *Bathe* (though loth)
To lend some comfort in his dolie dayes,
The stedfast friend sticks fast at all assayes:
Yet was I loth such time to spend in vaine,
The cause whereof, lo here I tell you playne.   35

By proofe I found as you may well perceive,
That all good counsell was but worne in wast,
Such painted paines his passions did deceive,[1]
That bitter gall was mell to him in tast,
Within his will such rootes of ruine plast,   40
As graffes of griefes were only given to growe,
Where youth did plant and rash conceite did sowe.

I sawe[2] long since his eares were open aye
To every tale which fed him with some hope,
As fast againe I sawe him turne away   45
From grave advise, which might his conscience grope,
From reasons rule his fansie lightly lope,
He only gave his mind to get that gaine,
Which most he wisht and least could yet attayne.

Not I alone, but many mo with me,   50
Had found what ficklenesse his Idoll used,
And how she claimed *Cressides* heire to be,
And how she had his great good will abused,
And how she was of many men refused,
Who tride hir tricks and knew hir by the kinde,   55
Save only him she made no lover blinde.

But what for this? whose face is plainer seene,[3]
Than he which thinks he walketh in a net?
Or who in bale hath ever deeper beene,
Than he which thought his state might not be bet,   60
In such a jealosie these lovers jet,
That weale to them doth seeme to be but wo,
And griefe seemes joy, they feede their fancies so.

Tell him that reason ought to be his rule,
And he allowed no reason but his owne,   65
Tell him that best were quickly to recule,
Before all force by feare were overthrowen,
And that his part. &c.

I Have not (hitherto) recovered a full ende of this discourse, the author thereof
being more curious in deliverie of the same, than he hath bene heretofore
in any other of his doings. But since my trust is that you will use that
and the rest but for your owne private commoditie, I am the bolder
to present you with a copie therof unperfect as it is, and nowe
having finished this written regyster, it amounteth to a good
rounde vollume, the which some woulde judge worthy
the Imprinting, but hoping of your curtesie
(ut supra) I ceasse wyshing you no
lesse profyte than pleasure in
readyng and perusying
these tryfles.

(∴)

FINIS

IMPRINTED AT LON-
don for Richard Smith.

TEXTUAL NOTES

INTRODUCTION

The text of this reprint is based on the original in the Library of Emmanuel College, Cambridge and is here reproduced by the kind permission of the Librarian. This original has been collated with five other copies which are listed below.

The editor's purpose has been to provide a text of *A Hundreth Sundrie Flowres* which would represent as accurately as possible the author's original intention. It should be clearly understood that no attempt has been made to present a definitive text of the material which appeared in *A Hundreth Sundrie Flowres*. All variants found in *The Posies* of 1575 are, however, printed in a separate section of the notes following the present Textual Notes. As has been pointed out in the Introduction (*supra*, pp. 19-39) Gascoigne altered, rearranged, and augmented the contents of *A Hundreth Sundrie Flowres* when he prepared the copy for *The Posies*. The reasons for this alteration and rearrangement have also been discussed in the Introduction and the inclusion of the variants found in *The Posies* will enable the reader to understand more clearly the nature of the alterations and rearrangements. Variant punctuation and spelling found in *The Posies* have not been included.

As will appear from the ensuing Textual Notes, the text of *A Hundreth Sundrie Flowres* as found in the copies collated is remarkably accurate. In all the six copies examined only two formes of two sheets in one copy survive in an unrevised state: the inner forme of "Bb" and the outer forme of "Cc" in the Cambridge University Library copy. Evidently, then, Gascoigne followed his usual custom of being in attendance at the printing house during the printing.

Two general observations on his proofreading may, however, be made. The first has to do with the rapidity of the printing, which has been noted in the Introduction (*supra*, pp. 13-17). A number of variants which affect the scansion of individual lines are found in *The Posies*. For example, in poem no. 69, note 23 will be found a reading from *The Posies* which adds a word not found in the *Flowres* thus giving the line the correct number of syllables. That Gascoigne was trying to correct such errors appears in note 2, poem no. 70, where a similar correction was made in the *Flowres* when the poet corrected the outer forme of "Cc." Note 1, poem no. 71, shows another correction aimed at proper scansion which escaped notice in the *Flowres* and was only caught in *The Posies*.

Omissions which have a bearing upon meaning are observable in the prose of "F.J." For example, page 60, note 1; page 62, note 2; page 68, note 3—all record omissions which were corrected in *The Posies*. These and such errors as repetitions of words (p. 59, n. 2; p. 60, n. 2; p. 73, n. 2), incorrect words (p. 65, n. 1; p. 68, n. 1; p. 96, n. 1; poem no. 46, n. 5), and compositors' errors in turning letters and the like, seem the result of the rapid printing and resultant hasty correction. These errors are comparatively few, but they are greater in number than similar errors in *The Posies*, whose printing Gascoigne was able to supervise in more leisurely fashion. Clearly, then, it would seem that Gascoigne's need for haste in the printing of his work is mirrored in the text of *A Hundreth Sundrie Flowres*.

Even more interesting, perhaps, is the fact that the text also reveals the approximate time of Gascoigne's departure for Holland. Beginning with poem no. 74, *Gascoignes voyage into* Hollande, which the poet sent to the printer from Holland (*supra,* p. 14), the reader will see that the number of errors which were first corrected in *The Posies* begins to increase. Such an increase is observable in the rest of the volume, as may be readily seen in the Textual Notes. The explanation seems to be that with Gascoigne away from the printing house, the corrections were less accurately made. This indication of the poet's absence confirms and is confirmed by the external evidence which shows that Gascoigne sent back to the printer from Holland the copy for poem no. 74 and "Dan Bartholmew of Bathe" (*supra,* pp. 13-14).

Finally, an examination of the text of the *Flowres* in comparison with that of *The Posies* gives a slight clue to the manner in which Gascoigne prepared the copy for the latter. It will be remembered that in the Introduction (*supra,* pp. 28-39) evidence was presented to show the purpose and method of Gascoigne's alteration in *The Posies* of the original sequence of his poems. One such alteration is found in poem no. 10, which has the following introduction in the *Flowres*:

> He began to write by a gentlewoman
> who passed by him with hir armes
> set bragging by hir sides, and left
> it unfinished as followeth.

In *The Posies* this poem, preceded by no. 19 and followed by no. 11, has this introduction:

> The lookes of a lover forsaken:
> written by a gentlewoman who
> passed by him with hir armes
> set bragging by hir sides, and
> lefte it unfinished as followeth.

The alteration of the introduction in *The Posies* is part of the process whereby Gascoigne sought to break the sequence of the original order. In this instance, by placing poem no. 10 some pages away from no. 9 he sought to avoid any connection between the two. This change in sequence required a word or phrase to take the place of "He began to write." In making the substitution Gascoigne was obviously using either the MS of the *Flowres* or a copy of the printed text, since only by such means could the verb and object, "lefte it," have acquired the ungrammatical structure they have in *The Posies.* Had he prepared a new MS he would have rewritten the entire introduction and would have most certainly noted the error.

A similar use of the original MS or a copy of the *Flowres* as the copy for *The Posies* is found in the new beginning of "F.J." where we find this unusual statement:

> And bicause I do suppose that *Leonora* is the same name whiche wee call *Elinor*
> in English, and that *Francischina* also doth import none other than *Fraunces,*
> I will so entitle them as to our own countriemen may be moste perspicuous.

Why does the feigned "translator" give the English names of Leonora and Francischina and not that of Ferdinando? It seems clear that too much revision would have been required to alter the original Elinor and Fraunces. For example, poem no. 8 if the heroine's name were altered to Leonora. The elimination of F.J. was requisite with its confusion about Hellen and Elinor would have created something of a problem, on two counts: first, on too many occasions the name, "F.J.", was coupled with the remarks of *G.T.*, which, of course, had to be deleted; secondly, the separation of Gascoigne and F.J. had to be made clear. Thus we see that Gascoigne made as few changes as possible in the original MS or printed text of the *Flowres* of which he made the copy for *The Posies*.

Although endeavor has been made to follow the original as closely as possible, certain emendations have seemed necessary. Long "s" is printed as modern "s," and "vv" as "w." To be consistent, "u" and "v" are distinguished according to modern usage, as are consonant and vowel "i." This last distinction justifies the use of the initials "F.J." for the hero of the prose tale, since the printer in his letter to the reader suggests "Freeman Jones" as a possible name.

The original spelling is preserved with few exceptions. First are those resulting from the use of modern letters. Abbreviations involving the omission of a nasal consonant have been silently lengthened, since their use is primarily a printer's device to justify the line. In like manner, abbreviated prefixes have been lengthened. On the other hand, the abbreviations y^e, y^t, w^{th}, w^{ch}, and w^t, which are frequent in Elizabethan manuscripts, have been retained. The form "qd" for "quod" appears in the original with an especial form of the letter "d" to indicate the abbreviation. Since it is difficult to reproduce this form, a period is supplied, *e.g.* "qd." No capitals are altered to lower case, but several lower case letters are, as noted, changed to capitals.

The punctuation is emended only where it seems absolutely essential to do so. There are several instances of the line length of the original preventing the insertion of punctuation or blurring the punctuation with the tail of the last letter. These are emended and noted as are the occasions when the original punctuation did violence to the meaning. As Dr. McKerrow observed, in his *Introduction to Bibliography*, the rules of punctuation varied among Elizabethan printing houses and no apparent standard existed. If we may judge by the two holograph letters in the Public Record Office, Gascoigne used little or no punctuation.

The original was printed in black letter with occasional use of italic and roman. These last were used to indicate letters, certain poems, proper names, and editorial information. As it is undesirable to reproduce the black letter of the original, roman has been substituted for it in all cases. The treatment accorded the original roman and italic requires some explanation. In general, roman was employed for the introductory comments which prefaced each poem and italic was used to emphasize proper names or dates which appeared within a passage of roman so used. Since the intention of the original was evidently to distinguish between poem and introduction by means of a different type face, it has seemed best to preserve this distinction by using italic for the original roman. To preserve the original distinction given to proper names and dates, roman has been employed for the original italic wherever the original italic appeared within a passage set in roman. All other instances of original italic are here reproduced in italic.

Finally, the line length of the original has not been preserved; and inconsistencies of indentation have been silently corrected.

The following system of abbreviations has been employed to indicate the copies collated

A: Emmanuel College Library
B: Cambridge University Library
C: British Museum (George III copy)
D: British Museum (Grenville copy)
E: Harmsworth (in the Folger Shakespeare Library)
F: Folger
P: *The Posies of George Gascoigne* (Folger copy)

Page	Note	
46	1	D,F: "co ntents"
	2	A,B: "Suppos es"
	3	C: omits "401".
	4	A-F: "discourseof"
	5	A,B,D,E,F: "farewel"
	6	C: omits "412".
47	1	C: "grey heared"
	2	A-F: omit final bracket.
50	1	A-F: "Lawrell."
51	1	A-F: *"frowardnes."; Faultes escaped:* "forwardnes"
53	1	A-F: *"work e,"*
	2	A-F: *"requ est."*
54	1	C,D: "portrayed"
	2	A-F: "recr eant"
	3	A-F: "werewide"
55	1	A-F: *"caught"; Faultes escaped:* "coucht"
	2	A-F: "lip."; P: "lip,"
	3	A,B,C,D,F: "st ay."
56	1	A-F: *"winges"; Faultes escaped:* "twigges"
	2	C,D: *"Till"*
	3	A-F: "Frances,"
	4	A-F: "reuereuce,"
57	1	A-F: "bleeding,"; P: "bleeding"
59	1	A-F: "strauunge."; P: "straunge."
	2	A-F: "is is"; P: "is"
	3	A-F: "packet"; P: "pocket"
60	1	A-F: omit "I"; P: "I".
	2	A-F: "once once"; P: "once"
61	1	A-F: "she"; *Faultes escaped:* "he"
62	1	A-F: "he"; P: "he"
	2	A-F: omit "to"; P: "to".
	3	A-F: "andcalling"
	4	A-F: *"please"*; P: *"pleasde"*
63	1	A-F: *"reitre"*; P: *"retire"*
64	1	A-F: *"hat h"*
65	1	A-F: "unfolded"; P: "foulded"
	2	A-F: "Frauuces"

Page	Note	
66	1	A-F: "pleased and:"; P: "pleased: and"
67	1	A-F: "friend s,"
	2	A-F: omit final bracket.
68	1	A-F: "son"; P: "some"
	2	A-F: "Ladi"
	3	A-F: omit "I"; P: "I".
69	1	A-F: "fyue"; P: "fine"
70	1	A-F: "gare," Since "gare" here has no meaning, it seems to be the error of a compositor who mistook a script "z" for "r".
71	1	A-F: *"Q ueene,"*
73	1	A-F: "trnst"; P: "trust"
	2	A-F: "dame Dame"; P: "Dame"
	3	A-F: *"Frañces?"*
74	1	A-F: "dame"; P: "Dame"
	2	A-F: *"T That"*; P: *"THat"*
	3	A-F: *"go:"*
75	1	A-F: *"setforth"*
	2	A-F: *"shield"*; P: *"shield."*
76	1	A-F: "ifhis"
	2	A-F: "diver s"
77	1	A-F: *"peeres"; Faultes escaped:* "pearles"
	2	A-F: "inexpriuable"; P: "inexprimable"
	3	A-F: "contentatious"; P: "contentations"
	4	A-F: "imemdiatlye": P: "immediatlye"
80	1	A-F: "sufficcieni"; P: "sufficient"
	2	A-F: omit initial bracket.
	3	A-F: "health?"; P: "health,"
82	1	A-F: "s kalde,"
90	1	A-F: "nenew"; *Faultes escaped:* "renew"
91	1	A-F: "whowold"
92	1	F: "at all these whot speches,"
	2	A-F: "encourage"; *Faultes escaped:* "enrage"

Page	Note	
93	1	A-F: "Secretaty"
	2	A-E: "far"
		F: "farre"
94	1	A-D: *"Frances"*
		E,F: *"Fraunces"*
	2	A-F: "reasonable"; P: "reasonably"
	3	A-F: "Dawe"; P: "Dame"
95	1	A-F: "Dam"; P: "Dame"
96	1	A-F: "pleasure"; *Faultes escaped*: "displeasure"
98	1	A-F: "hus band"
	2	A-F: "pocked,"; P: "pocket,"
	3	C: "still"
99	1	A-F: "hus band"
	2	A-F: "towars"; P: "towards"

[From this point on, the notes refer to poems rather than to pages, and are consecutively numbered for each poem.]

Poem	Note	
1	1	A-F: "let". The original Italian (cf. "Critical Notes") reads "sorte"; therefore I emend to "lot".
2	1	A-F: "wher eto"
3	1	A-F: "flittering"; *Faultes escaped*: "flytting"
4	1	A-F: "migh"; P: "might"
	2	C: "plaintes,"
		A,B,D,E,F: "plaintes"
6	1	A-F: "me lts"
7	1	A-F: "English) dames"
8	1	A-F: "it"; P: "yet"
	2	A-F: "c ar efull"
	3	A-F: "that descends,"; P: "that he descends,"
	4	A-F: "yet"
9	1	A-F: "more of bright hewe."; P: "more bright of hewe."
10	1	A-F: "fr esh"
13	1	A-F: "bauties"; P: "beauties"
14	1	A-F: "wrong"; P: "wrong."
	2	A-F: "god". Lower case used because of line length.
	3	A-F: "wil". As in preceding note.
15	1	A-F: "s kip"
16	1	A: "G.,G."
		B: in modern MS at this point.
		C-F: "G.G."
19	1	A-F: "were"; P: "where"

Page	Note	
	3	A-F: "shhe"
101	1	A-F: *"J.F."*
	2	A-F: "conceitps:"; P: "conceipts:"
102	1	A-F: *"Fraunces,"*; P: *"Fraunces,)"*
	2	A-F: "wrot"; P: "woote"
	3	A-F: "accasion"; P: "occation"
	4	A-F: *"redesse"*; P: *"redresse"*
103	1	A-F: *"toshed"*
104	1	A-F: "recant:itas"; P: "recant it, as"
	2	A-F: "determed"; P: "determined"
105	1	B: *"meo"*
	2	A-F: "fnrther"
	3	A-F: "easely,"

Poem	Note	
21	1	A-F: "Phil lip"
	2	A-F: "newfond"; P: "new found". The A-F reading might easily be an error for "newfoud" printed with the nasal sign over the u.
	3	A,B,D,E,F: "by the-rood," C: "by-the.rood" P: "by the rood,"
	4	A-F: "blame."; P: blame,"
24	1	A-F: "Dame"
	2	A-F: "she ("
25	1	A-F: "some for sing"; P: "some sing for"
26	1	A-F: "par agon"
	2	A-F: "and". Lower case used since line is long.
27	1	A-F: "so wen,"
28	1	A,C,D,E,F: "welwas"
	2	A,C,D,E,F: "prov'd" B: in MS. P: "prov'd."
29	1	A,C,D,E,F: "breede s" B: in MS.
33	1	A-F: "bani sh"
35	1	A-F: "mnst"
37	1	F: "wrouged"
	2	A,C,D,E,F: "almo st" B: in MS.
	3	A-F: "sorte,"
	4	A-F: "louely"; P: "louely". Although this is not altered in P, I think the "n" has been turned.

Poem Note

38 1 A-F: "bold". Since this line ends with "bolde" I have concluded that this first must originally have been "bald."

2 A-F: "s weete,"

3 A-F: "blame". I have inserted a colon following the punctuation of previous stanzas.

40 1 A-F: "and"

41 1 A-F: "I."; P: "I,"

43 1 A-F: "c olde"

45 1 A-F: "chase". Since 1. 19 refers to "the cheare of company," I have emended the introduction to suit this reading.

2 A-F: "wile"; P: "will"

46 1 A-F: "Aud"

2 A-F: "es,"; P: "yes,"

3 A-F: "wisedom e"

4 A-F: "shoon,"

5 A-F: *Corma*"; P: "*Corinna*". I print *Corina* since the compositor's error indicates "in" misread as "m".

47 1 A-F: "lo ver"

48 1 A-F: "hts"

49 1 A-F: "*N ever.*"

51 1 A-F: "*Lorde*"; *Faultes escaped*: "Lady"

52 1 A-F: "renue"; P: "relieve"

53 1 A-F: "to"; P: "loe"

2 A-F: "fast"

54 1 A-F: "Dame"; *Faultes escaped*: "Dan"

2 A-F: "worth"

3 A-F: "purest"; P: "poorest"

55 1 A,C-F: "Witth"
B: in MS.

2 A,C,D,E,F: No indentation of this stanza, but the last line of the preceding stanza is indented.
B: in MS.

3 A-F: "*N ever*"

58 1 A-F: "strives"; P: "sterves"

2 A-F: "soyle"; P: "spoyle"

60 1 A-F: "soyle"; P: "soyle"

2 A-F: "and and"; P: "and"

3 A-F: omit.

61 1 A-F: "cause, why". The caesural comma seems misplaced.

2 A-F: "furring"

62 1 A-F: "leafe"; P: "leafe"

2 A-F: "neeed,"

Poem Note

63 1 A-F: No indentation of stanzas 2, 5, and 9.

2 A-F: "darkesome stormes"; *Faultes escaped*: "darksomnesse"

64 1 A,C: "*de-/nyse*"
B,D,E,F: "*de-/uyse*"

66 1 A-F: "A"; P: "On"

2 A-F: "Douty"; *Faultes escaped*: "Doughty"

3 A,B: "suc he"
C,D,E,F: "suche"

4 A-F: "crease,"; *Faultes escaped*: "creast"

5 A-F: "money"; *Faultes escaped*: "muze"

67 1 A-F: "stande"; P: "stayde"

68 1 A-F: No indentation.

69 1 A-E: "always"
F: "alwaies". Thus the inner forme of Aa has been revised in A-E to give better spacing to a long line by shortening "alwaies" to "always."

2 A-F: "st riving"

3 B: "stand". This and the subsequent variants found in B indicate that the inner forme of sheet "Bb" here survives unrevised. Similarly, the variants noted in poem 70 show the outer forme of "Cc" surviving in a similar state. No other formes in any copy have a comparable number of errors; thus it seems reasonable to conclude that the few errors noted elsewhere, either survived revision or crept in during revision. B thus has the only two fully unrevised sheets found in any of the six copies.

4 B: "yoke:"

5 B: "slaveryes"

6 B: "then"

7 B: "sacrifice."

8 B: "he"

9 B: "lokte"

10 A-F: "For,"

11 A,C,D,E,F: "leau ehim". Here an error has crept into the revised sheet. Cf. note 3 above.

12 B: "sins"

13 B: "men,"

14 B: "so,"

Poem Note

69   15   B: "awhile,"
    16   B: "durst,"
    17   B: "Tnrks"
    18   B: "laiden"
    19   B: "aire."
    20   B: "abhor"
    21   B: "pearce."
    22   B: "mo:"
    23   A-F: "myghtie God"; P: "mighty hand of God". Extra words needed for scansion.
    24   A-F: "u pon". An error that escaped revision. Cf. note 3 above.
    25   A,C,D,E,F: "cosin"
        B: "cosen". This variation occurs on the outer forme of sheet "Cc", and it is difficult to tell which is the revised form.

70   1   A: "wilton."
        B-F: "wilton"
    2   B: "butned"
        A,C,D,E,F: "buttened". The scansion requires the longer word. Such a correction, plus the other corrections noted below, shows an unrevised outer forme of "Cc."
    3   B: "things"
    4   B: "vaine"
    5   D: "coutent"
    6   B: "maystrieers"
    7   B: "pricke."
    8   B: "arise."

71   1   A-F: "floures fresh"; P: "floures most fresh". Scansion requires "most".
    2   A-F: No indentation of this stanza.
    3   B: "Gardin". This seems to be an error on the inner forme of "Cc".

72   1   A-F: "there"; P: "here"
74   1   A-F: "me". A turned "w".
    2   A-F: "moreth an"
    3   A-F: "Dausk". A turned "n"; see Critical Notes.

Poem Note

74   4   A-F: "be"; P: "by"
    5   A-F: "by"; P: "be"
    6   A-F: "pufft"; P: puffe"
D.B.1   1   A-F: omit indentation for this, and stanzas 3, 8, 17, 18.
    2   A-F: "childe"; P: "cheife"
    3   A-F: "whe rein"
D.B.2   1   A-F: "was"; P: "were"
D.B.11   1   This link by the Reporter evidently arrived at the printer's too late to appear in its proper place (*vide supra*, Introduction, p. 14); cf. also *George Gascoigne*, p. 212) and was printed between nos. 10 and 12. I here print it in the position indicated by its original heading, "*This should have bin placed in the dolorous discourse, before the Supplication to Care in Folio. 430.*" I have, however, numbered it according to its original place in the sequence.
    2   A-F: "ge ason"
D.B.3   1   C,F: "disco urses"
    2   A-F: "fansi es"
    3   A-F: "bene."
    4   A-F: "facyes"
    5   A-F: "ofsuch"
D.B.4   1   A-F: "swell"; P: swelt". Cf. D.B.3, 1. 124, 1. 344.
    2   A-F: "breath,"; P: "breache,"
D.B.5   1   A-F: "hed"; P: "head."
D.B.6   1   A-F: "warnde"
D.B.7   1   A-F: "Are"; P: "Is"
    2   A-F: "we"; P: "wo"
    3   A-F: "go."; P: "go,"
D.B.8   1   A-F: "best"; P: "rest"
    2   A-F: "TheS ubscription"
D.B.8   3   A-F: "fame,"; P: "flame,"
D.B.12   1   A-F: "dece ive,"
    2   A-F: "sa we"
    3   A-F: "seen e"

Instead of the introductory letters (p. 49, l. 1—p. 51, l. 39) P has the following beginning for the tale.

The pleasant Fable of *Ferdinando Jeron[i]mi and Leonora de Valasco*, translated out of the Italian riding tales of *Bartello*.

IN the pleasant Countrie of *Lombardie*, (and not farre from the Citie of *Florence*) there was dwelling sometimes a Lorde of many riche Seignories and dominions, who nevertheless bare his name of the Castle of *Valasco*: this Lord had one only sonne and two daughters: his sonne was called (during the life of his father) the heyre of *Valasco*, who married a faire Gentlewoman of the house of *Bellavista* named *Leonora*: the elder daughter of the Lord of *Valasco* was called *Francischina*, a yong woman very toward, bothe in capacitie and other active qualities. Nowe the Lord of *Valasco* having already maried his sonne & heyre, and himselfe drawing in age, was desirous to see his daughters also bestowed before his death, and especially the eldest, who both for beutie and ripenesse of age might often put him in remembrance that shee was a collop of his owne fleshe: and therefore sought meanes to draw unto his house *Ferdinando Jeronimi* a yong gentleman of *Venice*, who delighting more in hawking, hunting, and such other pastimes than he did in studie, had left his owne house in *Venice*, and was come into *Lombardie* to take the pleasures of the countrie. So that the Lorde of *Valasco* know-ing him to be of a very good parentage, and ther withall not onely riche but adorned with sundr good qualities, was desirous (as is sayd) to draw him home to his house (under pretence of huntin and hawking) to the end he might beholde his fay daughter *Francischina*: who both for parentage ar other worldly respects, might no lesse content h minde, than hir beautie was likely to have allure his liking. But it fell oute farre contrary to h desire, for *Ferdinando Jeronimi* beholding the Lac *Leonora*, who was in deede very fayre, and of very courtlike behaviour, became enamoured of hi and forgetting the curtesie that the Lorde of *Valasco* had shewed him in entertayning him and h servaunts, with their horses, by the space of .iii moneths (whiche is a rare curtesie nowe adayes, an especially in suche a countrey) he sought all meane possibly to make the heyre of *Valasco* a *Becco*. An to the end that all menne may perceive what frute growe on suche trees, and what issues come of suc intents, I will set downe in English the fable as is written in Italian by *Bartello*. And bicause I d suppose that *Leonora* is the same name whiche we call *Elinor* in English, and that *Francischina* als doth import none other than *Fraunces*, I will s entitle them as to our own countriemen may b moste perspicuous. Understand you then, tha *Ferdinando* having nowe a hote affection unto th sayde Dame *Elynor*, and thinking it meeter to utte his firste conceipts in writing than in speache, di write unto hir as followeth.

Page	Line			Page	Line		
51	40	"MIstresse"; P: "FAyre Lady"		54	25	"my ... F.J."; P: "Ferdinando Ieronim	
	41	"these parties"; P: "this Countrie"			40	"as ... F.J."; P: "Ferdinando"	
52	14	"(as ... say)"; P: omits.		55	2	"my ... F.J."; P: "the Venetian"	
	24	"G.T."; P: omits.			3-5	"And ... that"; P: "For"	
	37-40	"I ... that"; P: omits.			16	"G.T."; P: omits.	
	41	"the sayd"; P: omits.		56	29	"F.J."; P: "Venetian,"	
	44	"unto him"; P: "him unto"			29	"hath"; P: "had"	
53	2	"F.J."; P: Ferdinando". This alteration continues throughout unless otherwise noted.			33	"one ... was"; P: omits.	
	8	"SHE:"; P: "Colei: which in english betokeneth SHE:"		57	26-30	"Well ... F.J."; P: "And Ferdinando	
					45	"G.T."; P: omits.	
	11	"G.T."; P: omits.		58	10	"I ... seene,"; P: "was doubtles"	
	25	"SHE."; P: "Colei: in english: SHE."			15	"(by ... F.J.)"; P: "(by the sam words that Bartello useth)"	
	26	"My ... that"; P: "FErdinando"			23	"London"; P: "Florence"	
53	27	"he"; P: omits.			25	"F.J."; P: "Ferdinando Ieronimi"	
	43	"G.T."; P: omits.			40	"F.J."; P: "Ferdinando Ieronimi"	
54	20-21	"(as ... declare)"; P: omits.		59	4	"therof,"; P: omits.	

Page Line

59 10 "(as . . . sayeth)"; P: "(as *Bartello* sayeth)"

    12 "my friendes"; P: "his"

    25 "strauunge"; P: "straunge"

    27 "is is"; P: "is"

    32 "packet"; P: "pocket"

    34 "*G.T.*"; P: omits.

60 6-8 ", I . . . pithy"; P: omits.

    17 "wil"; P: "I wil"

 23-24 "Knight . . . Castel"; P: "Lord of *Valas-co*"

    27 "once once"; P: "once"

    39 "*F.J.*"; P: "*Ferdinando Ieronimi*"

61 6 "*F.J.*"; P: "*Ferdinando Ieronimi*"

    22 "reason shall"; P: "reasons"

    24 "*Elinor*"; P: "*Elinor (a)*"; marginal annotation: "(a) as who sayeth"

    26 "*F.J.*"; P: "*Ferdinando Ieronimi*"

    30 "she"; P: "he"

62 1 "*F.J.*"; P: "he"

    10 "*F.J.*"; P: "he"

    19 "clappe the"; P: "clappe to the"

    34 "*G.T.*"; P: omits.

    41 "the"; P: "that"

    41 "please"; P: "pleasde"

63 9 "reitre"; P: "retire"

    20 "worthy"; P: "wotthie"

64 1-6 "These . . . it"; P: "BY these verses"

    16 "(as . . . saye)"; P: omits.

    22 "*G.T.*"; P: omits.

    33 "droppes"; P: "proppes"

65 2-6 "yet . . . it,"; P: omits.

    16 "unfoulded"; P: "foulded"

    18 "quod"; P: "quoth"

    21 "*F.J.*"; P: "He"

    28 "*F.J.*"; P: "hee"

    36 "*F.J.*"; P: "*Fardinando Ieronomy*"

66 9 "if so please"; P: "so if please"

    15 "pleasedand:"; P: "pleased: and"

    27 "*F.J.*"; P: "him,"

    33 "*H.D.*"; P: "*Hercule Donaty*"

    34 "*H.K.*"; P: "*Haniball de Cosmis*"

    36 "*F.J.*"; P: "his"

    38 "hir"; P: "*Bartelloes*"

    43 "*F.J.*"; P: "hym,"

67 1 "unto . . . kinswoman."; P: omits.

    3 "*F.J.*"; P: "*Ferdinando Ieronimy*"

    5 "be"; P: omits.

    8 "*F.J.*"; P: "he"

    14 "my . . . *F.J.*"; P: "*Ferdenando*"

    17 "*F.J.*"; P: "he"

    39 "*F.J.*"; P: "he"

Page Line

67 39 "at end"; P: "at that end"

    40 "now"; P: "how"

    40 "had shewed"; P: "had to plainely shewed"

    40 "to earnest"; P: omits.

    42 "walking"; P: "walked"

    42 "called"; P: "calling"

    44 "*F.J.*"; P: "he"

68 2 "quod"; P: "quoth"

    2 "here"; P: omits.

    4 "creature"; P: "ceature"

    7 "back"; P: "bark"

    7 "son"; P: "some"

    11 "and"; P: omits.

    21 "*F.J.*"; P: "he"

    31 "*F.J.*"; P: "hee"

    35 "*F.J.*"; P: "him"

    40 "qd."; P: "quoth"

    40 "adventured"; P: "I adventured"

69 15 "fyue"; P: "fine"

 25-37 "Were . . . depart."; P: omits.

    38 "*F.J.*"; P: "he"

    44 "did"; P: "laid"

70 2 "&"; P: omits.

    3 "that"; P: "the"

    7 "though F.J."; P: "thought *Ferdenando Ieronimy*"

    19 "also"; P: "well"

 23-28 "The . . . *G.T.*"; P: omits.

71 17 "And thus"; P: "So that"

72 6-13 "THis . . . judgementes."; P: omits.

    14 "*F.J.*"; P: "hee"

    19 "crowne"; P: "crowe"

    19 "bends"; P: "bandes"

    28 "*F.J.*"; P: "*Ferdinandos*"

    35 "*F.J.*"; P: "he"

    38 "towardes horsebacke"; P: "towardes the horsebacke"

    39 "*F.J.*"; P: "hee"

    39 "Madames"; P: "Madame"

73 6 "*F.J.*"; P: "he"

    10 "*J.*"; P: "*Ieronomy*"

    10 "soberer"; P: "sober"

    17 "*F.J.*"; P: "he"

    18 "*F.J.*"; P: "he"

    23 "trnst"; P: "trust"

    39 "*F.J.*"; P: "he"

    40 "*F.J.*"; P: "*Ieronomij*"

    45 "*F.J.*"; P: "him"

74 2 "*F.J.*"; P: "he"

    2 "dame"; P: "Dame"

    3 "with"; P: "of"

Page Line

74 11 "F.J."; P: "Ieronimy"
16 "F.J."; P: "hir servaunt"
16 "well"; P: omits.
23 "After"; P: "afterward when"
27 "G.T."; P: omits.
75 1-2 "THis . . . &c."; P: omits.
4 "I . . . affirme"; P: "it should seeme"
8 "G.T."; P: omits.
38 "foyl"; P: "stil"
76 10 "I . . . declare,"; P: "Bartello writeth,"
13 "opinions,"; P: "opinions, among the Venetians"
14 "world,"; P: "world."
14 "although . . . consent."; P: omits.
16 "by . . . F.J."; P: omits.
18 "and is"; P: "sayeth Bartello"
19-20 "I . . . behalfe,"; P: "he thinketh"
21-22 "being . . . F.J."; P: "knowing also that he"
23 "with mee"; P: omits.
24 "F.J. . . . himselfe"; P: "mine aucthor affirmeth"
27-29 "that . . . continaunce,"; P: "all circumstances of histories and"
32 "F.J."; P: "him"
32-33 "(the . . . confesse)"; P: omits.
35 "Amen"; P: omits.
35-39 "but . . . adventure"; P: omits.
77 15 "F.J."; P: "Ferdinando Ieronimy"
16-20 "I . . . Sonet,"; P: omits.
25 "proffred,"; P: "proffred, and"
26-27 "whereof . . . alleged)"; P: omits.
29 "inexpriuable"; P: "inexprimable"
39 "contentatious"; P: "contentions"
41 "imemdiatlye"; P: "immediatlye"
78 10 "this"; P: "his"
13 "mee,"; P: "sight of ye world,"
16 "amongst . . .
79 16 . . . curious:"; P: omits.
16 "and"; P: "And"
17 "now"; P: omits.
19 "London,"; P: "Florence,"
19 "F.J."; P: "hir servaunt"
81 36 "F.J."; P: "him"
40 "conceyved:"; P: "received"
82 3-4 "(for . . . the beginning,"; P: "as I finde it in Bartello the beginning,"
25 "then"; P: "that"
83 16 "along"; P: "aloane"
84 9 "new"; P: "now"
9 "new"; P: "now"
28 "translation . . . song"; P: omits.

85 34-37 "THis . . . who"; P: "THus Ferdinando"
86 2 "devoyre"; P: "endevoyre"
42 "F.J."; P: "hee"
87 4-5 "and . . . rest,"; P: omits.
25 "whome . . . name"; P: "named"
90 1 "F.J."; P: "Ieronimy"
19 "F.J."; P: "Ferdinando Ieronimy"
26 "F.J."; P: "hee"
34 "F.J."; P: "him"
39 "F.J."; P: "him"
44 "F.J."; P: "his"
91 21 "But . . .
25 . . . death. It"; P: "And It"
27-28 "my . . . that"; P: "mine aucthor dreameth yt Ferdenando"
40 "F.J."; P: "Ieronimy"
92 15 "you and"; P: omits.
15 "other"; P: omits.
24 "at these whot wordes,"; P: "at al these whot speches,"
26-27 "onely . . . pike"; P: "one only blowe"
27 "so"; P: omits.
30 "now"; P: omits.
31-35 "drewe . . . curtesie."; P: "assayleth his enemies by force."
35 "when . . . selfe,"; P: omits.
36 "F.J."; P: "him in bedde"
45 "sayd"; P: "saye"
45 "London"; P: "Florence"
93 2 "F.J."; P: "Ieronimy"
15 "therby"; P: "there"
16 "such"; P: omits.
17 "F.J."; P: "Ferdinandoes"
22 "F.J."; P: "Ieronimies"
31 "F.J."; P: "him"
94 1 "F.J."; P: "Ieronimy"
8 "Master J."; P: "him"
17 "F.J."; P: "Ferdinandoes"
19 "F.J."; P: "he"
21 "F.J."; P: "Ieronemy"
21 "reasonable"; P: "reasonably"
22 "F.J."; P: "he"
24 "F.J."; P: "he"
31 "Dawe"; P: "Dame"
34 "F.J."; P: "master Ieronemy"
44 "J."; P: "Ieronimy"
95 3 "aryse:"; P: "rise."
20 "my"; P: "me"
29 "F.J."; P: "signor Ieronemy"
30 "cause of his"; P: omits.
41 "F.J."; P: "him"
41 "arise"; P: "rise"

Page	Line				

Page Line
96 10 "meetest"; P: "meete"
   16 "pleasure"; P: "displeasure"
   25 "F.J."; P: "Ieronimies"
   34 "quippes,"; P: "quibbes"
97 28 "Besse:"; P: "Lamia"
   30 "Besse"; P: "Lamia"
   39 "locke"; P: "lockte"
98 21-22 "fallen . . . Slippes."; P: "in Italie called a Caroline."
   27 "three . . . peny"; P: "smal"
   32 "emported"; P: "imparted"
   40 "pocked,"; P: pocket,"
99 7 "slip,"; P: "Caroline,"
   20 "towars"; P: "towards"
   21 "semblant"; P: "resemblaunt"
   23 "obteyne"; P: "optaine"
   28 "shhe"; P: "shee"
   38 "which passed"; P: "which had ever passed"
00 27 "slippes"; P: "Carolines"
   42 "it, but . . . all."; P: "it."
   44 "F.J."; P: "ye Venetiane"
01 12 "F.J."; P: "Ieronimy"
   23-24 "Here . . . that"; P: "And"

Page Line
101 29 "conceitps"; P: "conceipts"
   33-34 "conclusion, thus"; P: "conclusion: And thus"
102 3 "Fraunces,"; P: "Fraunces,)"
   3 "F.J."; P: "him"
   5 "wrot"; P: "woote"
   10 "F.J."; P: "he"
   14-16 "you, unlesse . . . already"; P: "you."
   17 "accasion"; P: "occation"
   18 "F.J."; P: "he"
   25 "G.T."; P: omits.
   32 "G.T."; P: omits.
   34 "redesse"; P: "redresse"
103 8 "F.J."; P: "Ferdinando Ieronimy"
   21 "arme"; P: "harme"
   28 "G.T."; P: omits.
   43 "F.J."; P: "Ferdinando Ieronimy"
104 19 "itas"; P: "it, as"
   25 "F.J."; P: "he"
   36 "F.J."; P: "Poore Ieronimy"
105 3 "G.T."; P: omits.
   28 "F.J."; P: "Ferdinando Ieronimy"
   29 P has the following ending.

THus Ferdinando being no longer able to beare these extreeme despites, resolved to absent himselfe, [a]swell for his owne further quiete, as also to avoide the occasion of greater mischiefes that might ensewe: And although the exceeding curtesies and approved fidelitie of Dame Fraunces had beene sufficient to allure the fast lyking of any man, specially considering that shee was reasonably fayre, and descended of a worthy father, who nowe well flatlye to move and solicite the same, yet such sinistre conceiptes had he taken by the frailtye of Dame Elinor, as that rejecting all proffers, and contempning all curtesies, he tooke his leave, & (without pretence of returne) departed to his house in Venice: spending there ye rest of his dayes in a dissolute kind of lyfe: & abandoning the worthy Lady Fraunc[ischin]a, who (dayly being gauled with the griefe of his great ingratitude) dyd shortlye bring hir selfe into a myserable consumption: wherof (after three yeares languishing) she dyed:

Notwithstanding al which occur[rente]s the Lady Elinor lived long in ye continuance of hir accustomed change: & thus we see that where wicked lust doeth beare the name of love, it doth not onelye infecte the lyght minded, but it maye also become confusion to others which are vowed to constancie. And to that ende I have recyted this Fable which maye serve as ensample to warne the youthfull reader from attempting the lyke worthles enterprise. I knowe not howe my rude translation thereof wyll delight the finest judgementes: But sure as Bartello writteth it in Italian, it is both pleasaunt and profitable: the which hath made mee adventure thus to publishe the same in such simple style as I am able to endite: Desiring the gentle reader, rather to take example of reformation therein, then to finde faulte at the homelye handling of the same.

Ever or never.

[From this point on, the notes refer to poems rather than to pages.]

Poem Line
1   P: omits.
2 Int. P: prefixes: "The Frute of reconciliation,"
3 Int.,
  l.4 "so"; P: omits.

Poem Line
4 17 "migh"; P: "might"
8 Int. P: prefixes: "The refusal of a lover, writen"
   5 "it"; P: "yet"
   14 "that descends,"; P: "that he descends,"

Poem	Line	
8	15	"I not"; P: marginal notation: "Know not."
	19	"thewes"; P: marginal notation: "Good qualities"
9	12	*Cleopatra*; P: marginal notation: "She was an Egiptian"
	18	"solle"; P: "soyle". See "Critical Notes."
	29	"I that"; P: "that I"
	43	"of bright"; P: "bright of"
10	Int.	*He . . . write,*; P: *"The lookes of a lover forsaken: written"*
	22	"thy"; P: "the"
	28	"refusd"; P: "reffuse"
12	10	"in,"; P: "to"
13	Int., ll.1-3	"Enough . . . with a"; P: "A"
	Int., ll.3-4	"which he"; P: omits.
	6	"floweth"; P: "flowes"
14	Int., l.1	*Written*; P: "Pride in Court written"
	12	"wrong"; P: "wrong."
15	Int., l.1	*From . . . certaine*; P: "Certaine"
	Int., l.5	*foloweth.*; P: "foloweth, being termed with the rest that follow the lokes of a lover enamoured."
16	Int., l.6	"G.G."; P: "the Aucthour"
	Int., l.15	"G.G."; P: "the Aucthor"
	8	"jelouse love"; P: "jelousie"
18	6	"bind, then"; P: "bind them,"
20		P: omits.
21	Int., ll.1-2	*He . . . followeth.*; P: *"The praise of Phillip Sparrowe"*
	21	"newfond"; P: "new found"
	39	"by-the-rood,"; P: "by the rood,"
	53	"others"; P: "other"
22	23	"the"; P: "thy"
23	Int.	
	ll.1-3	*To . . . wise.*; P: "To the same gentlewoman because she challenged the Aucthour for holding downe his head alwaies, and for that hee looked not uppon hir in wonted manner."
	15	*Spraeta . . . vivunt.*; P: *"Si fortunatus infoelix."*
24	55	*Spreta*; P: *Spraeta*
25	Int., ll.1-2	*The . . . complayneth*; P: *"The lamentation of a lover."*
	15	"for sing"; P: "sing for"
26	Int., l.1	*The*; P: "Farewell with a mischief written
	Int., l.2	*doth . . . determine*; P: "& therfor he determined"
	28	"none"; P: "no"
	45	"dragges"; P: "druggs"
27	35	*Spreta*; P: *Spraeta*
28	Int.	*writer therof,*; P: "Aucthour,"
29	Int.	*another Author.*; P: *"a Lover."*
30	Int.,	*The Lover*; P: "In trust is Treason written by a Lover,"
	Int.	*fayle, . . . lament.*; P: "fayle."
32	Int., ll.1-4	*Now . . . this*; P: "In"
34		P: This is placed in *"Dan Bartholmew of Bathe"*, entitled, "Dan Barthomewes his third Triumphe", where has the posy *Fato non Fortuna*.
35	Int.	*The . . . complayneth.*; P: "The doe of disdaine written by a lover disdainfully rejected contrary to former promise."
	14	"faithfull"; P: "faithfully"
	28	P: Marginal annotation: "Angelica fusing the most famous knights the whole worlde, chose at last Medo a poore serving man."
	44	"That"; P: "But"
36	Int.	*An . . . complayneth.*; P: "Mars despite of Vulcane written for an a sent lover (parted from his Lady Sea.)"
38		P: omits.
39	Int.	*An*; P: "Patience perforce wherein a
41	Int.	*Three Sonets*; P: "Davids salutacio to Berzabe wherein are three sonet
	5	"a gaine"; P: "againe"
43	Int., l.1	*To*; P: "The fruite of foes written t
	15	"cured"; P: "recured"
44	Int.	*An*; P: "Soone acquainted, soone fi gotten, As appeareth here by an"
	Int.	*unconstant*; P: "inconstant"
45	16	"wile"; P: "will"
	22	"plaster"; P: "plasters"
46	21	"es,"; P: "yest,"

Poem Line

46 23 "nam"; P: marginal annotation: "Am not"
    40 "*Corma*"; P: "*Corinna*"
    47 "I"; P: "to"
47 Int. "*The . . . followeth.*"; P: "*The shield of Love. &c.*"
48 Int. "*I . . . Anatomie*"; P: "*The Anatomye of a Lover.*"
    13 "are . . . now,"; P: "quite braunfalne are,"
    16 "his"; P: "this"
    23 "can beare"; P: "sustaine"
49 Int. "*Gascoignes araignement.*"; P: "*The arraig[n]ment of a Lover.*"
    15 "Here"; P: "Wyll"; marginal annotation in P: "Wyll is dame bewties chiefe Justice of Oyre and terminer."
    50 P: marginal annotation: "Common Bayll."
50 Int. "*Gascoignes*"; P: "*In*"
51 Int. "*Gascoignes*"; P: "*In*"
    Int. "*Wilton.*"; P: "Wilton whome the auctor found in a homely house."
52 Int. "*Gascoignes passion.*"; P: "*The passion of a Lover.*"
52 43 "Ectyck"; P: marginal annotation: "There is in deede suche a kinde of fever."
    54 "renue"; P: "relieve"
    60 *Gascoignes*"; P: "my straunge"
53 Int. "*Gascoignes . . . Divorce.*"; P: "*The Divorce of a Lover.*"
    7   "to"; P: "loe"
    8   "wherein"; P: "in which"
    19 P: marginal annotation: "Such a sect there is that desire no longer lyfe then whiles they are in love."
54 25 "hir not"; P: "not hir"
    31 "purest"; P: "poorest"
55 Int. "*Gascoignes Lullabie.*"; P: "*The Lullabie of a Lover.*"
    48 "Gascoignes"; P: "then this"
56 Int. "*Gascoignes Recantation.*"; P: "*The Recantation of a Lover.*"
    32 "Astolfe"; P: marginal annotation: "Astolf being the goodliest personne in the worlde founde a dwarfe lying with his wife"
57 Int. "*I . . . written*"; P: "*Gascoignes Memories, written*
58 11 "strives"; P: "sterves"
    12 "povert"; P: "povertye"

58 32 "soyle"; P: "spoyle"
    40 "prove"; P: "poore"
60 55 "The bough,"; P: "They bought,"
    86 "silly"; P: "simple"
61 36 "He says"; P: "He say"
    41 "pens"; P: "pence"
62 Int. "*wherein . . . these*"; P: omits.
    Int. "*verses,*"; P: "verses, devised"
    Int. "*Inne,*"; P: "Inne:"
    Int. "*a . . . works.*"; P: "and therefore called Gascoignes memories."
    Title "*Gascoignes*"; P: "A"
    23-24 "He . . . gold."; P: omits.
    27-28 "He . . . neede:"; P: omits.
    33-34 "They . . . decreede."; P: omits.
    94 "Hallontyde,"; P: "Hollontide,"
    94 "wynters"; P: "winter"
    100 "his . . . best."; P: "himselfe at rest."
63 21 "we"; P: "you"
    35 "all"; P: "and"
64 Concl., ll.1-6 "*These . . . rehersed.*"; P: omits.
65 Int. "*Gascoignes . . . followeth.*"; P: "The introduction to the Psalme of Deprofundis."
66 Int. "*Gascoignes councell*"; P: "Councell"
    Int. "*him*"; P: "the aucthor"
    24 "A"; P: "On"
    28 "Hellycon"; P: marginal annotation: "The Hill where poetes fayne that the Muses sleepe."
    45 "Etymologie,"; P: marginal annotation: "A true exposition."
    46 "Surquydrye."; P: marginal annotation: "Overweening"
67 Int. "*Gascoignes councell*"; P: "Councell"
    39 P: marginal annotation: "There are to many of them in every countrey."
    50 P: marginal annotation: "A Misterie."
    94 "but . . . bones,"; P: "but bloud and leaves the bones,"
    117 "stande"; P: "stayde"
    119 "soule and bodie"; P: "bones and bodie"
    120 "faultes"; P: "blots"
    121 "this . . . P,"; P: "this P, can beare no blockes,"
    122 "my"; P: "me"
    123 "Papistrie," P: "piles and pockes"
    127 "the . . . infecte"; P: "such Spanish buttons can infect"
    129 "theyr . . . glosse,"; P: "those sunnes do mellowe men so fast"
    130 "per Papist,"; P: "very ripe"

Poem Line

67 131-132 "Or . . . Atheist:";
P: "Although (by sweate) they learne
to live and last
When they have daunced after
Guydoes pype:"
146 "Pencoyde:"; P: marginal annotation:
"Sir William Morgan of Pencoyde."
68 Int. *"Gascoignes"*; P: *"An"*
11 "Do"; P: "Doth"
27 "Gods"; P: "his"
33 "quoth"; P: "quod"
69 Int., l.1 *"Gascoignes"*; P: *"A"*
Int., l. 2 "(as . . . declare)"; P: omits.
Int., 12-13 *"Master Gascoigne"*; P: "The
Aucthour"
Int., l.15 *"Master Gascoigne"*; P: "The
Aucthour"
45 *"Zechynes"*; P: marginal annotation: "A
peece of golde like the Crusado"
68 "idlenesse,"; P: "ydle rest,"
82 *"Famagosta"*; P: marginal annotation:
"The chiefe Cittie in Cyprus."
101 "quoth"; "quod"
113 "quoth"; P: "quod"
121 "quoth"; P: "quod"
130 "first"; P: "styll"
156 *"Bragadine,"*; P: marginal annotation:
"The governour of Famagosta."
158 *"Mustaffa"*; P: marginal annotation:
"The generall of the Turkes."
171 "tirannie"; P: "traine"
210 "for"; P: "of"
224 "these"; P: "theie"
247 "lefte landes,"; P: "lefte his landes,"
257 "myghtie God"; P: "myghtie hand of
God"
261 "do"; P: "dyd"
263 "those"; P: "these"
280 P: marginal annotation: "The Monta-
cutes and capels in Italye do were
tokens in their cappes to be knowen
one from another."
309 *"Gondalaes,"*; P: marginal annotation:
"Venetian botes"
316 "our"; P: "the"
70 Int., l.4 *"master Gascoigne"*; P: "the Aucthor"
Int., l.6 *"master Gascoigne"*; P: "the Aucthor"
79 "stop"; P: "stoupe"
100 "bet"; P: marginal annotation: "better"
71 8 "floures fresh"; P: "floures most fresh"
72 1 "there"; P: "here"
74 5 *"Alderlievest"*; P: marginal annotation:
"best beloved"

Poem Line

74 12 *"(en bon gré)"*; P: marginal annotation
"in good worth"
52 "Fadome"; P: marginal annotation
"Fadom & a half, three ho."
66 *"Hull"*; P: marginal annotation: "Whe
all sayles are taken downe."
72 *"Ghy zijt te vroegh"*; P: marginal a-
notation: "You be to soone"
73 *"Tis niet goet tijt"*; P: marginal anne
tation: "It is not good tide."
81 *"Alba"*; P: marginal annotation: "th
Duke"
107 "unkouth,"; P: marginal annotation
"unknowen"
120 *"Die tijt is goet, dat heb ick weell be
kend."*; P: marginal annotation: "It i
good tide that know I well"
132 *"Edell Bloetts"*; P: marginal annotation
"Lusty gallants"
203 "My chiefe companions"; P: margina
annotation: "Yorke and Herle."
238 "carke,"; P: marginal annotation: "care"
259 "be"; P: "by"
283 "by"; P: "be"
283 "pynke"; marginal annotation: "A Smal
bote."
295 "As"; P: "And"
299 "pufft"; P: "puffe"
D.B. Int., ll.1-3 *"And . . . it."*; P: *"The delectabl-
history of sundry* adventures passed by
Dan Bartholmew of Bathe."
D.B.1 17 "childe"; P: "cheife"
25 "now"; P: "(neare)"
47 "had"; P: "hath"
140 "lacke"; P: "sport", marginal annota-
tion: "Lacke."
D.B.2 Int. *"Dan . . . Triumphes."*; P: "Dan Bar-
tholmew his first Triumphe."
28 "seeke"; P: "selfe"
67 "was"; P: "were"
D.B.
2-3 Bet. P here inserts: "Dan Bartholmew his
second Triumphe."; and "Dan Bar-
tholmewes his third Triumphe." which
appears in the *Flowres* as poem 34 (see
above, p. 131). I give here the
"second Triumphe."

FYe pleasure fye, thou cloyest me with delight,
Thou fylst my mouth with sweete meates overmuch,
I wallowe styll in joye both daye and night.
I deeme, I dreame, I doe, I taste, I touch:
No thing but all that smelles of perfect blisse,
Fye pleasure fye, I cannot like of this.

To taste (sometimes) a baite of bytter gall,
o drinke a draught of sower Ale (some season)
o eate browne bread with homely handes in Hall
oth much encrease mens appetites by reason:
nd makes the sweete more sugred that ensewes,
ince mindes of men do styll seeke after newes.

The pampred horse is seldome seene in breath,
hose maunger makes his greace (oftimes) to melt,
he crammed Fowle comes quickly to his death.
uch coldes they catche in hottest happes that swelt.
nd I (much like) in pleasure scawled styll,
oe feare to starve although I feede my fill.

It might suffice that love hath built his bowre,
etwene my Ladies lively shyning eyes,
 were inough that Bewties fading flowre:
rowes ever freshe with hir in heavenly wise.
 had bene well that shee were faire of face,
nd yet not robbe all other Dames of grace.

To muse in minde, how wise, how faire, how good,
ow brave, howe franke, how curteous, and how true,
Iy Lad[y] is: doth but inflame my blood,
'ith humors such, as byd my health adue.
nce happe alwaies when it is clombe on hye,
oth fall full lowe, though earst it reachte the Skye.

Lo pleasure lo, lo thus I leade a life,
hat laughes for joye, and trembleth oft for dread,
hy panges are such as call for changes knife,
o cut the twist, or else to stretch the thread,
hich holdes yfeere the bondell of my blisse,
ye pleasure fye, I dare not trust to this.
            Fato non Fortuna.

oem Line
.B.3 83 "Askaunces lo,"; P: marginal annotation: "As who should say:"
    85 "them"; P: "this"
    111 "seeke"; P: "like"
    161 P: marginal annotation: "These thinges are mistical and not to bee understoode but by Thaucthour himselfe."
    194 "ghostlike"; P: "ghostly"
    236 P: marginal annotation: "Another misterie."
    271 P: marginal annotation: "Another misterie."
    293 P: marginal annotation: "Another misterie."
.B.4 12 "swell"; P: "swelt"
.B.4 17 "breath,"; P: "breache"
.B.5 13 P: marginal annotation: "Another misterie."

Poem Line
D.B.6 48 P: marginal annotation: "Hope is ever contrary to a lovers Passion."
D.B.7 24 "Are"; P: "Is"
    28 "we"; P: "wo"
D.B.8 53 "best"; P: "rest"
    79 "fame"; P: "flame,"
D.B.12 17 "am"; P: "was"
    17 "prove unto"; P: "proved to"
    19 "am"; P: "was"
    21 "am"; P: "was"
    43 "long since"; P: "at first"
    61 "jealosie"; P: "jollitye"
    67 "feare"; P: "feares"
    68 "And that his part. &c."; P: rewords this line and completes the "reporters conclusion".

And that his bale were better overblowne,
Then thus to pine remedylesse in griefe,
And he would saye that griefe was his reliefe.

Short tale to make so long he lyved thus,
Tyll at the last he gan in deede to dye,
Beleeve me Lordes (and by him that dyed for us)
I sawe him give to close his dying eye,
I sawe him stryve and strangle passingly.
And suche a griefe I tooke, that yet I not,
If he or I had then more griefe ygot.

But who hath seene a Lampe begyn to fade,
Which lacketh oyle to feede his lyngring lyght,
And then againe who so hath seene it made,
With oyle and weecke to last the longsome night.
Let him conceyve that I sawe such a sight.
Whereof to thinke (although I sighde erewhile)
Loe nowe I laughe my sorrowes to beguile.

Upon the stones a trampling steede we heard,
Which came ful straight unto our lodging doore,
And straight therwith we heard how one enquirde,
If such a Knight (as I describde before)
Were lodged there: the Hoast withouten more,
Sayd yes forsooth, and God he knowes (quod he)
He is as sicke as any man maye bee.

The messenger sware by no bugges I trowe,
But bad our hoast to bring him where he laye,
(Quod I to *Bartholmew*) I heare by lowe,
A voice which seemes somewhat of you to saye:
And eare that past not full a furlong waye,
Behold the man came stowping in at doore,
And truth to tell he syked wondrous sore.

At last from out his bosome dyd he take,
A Letter sealde yfolded fayre and well,
And kyssing it (I thinke for Mistresse sake)
He sayd to *Bartholmew*: Syr Knight be well,
Nowe reade these lines the which I neede not tell,
From whence they come: but make an ende of mone,
For you are sicke, and she is woe begone.

The theefe condemnde and gone to gallowe tree,
(If one crye *Grace*: lo here a *Pardon* prest)
Doth dye sometimes, when most he seemde to be,
From death redeemd, such bronts may breede in brest,
Twyxt sodaine joye, and thoughts which paine opprest,
The *Romaine Widdowe* dyed when she beheld,
Hir Sunne (whome earst She compted slaine in field).

So *Bartholmew* tweene griefe and sodaine joye,
Laye styll in traunce, me thinkes I see him yet,
And out of doubte it gave me such anoye,
To see him so, him selfe in fancies fret,
That sure I thought his eyes in head were set.
And that he laye (as some saye) drawing on,
Untill his breath and all were past and gone.

But high de[c]rees of heaven which had ordainde,
(For his decaye) a freshe delaye of paine,
Revived him: yet from his eyes downe raind,
Such rewfull teares as moved me to plaine,
The dolefull plight wherein he dyd remaine.
For trust me now, to see him sorrowe so,
It might have made a stone to melt in wo.

Thrise dyd his tongue beginne to tell his thought,
And thrise (alas) it foltred in his mouth,
With stopping sobbes and skalding sighes he sought
To utter that which was to me uncouth.
So staies the streame, when furiouslie it flouth.
And filles the dikes where it had wont to swimme,
Untill by force it breakes above the brimme.

At last (with paine) the first word that he spake,
Was this: *Alas,* and therewithall he stayed,
His feebled Jawes and hollowe voyce could make,
None other sounde, his thoughtes were all dismayed,
His hearye head full lowe in bosome layed.
Yet when he sawe me marke what he would saye,
He cryed right out *Alas and welawaye.*

Alas (quod he) deare friend behold this bloode,
And with that word he gan againe to sorrowne:
The messenger which in a studdye stoode,
Awakt at last: and in mine eare dyd rowne,
Saying: those lines which I have there throwen downe.
Were written all with blood of hir owne hande,
For whome he nowe in this distresse doth stande.

And since (quod he) She hath vouchsafed so,
To shead hir blood in witnesse of hir griefe,
Me thinkes he rather should relieve hir wo:
Then thus deny to send hir some reliefe.
Alas alas (quod he) she holdes him chiefe.
And well wote I (what ere his fansie bee)
There sittes no man so neere hir heart as hee.

Therewith he raysde his heavy head alight,
Askaunces Ha? in deede and thinkst thou so?
But out alas his weake and weary sprit,
Forbad his tongue in furder termes to go.
His thought sayd *Haight,* his sillie speache cryed *H*
And thus he laye in dompes and dolefull trance,
Tyll darksome night dyd somewhat change his chance

For when the light of day began to fade,
And courtins round about his bed were drawne,
A golden slomber dyd his lymmes invade,
And held him husht tyll daye againe gan dawne,
Whereby Dame quiet put him in a pawne,
To set his thoughts (which strived earst) at one,
And bad debate be packing to be gone.

Percase sweete love dyd lull him so on sleepe,
Perhaps Dame fansie rockt the Cradell too,
How so it were I take thereof no keepe,
With such conceiptes have I nothing to doo,
But when he wakt he asked plainly who,
Had brought him so from rage to quiet rest,
And who had borne the torments from his brest?

(Quod I) my friend: here is a letter lo,
Behold it here and be all hole againe,
What man were he that wyther would in wo,
Which thus might prosper in despite of paine?
Were he not worse then mad which would complaine
On such a friend as this to me doth seeme?
Which (for thy health) hir blood doth not esteeme

Thus much I sayd to comfort him God knowes,
(But what I thought that keepe I cloose in hold)
Sometimes a man must flatter with his foes,
And sometimes saye that brasse is bright as Gold
For he that hath not all thinges as he would,
Must winke sometimes, as though he dyd not see,
And seeme to thinke thinges are not as they bee.

Dan Bartholmew gan take the briefe in hand,
And brake the seale, but when he saw the blood,
Good Lord how bolt upright his heere dyd stand?
For though the friendly wordes therein were good
Yet many a thought they moved in his moode,
As well appeared by his flecked cheekes,
Nowe cherrye redde, nowe pale and greene as leekes

I dreamt (quod he) that I was done to death,
nd that I laye full colde in earth and claye,
ut that I was restored unto breath,
y one that seemde lyke *Pellycane* to playe,
ho shed his blood to give me foode alwaye,
nd made me live in spite of sorrowe styll,
e how my dreame agrees now with this byll?

His feebled wittes forgotten had there whyle,
y whome and howe he had this letter first,
ut when he spyde the man, then gan he smile,
r secreete joye his heart dyd seeme to burst,
ow thought he best that (earst) he compted worst.
nd lovingly he dyd the man embrace,
nd askt howe farde the roote of all his grace?

See sodaine chaunge, see subtile sweete disceipte,
ehold how love can make his subjectes blinde,
t all men marke hereby what guilefull baite,
an *Cupide* layeth to tyse the lovers minde:
acke alacke a slender thread maye binde,
at prysonor fast, which meanes to tarrye styll,
lytle road corrects a ready wyll.

The briefe was writte and blotted all with gore,
nd thus it sayde: *Behold howe stedfast love,*
ath made me hardy (thankes have he therefore)
write these wordes thy doubtes for to remove,
ith mine owne blood: and yf for thy behove
ese bloody lynes do not thy Cares convert:
vowe the next shall bleede out of my heart.

I dwell to long upon this thriftlesse tale,
r *Bartholmew* was well appeasde hereby,
d feelingly he banished his bale,
king herein a tast of remedy,
y lyte and lyte his fittes away gan flye.
d in short space he dyd recover strength,
stand on foote and take his horse at length.

So that we came to London both yfere,
d there his Goddesse tarryed tyll we came,
am to blame to call hir Goddesse here,
nce she deserved in deede no Goddesse name,
ut sure I thinke (and you may judge the same)
e was [to] him a Goddesse in his thought,
though perhaps hir Shrines was overbought.

I maye not write what words betweene them past,
ow teares of griefe were turnde to teares of joye,
r how their dole became delight at last.
r how they made great myrth of much anoye,
r how content was coyned out of coye,
t what I sawe and what I well maye write,
at (as I maye) I meane for to endite.

In lovely London love gan nowe renew,
This blooddye Letter made it battle much,
And all the doubtes which he in fansies drew,
Were done away as there had bene none such,
(But to him selfe) he bare no body grutch.
Him selfe (he sayde) was cause of all this wo,
Withouten cause that hir suspected so.

O loving Youthes this glasse was made for you,
And in the same you may your selves behold,
Beleeve me nowe not one in all your crew,
Which (where he loves) hath courage to be bold,
Your *Cressides* climes are alwaies uncontrold.
You dare not saye the Sunne is cleare and bright,
You dare not sweare that darkesome is the night.

Terence was wise which taught by *Pamphilus,*
Howe courage quailes where love beblinds the sence,
Though proofe of times makes lovers quarelous,
Yet small excuse serves love for just defence.
These *Courtisanes* have power by pretence
To make a Swan of that which was a Crowe,
As though blacke pitche were turned into Snowe.

Ferenda, She whome heaven and earth had framde,
For his decaye and to bewitche his wittes,
Made him nowe thinke him selfe was to be blamde,
Which causeles thus would fret himselfe in fittes,
Shee made him thinke that sorrowe sildome sittes,
Where trust is tyed in fast and faithfull knottes,
She sayd *Mistrust* was meete for simple sottes.

What wyl you more shee made him to beleeve,
That she first loved although she yonger were,
She made him thinke that his distresse dyd greeve,
Hir guiltlesse minde: and (that it might appeare,
Howe these conceiptes could joyne or hang yfere)
She dyd confesse howe soone shee yeelded his,
Such force (quod she) in learned men there is.

She furder sayde that all to true it was,
Howe youthfull yeares (and lacke of him alone)
Had made hir once to choose out brittle glasse,
For perfect Gold: She dyd confesse (with mone)
That youthfully shee bytte a worthlesse bone.
But that therein she tasted deepe delight,
That sayde shee not, nor I presume to write.

She sware (and that I beare full well in minde)
Howe *Dyomede* had never *Troylus* place,
Shee sayd and sware (how ever sate the winde)
That *Admirals* dyd never know hir case,
She sayd againe that never *Noble Face,*
Dyd please hir eye nor moved hir to change,
She sayd her minde was never geven to range.

She sayd and sayd that *Bracelettes* were ybound,
To hold him fast (but not to charme his thought)
She wysht therewith that she were deepely drownd,
In Ippocrace: if ever she had sought,
Or dronke, or smelt, or tane, or found, or bought,
Such *Nectar* droppes as she with him had dronke,
(But this were true) she wisht hir soule were sonke.

And to conclude, she sayde no printed rymes,
Could please hir so as his brave *Triumphes* dyd:
Why wander I? She cov'red all hir crimes,
With deepe disceipt, and all hir guiles she hyd,
With fained teares, and *Bartholmew* she ryd
With double gyrthes, she byt and whyned both,
And made him love where he had cause to loth.

These be the fruictes which grow on such desire,
These are the gaines ygot by such an art,
To late commes he that seekes to quenche the fire,
When flames possesse the house in every part,
Who lyst in peace to keepe a quiet hart.
Flye love betimes, for if he once oretake him,
Then seeld or never shall he well forsake him.

If once thou take him *Tenaunt* to thy brest,
No wrytte nor force can serve to plucke him thence,
No pylles can purge his humour lyke the rest,
He bydes in bones, and there takes residence,
Against his blowes no bucklar makes defence.
And though (with paine) thou put him from thy
    house,
Yet lurkes he styll in corners lyke a Mouse.

At every hole he creepeth in by stelth,
And privilye he feedeth on thy crommes,
With spoiles unseene he wasteth all thy welth,
He playes boe peepe when any body commes,
And dastardlik he seemes to dread the drommes,
Although in deede in *Embushe* he awaytes,
To take thee stragling yf thou passe his straites.

So seemed now by *Bartholmews* successe,
Who yeelded sone unto this second charge,
Accusing styll him selfe for his distresse,
And that he had so languished at large,
Short worke to make: he had none other charge
To beare loves blowes, but styll to trust hir tale,
And pardon crave because he bread hir bale.

And thus he lyvde contented styll with craft,
Mistrusting most, that gave least cause of doubt,
He fledde mishappe and helde it by the haft,
He banisht bale and bare it styll about,
He let in love and thought to hold him out.
He seemde to bathe in perfect blisse againe,
When (God he knowes) he fostred privie paine.

For as the Tree which crooked growes by kin
(Although it be with propping underset)
In trackt of time to crooked course wyll twinde,
So could *Ferenda* never more forget,
The lease at large where she hir flinges had fet.
But rangde againe, and to hir byas fell,
Such chaunges chaunce where lust (for love) d
    dwell.

And as it hapt (and God his wyll it was)
Dan Bartholmew perceyvde it very plaine,
So that perforce he let his pleasures passe,
And strave no more against the streame in vaine
But therewithall he purchased such paine,
As yet I shrinke in minde thereof to muse,
And marvaile more howe he the same could use.

His lustlesse limmes which wonted were to syt
In quiet chaire, with pen and paper prest,
Were armed nowe with helme and harnesse fyt,
To seeke adventures boldly with the best,
Hee went to warres that wont to live in rest.
And warres in deede he made withouten blowes,
For why his friendes were nowe become his foes.

Such was his hap to warre both night and day
To watche and warde at every time and tyde,
Though foes were farre yet skowted he alwaye,
And when they came he must their brontes abide
Who ever fled he would his head not hyde.
For sure dispayre his corpse so close had armed,
That by deathes darte he could no whit be harm

In his *Ensigne* these collours gan he chuse,
Blacke, white, and greene, first blacke for morni
    mone,
Then white for chaste, because he did refuse,
(Thenceforth) to thinke but even of hir alone.
A bende of greene: for though his joyes were go
Yet should it seeme he hoped for a daye,
And in that bende his name he dyd displaye.

That selfe same name which in his will he wro
(You knowe my minde) when he was out of *tune*
When he subscribde (which may not bee forgote)
Howe that his name was *Fato Non F[o]rtuna.*
And as I gesse bicause his love was *Una*,
That played hir pranckes according to hir kinde,
He wrote these wordes hir best excuse to finde.

As who should saye, lo destenies me drive,
And happe could not have overthrowen me thus
I constrew this because I do beleeve,
That once againe he wyll bee amorous,
I fere it muche by him that dyed for us,
And who so doubtes that causeles thus I faint
Let him but reade the greene Knights heavy plai

Bartello he which writeth ryding tales,
ringes in a Knight which cladde was all in greene,
hat sighed sore amidde his greevous gales,
nd was in hold as *Bartholmew* hath beene.
ut (for a placke) it maye therein be seene,
hat, that same Knight which there his griefes begonne,
Batts owne Fathers Sisters brothers Sonne.

Well since my borrell braine is all to bloont
o give a gesse what ende this man shall have,
nd since he rageth not as he was woont,
lthough sometimes he seeme (alite) to crave,
et wyll I not his doinges so deprave,
s for to judge (before I see his ende)
hat harder happe his angrie starres can sende.

And therewithall my wearye muse desires,
o take her rest: and pardon craves also,
hat shee presumde to bring hir selfe in bryers,
y penning thus this true report of wo:
ith sillye grace these sorye rimes maye go,
 such a rancke as *Bartholmew* hath plast,
 that shee feares hir cunning is disgrast.

But take them yet in gree as they be ment,
nd wayle with mee the losse of such a man:
coumpt him lost because I see him bent.
o yeld againe where first his greefe began,
nd though I cannot write as others can
me mournefull verse to move you mone his fall,
et weepe (with me) you faythfull lovers all.
        Finis.   quod Dixit & Dixit.

Lenvoye

SYr *Salamanke* to thee this tale is tolde,
Peruse it well and call unto thy minde,
The pleasaunt place where thou dydst first behold
The rewfull rymes: remember how the *Winde*
Dyd calmelye blowe: and made me leave behinde,
Some leaves thereof: whiles I sate reading styll,
And thou then seemdst to hearken with good wyll.

Beleeve me nowe, hadst thou not seemd to lyke
The wofull wordes of *Bartholmews* discourse,
They should have lyen styll drowned in the dyke,
Lyke *Sybylls* leaves which flye with lytle force,
But for thou seemdst to take therein remorce,
I sought againe in corners of my brest,
To finde them out and place them with the rest.

Such skyll thou hast to make me (foole) beleeve,
My bables are as brave as any bee,
Well since it is so, let it never greeve
Thy friendly minde this worthlesse verse to see
In print at last: for trust thou unto mee,
Thine onely prayse dyd make me venture forth,
To set in shewe a thing so litle worth.

Thus unto thee these leaves I recommend,
To reade, to raze, to view, and to correct,
Vouchsafe (my friend) therein for to amend
That is amisse, remember that our sect,
Is sure to bee with floutes alwayes infect.
And since most mockes wyll light uppon my muse,
Vouchsafe (my friend) hir faultes for to peruse.
        Tam Marti quam Mercurio.

CRITICAL NOTES

The *Critical Notes* are designed to elucidate those passages whose meanings time has obscured, and to identify Gascoigne's references to persons and places. In general, single words are not explained in these notes but are listed in the Glossary.

The *Oxford English Dictionary* is the chief source of the notes on the meanings of words and phrases. Works of the period and the labors of editors of many such works have also been utilized and references are included.

Page	Line	
47		This introductory letter by the printer and those of *H.W.* and *G.T.* are discussed in the Introduction to this volume and in the present editor's study, *George Gascoigne*. In the Introduction discussion will be found in the following sections: Bibliographical Problems, The Original Contents, and Authorship.

The reasons for the omission of all these letters in *The Posies* are quite clear: that of the printer applies specifically to the *Flowres*; those of *H.W.* and *G.T.* were part of the mask of anonymity adopted by Gascoigne in publishing the *Flowres* and had no place in the revised and acknowledged *Posies;* furthermore, the transformation of "The Adventures of Master F.J." into a feigned translation from the Italian eliminated *G.T.*'s original introduction to the story.

28-30   *And as the venemous . . . weede*] Cf. Gascoigne's letter "To al yong Gentlemen," (*Works,* I, 12) where the same Euphuistic conceit is employed. This popular conceit appears in Erasmus' *Parabolae* (in Lycosthenes' *Apophthegmata*, ed. 1574, pp. 1216, 1247, 1284); in Lyly's *Euphues* (*Works*, ed. Bond, I, 309); and in Nashe's *Anatomie of Absurditie* (*Works*, ed. McKerrow, I, 30).

31   *harebraind*] wild or giddy, derived obviously from "the brain of a hare."

48   Following this letter the original contained *Supposes* and *Jocasta*. For the omission of the two plays, see The Original Contents in the Introduction to the present work.

3   *Freeman Jones*] apparently the equivalent of the modern "John Doe."

49   3   *H.W.*] This and the other initials of these letters—*G.T.* and *A.B.*—were obviously chosen because they were common and could suggest any number of possible identifications.

22-23   *the fond devises . . . fantasie*] *fantasie* here seems to mean love; *golden fetters,* the bonds of love—perhaps an echo of Petrarch's *Trionfo D'Amore* in which Cupid appears as the returning Roman conqueror with his captives in chains. There is a pictorial representation of this in Gascoigne's own copy of Petrarch (*vide* frontispiece of *George Gascoigne*).

24   *they walke unseene in a net*] a proverbial phrase meaning, "they think themselves unseen although they are only covered by a net through which anyone can see." There seems to be some connection with

Page   Line

                the story of Venus and Mars trapped in the net cast by the jealous
                husband, Vulcan, although in this instance the guilty pair had no
                illusion as to their being on view.

49   30-31   *gained . . . Choler*] a proverbial expression. The use of liquid measure
                for *choler* is obvious, but not dry measure for *good will*.

50   17 ff. This didactic view of literature is discussed in *George Gascoigne,* pp.
                82 ff. See also J. E. Spingarn's *Literary Criticism in the Renaissance,*
                chs. i, ii.

        26   *Sir Geffrey Chaucer*] Such a view of Chaucer arises from the retraction
                and the closing lines of *Troilus and Criseyde.* For a discussion of
                the retraction and its interpretation see Robinson's *Chaucer,* Notes,
                p. 880. For the typical nature of this view in Mediaeval and
                Renaissance critical theory cf. C. S. Lewis, *The Allegory of Love,*
                pp. 43 ff.

        34   *a passover praise*] a negligible praise, one that can be casually passed
                over.

        38   *to be crowned with Lawrell*] perhaps the designation of poet laureate
                to which Gascoigne aspired. See the drawing (*Works,* II, 473)
                which prefaced *Hemetes,* wherein Gascoigne appeared kneeling before
                the Queen with a laurel wreath suspended over his head.

51   1   *Opere precium*] a work of value.

        4-5   *to participate the sight*] to share the reading of.

        13   *the Sundry lots of love*] Dr. Bowers (*Harvard Studies and Notes,* XVI,
                14) thinks that this refers to "Dan Bartholmew of Bath." If this is
                true, why was "D.B." included in the volume? I can see no reason
                for noting unknown works unless it be to whet the reader's appetite
                for subsequent volumes. Perhaps Gascoigne had not meant to
                include "D.B." when he wrote these letters. The problem is obscure
                and I can only suggest that "the *Sundry lots of love*" might have
                been a long poem or prose tale similar to "F.J." The unfortunate
                reception accorded this latter tale would have deterred further at-
                tempts. Dr. Bowers' theory is as valid as this, however.

        14   *The clyming of an Eagles neast*] Dr. Bowers (*ibid.,* p. 20) considers this
                a reference to "Dulce Bellum Inexpertis." In the first place there
                is no proof that this poem had been begun or contemplated when
                Gascoigne wrote this letter. Secondly, the figure of greater per-
                spective gained by a soaring hawk ("Dulce Bellum," stanza 34)
                has nothing to do with this phrase. "Climbing of an eagle's nest"
                was an Elizabethan figure for ambition. For indication of this see
                the quotation from the letter of *N.W.* in Daniel's *The Worthy Tract
                of Paulus Iovius* (*supra,* p. 32), and John Grange's *The Golden
                Aphroditis* (ed. Rollins, p. 20): The lover, rebuked by his lady for
                winking at her, replies: "Not so (dere dame) I winke for feare,
                least my too much contemplation of thy wonderful beautie daze

Page   Line

my greedy eyes, for by proofe I fynd it not over easy to clyme the Egles nest, and thy great curtesie is a ready repulse to my rudenesse. . . ." The meaning of the phrase is unmistakable in both instances. Therefore, it seems to me that the work referred to would be connected with ambition; either the work was a study of ambition or its purpose was to fulfill the author's ambition. As in the preceding note, there is no reason to think that either of these works ever appeared in print. If we must choose some published work, I should suggest *The Grief of Joye* which belongs to the period before 1574 much more than to that of the moral tracts, and certainly its purpose was to fulfill the author's ambition.

51   23   *Youres or not his owne*] a valediction expressing the contemporary idea of friendship. *Youres* and *not his owne* are synonymous: *G.T.* belongs to *H.W.* and not to himself. Lauren Mills' *One Soul in Bodies Twain* examines at length Elizabethan concepts of friendship.

        25   A consideration of the literary significance of the ensuing prose narrative is contained in *George Gascoigne*, pp. 198-212.

        29   *Aliquid Salis*] something of salt, *i.e.*, something of value.

        35   *The said F.J.*] The second edition (*The Posies*) abandoned this casual beginning and established an Italian background, with introduction and names all in keeping with Gascoigne's fiction that the tale was a translation. All variants in *The Posies* are noted above in those notes entitled Variants in *The Posies*.

        44   *So that consideringe*] This antithesis of the cold climate and the heat of love's fire is a familiar one and may be found in Petrarch (*Rime*, ed. Salani, XXX, "Giovene donna").

52   9   *safe garde for your sampler*] Safeguard was the name of a large petticoat worn over the other clothes to protect them from dirt. Therefore, the letter wrapped around a sampler would act as a protective covering.

        9-10   *a bottome to wind your sowing silke*] Cf. Grange's *Golden Aphroditis* (*op. cit.*, Diiij^v) where the lover presents a letter to his lady saying: "if she wanted a bottome whereon to winde hyr silke, that waste paper would aptly serve hir turne. Whereat (she plucking foorth hir sampler) accepted his wryting willingly. . . ."

        22   *brake the braule*] A brawl was a kind of dance, brought from France about the middle of the sixteenth century. Cotgrave translates *bransle*, "a brawle, or daunce wherein many, men and women, holding by the hands, sometimes in a ring, and otherwhiles at length, move altogether."

Good fellowes must go learne to daunce,
The brydeal is full near-a;
There is a *brall* come out of Fraunce,
The fyrst ye harde this yeare-a.
Good Fellowes, a Ballad, 1569.

52 25 This idea of comparison with famous lovers is expanded in poem no. 46, and seems to me another indication that the present poem is an early attempt.

The David and Bersabe figure is used again in no. 41 where it is blatantly applied to the poet's affair with a "gentlewoman." Wyatt had translated the story in his "Penetential Psalmes," while the 1537 Bible had an illustration of the tale at the beginning of *Psalmes.*

26 *With deawe*] a frequent figure in Petrarchan love. Love shot, from the beauteous aspect of the beloved, beams which entered the lover's eyes. The intensity of these beams was such that often the lover's eyes, unable to stand the strain, filled with tears.

37-42 These lines, omitted in *The Posies,* may be considered as typical of two important aspects of "The Adventures of Master F.J." The reason for their omission in *The Posies* is quite clear: they show that the tale is not a translation from the Italian as Gascoigne would have the reader of the revised edition believe. The true author is, of course, Gascoigne, and the tale is autobiographical as I have shown elsewhere (*George Gascoigne,* pp. 189-98).

The second fact of importance found in these lines concerns the time of the affair between Gascoigne and "Lady Elinor." Clearly these lines indicate that the preceding poem was the first love poem written by Gascoigne. Similarly, poem no. 8 is described as having been composed "in the first beginning of his writings" (*supra,* p. 76). Thus, if my conclusions, that the poems concern the affair with Elinor (*George Gascoigne,* pp. 196-97) be accepted, then clearly Gascoigne's first love affair—at least the first which inspired him to verse—was this with the Lady Elinor.

Although there is no external evidence by which to date this affair, it probably belongs in the first Gray's Inn period (1555-58), since, shortly after 1558, Gascoigne was at court, and most likely enjoyed a number of amorous intrigues.

53 8 *SHE*] *The Posies* substitutes "COLEI:" and adds, "which in english betokeneth SHE:" Colei is the feminine singular of the demonstrative pronoun in Italian. Gascoigne, in the revised story, substitutes the Italian, in keeping with the fiction that the tale is a translation from the Italian. The term *in Romaine* which appears in both editions apparently indicates the use of the italic rather than cursive script. This substitution of *COLEI* for *SHE* is made consistently in *The Posies.* For all such instances see Variants in *The Posies.*

19, 20 *coales to kyndle such sparkes of fire*] Italian love poetry had this as one of its tenets of faith. The beauty of the lady created a fire in her lover's heart. For a rather ridiculous but logical development of this cf. poem no. 48. The ramifications of this "fire" figure are infinite: sighs both flame and smoke, fires turn to ashes, tears drench the fire, while antithetical "ice" often appears.

53   31   *discipher*] reveal.

33   *as the perfect hound*] The same figure appears in "Dan Bartholmew" poem 3, ll. 129 ff. Gascoigne makes considerable use of the figures of hunting.

36   *to bringe this Deere*] It was customary to drive the deer past a place where the hunting party, armed with bows, were waiting.

40   *written in counterfeit*] written in a disguised hand.

54   10   *like unto Narcissus*] an allusion to the myth of Narcissus enamoured of his own reflection. Classical allusions, while not frequent in Gascoigne, are to well-known stories.

19   *faye written over*] copied in a neat hand.

23, 24   *Ambassade and Camnassado*] These military terms suggest that the prose links were written after experience in war. The first term is obvious;· the second means a surprise attack by night, the term being derived from the practice of wearing white shirts as a means of identification. Cf. poem 10 and "D.B." poem 3.

Aretino (*I Sonetti Lussuriosi*) similarly uses military figures.

25-26   *overcome by ye beautifull beames*] Cf. note l. 26, p. 52

55   7   *to subject his libertie*] The Italianate lover becoming enamoured, lost his liberty by becoming a slave of the lady.

12   *Bezo las manos*] kiss on the hands (Sp.). Cf. Puttenham (*Arte*, ed. Willcock and Walker, p. 286).

13   *zuccado dez labros*] kiss on the lips (Sp.).

15   *Terza sequenza*] a sequence of three (It.).

23   *where snares*] another allusion to the sport of hunting. Nets were a common means of taking birds. Cf. *The Gentleman's Recreation—Fowling*, p. 4.

32   *It . . . heaven*] it is heavenly.

34   *It . . . world*] it is a wonder. Cf. *Taming of the Shrew*, II, 1.

34   *hang the lip*] exhibit vexation.

37   *boorden*] made of boards, *i.e.* wooden.

38   *mishape*] rhymes with trap (l. 11) but it did not seem justifiable to alter the spelling.

43   *Till . . . stay*] until death ends her frantic efforts to escape.

44   *linkes of love*] Cf. note to p. 49, l. 22.

45   *stryve with the streame*] a proverb denoting impossibility, greatly used by Gascoigne.

56   11   *lymed twigges*] another method of taking birds. Cf. *The Gentleman's Recreation—Fowling*, p. 7. Frequently used in Italianate love poetry

(cf. *Orlando Furioso*, XXIII, 105, ll. 1-6; Ronsard, *Le Bocage*, opening lines).

56   21   *the smithie*] one of the many analogies which infest Gascoigne's poetry. In the use of these, proverbs, and antithetical structure, Gascoigne is well on the way to Euphuism.

        26   *Dame Venus*] Astronomical and astrological figures are frequent. Cf. poem no. 24.

        29   *hath*] *The Posies'* reading of *had* seems another instance of Gascoigne's attempts at concealing, in his revision, the autobiographical nature of the present tale.

        44   *rounding*] whispering.

        45   *Hazell sticke*] I have been unable to find any explanation of this remedy for the nose-bleed. Lupton's *A Thousand Notable Things* (1567) contains many cures for nose-bleed but not this. Perhaps there may be some relevancy in the fact that a hazel wand was thought to have magical properties. At any rate, F.J.'s cure was based on the principle of reducing the amount of blood in the head by relaxation.

57   26-30   *Well . . . tale*] These lines, omitted in *The Posies*, clearly reveal the true nature of the tale. Gascoigne could not deny himself his hour of triumph. In the revision such a passage had to be omitted, if the fiction of a translation were to be maintained.

        42   *an unknown humour*] This is an allusion to the medical theory of the four fluids or humours—blood, phlegm, choler, and melancholy—which were supposed to determine a person's health or temperament.

58   10   *I have seene*] another indication, omitted in *The Posies*, of the true character of the tale.

        16   *Hee was* etc.] Gascoigne's bitter hatred of his rival is only too apparent in this vituperative description.

        35   *his Mistresse, being Queene*] Dr. Bradner (*P.M.L.A.*, XLV, 549) discusses this and subsequent appearances in literature of the pastime of *Questioni d'amore* which was widespread throughout the Mediaeval and Renaissance periods. T. F. Crane (*Italian Social Customs of the Sixteenth Century*, New Haven, 1920) is excellent on this subject. See also Violet Jeffery's *John Lyly and the Italian Renaissance* (Paris, 1929), ch. iv, "Italian Social Customs."

        43   *is . . . halfpeny*] proverb meaning, to have a particular object in view.

59   12   *somewhat mistie*] This tendency to obscure the meaning by half truths and veiled references is not only frequent in Gascoigne (cf. poems nos. 8, 14, 20, 38, 47, 67 and D.B." no. 3), but is characteristic of the age.

        19-20   *byting uppon the bit*] proverb meaning, to be impatient.

        29   *Cocklorells musicke*] music of little worth. The phrase derives from *Cocke Lorelles Bote* (c. 1510), a humorous imitation of Barclay's *Shyp of Folys* (1509).

poem no. 3   Of this, *G.T.* says: "I have heard F.J. saye that he borowed th'invention of an Italian." Actually it is very close to a poem of Petrarch's, which was translated by Wyatt.

> Amor, fortuna e la mia mente schiva
>> di quel che vede e nel passato volta
>> m'affligon si, ch'io porto alcuna volta
>> invidia a quei che son su l'altra riva,
>
> Amor mi strugge 'l cor, fortuna il priva
>> d'ogni conforto: onde la mente stolta
>> s'adira e piange; e cosi in pena molta
>> sempre conven che combattendo viva.
>
> Nè spero i dolci di tornino in dietro,
>> ma pur di male in peggio quel ch'avanza;
>> e di mio corso ho già passato 'l mezzo.
>
> Lasso! non di diamante ma d'un vetro
>> veggio di man cadermi ogni speranza,
>> e tutt' i miei pensier romper nel mezzo.
>> (Petrarch, *Rime,* ed. Salani, CXXIV)

Wyatt's version is found in vol. I, p. 29 of Miss Foxwell's edition.

Page	Line	
60	6-8	These lines, omitted in *The Posies,* again reveal the method of composition of the original as well as Gascoigne's careful revision which made the tale seem a translation.
	13-14	*cause of my mallady*] *Brewer's Dictionary of Phrase and Fable* says that nose-bleed was a sign of being in love. This reference to Elinor's sickness would seem to confirm that supposition.
	18	*teach you the ful order* etc.] The ensuing seduction in the same gallery leaves little doubt that this is a double-entendre on the cause and cure of falling in love.
	34	*cheekes wold be much thinner*] The lover was supposed to consume himself in suffering as is shown by poem 48 and by "D.B." poem 3.
61	4-5	*Image of S. Fraunces . . . and S. Elynor*] Mediaeval love convention, as well as the Petrarchan, combined the figures of the lovers' mythology and world with the attributes of the Christian.
	6	*pavion*] the pavane, a slow or stately dance or the music for such a dance. Cf. Puttenham's *Arte* (ed. Willcock and Walker), pp. 46, 47.
	19-20	*I am sory . . . all his lawes*] The fate of him who denies Love is clearly shown in "D.B." no. 6.
	26	*braule*] Cf. note to l. 22, p. 52.
	36-37	*myne instructers . . . your words*] This may possibly be considered as an indication of Gascoigne's youth at the time and his not too distant days at Cambridge.
62	4	*bone to gnawe on*] proverb meaning, to puzzle over.

Page	Line
62	4-5

62   4-5   *to halt before a Creple*] Cf. Chaucer's *Troilus*, IV, ll. 1458 ff.:

> It is ful hard to halten unespied
> Byfore a crepel, for he kan the craft;

Halt is used in the sense of walk with a limp.

6   *to hop*, etc.] To run for the bell means to try for a prize; thus the present meaning seems to be that evil will result from trying to interfere with those who seek for a prize.

7-8   *to hang the Bell*] Elinor seems to jibe at F.J. with the implication that he is running for more than one prize.

10   *Gallyard*] The galliard was a gay or merry dance in contrast with the *pavane*. (Cf. W. S. Pratt, *History of Music*, p. 155 and Puttenham's *Arte*, pp. 46, 47.)

16   *congey*] farewell.

21   *a corosive*] A plaster was applied to heal a wound, but a corrosive would make it worse.

24   *to drive etc.*] Cf. *Orl. Fur.* XLV, 29, l. 6: "Talor chiodo con chiodo cacciar fuore."

28   *Bargynet*] a rustic dance accompanied with a song.

31   *Tyntarnell*] The authorities are in dispute as to the origin of this word. Halliwell claimed a derivation from the Italian *tintinno*. The *O.E.D.* says this has no sanction. At any rate, it is obviously a dance measure to which words are sung. Its Italian origin is pointed by *Alla Napolitana*, "in the Neapolitan fashion."

35   This is one of the poems which Thomas Watson (*The Tears of Fancie*, ed. Arber, p. 179) turned into a sonnet and passed off as his own composition.

42   *The coales etc.*] The fire of love figure is here so trite that we can well believe G.T.'s statement that it concerned first love.

63   6   *The Rose and Lilly*] This figure is frequent in Petrarch but by Gascoigne's time had become hackneyed.

12   *to hop etc.*] one of Gascoigne's favorite proverbs meaning, to attempt a difficult task.

23   *Faucon gent*] one of the seven kinds of falcons, so called for her gentle disposition. Cf. *The Gentleman's Recreation—Of Hawking*, p. 178.

25   *The fayrest Woulf etc.*] According to Turbervile (*The Noble Arte of Venerie*, Oxford, 1906, p. 206) this refers to the peculiar habits of the wolf. At the clicketing season the female allows a group of males to follow her in a chase that lasts for eight or ten days. When the males are exhausted, they lie down and sleep, and at this time the female, after inspection, wakes that one whom by the dirtiness and foulness of his appearance, she judges to have followed her longest and most faithfully. Lyly employs no figure from natural history any more far-fetched than this.

Page	Line	
64	1-6	*These verses . . . by it*] These lines, omitted in *The Posies,* are important in showing that this was Gascoigne's first love affair.
	3-4	*continua oratio*] an unbroken (*i.e.*, complete) account (Lat.).
	6	*in cloudes to discipher*] to reveal in a vague and intangible manner. Cf. note to l. 12, p. 59.
	12	*choller*] one of the humours. Cf. note to l. 42, p. 57.
	23	*coste*] coast. The figure is involved but it seems that the poet sees his life and fortune as a sea coast that is overcast by a cloud of care, threatened by storms of strife, and washed over by waves of woe.
	27	*chippes* etc.] The figure suddenly changes to one of woodmanship.
	32	*lot*] fate.
	39	*care* etc.] Care, the carving knife that will cut the thread of life, is one of Gascoigne's favorites and appears frequently in "D.B." Cf. "D.B." no. 3.
65	2-6	*yet have I . . . presented it*] The omission of these lines in *The Posies* is easily understood, but the lines are puzzling. The military figures would suggest a date of composition for the prose subsequent to Gascoigne's experiences in Holland. What one word in the poem Gascoigne regretted is another "misterie" whose secret is well hidden.
	19-20	*evensong . . . morrow masse*] another instance of the use of christian terminology in the religion of love. Cf. note to ll. 4-5, p. 61.
	20	*Saint*] see preceding note.
66	14	*Trust*] Cf. Grange, *Golden Aphroditis,* (*op. cit.*) Eiiii^v, where N.O. calls A.O. "his *Trust* (for so he had termed hir)."
	31	*holyest Idoll*] the beloved identified with a religious image. Cf. note to ll. 19-20, p. 65.
	33-34	*H.D.* and *H.K.*] I can offer no identification of these former lovers. In *The Posies* they appear under the Italian names, Hercule Donaty and Haniball de Cosmis.
	39	*woorthy to have the severall use* etc.] By using the figure of enclosing a common field to his own private use, Frances implies that F.J. is not worthy of being cuckolded by the Secretary.
67	1	*unto F.J. a kinswoman*] This relationship, omitted in *The Posies,* was I think a true one, with Elinor no kin, except possibly by marriage, to Gascoigne or his family.
	26	*per misericordiam*] chastened (Lat.).
	27	*lap*] end or overlapping part of a garment.
	31	*supersedias*] a writ for a stay of legal proceedings (Lat.).
	36-37	*Italian dittie* etc.] This passage occurs in *Orlando Furioso,* XLIV, 61.
	44	*My Fathers Sisters* etc.] Cf. *Works,* I, 136:

> *Bartello* he which writeth ryding tales,
> Bringes in a Knight which cladde was all in greene,
> That sighed sore amidde his greevous gales,
> And was in hold as *Bartholmew* hath beene.

But (for a placke) it maye therein be seene,

That, that same Knight which there his griefes begonne,

Is *Batts* owne Fathers Sisters brothers Sonne.

This seems to show another link with Gascoigne since he and the greene Knight are the same.

68   9   *without touch . . . nip by the hart*] an emotional rather than a physical "nip."

12   *playster*] the familiar figure of a wound which is helped by a plaster or made more grievous by a corrosive.

15   *sickly*] pale.

18   *knot* etc.] Her affections are tied to him or to anyone else by a slip knot which is easily loosed.

20-25   *I drempt . . . myne adventures*] an involved and "cloudie" or "mistie" reference. F.J. is uncertain as to the meaning of Elinor's proposal (*the hope hanging in the ayre*) and he tells her that he has attempted to discover the truth by means of astronomy (astrology).

69   25-37   *Were it not . . . loth to depart*] excised in *The Posies* presumably because of moral objections to which reference is made by Gascoigne in the prefatory letters of *The Posies* (*Works*, I, 7).

28   *Enaeas*] presumably a reference to the episode of Dido and Aeneas in the cave.

40   *base court*] outer or lower courtyard.

70   23-28   *The occasion . . . G.T.*] For the significance of these lines as well as the reason for their omission in *The Posies* see *George Gascoigne*, p. 195.

72   6-13   *This . . . judgementes*] In these lines, omitted in *The Posies*, Gascoigne reveals one of his artistic principles: a love of the elaborate conceit. As he proudly says *it hath great good store of deepe invention,* and indeed the involved explanation of Phoebus' hatred of the lady with its jargon of Petrarchan love can well be called *deepe.* The poet has some reticence with his concessive *dyddeldome* (a trifling hummed tune).

18   *with a coyfe* etc.] an excellent example of a livery. The significance of Elinor's cap trimmed with cloth of gold in the Piedmont manner and its one word would only be apparent to the lover who, of course, knew at once why his mistress thus arrayed herself. Samuel Daniel (Intro. to his translation of Paolo Giovio) discusses similar costumes. Cf. Introduction, pp. 28-29, 32.

26   *reconninges . . . the accompt*] a play on "reckonings" (the sum total of the account) and the account itself (F.J.'s seduction of Elinor).

27   *omnia bene*] everything went well (Lat.).

29   *pretie trippe*] a mistake or error.

38   *going towardes horsebacke*] going to mount their horses.

40   *in trip*] catching himself giving away a secret.

41   *conceipt*] apprehension.

Page	Line	
73	27	*a gard*] a band of material to serve as a trimming. Here it seems to be a trimming embroidered with swords.
	31-32	*God Mars* etc.] an allusion to Mars' seduction of Venus and deception of Vulcan, her husband. The hammer is here a reference to cuckoldry. I can find no significance beyond the express idea of the phrase.
	36-37	*that dreames* etc.] another astrological reference. The use of dreams and their significance is somewhat reminiscent of Chauntecleer and Pertelote.

F.J. is, of course, trying to discover if Frances really did see him. Deloney (*Works*, ed. F. O. Mann, p. 8) uses a similar device in *Jacke of Newberie.*

	39	*gesse, like a young scholler*] probably proverbial, but the phrase may also be an indication of Gascoigne's youth at the time.
74	16-23	*well I dwell . . . uppon this occasion. After*] again a comment on the manner of composition which Gascoigne deleted in *The Posies.*
	28	Poem no. 7. The reference to Friday and the fifth line in particular suggest Petrarch's celebration of his Good Friday's meeting with Laura: "Benedetto sia 'l giorno e 'l mese e l'anno." There is also a poem in *Tottel's Miscellany* (ed. Arber, p. 230) that celebrates a lover's meeting on Good Friday. If Gascoigne is following Petrarch, he is almost blatantly sacreligious.
75	9	Poem no. 8. There is considerable editorial comment on this poem on p. 76. A difficulty arose when Elinor became suspicious of the praise rendered Helen. She doubted Gascoigne's explanation that Helen and Elinor were really the same person. The trouble arose from Gascoigne's acknowledged practice of basing a complimentary poem on a mythological figure. Being unable to find any famous Elinor, he chose the familiar Helen.

Another editorial comment of interest is that which tells of a confusion between Elinor and a later love named Helen. Some of Gascoigne's poems were evidently circulated in MS soon after the affair with Helen and those who read this particular poem were uncertain as to the identity of the lady therein praised. Gascoigne tries to settle the problem by his editorial comment and makes two assertions that are of biographical and literary importance. First, he says (p. 76, ll. 27-29) that the present poem was among his first compositions. Secondly, he says (p. 76, ll. 33-34) that he might adapt this poem to apply to Helen. Such an adaptation was made and it appears in this volume as "Dan Bartholmew's Triumphes." One need only compare the two to realize that the "Triumphes" is the later poem since it develops as fully as possible the method of "Beautie shut up thy shop." If the figures of this latter poem seem elaborate, those of the adaptation are a veritable maze.

There remains the problem of the identity of Helen. Presumably

that was the real name of Ferenda Natura, the lady of "Dan Barthol-
mew," since the poem celebrating her thus appears in "Dan Barthol-
mew." The method of composition of this verse narrative renders
any conclusion indefinite. For a further discussion of these two poems
see *George Gascoigne,* pp. 139, 194, 213-214.

75   10   *left thee in the lash*] left you in the lurch.

       13   *paynted pale*] pallor alleviated by cosmetics.

       15   *bodies* etc.] It was customary to pad clothes with bumbast, a stuffing.

       16   *rowles*] a cushion or pad of hair.

       16   *Ruffes*] the familiar neck-ruff.

       16   *caules* and *coyfes*] close-fitting caps or headdresses.

       16   *Jerkins*] garments with or without sleeves worn over the doublet.

       16   *jagges*] the slashings on garments to show another color underneath.

       17   *curling* and *cost*] the curling of the hair and attendant expense.

       17   *frisling*] to curl hair in small close curls.

       17   *fare*] appearance.

       26   *bayte* etc.] a mixture of figures. The lover is a fish: he gazes as a man
but swallows the bait as a fish.

       27   *slipt*] have cut off a flower for propagation elsewhere.

       28   *corne, chaff*] The homely agricultural figure is frequent. This one ap-
pears again in "D.B." no. 2, l. 10. Petrarch and Wyatt employ the
crop, root, seed, fruit figures, but Gascoigne is here drawing from
his own experience and is specific in the use of a wide range of such
figures.

       33   *Theseus, Paris*] Helen, daughter of Zeus and Leda, was carried off by
Theseus. Recovered by her brothers, she married Menelaus but was
later seduced by Paris.

       35   *Mars*] another reference to the seduction of Venus by Mars. It is fre-
quent in Gascoigne.

76   1-2   *proud challenge to Beautie*] Poem no. 49, "Gascoignes araignement,"
seems to have resulted from this challenge; another example of the
manner of composition of "F.J."

       11   *by*] about, concerning.

       11   The question of the poem and the name is discussed in the note to p. 75,
l. 9.

    16-17   *yet never a barell* etc.] proverb meaning, nothing to choose between them.

    17-19   *that other Hellen* etc.] This does not agree with what we learn elsewhere
about Ferenda Natura. See note to p. 75, l. 9, and *George Gascoigne,*
pp. 219-20.

       33   That such an adaptation took place is shown by poem 2 in "D.B." which
is an expansion of the idea of this. Cf. note to p. 75, l. 9.

Page	Line	
77	17	There were similar "inventions" by any number of Italian and French poets. Probably the best known is Ariosto's description of Alcina (*Orl. Fur.*, VII, 11-14), part of which I quote. Other examples of this description of a woman are Petrarch's "O dolci sgardi" and "Quel che d'adore"; Du Bellay's *L'Olive*, VII, LXXI; and three sonnets by Ronsard: *Amours* I, CLVI, XLVI, XCV.

> Sotto quel sta, quasi fra due vallette,
> La bocca sparsa di natio cinabro:
> Quivi due filze son di perle elette,
> Che chiude ed apre un bello e dolce labro:
> Quindi escon le cortesi parolette
> Da render molle ogni cor rozzo e scabro:
> Quivi si forma quel suave riso
> Ch'apre a sua post in terra il paradiso.

	16-20	*I . . . Sonet*] Omitted in *The Posies* for obvious reasons.
	36-37	If the poems printed were not considered to reveal "the luckie lottes of love," the imagination wonders at the thought of those which were suppressed. It appears that lip service, at least, is being paid to that great principle of courtly love, secrecy.
	43	*Potycaries pot*] a figure worthy of Lyly.
78	16	*amongst other . . .*
79	16	*. . . be to curious*] omitted from *The Posies* on moral grounds. Cf. note to ll. 25-37, p. 69.
78	18	*kept Cut*] The *O.E.D.*'s explanation, "to keep one's distance," hardly suits the present use; rather it would seem to mean that the husband returned and stayed at home.
	23	*greene*] This appears to have been the poet's favorite color since he later appears as the greene Knight and in "Dulce Bellum" as *die groene Hopman.*
	26	*moulting* etc.] This facetiousness in referring to the horns of the cuckold is continued throughout the episode. For a full discussion of the horns and their origin, see F. L. Lucas' exhaustive note in his edition of John Webster's *Works* (*The White Devil*, p. 206).
	31	*comming*] I can find no authority for the obvious meaning which appears to be "blowing."
	35	*rechate*] a series of notes to call the hounds together. Turbervile (*Art of Venerie, op. cit.,* t^v) gives the notes for this on a musical scale.
	38-39	This pride in speedy composition is shown elsewhere by the poet. Cf. poem 70 and *Works*, II, 177
79	12	*Rye*] The *Booke of Sparhawkes* (1575) describes, according to the *O.E.D.*, a disease among hawks, known as "Rye," which appears as a swelling of the head. There may be a pun between this and Rye used as an aphrodisiac. Also wry.

Page   Line

The following lines by Nicholas Breton, Gascoigne's stepson, may be of some value in explaining the matter.

The pastrie is a place of open patcherie;
An other trumperie, an other mockerie,
And baudrie too; and yet the best is but a kinde of rye,
Wherof the meale is made, that maketh Fancies bread;
And that is baked in the braine of a hot foolysh head.
A Floorish Upon Fancie (1582)
(Rprt. in *Heliconia*, ed. T. Park, 1815, I, 47-48)

79   27-28 *The lover* etc.] This love sickness can be found in practically any of the French and English imitations and translations of the Italian *novelle*. Its addition by those who were following a literary rather than an oral model is characteristic of the tastes of the generation before Shakespeare.

80   3   *tractable yong scholler*] Cf. note to l. 39, p. 73.

81   22-23 *professed his service*] The lover entered the service of Cupid as a priest did holy orders or as a knight into feudal allegiance and homage.

      36   *Mythrydate*] An electuary serving as a remedy or preservative against poison, compounded of a great number of drugs, and used extensively as a cordial, opiate, or sudorific. The name derives from Mithridates, the king of Pontus, who, by taking daily minute doses of poison, inoculated himself against its effect.

      45   *willow braunce*] The willow was universally a symbol of bad fortune in love.

To me most unhappy, still spurnde by dispight,
Is given writhed Willows to expresse my state right.
(*Howells Devises* 1581, "All of greene Willow")

A green willow must be my garland
(*Othello*, IV, iii, 50)

82   3-4   The reference to Ariosto is omitted in *The Posies* and Bartello is substituted. This was, of course, done to preserve the fiction of translation. It was rendered possible by the fact that the story of Suspicion did not appear in the ordinary editions of the *Orlando Furioso* but in the *Cinque Canti*, a variety of material which was designed to appear in the *Orlando* but which was excised, and appeared separately. In the Venice edition of 1566 (Gio. Varisco) it occupies sigs. Aaa 7^v—Bbb 5^r. I do not print the original because of the length; however, Gascoigne's version is a close translation from the Italian.

      31   *Carone . . . Radamanthus*] the familiar characters of the underworld: Charon, the ferryman, and Radamanthus, the judge. Cf. *George Gascoigne*, pp. 210-11, for notice of the literary significance of this interpolated tale.

Page	Line	
83	23	*Ganymedes*] Zeus' cupbearer who was stolen from earth and borne to Olympus by the eagle, bird of Zeus.
	29	*Via Appia . . . Flaminia*] two of the great roads which led to and from imperial Rome.
84	28	*Ariostoes xxxi. song*] This is not in *The Posies,* a further attempt to conceal the authorship of the tale. The first five stanzas are a literal translation of the first five stanzas of Canto XXXI of *Orlando Furioso.* The sixth is an envoie or interpretation which points the moral. This is a frequent trick of Gascoigne's and appears to have been suggested by the Pléiadistes who were fond of the device. (Cf. Alice Cameron, *Influence of Ariosto on Ronsard,* Baltimore, 1930, p. 97.)
85	22	*Zoroastes*] Zoroaster—the founder of the Persian cult of Mazda, the god of light.
	27	*Troylus sect*] Those who, like Troylus, were deceived by women.
	36	*tyed to the invention*] tied, meaning compelled. He was compelled to follow the translation.
86	10	*damaske water*] water distilled from damask roses.
	18	*casting bottle*] There is a strong temptation to think of the casting bottle over which Dame Margaret Gascoigne fought with her sister. Cf. *George Gascoigne,* p. 13.
87	4-5	*and that . . . disclose the rest*] Here is a clue to the fact that the story does concern real people. Even in this first edition Gascoigne was somewhat careful.
	6	The *questioni d'amore* have been referred to in the note to l. 35, p. 58. T. F. Crane (*Italian Social Customs of the Sixteenth Century,* pp. 66 ff.) discusses the matter of the choosing of a Governor.
	26-27	*least hir name . . . of all waters*] Again (cf. note to ll. 4-5, p. 87) we have an indication of the autobiographical nature of the tale. *To brode before* means too obvious, and is so used by Gascoigne in poem 19: "For Lemmans beare their name too broad before;" and again in poem 74: "I name no man, for that were brode before." This last is quoted by the *O.E.D. "Might not drinke of all waters,* according to the *O.E.D.,* means "might not suit everyone."
88	2	*daungerously*] Danger had a variety of meanings in mediaeval love allegory. (Cf. C. S. Lewis, *The Allegory of Love,* Appendix II.) Here the meaning seems to be—with selfishness, refusing to grant love, difficult as opposed to affable.
	9	*Ardena*] St. 78 of *Orl. Fur.,* Canto I, describes two fountains in the forest of Ardenna: the water of one, when drunk, inspires love; the other, hate. The single fountain which inspires hate is found in Boiardo's *Orlando Innamorato.*

Page Line
88   7, 12 The use of "seven yeares" and "apprenticehode" shows the artificial
          nature of this tale. Mediaeval love allegories made frequent use of
          the seven year period. The purpose of the story in the tale of "F.J."
          is obscure; it is unlikely that Pergo would tell such a tale about
          herself, and it is possibly an attack on Frances, since we find later
          several disputes between these two.
              A story with a similar point to this is found in Boccaccio's
          Filocolo and is discussed by T. F. Crane (*It. Social Customs*, pp.
          70-72). Two sisters loved two noble youths. The lover of the
          elder was banished and she was unable to follow; the other sister
          was prevented from enjoying her love by reason of jealousy. The
          question becomes, who endured the greater grief? The ensuing
          judgment of the Queen is similar to that of F.J. in the present
          instance.
      26 *haggard Faulcon*] a falcon still in its wild state.
      39 *cheines*] Cf. note to ll. 22-23, p. 49.
89   15 *lead Apes in Hell*] the fancied consequence of dying an old maid. The
          origin is obscure but the phrase appears in Lyly (*Euphues*, ed. Arber,
          p. 87) and in Shakespeare (*Taming of the Shrew*, II, i, 34; *Much
          Ado About Nothing*, II, i.)
      28 *tip for tap*] modern tit for tat.
90   21 Cf. note to l. 43, p. 58.
91   21-25 *But . . . of death*] Omitted in *The Posies*, which reads "And It." The
          two capitals would indicate that *The Posies* was therefore set from
          a copy of *A Hundreth Sundrie Flowres* which Gascoigne had cor-
          rected. Such an error could hardly have resulted from Gascoigne's
          MS since in his letters which survive he made little or no use of
          capitals at the beginning of sentences. Textual Notes, p. 222.
      27-28 *For . . . that*] The *Posies* has the very awkward "For mine aucthor
          dreameth y^t *Ferdenando*." This alteration, designed to support the
          fiction of a translation, reveals itself, by its very awkwardness, and
          defeats its own purpose. We might also conclude that Gascoigne
          made his revision in some haste since he did not trouble to find
          a better fashion of eliminating the obvious autobiographical reference.
92   31-35 *drewe uppon . . . enemies curtesie*] omitted in *The Posies*, another ex-
          ample of the purgation of "wanton speeches."
      33 *prepare the warde*] prepare a defense.
      33 *thrust . . . both hands*] pushed against her with both hands.
93   11 *the xi. article of hir beleeve*] The eleventh article in the code of love of
          Andreas Capellanus was opposed to loving a person whom one
          would be ashamed to marry. This certainly cannot apply in the
          present instance. I can suggest two possible explanations: (1) the
          eleventh of Capellanus' judgments of love which posed the question
          of a lady sued in love by a good and prudent man; afterwards by

a worthier man; which is to be preferred? or (2) the ninth article of Cappellanus' code (assuming that xi. is a transposition of ix.) which states that no one can love unless he is compelled to do so by the persuasion of love.

93   13   *reformation of hir religion*] a continuation of the "religion of love" concept. Cf. notes to ll. 4-5, p. 61; ll. 19-20, p. 65; l. 31, p. 66.

15ff. This double-entendre in musical terminology was left intact in the second edition.

16   *faburden*] a droning undersong or accompaniment. From the French "faux-bourden," false base, an octave removed from the true base.

17   *descant*] a melody or counterpoint sung above the plain song of the tenor. From the French "deschanter."

17   *playne song*] the simple melody, without other parts.

27   *una voce*] with one accord (It.).

36   *Cuckoe*] There follows considerable play on this song of the cuckoo, based, of course, on the derivation of "cuckold" from the cuckoo's custom of laying its eggs in other birds' nests. Cf. note to l. 26, p. 78.

94   3   *he is not maried*] This would place the date of the story's action sometime before 1561-2, when Gascoigne married Elizabeth Bretton.

4   *envieth*] bears a grudge against.

14   *the trees* etc.] The time has been well established by the reference to the cuckoo's departure and this well-integrated sign of autumn. Both references to time are extremely well done; so too is that on p. 70 to the spring. The limits have thus been indicated. Cf. *Works*, I, 384, where "iiii. moneths" is given as the duration of F.J.'s visit. This period of time is suggestive of the Long Vacation granted by the Universities and the Inns of Court.

95   15   *salve for that soore*] Cf. note to l. 12, p. 68.

38   *her conceipt*] her opinion.

43   *a Dio*] farewell (It.).

43   *courte*] the group of the company, not the royal court.

96   1-4   A foreshadowing of the tale which angered Pergo. Cf. note to ll. 38-39, *infra*.

1   *cast out some bone*] Cf. note to l. 4, p. 62.

9   *overseene*] mistaken.

31   *lure*] The apparatus used by falconers to recall their hawks; it was constructed of feathers to resemble a bird and a young hawk was fed with meat pushed through the structure. It was whirled in the air by means of a long cord and so attracted the hawk.

Page Line
96   38-39 *not fayned . . . of late daies*] This idea of a true story is found elsewhere
             in Gascoigne. The opening lines of "Dan Bartholmew" make quite
             clear the Renaissance critics' view of a fictitious story.

> TO tell a tale without authoritye,
> Or fayne a Fable by invention,
> That one proceedes of quicke capacitye,
> That other proves but small discretion,
> Yet have both one and other oft bene done.
> And if I were a Poet as some be,
> You might perhappes heare some such tale of me.

Again (p. 51), "The Adventures of Master F.J." are described
as a "history," which thus would indicate that they were true. It seems
no accident, therefore, that in *The Posies* we find this title, "The
pleasant Fable of Ferdinando Jeronimi and Lenora de Valasco trans-
lated out of the Italian riding tales of Bartello." Not only has the
tale become a translation but it is described as a "Fable" which,
according to the lines of "Dan Bartholmew" quoted above, means
that it has been "fayned by invention."

Such careful differentiation in terminology is, of course, part
of the Renaissance critics' attempts to free literature from the
strictures of Plato which had been emphasized by the Church
Fathers. As far as I know, little has been made of this point in
connection with Renaissance prose fiction.

I cannot agree with Dr. Bradner's interpretation of this tale
(*P.M.L.A.*, XLV, p. 549) as Frances' exposure of F.J. and Elinor.
It is directed at Pergo, as the discussion (p. 100) shows; probably
Pergo was one of the busy-brained sisters.

It is worth noting that the line length of this story as found in
the *Flowres* is reproduced exactly in *The Posies*. Of no other ex-
tended passage is this true.

97   28   *Besse*] This must have been a real name, since it is the only Christian
             name changed in *The Posies*, where it appears as "Lamia."

      34-35 *began . . . grease*] proverb meaning, to exhaust themselves by their own
             violence.

98   5   *mystery*] what the maid has seen is to be a secret.

      11   *dranke up his owne swette*] suffered in silence.

      22   *Slippes*] a counterfeit coin worth three halfpence. This was changed in
             The Posies to "Carolines": a small silver coin current in Italy. The
             Italianization of the tale was carefully done.

99   35   *beaten hir braynes*] exerted herself in thought.

100   25-29 T. F. Crane (*It. Soc. Customs, op. cit.*, p. 10) notes a similar question
             found in Provençal poetry: a husband learns that his wife has a
             lover; the wife and lover perceive it—which of the three is in the
             greatest strait?

Page	Line	
100	32	Here again the differentiation between a tale and a history. Cf. note to ll. 38-39, p. 96.
	39-42	The relation of the preceding history to Dame Pergo is here hinted at.
	40	*smyled in hir sleeve*] The same expression is in use today.
102	33	*I could not though I would*] The intricate play on such words seems to have been a great pastime for the Elizabethans. Joan Evans (*English Posies and Posy Rings,* London, 1931, xvii-xviii) says, "How far posy-writing had become a literary exercise is evident in such a series as *If so I may, I will not say nay; I would if I might; I may not if I would,* and *I may and will not."*
	36	*gallies* etc.] Galleys, being propelled by oars, can go where the captain wishes; sailing vessels are dependent on the wind.
	39	An allusion to the belief that the nightingale sings with a thorn at her throat to keep her awake.
103	2	*if good . . . power is*] If good will were as ready as the power to do a thing.
	16	*Bezo las manos*] Cf. note to l. 12, p. 55.
	17	*allo solito*] as was her wont (It.).
	40	*Cat*] slang for prostitute. Thus the proverb: never does a prostitute change her nature.
	42	*Woon* etc.] A proverb denoting a quick conquest and a quick loss, equivalent to the modern, "easy come, easy go." Cf. *Euphues* (ed. Arber, p. 41): ". . . if he perceive thee to be won with a nut, he will imagine that thou wilt be lost with an apple; if he find thee wanton before thou be wooed, he will guess thou wilt be wavering when thou art wedded."
104	10	*conformitie*] He conforms to the general pattern of a rejected lover.
	19	*Surquedry*] overweening pride.
	25	*to drinke* etc.] Cf. note to l. 11, p. 98.
	26	*I like . . . fantasie*] Frances likes his decision to have done with the affair better than his determination to suffer in silence.
	28	*garded*] Cf. note to ll. 27-28, p. 73.
	30	*smelt* etc.] saw how matters proceeded.
	41	*bone . . . uppon*] Cf. note to l. 4, p. 62.
105	11	Cf. note to l. 35, p. 99.
	29	The ensuing conclusion does not appear in *The Posies,* whose entirely different ending is found in *Variants in The Posies.*
	32	*to plaine*] Another reference to the truth of the story.
	37	*domine*] lord.

[From this point on, the notes refer to poems rather than to pages, and the line numbers are given for each poem.]

Poem Line
1   This is a literal translation of *Orl. Fur.* XXXIII, sts. 62, 63, and 64,
         which are quoted below. Du Bellay translated 63 and 64 in a sonnet
         which I also quote to the end that a comparison between Italian,
         French, and English may be easily available. The custom of an
         appended envoie or interpretation is discussed in the note to l. 28,
         p. 84. Why this poem did not appear in the second edition is ob-
         scure; certainly it is not lascivious. I can only suggest that its con-
         fession of love was either too intimate or else the poet repented
         of his vow of faithful love. The scene described by Ariosto explains
         itself; so I can only add that Bradamant is the female warrior of the
         Orlando who falls in love with the pagan knight Ruggiero.

> Rinova allor i pianti la donzella,
> E ne la mente sua cosi favella:
>
> Fu quel che piacque, un falso sogno; e questo
> Che mi tormenta, ahi lassa! è un veggiar vero.
> Il ben fu sogno a dilequarsi presto;
> Ma non è sogno il martire aspro e fiero.
> Perchè or non ode e vede il senso desto
> Quel ch'udire e veder parve al pensiero?
> A che condizione, occhi miei, sète,
> Che chiusi il ben, e aperti il mal vedete?
>
> Il dolce sonno mi promise pace;
> Ma l'amaro veggiar mi torna in guerra:
> Il dolce sonno è ben stato fallace;
> Ma l'amaro veggiare, oimè; non erra.
> Se 'l vero annoia, e il falso si mi piace,
> Non oda o vegga mai piu il vero in terra:
> Se 'l dormir mi da gaudio, e il veggiar guai,
> Possa io dormir senza destarmi mai.
>
> O felice animai ch'un sonno forte
> Sei mesi tien senza mai gli occhi aprire!
> Che s'assimigli tal sonno alla morte,
> Tal beggiare alla vita, io non vo'dire;
> Ch'a tutt'altre contraria la mia sorte
> Sente morte a veggiar, vita a dormire:
> Ma s'a tal sonno morte s'assimiglia,
> Deh, Morte, or ora chiudimi le ciglia!

——x——

> Le doulx sommeil paix & plaisir m'ordonne,
> Et le reveil querre & douleur m'aporte:
> Le faulx me plaist, le vray me deconforte:
> Le jour tout mal, la nuit tout bien me donne.

Poem   Line

> S'il est ainsi, soit en toute personne
> La verité ensevelie & morte.
> O animaulx de plus heureuse sorte,
> Dont l'oeil six mois le dormir n'abandonne!
>
> Que le sommeil à la mort soit semblant,
> Que le veiller de vie ait le semblant,
> Je ne le dy, & le croy' moins encores.
>
> Ou s'il est vray, puis que le jour me nuist
> Plus que la mort, ô mort, veilles donq' ores
> Clore mes yeulx d'une eternelle nuit.
>
>   (Du Bellay, ed. Chamard, I, 66, XLVII.)

1   23-24 A reference to hibernating animals.

    40   *Si fortunatus infoelix*] if one is fortunate, one is unhappy.

2   6   The figure is mixed but it seems to depend on true friendship being like the intertwining of the threads of life. Anger (*choller*) has twisted the threads into a crooked knot.

    15   This reference to youth and the mood of resignation and reconciliation of these first two poems seem to indicate a fairly late date of composition, when considered in connection with poem 3. The struggles, anger, and rivalry of "D.B." seem over and done with.

    20   *grutch of grief*] the complaining or grumbling caused by grief. A frequent phrase in Gascoigne.

3   Intro. A reference to the Elizabethan sport of tilting or running at the ring. The tilter, mounted on horseback, rode at full speed endeavoring to pass the point of his lance through a small ring suspended from a horizontal cross-bar. Three courses or attempts were allowed to each competitor. (Cf. Strutt, *Sports and Pastimes of the People of England,* pp. 123-25.)

    2ff. This view of war resembles that found in poem 70, where Gascoigne resolved not to return to the Dutch wars. It may be, then, that both this poem and no. 70 belong to the winter of 1572-73. (Cf. Introduction, pp. 16-17.)

    22   *to teare* etc.] The *O.E.D.* cites, "I teare my time (ay me) in prison pent," from Gascoigne's "fruit of Fetters" (*Works,* I, 367) and interprets the meaning as "to weep for." This meaning does not suit the present use which seems to indicate "to waste" *i.e.,* to tear into shreds.

    26   If *Pan* (rural pursuits) is so strong as to conquer Dame *Pallas'* lore (intellectual pursuits).

    30   *when shadowes make thee sure*] when you believe in shadows *i.e.,* go to the wars when you are no longer in your right mind.

4   Intro. This journey to the west and the reference to Exeter in poem no. 5 may, perhaps, have some connection with Bath and "Dan Bartholmew."

Poem	Line	

4   1   *Lachesis*] Gascoigne frequently uses the fable of the three fates, Clotho, Lachesis, and Atropos, who respectively held the distaff of the thread of man's life, spun out the thread of events, and finally cut the thread.

3   *webb*] The idea of the fates making a web or cloth of the thread of life is found in *Orl. Fur.* XXXIV, sts. 88-92.

4   *wale*] the ribbing or grain of the cloth. Gascoigne is carrying forward the figure of the cloth of his life which was woven by the fates.

15   *slipper* etc.] again the idea of the threads of life which may become knotted, sometimes in crooked knots (poem 2, l. 6) or as here a slippery knot that does not bind people together.

23   *forsight in dreames*] He has dreamed of approaching death.

31-36   Cf. Petrarch "Io non fu d'amor" and Wyatt's translation of this (ed. Foxwell, I, 16) for a similar idea.

5   1   *in course . . . kind*] suns (*i.e.* days) not sons. *Course* means in sequence; *kind,* nature.

7   Cf. l. 6, poem 4.

11   In the illustrations of the mediaeval *Dance of Death,* Death is usually shown armed with a dart.

6   Intro.   The Palace of Fontainebleau was begun in 1528 for Francis I by Gilles Le Breton and was extended during the century. The interior decorations by Italian and French artists were so lavish that the style of art became known as The School of Fontainebleau.

3   *Syrriane towers*] the tower of Babel. A mixture of the Biblical with the Greek myth of the Titans waging war against the gods and trying to reach Olympus by piling Ossa on Pelion.

5   *ports*] I can find no reference to any gates famous at this time.

8   *Apelles*] the famous Greek painter of the time of Alexander the Great. His most noteworthy paintings were a picture of Venus Anadyomene for a temple at Cos which Augustus placed in the temple of Caesar at Rome, and one of Alexander wielding a thunderbolt. The first is probably referred to here since the temple of Caesar could be considered as Caesar's *toome.*

12   *Phoebe*] This should be Phoebus, but for the scansion.

7   Intro.   I can see no reason to doubt that Gasciogne at some time went to France, and might well have known a "Skotish Dame." A possible identification might be one of the daughters of John, Baron Fleming, Queen Mary's ambassador at the French Court. There were, however, any number of Scots in France at the time. In *The Grief of Joye* (*Works,* II, 532) Gascoigne recalls the ladies he has known and says, "From Skotland *Flemyng,* woulde appeare in sight."

11, 12   The flames of love which Petrarch felt have here become the subject of an ingenious but utterly artificial conceit. This practice of twisting the conceit into the distortions of Laöcoon is characteristic of Gascoigne and his contemporaries.

Poem   Line

8   Intro.   *bewrayeth in cloudes*] reveals in a mysterious fashion. In view of Gas-coigne's general method of concealment, I offer the following ex-planation which identifies the lady as Elizabeth Bacon Bretton Boyes Gascoigne, the husband as Edward Boyes, and the rejected lover as Gascoigne. Line 18 (*of stature small* etc.) might well describe a boy (Boyes). "Thewes" (l. 19) was used by Turbervile as meaning "thighs," and a name for a horse's thighs was "gaskins." Thus "Boyes" is unfavourably compared with "Gascoigne" (*of stature with the most*—"Long George"). If we add to this the illustrious lineage (l. 14) which would certainly apply to the poet, and consider the lesser fame of the Boyes family, the identification seems strengthened. Finally, l. 16 with its "bycause I love him well" is close to the "riddle" of "F.J." (l. 44 ff., p. 67) and that in the completed ver-sion of "D.B."

        sweete gloves and broken ringes] Perfumed gloves were frequent gifts at the time. Lovers were in the habit of breaking a ring, one-half of which was kept by each.

    10   *gorged haukes*] The hawk's crop was called a gorge; thus the hawk that has fed has no further desire for food. For "lure" see the note to l. 31, p. 96.

           Mr. Fleay, (*Biogr. Chron. of the English Drama*, I, 238 ff.) referring to the hidden names, says, "I cannot find them, unless the 'gorged hawk' alludes to Helen Suavemberg's second marriage with Thomas Gorge." Mr. Fleay identifies Ferenda Natura as Helen Suavemberg because in *The Grief of Joye* (*Works*, II, 530) Gas-coigne applies to Ferenda the epithet "My *Hollow tree*." Fleay takes this to be the heraldic name of a boat and since a boat figured in Helen Suavemberg's arms, she becomes Ferenda. This is hardly evidence.

    19   *thewes*] A marginal note in *The Posies* reads, "Good qualities."

    26   Wyatt's fifth Epigram notes the custom of a gift of gloves:

> She take from me an hert; and I a glove from her;
> Let us se nowe, if thon be wourth thother.
>   (ed. Foxwell, I, 47)

    33   *griefe . . . game*] Grief for game is a frequent proverb in Gascoigne. It means that a thing originally thought to be good or pleasurable be-comes a matter for sorrow, on second thought.

    39   *Troylus*] The story of Troylus deceived by false Cressida was a handy reference for practically all Elizabethan poets in their attacks on false ladies.

9   Intro.   *fayre*] Firenzuola described the ideal beauty as possessed of light hair, bright and clear skin, and black eyes. The fact that Queen Elizabeth had light hair and complexion enforced the idea in England. How-

Poem   Line

ever, Sir John Harington, in a notation on Ariosto's description of
Alcina's dark eyes (*Orl. Fur.*, VII, 12), says black eyes and light
hair are monstrous together.

hard favored] well favored.

9   4   *Pompeia*] probably the wife whom Caesar divorced for intriguing with
               Clodius.

        5   *Marcus*] Marcus Aurelius, the philosopher emperor. Thus known from
               the *Golden Book of Marcus Aurelius.*

        6   *Boemia*] possibly mediaeval romances connected Marcus Aurelius with
               a Queen of Bohemia.

        10   *Antonius*] Marc Antony, the conqueror of Egypt and lover of Cleopatra.

        16   *foyle*] a setting for a jewel. It is difficult to determine whether a long
               "s" or an "f" was intended. Soil giving the meaning of a dark skin
               may be intended.

        18   *solle*] the sun. The sun was the cause of her brown skin. *The Posies'*
               reading of "soyle" seems an error, although the meaning might then
               be that the land (soil) of Egypt produced dark skinned people.

        22   *Faustine*] probably Faustina, the wife of Marcus Aurelius, noted for her
               profligacy.

        25   *Lucrece*] Even Lucrece, who committed suicide after being raped by
               Tarquin, would have loved Antony.

        26   *lure*] Cf. note to l. 31, p. 96.

        26   *Fist*] The falconer held the hawk on his wrist.

        39   *Allegoria*] Cf. note to l. 28, p. 84.

        40ff. Gascoigne follows the method which he advocated (*Works*, I, 466) of
               finding a classical example by which a fault might be explained to
               the lady's advantage. He gives the classical example to which he
               applies the case at hand.

        43   The lady has a lighter skin than Cleopatra but she is not a blonde.

        44   *grey as glasse*] Thus Chaucer (ed. Robinson, p. 20, l. 152) describes the
               eyes of the Prioress.

        49   Gascoigne judges Cleopatra on the basis of her faithfulness in love.
               Nothing else mattered as long as she followed the code of Courtly
               Love.

10   Intro. *bragging*] swaggering.

        1   *on hoygh*] This seems to mean "on high" *i.e.*, supercilious or proud, al-
               though it is difficult to account for the spelling.

        26   *bulwarks*] The martial figure applied to individual physical conquest is
               fully amplified by Aretino (*I Sonnetti Lusuriosi*) and is used to some
               extent by Gascoigne. Cf. note to l. 24, p. 54.

        29   A reference to the common belief that the lion will not hurt defenceless
               creatures. Cf. Wyatt:

               The fierce lion will hurt no yelden thinges
               (ed. Foxwell, II, 42)

Poem	Line	
12	Intro.	*An other Sonet*] The preceding is not a sonnet and since Gascoigne defined the form of a sonnet (*Works*, I, 471), we can only conclude that this means "An other poem, a Sonet."
13	1-4	A mixture of figures. Beauty like a spider weaves a web wherein eyes like flies are caught.
	5	*gite*] gown. This word, used by Chaucer, appears frequently in Gascoigne but seldom in the writings of his contemporaries.
	6	*tysing*] enticing.
	6	*Pallas pooles*] pools of Pallas Athene. This seems to mean that the enticing conversation was concerned with intellectual matters, but the figure is obscure.
	7	*painted pale*] Cf. note to l. 13, p. 75.
	9	*eld*] old age.
	10	*beauties blaze*] golden hair.
	11	*Had I wist*] had I known. A frequent theme: Skelton's *Magnyfycance* (ed. Dyce) II, 12, 66; Tottel (ed. Arber) p. 244.
14	1	*daunger*] Cf. note to l. 2, p. 88.
	5	*to hop*] Cf. note to l. 12, p. 63.
	18	*roome*] position.
	29	*cart*] home again to the country.
15	10	Love is the fisherman and the lover's mind the fish's throat.
16	Intro.	*knowing . . . purposes*] The popularity of handbooks teaching witty and sparkling conversation is noted by Louis B. Wright, (*Middleclass Culture in Elizabethan England*, pp. 132-33) who mentions T.T.'s *The Schoolemaster, or Teacher of Table Philosophie* (1576) as an outstanding example of the genre. *The Schoolemaster*, he says, "provides in Book I a discussion of foods and drinks, with stray bits of curious information about them; in Book II a description of the manners and customs of various people; in Book III witty questions and answers; and in Book IV merry jests."

making of purposes] a game of questions or riddles and answers.

Riddles] Wyatt wrote several riddles which are among his epigrams and the custom was a popular one.

> A ladye gave me a gyfte she had not
> And I receyved her guifte I toke not
>   (ed. Foxwell, I, 49)

drave out one nayle with another] answered one question with another. Cf. note to l. 24, p. 62.

17	1	Presumably she refers to poem 34.
18	Intro.	The ensuing sequence depends on the pun of lemon and lemman (lover, in a bad sense).
	1	*peat*] a spoiled or pampered girl; from the French "petite."
19	2	*to broad before*] Cf. note to ll. 26-27, p. 87.

Poem	Line	
20		This poem was omitted in *The Posies* presumably because it contained such definite references as made identification of the persons involved possible. Cf. Puttenham's remarks above in the Introduction, n. 99.
	6	*painted shadow*] picture.
	7, 8	These lines suggest some connection with poem 24, *q.v.*
21	1, 2	Catullus' "Lugete, Veneres Cupidinesque" and Skelton's "Phylyp Sparowe" come at once to mind. However, Gascoigne's poem is far from being a lament.
	2	"Phillip" was a familiar name for a sparrow and was probably derived from "phip," an imitation of the chirp of a sparrow.
	23	*fend* etc.] fencing terms.
	24	*peat*] Cf. note to l. 1, poem 18.
22	Intro.	The easily demonstrable use of the family crest in poem 47 inclines me to consider the present poem as an example of the same sort of thing, and we find the crest of Knolles to be a hawk (merlin) seizing a partridge. In *The Grief of Joye* (*Works*, II, 527) we find a marginal notation of the initials E.K. for the stanza devoted to "my *Ladie per a mount.*" The next stanza begins "Of selfe same lyne, a Countesse doth appeare" and the initials are "C. of Ess." This last can only be Lettice Knollys and the preceding seems to be her sister, Elizabeth Knollys. It may be, then, that Elizabeth Knollys was one of the poet's loves and that this poem was written to her. A poem on the same theme is in *Tottel's Miscellany* (ed. Arber, p. 132).
	36	*seale*] presumably the posy, *Spraeta tamen vivunt,* which means "Despised things may live."
23	Intro.	In *The Posies* this poem appears after no. 12 and has its posy altered to *Si fortunatus infoelix.* In an obvious attempt to link it to no. 12, the introduction in *The Posies* reads *To the same gentlewoman.* By such alterations it seems clear that there was a certain unity in the original order and sequence of posies which Gascoigne altered to prevent the identification of people and events.
24	1-6	Puttenham (ed. Arber, pp. 203-04) criticizes this beginning as an example of "Periphrasis," since the poet spends a stanza to describe the time as spring which everyone knew the moment the word "March" appeared!
		More important is the fact that elsewhere (*ibid.*, p. 265) Puttenham reveals a certain personal knowledge of Gascoigne. He says: "His intent was to declare how upon the tenth day of March he crossed the river of Thames, to walke in Saint George's field, the matter was not great as ye may suppose." Nothing in the poem shows what part of the river Gascoigne visited, so it may be concluded that Puttenham knew Gascoigne well enough to know the

circumstances of this poem. This naming of a place may suggest who the lady was. Viscount Montague had large holdings in South-wark and built there a residence called Montague House. The masque (poem 69) written by the poet for the Montague marriage shows that the marriage took place at this residence, therefore it may be that the lady whom Gascoigne describes was one of the daughters of this nobleman.

This poem is another of those paraphrased by Watson and printed as his own in *The Tears of Fancie* (ed. Arber, p. 202).

24   5   *Thames*] This reference to the river may indicate that the lady of poem 20 is identical with the one of this present poem.

       26   *graffes of grief*] not the ordinary pleasures of spring grow in her mind, instead the grief that has been grafted onto her mind.

       31   *Ver*] spring (Lat.).

       36   *mould*] earth. The figure is again pressed to a conclusion.

       49   This concluding stanza shows the poet's connection with the Court.

25   1   This answers the last line of the first stanza of "D.B." no. 4 (*q.v.*). Cf. *George Gascoigne*, p. 215.

    7-11 Plagiarized by Watson (*Tears of Fancie*, ed. Arber, p. 207).

       9   *Bolte*] the missile of the cross-bow.

26   16   *mew*] coop, pen.

       16   This and the other charges made against the lady together with the rival are almost identical with the charges which Dan Bartholmew brings against Ferenda ("D.B." no. 3). Is this poem therefore part of the same story? It may well be, since it could not be included in "Dan Bartholmew" without being redundant. Cf. *George Gascoigne*, pp. 220-21.

       26   *Peacocke foole*] It was a familiar belief that the peacock, in spite of his fine feathers, was ashamed of his ugly feet. Cf. Nashe, *Works*, ed. McKerrow, II, 112; and Deloney, *Works*, ed. Mann, pp. 29, 514.

       45   *dragges*] drugs.

27   3   *hooded Hauke*] the hawk's head was covered until it was released to pursue a particular bird.

       6   *to hop* etc.] Cf. note to l. 6, p. 62.

       7   *disdayne*] regularly used as the antithesis of love.

       22   *slippe*] leash.

       31   *lease of libertie*] The lady is not free to be with her lover.

       33   *in gree*] in kindness, from the French "gré."

       33   *playnsong*] Cf. note to l. 17, p. 93.

28   1   *Despysed things may live*] a translation of *Spreta tamen vivunt*.

       11   *set full light*] held in no esteem.

  13-14 *Diomede . . . Cressydes . . . Troylus*] Cf. note to l. 39, poem 8.

  17-24 A series of examples of the rule of change which could be duplicated in any number of Mediaeval and Renaissance writers.

Poem	Line	
28	24	*fortunes wheele*] Many woodcuts survive which show a wheel turned by the goddess Fortune which lifts men up only to hurl them down again. On this concept of tragedy see Willard Farnham's *Mediaeval Heritage of Elizabethan Tragedy.*
29	1	The entire poem is a play upon the antitheses of love, which were the stock in trade of every versifier. Wyatt's "Twenty-fourth Epigram" (ed. Foxwell, I, 59) contains an excellent series of these antitheses.
	16	*gruch*] grutch, grudge.
	25	*Philomene*] The story of Progne and Tereus was made into a long poem by Gascoigne (*Works*, II, 175 ff.). Philomene, the sister of Progne, was seduced by Tereus, Progne's husband. Progne learned of this, killed her son. Tereus then pursued the sisters, but the gods changed them into birds. Philomene became the nightingale. Cf. *George Gascoigne*, pp. 251-63.
	37	*Ferenda Natura*] This posy is explained in "D.B." (poem 1, st. 14) as signifying that Nature bears the blame for the lady's fickleness.
30		For a discussion of this poem see *George Gascoigne*, pp. 140-41.
	18	*to mend the breach* etc.] The breach can never be mended before the flood tide returns.
32		Here Gascoigne is following his avowed method of finding some supernatural reason for praising the lady (*Works*, I, 465-66). Pallas is jealous; Mars is in love with her; Phoebus dreads her beams, and Dame Cynthia disappears.
	8	*invention*] an elaborate conceit.
	13	*Pallas*] Pallas Athene, goddess of wisdom.
	20	*Joves daughter*] Venus of line 22.
	23	*Vulcane*] The legend was that Mars seduced Venus from her husband Vulcan.
	25	*Dan Phoebus*] the same idea as "F.J." poem 6.
	37	*Meritum petere, gravè*] To seek reward is serious. It was of this posy that Gabriel Harvey wrote: "Meritum petere, vile." Harvey went on to remark that in this world it is not a question of talking about rewards, but of doing something to deserve them. (*Marginalia*, ed. Moore-Smith, p. 167.)
33	1	*coulors black and whyt*] The symbolism of these colors is noted in John Grange's *Golden Aphroditis* (D. ij) in the following passage: "Thus takyng his leave, he marched towarde his chamber, whiche he founde all hanged with whyte and blacke. Who knowing well the vertue of eche coloure, and the myrting of the same, thought veryly hee swymmed agaynst the streame. For (as I have heard some say) these colours pretended virginitie unto death." Cf. also Nicholas Breton's lines, "When first I saw the clad in colors black and white" (*A Floorish Upon Fancie*, 1582, Rpt. in *Heliconia*, ed. T. Park, 1815, I, 116).

Poem	Line	
34		In *The Posies,* this poem is incorporated into "Dan Bartholmew" and is there entitled "his third Triumphe." Cf. *George Gascoigne,* p. 213.
	11	*Meritum petere, gravè*] In *The Posies,* where this poem is inserted in "Dan Bartholmew," the posy becomes *Fato non Fortuna.*
35	1	Puttenham (*Arte,* ed. Arber, p. 261) criticizes the excessive alliteration of these first lines.
	10	*plainsong*] Cf. note to l. 17, p. 93.
	28	*Angelica*] In *The Posies* Gascoigne appended this marginal notation: "Angelica refusing the most famous knights in the whole worlde, chose at last Medoro a poore serving man." The Angelica-Medoro story is found in *Orl. Fur.,* XXIII, sts. 100-122.
	36	*Orlando*] The story of Orlando's love for Angelica was begun in Boiardo's *Orlando Innamorato* and was continued by Ariosto.
36	2	*Leander*] a reference to the story of Hero and Leander, later told at length by Marlowe.
	4	*behove*] advantage.
	37	Cf. note to l. 28, p. 84.
	41-42	*Mars . . . Vulcane*] This reference would seem to mean that the lady went overseas with her husband (Vulcan) and the poet as her lover (Mars) wishes her to return to him.
37		Wyatt (ed. Foxwell, I, 266) writes a poem ostensibly by a woman. The present poem is presumably one written for someone else, and the recital of the story is necessary in order that the ladies of the Court (l. 51) may fully understand her plight.
	12	*behove*] advantage.
	41	*towers*] perhaps the Tower of London.
	51	*Ladies*] A number of poems appeal to the ladies of the Court, presumably because of their power of scandal and influence, and also because the subject of the poem is one of their number. Cf. nos. 24, 54, 56.
38		This poem is omitted in *The Posies* presumably because it relates to Gascoigne's affair with Elizabeth Bacon Bretton and Edward Boyes.
	1	*christs crosse rowe*] the alphabet.
	2	*B.*] This probably refers to Edward Boyes.
	4	*A.O.G.N.C.S.*] an anagram for "Gascon."
	6	*thinckest*] The last syllable of this word must be slurred for proper scansion.
	25	*highest place*] the "G" cliff as opposed to the base.
	27	*sol, re, ut*] The names of the notes of the scale are taken from the first two letters of the words of a hymn to St. John the Baptist: *Ut* queant laxix *Re*sonare fibris *Mi*ra gestorum *Fa*muli tuorum, *Sol*ve polluti *La*bii reatum, Sancte Johannes. (W. S. Pratt, *History of Music,* pp. 67-69). The present arrangement signifies a chord.
	35	*dooble G.*] G(eorge) G(ascoigne).

Poem	Line	

38 39, 40 This description of himself and Boyes does agree with the charges made in "D.B." no. 3.

40 Intro. The title indicates a poem written for someone else, as does the poem itself.

10 This line suggests Dr. Faustus' famous apostrophe to Helen.

41 Intro. Richard Adlington's translation of *The Golden Asse* of Lucius Apuleius was first printed in 1566, and it may have been this version which the poet presented to his lady. The sequence gives the main details of the story of the transformation of Apuleius into an ass. Lucius Apuleius arrived in the city of Hipate and lodged with one Milo whose wife was an enchantress. In the same city there lived Birhena, Apuleius' cousin, who tried to persuade him to leave the house of Milo and lodge with her. He was unwilling to do so for he had fallen in love with Milo's servant girl, Fotis. Lucius witnessed the enchantress' transformation into an owl, and desired a like transformation; however, by a trick of Fotis' he became, instead, an ass.

11 *foyld*] overthrown.

13 *gadding*] going about or on a pilgrimage. A hopelessly mixed figure.

19 *fitte*] experience. An extension of the ordinary meaning, "painful experience."

22-23 *set . . . in brake*] control his brains. Brake, meaning a horse's bit, appears in Surrey's poem, "Lyke as the brake within the riders hands." Gascoigne's use seems close to the modern sense of the word.

31 *whitled*] drunk. So used by Lyly in *Mother Bombie*, III, 3, "The best was our masters as well whitled as wee, for they yet lie by it."

35 *greasd this gest*] tricked this guest.

39 *foule*] fowl, bird.

41 *bobbing blocke*] a thing to be struck or hit.
beating stocke] a senseless person.

49 *David*] The use of the David and Bersabe figure suggests some relation to the first poem in "F.J."

42 The answer to the riddle seems to be a kiss.

43 4 *put their . . . barck & tree*] put their hands (intercede) between the bark and tree (two lovers).

44 9 *Cressyde*] Cf. note to l. 39, poem 8.

45 The story told in this poem is very close to that of Dan Bartholmew, particularly as it is found in the "Dolorous discourses." Cf. *George Gascoigne*, p. 220.

9 *not to bleede*] Wounds inflicted by Cupid did not bleed.

16 *will*] passion, desire.

22 *Dame pleasures plaster*] Having sought solace (a plaster) for his sorrow (wound), he finds that the plaster is not helpful but is a corrosive in that it aggravates the wound.

Poem	Line	
45	26-30	a series of proverbs.
	30	*gorged Hauke*] Cf. note to l. 10, poem 8.
46		The idea and some of the famous people here noted are amplified from the first poem in "F.J." (*q.v.*). The idea was a frequent one and an excellent example is found in *The Palace of Pleasure* (ed. Haslewood, III, 597).
	19-20	*Saloman . . . Pharaos daughter*] a reference to the Biblical story of Solomon and the Queen of Sheba (I Kings, x).
	23	*nam*] am not, thus from a marginal annotation in *The Posies*.
	25	*Assirian Knight*] Holofernes of line 29. The story is found in Judith, iv.
	32	*Sampson*] The Samson-Delilah story is found in Judges, xvi.
	35	*Deyanyraes*] Deianira was won as wife by Hercules who fought Achelaus for her. She was the unwitting cause of the hero's death in giving him the poisoned robe which she received from the centaur Nessus.
	37	*Nasoes*] Publius Ovidius Naso, whose love, Corinna, figures in his *Amores*.
	42	*Cressides*] Cf. note to l. 39, poem 8.
47	Intro.	The name disciphered is "Scudamore" as has been shown above in the Introduction, "Authorship" (*q.v.*, pp. 26-27). Sir John Scudamore was a student of the Middle Temple (*Students Admitted to the Middle Temple 1547-1560*, p. 36) at about the same time that Gascoigne was at Gray's Inn. Scudamore held many positions at Court: he was standard bearer to the honorable band of Gentlemen Pensioners, a member of the Council for the Marches of Wales, and was Custos Rotulorum and High Sheriff of Herefordshire. He received, as one of the unofficial perquisites of a courtier, the wardship of John Appary. This brought him into dispute with James a Parry, the child's uncle, who may be the person referred to in poem 70 (*q.v.*). (P.R.O. St. Ch. 5, A55/33, S32/40.) Sir John was a friend and benefactor of Sir Thomas Bodley. (Matt. Gibson, *A View of . . . the Churches of Door, Home-Lacy and Hempsted*, pp. 55-62.)
	1	*L'Escü d'amour*] the shield of love (Fr.).
	5	*targe*] shield.
	31	*Lenvoie*] Cf. the note to l. 28, p. 84.
48	Intro.	*so many more* etc.] These words show clearly that the preceding poems are Gascoigne's. Cf. pp. 19-28 in the Introduction. Gascoigne said (*Works*, I, 11) that both the "areignment and divorce of a Lover . . . [were] written in jeast," so the present poem may equally well have been written in a like spirit, since all three have the same mock heroic tone.
	8	*tewed*] employed.
	13	*braunfalne*] thin. The brawny or muscular part of the arms has disappeared.

Poem   Line

48   18   *lights*] lungs. This type of pleonasm is a common stylistic device.

        29   *Ever or Never*] a posy liable to a variety of interpretation. Cf. Introduction, pp. 28-39.

49   As has been noted in the comment on the preceding poem, this "araignement" was written in jest. It would seem to be the result of Gascoigne's gross flattery in poem no. 8 of "F.J."

                Petrarch's canzone "Quell' antiquo mio dolce empio Signore" tells how the poet brought Love before the bar of Reason and the former delivered a eulogy of Laura. Wyatt translated this.

        10   *doome*] judgment.

        13   *sitteth not*] is not fitting.

        15   *Justice*] *The Posies* has the following marginal annotation: "Wyll is dame bewties chiefe Iustice of Oyre and terminer."

        19   *crafte the cryer* etc.] *crafte* (trickery) empanels a jury made up of falsehood and a pack of *pickethankes* (tale-bearers).

        24   *trust*] trussed up, hung.

        28   *heavie hill*] Tyburn hill, where were the gallows.

50   The invention employed in this poem follows Gascoigne's own recommendation that a supernatural cause for an imperfection should be used so that praise may accrue to the lady (*Works*, I, 466).

        Intro. *Bridges*] Catherine, daughter of Edmund, Lord Chandos, married William, Lord Sands (Dugdale, *Baronage*, II, 395). One is tempted to wonder if Gascoigne numbered among his riotous friends "one Sands, a young son of Lord Sands [who] was hanged at St. Thomas of Watering for robbery [in 1566]" (Stow's *Annales*, 1631, p. 628).

        2   *beares yᵉ bel*] takes first place. This derives from the bell worn by the leading cow or sheep of a flock.

        8   *the blemishe*] obviously a birth mark.

        14   *Apelles*] Cf. note to l. 8, poem 6.

51   Intro. *Zouche*] Dorothy Zouche, illegitimate daughter of Richard, Lord Zouche of Haryngworth and wife of Arthur, Lord Grey of Wilton. Lord Grey was remarried sometime before 1572 to Jane Sibilla Morysin, the widow of Edward, Lord Russell. (G.E.C., *Complete Peerage*, VI, 186.)

52   7   *find nor peace*] Cf. Petrarch's "Pace non trovo" which contains this line as well as others in this poem.

        13   *hope, yet live in dread*] Cf. Wyatt (ed. Foxwell, I, 24) for a parallel to this stanza.

        16   *for why*] because.

        19   The series of rhetorical questions is frequent in Wyatt (ed. Foxwell, I, 178).

        29-30   Cf. Wyatt (ed. Foxwell, I, 133) for a whole poem on this theme.

        43   *fever Ectyck*] *The Posies* has a marginal annotation reading, "There is in deede suche a kinde of fever." In fact, our modern "hectic" had

Poem   Line

its origin in the Greek "hektikos" which means a recurrent or
habitual fever. Wyatt describes such a fever in these lines:

> I sit alone, save on the second day
> My fever comes, with whom I spend the time
> In burning heat while that she list assigne.
> (ed. Foxwell, I, 43)

52   60   *past*] is past all others.

53   Cf. notes to poem 48 which show that this is a humorous mock-serious
                poem. The legal figure is here continued, and the absurd conceits of
                love are ridiculed. Cf. also "D.B." no. 6.

        Intro. *libell*] libellus, bill, a legal petition.
        12   *beares the bell*] Cf. note to l. 2, poem 50.
        22   *make*] mate.
        39   *dart*] Cf. note to l. 11, poem 5.

54   The first lines of this contain the familiar figures of unfortunate lovers
                found in "F.J." no. 8 and "D.B." no. 2.
        1   *Paris*] An allusion to Paris' choosing Venus the most beautiful of the
                three goddesses, and receiving from her in return Helen, wife of
                Menelaus, whose departure to Troy caused the Trojan War.
        5   *Priams younger son*] Troilus.
        10   *never gropes* etc.] never seeks for the engrafting of grace.
        25   *Ladies*] Ladies of the Court. Cf. poems 24, 37, and 56.
        26   *as Tytan* etc.] as the sun surpasses a star.
        34   *I seeke* etc.] an expression of futility.
        36   Proverbs denoting futility.
        41   *Attamen ad solitum*] But nevertheless with regard to what is usual. This
                is presumably part of a larger Latin quotation. The posy has little
                meaning by itself, and appears only this once in the entire volume.

55   7   *wanton babes*] youthful years, gazing eyes, wanton will, and loving boy.
        34   *Robyn*] *not* his son.

56   Intro. *Recantation*] A recantation was traditional; Chaucer, Petrarch, and Wyatt
                could serve as examples. Gascoigne, however, chose his own idea
                of recanting and we have another of his mock-serious poems with
                legal figures. Cf. poems 48, 49, and 53.
        8   *turning cap*] proverb meaning, to change one's mind.
        19   *Anatomie*] poem 48.
        21   *araignde*] poem 49.
        24   *I Bathe in Blisse*] poem 29.
        28   *tippet*] cap; again, to change one's mind.
        32   *Astolfe*] *Orl. Fur.*, Canto XXVII, contains the story of the cuckolding
                of Astolfo, King of Lombardy, by his dwarf.
        37   *Haud ictus sapio*] Although beaten, I have not learned wisdom.

Poem	Line	

57   Intro.   *Greyes Inne*] Gascoigne first entered Gray's Inn in 1555 and probably remained in residence for two or three years. His resumption of his studies in 1564-65 was the occasion for writing the five theme poems which ensue. (Cf. *George Gascoigne*, pp. 17, 32-34.)

theames] The theme was a standard school-boy exercise, an example of which may be found in Gascoigne's *The Glasse of Government* (*Works*, II, 55-58).

Francis Kinwelmarshe] Kinwelmarshe was admitted to Gray's Inn in 1557 and collaborated with Gascoigne in the translation of *Jocasta*. His other literary work consisted of a number of poems in *The Paradise of Dainty Devises* (ed. Rollins, poems 9, 11, 13, 18, 19, 21, 40, 41, 75, and 98). (Cf. *George Gascoigne*, pp. 32-33, 148-150.)

Audaces fortuna iuvat] Fortune favors the brave.

5   *Menelaus*] If Menelaus had not tried to recover Helen, there would have been no Trojan war.

10   *Prince*] Aeneas.

11   *Ascanius*] son of Aeneas and founder of Rome.

15   *Sic tuli*] Thus I bear (my burden).

58   Intro.   *Antonie Kynwelmarshe*] Admitted to Gray's Inn in 1561, Anthony Kinwelmarshe was probably the brother of Francis and may have been the Anthony Kinwelmarshe of Wing, Buckinghamshire, who was friendly with the Dormer family. (Cf. *George Gascoigne*, p. 33.)

Satis sufficit] Enough is enough or, as Gascoigne says, "I coumpt enough as good as any feast."

3-4   *and beates . . . dignitie*] and keeps the restless mind searching all means (*endlesse driftes*) to support wordly reputation.

8   *Dan Croesus*] King Croesus.

12   *povert*] poverty.

15   *store*] any possessions "stored" away.

26   *shente*] injurious. The Middle English "shenden," of which "shente" is the participle, means to harm or injure. Gascoigne seems to have made an adjective of the participle.

59   Intro.   *John Vaughan*] John Vaughan entered Gray's Inn in 1562/3 but little more is known about him since there is no other evidence than his residence at the Inn which might serve to identify him. (Cf. *George Gascoigne*, p. 33.)

Magnum vectigal parcimonia] Thrift is a great source of revenue.

2-3   *a bottel . . . wofull ende*] the attributes of a beggar.

4   *in bravery* etc.] to boast (*bragge*) of one's position by wearing fine clothes (*bravery*).

6-7   *spare . . . faster bound*] The contrast between *brinke* and *bottom* would seem to mean that even if you have money, don't spend it, for with the top of your supply gone, the bottom is that much nearer.

Poem	Line	
59	12	*Hick, Hobbe and Dicke*] equivalent to the modern "Tom, Dick, and Harry."
	13	*goonhole groates*] The *O.E.D.* quotes Mr. Barclay V. Head of the coin department of the British Museum to the effect that "goonhole" may be a corruption of some foreign proper name; "groates" were silver coins worth fourpence.
	15	*let their lease*] sell a lease for an immediate cash return.
	15	*tooke their rent before*] by receiving payments in advance, they must give a discount.
	16	*rappes a royall on his cappe*] hastens to spend a royal (a gold coin worth fifteen shillings) in the purchase of a cap. The Old English *hrepan* with its idea of seizing seems to explain the rather unusual construction here.
	23	*angells*] gold coins worth from six to ten shillings.
	25	*When orders fall*] when an office falls vacant.
	26	*haggard hawkes*] A haggard hawk was one first caught in its adult state. *The Gentleman's Recreation* (p. 171) is at pains to describe the manner of luring the haggard.
	26	*emptie hand*] without a lure.
	30	*Davie Debet*] a personification of debt.
	37	*Malmesey*] a sweet wine, originally obtained from Morea.
	39	*teynter hookes*] hooks passed through the edges of cloth so that it may be stretched (tentered).
60	Intro.	This poem shows an interesting use of the sonnet as a stanza form. The same thing is done in poem 41 but here the last line of one becomes the first line of the next.

Alexander Nevile] There is no record of Alexander Nevile's admission to Gray's Inn; Gascoigne's reference is, however, presumptive evidence of his being a member. There seems to be confusion regarding the identity of this young poet who, in the preface to his translation of Seneca (1560), gives his year of birth as 1544. *D.N.B.* describes him as brother to Thomas Neville, Dean of Canterbury, and son of Richard Neville of South Leverton, Notts., by Anne, daughter of Sir Walter Montell. I have found several Chancery Proceedings instituted by Alexander Neville of South Leverton, Notts., against his mother Anne, the widow of Sir Anthony Neville (Early Chanc. Proc. C1/1455, 21-25; C1/1455, 26-30). These date from 1553 and could hardly have been instituted by a boy born in 1544. There is need for a study of this secretary of Archbishop Parker (Strype's *Life . . . of . . . Parker*, II, 433) and author of *De Furoribus Norfolciensium Ketto Duce* (1575), and *Academiae Cantabrigiensis Lacrymae* (1587).

Poem	Line	
60	Intro.	*Sat cito, si sat bene*] literally, if it be well, let it be quickly (done). Gascoigne emphasizes the negative as well as the positive aspect by saying "No haste but good."
		Nimis cito . . . and . . . *Vix bene*] These two Latin tags mean "too quickly" and "scarcely well." In connection with the main theme and the story of his vain attempts to gain a position at Court, the meaning becomes clear. The poet sought high station too quickly and the means by which he sought favor were scarcely well planned.
	1	*when fyrste* etc.] Gascoigne probably became acquainted with the courtly world in 1557 or 1558. (Cf. *George Gascoigne*, pp. 20-21.)
	9	*saint*] Cf. note to ll. 4-5, p. 61.
	20	*trustlesse trace*] uncertain path (way of life).
	35	*badge of braverie*] fine clothes.
	47	*boughes of . . . oke*] Instead of preserving his property (pilles of provision) he sold the oak trees on his lands to purchase fine clothes.
	51	*ferme* etc.] For a full account of this squandering of his property see *George Gascoigne*, pp. 20-21.
	65-66	*expences* etc.] His expenses, like lumps of lead, pressed his purse against the ground.
61	Intro.	*Richarde Courtop*] All that is definitely known is that Courtop entered Gray's Inn in 1559. There was a Richard Courtop of Cranbrook, Kent, and the name also appears in a Chancery action. (Cf. *George Gascoigne*, p. 33.)
		Durum aeneum & miserabile aevum] the pitiless cruel age of brass (as opposed to the Golden or Silver age).
	2	*queste*] jury.
	13	*Licurgus*] the law-giver, whose brother Polydectus was king of Sparta. The latter's wife, after his death, proposed to Lycurgus that she kill her children if he would share the throne with her. At the birth of the posthumous son, Lycurgus proclaimed him king and left Sparta to avoid any suspicion.
	19	*Prince . . . babe*] perhaps a reference to Edward VI and the conspiracies of Warwick.
	25	*Cayphas* etc.] Gascoigne is comparing the contemporary world to that which crucified Christ. It is only natural that such an analogy should be presented as a mystery play with the characters of Cayphas, Herod, Pilate, and Judas. Such a play Gascoigne had probably seen many times.
	27	*vice*] the evil protagonist of the morality plays who figured equally in the interludes which were popular in Gascoigne's youth. In his *Glasse of Government* Gascoigne employed the character of the vice.
	28	*Tom Troth*] a personification of truth in the manner of the moralities and interludes. Having begun with the device of a mystery play,

Poem	Line	
		Gascoigne continues his strictures of the present by reference to the characters of the moralities and interludes.
61	29	*woman wantonnesse*] A harlot usually figured in the moralities and interludes. The other persons mentioned are also typical figures.
	33	*Simme Swash*] an alliterative name, probably coined by Gascoigne, for the braggart.
	34	*Climme of yᵉ Clough*] one of the characters of the famous ballad, *Adam Bell, Clym of the Clough, and William of Cloudesly*. Here used to represent rustic virtue.
	37	*treble parte*] highest of four voice parts. Presumably Pride sings this because of his vaunting nature.
	38	*meane*] The Golden Mean cannot compete with Pride and Extravagance and so mumbles.
	39	*Cost lost*] extravagance. He sings the Counter Tenor part (next highest to the treble) since he accompanies Pride.
	39	*counter Tenor*] There is an opportunity here for a pun on The Counter, the debtor's prison, and Nashe alluded to Gascoigne's wild youth by such a pun.

> I yeeld that I have dealt upon spare commodities of wine and capons in my daies, I have sung George Gascoignes Counter tenor; what then?
>
> (Nashe's *Foure Letters Confuted* 1593, ed. Grosart, II, 253)

	46	*crosier staffe*] a pun on a bishop's staff and the staff sign in music.
	Concl.	*he devised . . . undertake the like*] Gascoigne was evidently proud of his ability to compose quickly. The introduction to poem 10 of "F.J." reads, "And hereupon (before the fal of the Buck) [he] devised this Sonet following." The dedicatory letter of *The Complaynt of Phylomene* tells a similar story of the rapid production of "De Profundiis" achieved while riding from Chelmsford to London.
62	Intro.	*Dominus ijs opus habet*] The Lord has need of these.
	4	*glass*] mirror. The figure of the mirror is widespread in literature, but this is Gascoigne's first reference to it. The culmination of his satire is, of course, *The Steele Glas*—only a steel mirror would show things as they were.
	10	*beates his braine*] does everything possible.
	13	*Give Gave*] an alliterative personification.
	13	*what neede* etc.] but that's as far as it goes.
	17	*by gisse*] a corruption of the oath, "By Jesus."
	23-24	*He is . . . glister all of gold*] These lines were omitted in *The Posies* presumably because of their attack on the vestments of the clergy. It would seem, therefore, that there were objections to the *Flowres* on the grounds that it slandered the clergy.

Poem Line

62 27-28 *He likes . . . hath neede*] Why this attack on Popery was objected to is uncertain. Either the authorities wished to suppress all religious dispute or else Gascoigne wished to appease some of his Catholic friends such as the Viscount Montague and the Dormers. Poem 67 also contains anti-Catholic references which were excised in *The Posies.*

33, 34 *They shrinke . . . destenies decreede.*] omitted in *The Posies.* I see no reason for this omission.

37ff. *office falles* etc.] That this was a frequent complaint is shown by Holinshed's obituary notice on Sir Thomas Cheinie where that knight is praised because he did give offices to his dependents.

Practically all the charges made by Gascoigne in this poem are echoed by Holinshed, who praises Cheinie as the last to preserve the old virtues. (*Chronicles,* 1587, III, 1171.)

40 *durante bene placito*] subject to the grantor's pleasure.

63 *lubbers*] farm laborers. I can find no authority for this meaning, but it cannot here mean "one who lives in idlenesse" as the *O.E.D.* says.

69 *count*] account.

73 *tables end*] the lower end of the table, where the lesser dependents of a great lord ate.

91 *lubber*] Cf. note to l. 63 above.

94 *turne him up*] discharge him.

94 *Hallontyde*] All-hallows time, *i.e.* All Saints Day, November 1st.

102 *zore*] an early use of western dialect for rustics.

104 *measne land*] common land.

105 *saint Needam*] the name of a small town near Ipswich, used punningly with allusion to "need"; hence poverty, beggary.

107 *Ever or never*] Cf. note to l. 29, poem 48.

63 21 *glasse*] a mirror, showing the symbolic significance of the preceding.

23-24 This figure is repeated in ll. 26-27, poem 64.

64 27, 28 Cf. note to ll. 23-24, poem 63.

Concl. *These good . . . rehersed.*] omitted in *The Posies.*

65 Intro. *The occasion . . . here followeth.*] omitted in *The Posies.* The reason for the omission is puzzling, since this poem is referred to by Gascoigne in the introductory letter to his *The Complaynt of Phylomene* (*Works,* II, 177). Here the poet says that twelve or thirteen years before (1572-73) he began to devise his *Phylomene* while riding between Chelmsford and London. Overtaken by a sudden rain storm he changed over into the *Deprofundis.*

5 *yelds . . . reach*] yields dominion to the rain.

8 *doth rudenesse me apeach*] does rudeness accuse me of being rude.

66 Intro. The seat of the Dive family was at "Broomeham" in Bedfordshire, and Lewis Dive was a prominent figure in affairs of the county, as is shown by the mention of his name in various records. Through his

Poem   Line

mother, Lewis was a cousin to the Lord Grey of Wilton. With William, Lord Grey, he was present at the surrender of Guisnes. At Calais both Grey and Dive were captured and the necessary ransom cost Grey his estates at Wilton, and Dive, considerable litigation. The latter was by this time married to Mary, daughter of Sir William Strickland of York, by whom he had one son John Dive, who in turn married Douglas, daughter of Sir Anthony Denny of Hertfordshire, Knight Groom of the Stole to Henry VIII. Gascoigne dedicated *A delicate Diet* to Lewis Dive and in the dedication referred to "my Brother John Dive." Clearly then, the poet numbered the Dive family among his friends. Why the present poem adopts such a highly moral tone can only be explained on the ground that it was written when the poet's fortunes reached their ebb in the litigation of 1562-71 and when, as a result, Gascoigne's reformation had begun.

66   5   *puttocke*] a scavenging bird of the kite family.

        6   *kight*] kite, a scavenging bird of prey to which Gascoigne compares himself throughout this poem. The conceit is somewhat savagely developed, but it must be remembered that Gascoigne was at the ebb of his fortunes when this poem was written, probably in 1570 or 1571. The poem following is dated 1572.

        19   The kite was a common bird in London where he scavenged the streets for refuse.

        21   *hennes poore progenie*] The kite preyed on chickens.

        31   *of faulcon's kinde*] She possessed the noble qualities of the falcon.

        41   *alight*] a little.

        46   *Surquydrye*] peevish pride, as Gascoigne says. The word is frequent in Spenser and the following stanza will illustrate his usage of it.

> They were faire Ladies, till they fondly striv'd
>   With th'*Heliconian* maides for maistery;
>   Of whom they over-comen, were depriv'd
>   Of their proud beautie, and th'one moyity
>   Transform'd to fish, for their bold surquedry,
>   But th'upper halfe their hew retained still,
>   And their sweet skill in wonted melody;
>   Which ever after they abusd to ill,
> T'allure weake travellers, whom gotten they did kill.
>   (*Faerie Queene*, II, xii, 31)

        48   *row* etc.] frequent proverb denoting a limit to one's ability.

        59-60 *peacocke* etc.] Cf. note to l. 26, poem 26.

        62   *kepe close my creast*] keep my crest (continuing the kite analogy) at home.

Poem	Line	
66	72	*goonshot of calamitie*] This seems to enforce the idea that the poem was written when the poet was in financial straits.
	82	*tooth picke*] and yet in the next poem, l. 107, the toothpick is condemned as being Italianate!
67	Intro.	Professor Moore-Smith has done a notable piece of work in tracing the history of the Withypoll family as it appears in various records. From this I have derived all my information concerning the family and Bartholomew.

Prof. Moore-Smith suggests a possible explanation of this poem on the basis of the will of Edmund Withypoll, the father of Bartholomew. This document says that the second son is to enjoy, until the age of twenty-five, the revenue from certain funds invested in the Bank of St. George at Genoa. It was probably to get this revenue that Bartholomew was journeying to Genoa. Presumably he had been there before on a similar mission, since Gascoigne refers to "his latter journey to Geane." The connection of the family with Italy is obscure. Edmund is described several times as "Vedipolo," but why he possessed this alias is unknown. Certainly there is cause, in the present poem, to wonder if Bartholomew's journey was only concerned with his inheritance. This was, however, the last journey to Genoa for "Bat," since our next news of him is in the burial register of St. Margaret's, Ipswich, for the year 1573: "Bartholomewe Wythypoll, the sonne of mayster Edmunde Wythipol esquyer, and of maystres Elsabeth hys wyfe was buryed yn this Churche the xxvi day of the moneth of November beiynge Thursdaye."

	5	*gape*] jape. Puttenham's explanation of this word (*Arte*, ed. Arber, p. 260) clarifies Gascoigne's meaning: ". . . as one that should say to a young woman, I pray you let me jape with you, which is indeed no more but let me sport with you. Yea, and though it were not so directly spoken, the very sounding of the word were not commendable . . . for it may be taken in another perverser sense by that sorte of persons that heare it."

This seems to be Gascoigne's meaning as is witnessed by the "so plaine" of line 6. In fact, the whole poem seems a humorous teasing of "Bat" rather than a serious poem of advice.

	12	*bone*] to gnaw upon, to puzzle over.
	13-14	*grave advise . . . full geazon*] good advice which is lacking in his own head.
	22	*thy due*] the revenue from St. George's Bank?
	25	*Thy good Companion*] In l. 146 Gascoigne promises to pray for Pencoyde, who is identified by a marginal notation in *The Posies* as Sir William Morgan of Pencoyde. Lines 146-51 give the additional information that if one James a Parrye makes good what he has said, then Gascoigne will meet "Bat" and Morgan at Spa in August. What

Poem   Line

all this means I do not know, but it would seem that some adventure was afoot.

Sir William Morgan was a soldier of fortune in the wars in France and Holland and in the spring of 1573 went to Ireland in search of further adventures. It is known that Morgan was in England during the winter of 1572-73 and he may well have been there the previous winter.

Whether the date of 1572 means 1571/2 or 1572/3 is also uncertain. I had originally thought that it was 1572/3, but the tone of the poem, its lack of references to martial experiences, and the promise to meet in August now incline me to date it as 1571/2, before Gascoigne first embarked on his military career. Gascoigne would hardly have planned a trip to Spa in August during the winter of 1572/3 when he was so busily engaged in securing a patron and in publishing his works.

67   39   *them, whiche fled*] probably the Catholic exiles who fled from England during the early years of Elizabeth's reign.

    46   *Da, da, sir K*] The significance of these words I have been unable to ascertain.

    46   *maye not come at you*] may have nothing to do with you.

    49   *foolishe . . . boye*] perhaps "Batte" himself. Gascoigne may be alluding to a previous trip of Withypoll's.

    61   *poyson*] typical of the charges made by Englishmen against the Italians.

    64   *paper*] the bills of credit, mentioned in the next line. Cf. note on the Introduction to this poem.

    69   *the shelles of Christe*] Neither the shell worn by pilgrims to St. James of Campostella, nor the slang for money can explain this. What it does mean, I cannot say.

    73   *fico*] fig. Figs were a common means of poisoning. A rumour was current that Leicester poisoned Sir Nicholas Throgmorton by means of fig salad (Strickland, *Lives of the Queens of England*, IV, 589).

    73   *foysted*] concealed.

    75-76   *Beware therefore . . . a Letter*] feed on fish rather than eat the more desirable meat (*fyne fleshe*) which is accompanied by poison.

    78-80   *Spanishe soape*] This cannot mean Castile soap as the *O.E.D.* suggests for this passage; rather it is poisoned soap which leaves its poison in the clothes which are washed with it. The Spaniards, as well as the Italians, are villains!

    82   *Spanishe wooll*] wool steeped in poison which, stuffed in a saddle, would penetrate the clothing of anyone using it. Cf. preceding note.

    83   *toye*] a poisoned instrument which would infect the rider.

    84   *legges may swelle*] a symptom of poisoning.

    86   *before an other taste*] to avoid poisoned drink.

Poem	Line	
67	88	*Bumbaste*] stuffing for clothes but here presumably bumbast that has been poisoned.
	90	*haire . . . to glyde*] a common symptom of poisoning.
	91	*Straungers . . . feate*] strangers are clever in many a subtle trick.
	101-103	*oure Countreymen . . . Devils incarnate*] an echo of Ascham's words in *The Scholemaster*:

> . . . hear what the Italian saith of the Englishman, what the master reporteth of the scholar; who uttereth plainly what is taught by him and what is learned by you saying *Inglese Italianato è un diabolo incarnato*, that is to say you remain men in shape and fashion, but become devils in life and condition.

	107	*pyketoothe*] toothpick, but cf. note to l. 82, poem 66.
	109	*Coptanckt hatte . . . Flemmishe blocke*] a high crowned hat in the form of a sugar loaf made on a Flemish block or form.
	111	*slender sloppe* etc.] wide baggy pantaloons tightly fitted at the waist and over the buttocks.
	112	*curtold slipper*] pointed slipper. Slippers with great curling toes, some with bells hanging from the point of the curl, were among the extravagancies of dress which Ascham and others claimed were imported from Italy. It was indeed true that many an Elizabethan courtier wore his fortune on his back, and we can understand how Gascoigne came to squander his wealth in his attempt to follow the fashion at Court.
	114	*Marquise of al Beefe*] presumably a ridiculous name to indicate an upstart.
	121	*this . . . double P*] omitted in *The Posies*. Gascoigne's last "P" in the *Flowres* is "Papistrie," but in *The Posies* it is altered to "piles and pockes." All alterations are noted in Variants in *The Posies*.

> The reason for this alteration must be the same as that which caused the omission of the anti-Catholic references in poem 62. Cf. note to ll. 27-28, poem 62.

| | 132 | *Atheist*] The significance of the term "Atheist" is pointed out by Dr. Boas, who says: |

> The term 'Atheism' had in the sixteenth century much of the sweeping sinister associations that 'Bolshevism' has in the twentieth. It was a useful slogan with which to denounce doctrines or actions that challenged constitutional ecclesiastical or secular authority.
>
> (*Christopher Marlowe*, Oxford, 1940, p. 109)

> The charge of "Atheist" was directed at Gascoigne by his creditors. Cf. Introduction, p. 16.

| | 146 | *Pencoyde*] Sir William Morgan of Pencoyde, as a marginal note in *The Posies* tells us. |

Poem   Line

67   147   *James a Parrye*] Perhaps the same James a Parry who was involved in litigation with Sir John Scudamore (cf. notes to poem 47) and who fought with the justices of Hereford (St. Ch. 5, A 8/10, A 55/33, A 29/5).

       150   *Spawe*] Spa, near Liège in Belgium. What plans were afoot, we do not know. In August Gascoigne was engaged in the siege of Ramykins, a considerable distance from Spa.

       154   *Take it in gree*] take it in good part.

68   Intro. *capitaine Bourcher*] This captain was killed in a skirmish near Middleburgh in the late summer of 1573 (Sir Roger Williams, *Actions in the Lowe Countries,* p. 80).
                the tale of a stone] almost a macabre device when the "posy" is noted.

       27   *Gods foes*] Catholic Spaniards. This was altered to "his foes" in *The Posies.* Cf. notes to l. 121, poem 67, and ll. 27-28, poem 62.

       43   *Finis . . . Marblestone*] Since the epitaph is described as "the tale of a stone" this substitute for a regular "posy" is understandable.

69   Intro. *Viscount Mountacute*] Anthony Browne, Viscount Montague had his seat at Cowdray House, Midhurst, Sussex and his town house in Southwark. He was a prominent Catholic and had been a member of Queen Mary's Privy Council. The Dormers, likewise, were a Catholic family, although Sir William seems to have been leaning to the Protestant cause since we know that he and his wife were in dispute over this wedding. Sir William's daughter by his first marriage to Mary Sidney was Jane, Duchess of Feria, whose correspondence reveals that she favored the alliance since it would strengthen the position of the Dormers in the Catholic world. Perhaps his friendship with Montague, who was presumably instrumental in securing Gascoigne's election to Parliament, led to the excision of anti-Catholic references which has been noted in poems 62, 67, and 68.
                This double wedding took place sometime after Sept. 15, 1573, as we learn from a protest to the Revels Office by Thomas Giles, a haberdasher whose costume-renting business had been injured by competition from the Yeoman of the Revels. The Yeoman had lent "into the contre to the maryage of the dawter of my lorde Montague . . . the coper clothe of golde gownes" and another masque. None of these costumes were used in the present masque since Gascoigne tells us that one reason for his composition was to furnish an excuse whereby the eight gentlemen (relatives of Lord Montague) could utilize their Venetian garments.
                Giles' reference to "the contre" would at first indicate that the marriages were celebrated at Cowdray House, but reference to the masque shows that at least part of the festivities were cele-

Poem   Line

brated at Montague House, in Southwark. The storm-tossed voy-
agers explain their presence by saying that they made their way up
the Thames to London where the "pouer boy," the narrator, heard
of the wedding and so decided to attend with his Venetian relations.
The arrival in London on the day of the wedding and the appear-
ance of the masquers on the same day would suggest Montague
House, rather than Cowdray.

The source of the details regarding the siege of Famagusta has
been found by Dr. R. R. Cawley (*Modern Language Notes*, XLIII,
296-300). According to Dr. Cawley, Famagusta fell on August 15,
1571, and Count Nestor Martinengo who had been present wrote
a lurid account which was published at Verona in 1572. Sometime
in the same year William Malim, headmaster successively of Eton
and St. Paul's, made an English translation entitled *The true Report
of all the successe of Famagosta, of the antique writers called Tamas-
sus, a Citie in Cyprus . . . Englished out of Italian by William Malim
. . . Imprinted at London by John Daye. An. 1572.* Dr. Cawley
does not attempt to date this edition more exactly, but it seems likely
that Malim could hardly have been ready for publication much be-
fore the summer. The Italian edition appeared in 1572 and it was
necessary to bring a copy to England before translation began. Cf.
George Gascoigne, pp. 57-58, 173-77.

69   11   *glittering golden gite*] the elaborate costume (gite) of the masque.

        25   *Soldado*] soldier.

        37   *Rhodes*] the eastern Mediterranean island, a stronghold of Knights of
              St. John until 1525.

        41   *Chios*] one of the Aegean islands.

        45   *Zechynes*] a Venetian coin derived from "Zecca," a unit or place of coin-
              age.

        49, 50 The double commas indicate not a quotation but an important passage.

        56   *pheares*] fers, the old name of the Queen in chess.

        67   *rest*] residue, that which remained after paying his ransom.

        68   *idlenesse*] *The Posies* substitutes "ydle rest," presumably because of the
              rhyme.

        70   *Finestre*] the most westerly headland of Spain.

        71   *Marrocchus streights*] straits of Gibraltar.

        72   *Cyprus*] This eastern Mediterranean island was the scene of almost
              constant warfare between Turk and Christian.

        77, 78 Cf. note to ll. 49, 50.

        79   *sentence*] sententia (Lat.), platitude.

        88   *to give* etc.] to avoid such fury.

        97   Cf. note to ll. 49, 50.

        99   *pheares*] here the usual meaning of "companions."

Poem　Line

69　107　*fends*] fiends.

127　*braying*] harsh.

130　*groveling*] prone, from the Middle English adverb "grovelinge." Here an attitude of prayer.

138　*render*] surrender.

140　*sillie cage*] weak prison. Their ship is weak or simple (*sillie*) and it is indeed a prison.

153　*peece*] fortress, stronghold; so used by Spenser in *F.Q.*, II, xi, 14.

156　*Bragadine*] the governor of Famagusta. This detail of his torture is to be found in Malim.

158　*Mustaffa*] leader of the Turks. Cf. note to l. 156.

168　*Prelybassa*] one of the Turkish commanders.

169　*Pant*] Lepanto (?), the gulf of Corinth.

173　*Argostelly*] the gulf of Argos (?).

176　*October*] On Oct. 7, 1571 the Christian fleet under Don John of Austria defeated the Turks at Lepanto, near the Gulf of Corinth. This Christian victory ended the Turkish threat against the Western World. The use of the word "last" may mean that these lines were written in 1571 or before Oct. 7, 1572; however, there is also the interpretation of "last year."

182　*pight*] placed.

190　*cruddy*] resembling curded milk.

190ff.　These details of battle were taken from Malim's account of Famagusta and applied to the battle of Lepanto. Cf. Dr. Cawley's article.

192　*lime unsleakt*] used to blind the enemy.

196　*halberts*] a long-handled weapon headed with a point and axe-like face.

196　*bills*] a long-handled weapon with a hooked cutting edge.

197　*harquebush*] a primitive matchlock rifle.

209　*in pound was pent*] literally, enclosed in the pound, but here the meaning seems extended to "was in a dangerous situation."

210　*generall*] Don John of Austria.

211　*Prely Bassa*] Cf. note to l. 168.

247　*son Dieu son droit*] The son quotes his father's wrods: "So shall we pay the debt, which unto God is due."

259　*armes*] This point is also made in Gascoigne's introduction to the masque.

280　*this Token*] *The Posies* has a further marginal annotation: "The Montacutes and Capels in Italye do were tokens in their cappes to be knowen one from another." The Montague-Capulet feud was, of course, known in the English translations by Painter and Broke of the Romeo-Juliet story.

292　*Kentishe coast*] A strange journey from the Adriatic to the coast of Kent caused by one storm!

295　*Siate* etc.] The second half of the line translates the Italian.

Poem Line
69 308-320   They arrived by gondolas on the day of the wedding, therefore the
              masque must have taken place in London and not at Cowdray House
              at Midhurst in Sussex. The fact that Montague had a residence in
              Southwark fits these details.

    342   *drumme*] A drummer was an integral part of most masques.

    346   *Tho. Bro.*] Thomas Browne, brother of the groom. (B.M. Add. MS.
              5689 f. 154.)

    348   Cf. note to l. 295.

    356   *tronchman*] The *tronchman* made the complimentary speech. Here there
              seems to be a social distinction between the *tronchman* who is a
              Montague and the "presenter" (the "pouer boy") who is an actor.
              Neither Chambers in his discussion of masques in *The Elizabethan
              Stage* nor Miss Welsford (*The Court Masque*) note any such dis-
              tinction.

    366   *Gentilezza*] gentility, good breeding (It.).

    380   *Servidore* etc.] "And I your Servant kiss your hands."

70   This is one of the important pieces of evidence which show that Gas-
              coigne was in England during the winter of 1572-73. Lines 67-68
              read: "But flussing fraies have taught him such a parte, That now
              he thinks the warres yeld no such gaine." The first reference which
              the poet makes to his experiences in the Dutch wars in "Dulce
              Bellum Inexpertis" (*Works*, I, 160) is: "For I have seene full many
              a *Flushyng* fraye, And fleest in *Flaunders* eke among the rest." I
              have shown elsewhere ("Gascoigne in the Low Countries," *R.E.S.*,
              April 1935) that the skirmishes before Flushing in which the poet
              was involved took place in the summer of 1572. Since the *Flowres*
              was published in the spring of 1573, and since Gascoigne refers to
              events in the summer of 1572 in a poem printed in the *Flowres*,
              then he must have hunted with Lord Grey between the summer
              of 1572 and the spring of 1573. Therefore, it is inescapable that
              Gascoigne was in England in the winter ("winter deare") of 1572-73.
              His return to Holland in March, 1572/3 is celebrated in poem 74
              (*q.v.*).

    Intro.   *L. Grey*] Arthur, Lord Grey of Wilton, who had succeeded to the title
              Dec. 25, 1562. The family seat of Wilton in the Wye valley having
              been sold to pay his father's ransom to the French, his residence
              was chiefly at Whaddon in Buckinghamshire. This hunt may, how-
              ever, have taken place on his estate at Wrest in Bedfordshire.
              cum Pertinencijs] with appurtenances.

    5   *carren*] a doe with young and therefore unfit for eating.

    7   *barren*] a doe without young and therefore edible. Cf. preceding note.

    18   *Philosophie*] Presumably this refers to his days at Cambridge.

    21   *lawe*] the Gray's Inn period.

Poem	Line	
70	22	*Litleton*] Sir Thomas Littleton, a justice of the Common Pleas, temp. Ed. IV. His famous law book was *Littleton's Tenures*.
	23	*dawe*] a jackdaw, a simpleton.
	25	*Fitzharbert*] Sir Anthony Fitzherbert, famous barrister, who published in 1514 *La Grande Abridgement*, the first attempt to systematize the whole law. Gascoigne obviously found this work most difficult.
	26	*Tully*] Marcus Tullius Cicero.
	31	*slippe the string* etc.] By sighting incorrectly (*winked wrong*) and then loosing the string he shot his arrow wide of the mark.
	33	*courtly grace*] his attempt to become a courtier.
	49	*buttened with gold*] a gold button in his bonnet.
	53	*Peter pence*] formerly a tax of a penny payable by each householder in England to the papal see. Here it is used in the derogatory sense of money used for bribery.
	62	*souldier*] his ventures in the Dutch wars.
	67	*flussing fraies*] Flushing frays.
	73-84	His objections to war.
	78	*sheare* etc.] And give the soldier ragged sheets for his pay.
	79	*stop*] stoop.
	80	*groveling*] drunk.
	81-84	*He cannot . . . contrarie pretence*] He cannot take their spoil from pillagers, saying that he is angry at their offence and is taking their plunder as punishment, although he is really doing it for his own advantage.
	91	*boane to gnawe upon*] thing to worry over.
	95	*blacke houre*] The stars at his birth were unfavorable.
	96	*Whyche framed* etc.] Which made me a luckless man on earth.
	105	*Parkyns*] John Parkins of the Inner Temple, who published in 1530 a text book of law, *Perutilio Tractatus*.
		Rastall] William, son of John Rastell the playwright, printer, and lawyer. William wrote several legal treatises.
		Dan Bracten] Henry Bracton, famous jurist, who between 1235 and 1259 wrote *De Legibus et Consuetudinibus Angliae* which Tottel published in 1569.
	109	*maystries*] mastery of several skills.
	110	*pricke*] the wooden peg in the center of the target.
	112	*white*] the white circle surrounding the center peg.
	116	*mule*] The Lord Mayors, at this time, rode on mules.
	130	*carrion carkas*] Cf. note to l. 5.
71	3	*share*] degree.
	16	*beames* etc.] An involved figure: *braverie* (extravagance) is the scorching sun whose beams wither the plants (wealth).
	34	*muckte*] mulched.
	40	*ruffe*] exalted condition.

Poem	Line	
71	42	*molde*] earth.
73	Concl.	*did the coste*] composed. He did that which the devises cost, *i.e.*, he composed them.
		Quoniam etiam humiliatos, amoena delectant] Pleasant places delight even those of humble station.
74	Intro.	The date of this poem is shown by references found in lines 103-110 and 305-06.
		Lorde Grey] Cf. note to Intro. of poem 70.
	1	*conceyte*] Gascoigne is once again pleased with his device; this time the parallel between his own life and his voyage to Holland.
	4	*in hazarde of repreefe*] at the risk of reproof.
	5	*Alderlievest*] best beloved, according to a marginal annotation in *The Posies.*
	12	*en bon gré*] in good worth, explained as in the preceding note.
	18	*starting hole*] a hiding place from which one could quickly escape.
	30	*leapt to clime*] sought to advance myself.
	32	*last March*] March 19, 1572/3. Cf. notes to ll. 103-110, 305-06.
	34	*Quinborough*] Queenborough near Gravesend.
	42	*ferly chaunce*] a strange trick of fate.
	50	*gate*] course or channel.
	57	*had reacht* etc.] a realistic picture!
	61	*The sonder sings*] The sailor who is sounding calls out.
	62	*Aloofe, aloofe*] turn the helm to the windward.
	64	*streame*] current or channel.
	65	*extremes*] presumably the shallow water and the current.
	66	*to Hull*] According to a marginal annotation in *The Posies* this phrase means "When all sayles are taken downe."
	69	From here on there are constant rude remarks about the Dutch. An interesting exposition of the English view of the Dutch based on these and other references in Gascoigne is found in Huizinga's *Tien Studien* (Haarlem 1926), pp. 201-239.
	69	*butterbitten jawes*] a contemptuous reference implying great eating (biting) of butter.
	72	*Ghy zijt te vroegh*] You be to soone, according to a marginal note in *The Posies.*
	73	*Tis niet goet tijt*] It is not good tide, as in the preceding note.
	76	*Albaes*] the Duke of Alva, commander of the Spanish forces in the Low Countries.
	78	*to tice* etc.] to entice us into this danger.
	79	*him selfe* etc.] The pilot was in equal danger, and his reasons for treachery might have been spite, hate, or hope of gain.
	87	*wond*] moved (the ship).
	89	*Pylats crafte*] the craft of Pontius Pilate. A play on words with the *Pylots* experience of the preceding line.

Poem	Line	
74	94	*To runne on head*] to act rashly.
	100	*plight*] This seems to be an unusual form of the past tense of "plot," in the sense of "plot a course." I can find no authority but I feel this is a valid explanation.
	101	*Dansk*] The *O.E.D.* does not favor the meaning "Danzig" which had been suggested for other uses of this word, but prefers "Denmark." Here, however, the preceding word is Denmark, and the inference seems to be that Dansk is something else, not a repetition, hence Danzig seems credible.
	102	*Frize*] Friesland.
	103-110	English ships had been barred from the Dutch ports since 1568; but in January 1572/3 negotiations between England and Spain opened them to English ships and merchants (Camden, *The History of* . . . *Princess Elizabeth*, 1675, p. 191). This poem could not, therefore, have been written before the spring of 1572/3, and so we may add to the 19th of March, the year date 1572/3.
	107	*unkouth*] unknown. The master explains his lack of knowledge of the port and channel of Brill as due to the absence of travel to that port.
	109	*a gospell on that mouth*] a blessing on those words. Gascoigne expresses a pious hope that the reopening of Brill will be profitable to English merchants.
	111	*sowne*] sounding, the channel.
	116	*to Hull*] Cf. note to l. 66.
	120	*Die tijt* etc.] It is good tide that know I well, from a marginal note in *The Posies*.
	132	*Edell Bloetts*] Lusty gallants, as in preceding note.
	133	*takyng up the borde*] a pun on the two meanings: (1) to sit down at the table to eat; (2) to tack (nautical).
	139	*fleete and flowe*] drift with the tide or current.
	169	*engrave*] impress strongly.
	173-74	*But there were* etc.] This is nicely ironic when compared with lines 198-199.
	175	*griefe to game*] Cf. note to l. 33, poem 8.
	179	*in dust*] to ruin.
	191	*halfe fraighted*] half unloaded.
	203	*chiefe companions*] Yorke and Herle, according to a marginal annotation in *The Posies*. Rowland Yorke was a notorious London roisterer who, it is said, introduced duelling with rapiers into England. Perhaps his most disgraceful act was his betrayal of the town of Zutphen to the Prince of Parma in 1587.
		Herle was probably William Herle, an agent of Walsingham's. Cf. *George Gascoigne* (pp. 63-65) for further information on these two companions.
	227	*bowge*] to suffer fracture in the bilge or bottom of a ship's hull.
	231	*Hoye*] a sloop-rigged coasting vessel.

Poem   Line
74   231   *flynging fast*] sailing rapidly; from the Middle English "flingen," to rush.
       238   *in carke*] in care, according to a marginal annotation in *The Posies*.
       272   *Pylot . . . Pilate*] Cf. note to l. 89.
       280   *close in clynke*] an allusion to the prison, the Clynke, in Southwark.
       283   *pynke*] a small boat, according to a marginal annotation in *The Posies*.
       292   Cf. note to l. 69.
              Bulbeefe] a term of abuse based on the idea of the toughness, the un-
              desirability of the meat of bulls.
       293   *Butter* etc.] By their very nature, they are made soft by eating butter.
       295   *double beere*] beer of double strength?
       296   *butterd beare*] a beverage of sugar, cinnamon, butter, and beer brewed
              without hops.
       300-01 *Harlem*] The siege of Haarlem began Dec. 11, 1572 and ended July 14,
              1573 (Grimeston, *A General Historie of the Netherlands*, 1627, p.
              392). Thus there is further internal evidence to show that this poem
              must have been written after March 19, 1572/3. Since the original
              "contents" (*q.v.*) describe this as "Gascoines last voyage into Hol-
              land in Marche," we can be certain of both his presence in England
              prior to March 1572/3 and a previous journey to Holland.
       307-15 *As how they traine* etc.] This passage is rather obscure, but it seems to
              allude to attempts by some Dutchmen who, by pretending to be
              drunk, sought to gain secret information from certain Englishmen.
              It would seem that Gascoigne had witnessed such attempts and knew
              the person in question, who may have been dissembling and giving
              false information.
       311   *brode before*] Cf. note to ll. 26-27, p. 87.
       323   *Masse* etc.] probably secret Catholic sympathies are indicated.
       328   *mother B*] presumably some notorious procuress.
       330   *Re: ceive*] Receive the first half of the word which ends the preceding
              line and let the rest of the word go.
       334   *Edel Bloetts*] lusty gallants.
       336   *met v: and anders niet*] with you and not otherwise. Each tells you and
              everyone else that she is chaste. Not glossed in *The Posies*.
       339   *Rouland Yorke*] From what is known of Rowland Yorke (cf. note to
              l. 203) this charge is probably true.
       344,345 *John Zuche . . . Ned Dennye*] Apparently *John Zuche* and *Ned Dennye*
              were companions of his former adventures in Holland, and are not
              with him on this trip. John Zouche may have been the younger
              son of John, Lord Zouche of Haryngworth. This nobleman died in
              1550, and thus may have had a son of an age to venture in the Dutch
              wars. Ned Denny was probably the illegitimate son of Sir Anthony
              Denny, and brother to Douglas Denny Dive. Such a man appears
              in letters of Arthur, Lord Grey and Sir Philip Sidney (Wright's
              Queen Elizabeth and Her Times, II, 147-48, 157-58). Both of these

Poem   Line

men tried to help Ned Denny to secure lands in Ireland where he had taken part in the wars.

74   349   *master Moyle*] probably a humorous reference to Sir Thomas Moyle, a Kentish man, and in temp. Henry VII Speaker of the House. He was famous as a heretic hunter and in this sense the reference would be appropriate! (Strype's *Ecclesiastical Memorials*, II, ii, 402; III, i, 156, 476.)

[From this point on, the notes refer to the poems of "Dan Bartholmew of Bathe" in sequence.]

"D.B."
Poem Line

Intro. *And nowe . . . of it*] Omitted in *The Posies* where is found this title instead: *The delectable history of sundry* adventures passed by Dan Bartholmew of Bathe.

historie] Cf. note to ll. 38-39, p. 96.

1   1-7   *To tell* etc.] Cf. note to ll. 38-39, p. 96.

20   *on*] to.

25   *now*] *The Posies* reads "neare." Such alteration might mean that the affair was continuing in 1575 when *The Posies* appeared or else that Gascoigne wished to emphasize the vacillations of the affair.

39   *did skamble there in skath*] struggled wildly. *Skamble* is an old form of scramble and *skath* means harm or damage.

43   *learned lore* etc.] Cf. ll. 101-04, poem 70.

49   *fastned fansie* etc.] turned his fancy (heart, disposition to love) to thoughts of love. The significance of the eyes and looks in the code of love is frequently noted by Gascoigne. Cf. note to l. 26, p. 52 and poems 11, 12.

57-84 *First for hir head . . . fond fooles apace*] This description of the lady is paralleled in many Renaissance poets. Cf. note to l. 17, p. 77.

57   *heares* etc.] This conceit of hair being wires of any one of a variety of metals was one of the most popular of the time. Wyatt (ed. Foxwell, I, 185), Turbervile (*Tragical Tales*, Rprt. of 1837, p. 296), Lilly (ed. Bond, I, 423), *Paradise of Dainty Devises* (ed. Rollins, p. 41)—all use the conceit in various ways. Shakespeare's "If hairs be wires, black wires grow on her head" laughs the figure out of court.

59   *crinet*] an individual hair.

68   *flinging fault*] grievous or disappointing fault. This seems to be an extension of the meaning of flingen—to rush.

69   *kits of Cressides kind*] loose, faithless women like Cressida. *Kit* was a slang term for a prostitute. Cf. note to l. 40, p. 103.

71, 72 *Dame Natures frutes* etc.] Her true character of faithlessness was never revealed in her face.

Poem	Line	
1	76	*That all* etc.] The lover could not see the arrow which had hit him, nor could he see fault in his lady.
	92-98	*Ferenda Natura*] the origin and significance of the name.
	100	*links of love*] Cf. note to ll. 22-23, p. 49.
	111	*Saint*] Cf. note to ll. 4, 5, p. 61.
	121	*stoupe*] strike or pounce.
	124	*pricke of kynde*] The goad of natural desire can never be eliminated.
	137	*webbe* etc.] probably an allusion to the proverb "walk unseen in a net." Cf. note to l. 24, p. 49.
	143	*marte*] martyrdom or smart. I can find no example of the use of this word, but its meaning seems clear.
2		This poem is an elaboration of the last half of "F.J." poem 8. The same persons and figures are here employed.
	1	*Pryams sonnes*] Paris and Troilus.
	7	*Shepheard*] Paris was tending sheep when he chose the most beautiful of the three goddesses, Juno, Minerva, and Venus.
	9	*first frutes*] a reference to Helen's abduction by Theseus.
	17, 18	*partched eares* etc.] a continuation of the agricultural figure of l. 10.
	19	*slivde*] stripped off the bough (*Slippe*).
	34	*Lollius*] the fictitious authority quoted by Chaucer (*Troilus and Criseyde*, I, 394 and VI, 1667).
	38	*leaper*] Thynne's *Chaucer* of 1532 contained Henryson's sequel to the Cressida story which told of her death as a leper. Howell (*Devises*, 1581, pp. 18, 19) also tells this story.
	65	*the writte* etc.] Cf. l. 366, poem 69.
	81	*Fato non Fortuna*] by fate not by fortune.
11	Intro.	I have placed this section by the Reporter where, according to its Introduction, it should have appeared in order to explain the transition between the "Triumphes" and the "Dolorous discourses." I have, however, numbered it according to its position in the *Flowres*. Cf. *Textual Notes*.
	4	*braggers boate*] a clear reference to the shipwreck described in poem 74, and which therefore shows that the remaining copy was sent to England soon after the poet's arrival in Holland. Further, the fact that by the time this arrived, it was too late to insert it in its proper place indicates that the printing was completed not long after April 1, 1573.
	22	*Saint*] Cf. note to ll. 4-5, p. 61.
	54	*greev'd* etc.] Cf. note to l. 33, poem 8.
3	1	*entreated care*] Strangely enough this entreaty is found as "D.B." poem 6 below.
	19-20	*When hote desire* etc.] Desire counted the torments which came from gazing at her less than the torments of lost freedom.
	26	*How I had layd* etc.] The ensuing account of the unhappy loves of his

Poem   Line

youth is directly opposed to the Reporter's statement that Dan Bartholmew had never been in love before ("D.B." 1, l. 100).

3   49-50 *goddesse of revenge* etc.] This theme is repeated in ll. 12-18, "D.B." poem 6.

55-56 *delight did . . . of thine*] Cf. l. 366, poem 69, and l. 77, "D.B." poem 2.

69-84 *I cannot now . . . thee resinde*] These lines tell practically the same story and employ much the same imagery as poem 10 (*q.v.*). For an explanation of these similarities see *George Gascoigne*, pp. 220-21.

89   *Tythe* etc.] Cf. l. 59, "D.B." poem 8.

94-110 Cf. poems 26, 38, and 45 for parallels to this.

119-124 *Cressides* etc.] the frequent Troilus and Cressida allusion. Cf. poems 28, 35, 39, 44, 46, 47, and 54.

128   *corosives*] the opposite of a healing plaster.

150   *Dover*] The fact that Edward Boyes, Elizabeth Bacon's second husband, came from Nonnington near Dover would seem to make this a reference to him, but for the objections to identifying "D.B." with Gascoigne, Elizabeth, and Boyes cf. *George Gascoigne*, pp. 219-220.

151   *Admyrall*] Lord Clinton was the Lord Admiral at this time, but there were a number of vice-admirals in many of the maritime counties. However, this might well be an allusion understood by only a few people.

161-67 *The Posies* has the following annotation: "These thinges are misticall and not to be understoode but by Thaucthour himselfe." Gascoigne has well preserved his secret!

163-64 *colours* etc.] evidently a livery. Vide Samuel Daniel's introductory letter to his translation, *The Worthy Tract of Paulus Iovius*. Cloth as well as color had significance. For an example cf. l. 19, p. 72.

181   *restlesse rest in Bathe*] In the *Grief of Joye* (*Works*, II, 530) Ferenda is apostrophized by Gascoigne as "my banishment to Bathe."

183   *skamble* etc.] Cf. note to l. 39, "D.B." poem 1.

199   *griefe for game*] Cf. note to l. 33, poem 8.

237   *I spy* etc.] *The Posies* has this annotation, "Another misterie."

242   *fazed*] unraveled.

245   *lace*] the bracelet which is braided, *i.e.*, laced.

272   *the noble face*] presumably the rival. I can offer no clue as to his identity.

280   *Surcuydry*] overweening pride. Cf. note to l. 46, poem 66.

289   *Graines*] the capsule of Amomum Meleguetta, also called Guinea grains.

292   *Ippocrace*] a beverage composed of red wine, spices, and sugar, said to be so named because a strainer was known as "Hippocrates sleeve."

293   *Ippocrace*] a pun between hypocrisy and Ippocrace which is continued for several lines.

338-343 Cf. note to ll. 19-20, p. 53.

4   This completely artificial effort must have been a very early poem since it uses seriously all the trite, ridiculous conceits which Gascoigne used humorously in poem 48 (*q.v.*).

Poem	Line	
4	6	*I cannot weepe, nor wayle my fill*] This lament is answered by poem 45 (*q.v.*).
	19-24	The mixture of figures in this stanza is nearly unintelligible: his thoughts are like a water wheel which cannot drown!
	31	*sorrowes smoke*] Cf. ll. 15-18, poem 48.
	43-48	*Wherefore I come* etc.] This seems to lead directly to "D.B." poem 6.
5		This seems to be a link composed at the time Gascoigne planned "D.B." Cf. *George Gascoigne*, pp. 212-13.
	13	*The rymes*] Another clue to the rival, but I can offer no solution. *The Posies* has this notation, "Another misterie."
6	Intro.	*libell*] This title is in keeping with Gascoigne's other legal poems. "Libell" is an anglicization of the latin "libellus" meaning a bill or petition presented to a court. Cf. other "legal" poems, 49, 53, and 56.
	4	*semerent sheete*] A semare was a loose white mantle worn by women; this seems to be an adjective from the noun, although I can find no other instance of its use.
	22	*webbe of . . . life*] Cf. note to l. 3, poem 4.
	41	*slept*] slipped.
	45	*hope*] A marginal annotation in *The Posies* reads, "Hope is ever contrary to a lovers Passion."
7		Another link probably written along with no. 5.
8		A legal poem in the same style as poems 49, 53, and "D.B." 6.
	1-4	Several scholars have tried to discover the poet's age from this. It would perhaps be feasible if we knew what date B.C. he used as that of the world's origin!
		For an interesting discussion of literary wills see E. C. Perrow's *The Last Will and Testament as a Form of Literature*, Trans. Wisconsin Acad. Arts and Sciences, XVII, Part I. The late Mr. E. Vine-Hall, from whose wide knowledge of sixteenth century wills I derived considerable information, discusses wills of the period in *Testamentary Papers*, London, 1928.
	15-22	*My bodie . . . do no more*] This elaborate conceit would undoubtedly have pleased the metaphysical poets of the next century.
	38	*fa-burden*] Cf. note to ll. 16-17, p. 93.
	59	*privie Tythes*] Cf. l. 89, "D.B." poem 3.
	64	*frydayes and wednesdayes*] fast days.
	69	*Supravisor*] the executors administered an estate, but were checked by a supervisor appointed by the deceased.
9		A link similar to nos. 5 and 7.
	4	*strings* etc.] a truly metaphysical conceit.
	5	*Christall yce*] I have been unable to find a similar use of this phrase which seems to be the soul or the life force.
	23-24	*It was thy will . . . yet but grene*] This reference to a youthful death is contrary to both the Reporter (ll. 50-51, "D.B." poem 1) and Dan

Poem   Line

Bartholmew himself (ll. 39-40, "D.B." poem 3). Certainly Gascoigne was not middle-aged as late as 1573, even by the standards of the day. It would seem that in writing the links Gascoigne did not bother to check the details by which he had attempted to conceal the autobiographical nature of the story, but rather relied on his own memory of what actually had happened. A similar lack of consistency is the Reporter's statement that Dan Bartholmew had never been in love before which assertion is contrary to Bartholmew's description of his previous love affairs.

10   The details here related show that this was written after nos. 3 and 8.

12   The unfinished nature of this shows haste in publication. It was probably sent back from Holland. The sudden ending may have resulted from the exigencies of war as did *The Grief of Joye* which ended in the middle of a line with the note *"left unperfect for feare of Horsemen."* (*Works*, II, 557.)

16   *on the mold*] on earth.

17-21   *I am . . . was borne*] All the verbs in these lines are changed to the past tense in *The Posies*. Such alteration may have resulted from one of two things: (1) Gascoigne wished to conceal that he was both the Reporter and Dan Bartholmew; (2) in 1573 when this was first written the affair may have been still in progress but by 1575, the date of *The Posies*, it was ended, and so at that time the past tense would be more accurate.

26   *And feele* etc.] Love's (*fansie's*) fire raises a smoke to make fools of my friends. Cf. poem 48.

29   *The force of frendship bound by holy oth*] Poem 20, which has this introduction, "This Sonet of his shall passe (for me) without any preface," uses almost identical words:

When stedfast friendship (bound by holy othe)
Did parte perforce my presence from thy sight.

When we add to this the facts that poem 20 was omitted from *The Posies*, and that the Reporter (ll. 50-56) confesses to a previous affair with Ferenda, we are faced with a mysterious problem. It would seem that Gascoigne and a close friend both loved Ferenda, but then the friend could hardly have been the rival of whom Bartholmew speaks in the "Dolorous discourses." Once again, we can only conclude with Gascoigne's own words, "These thinges are misticall and not to bee understoode but by Thaucthor him selfe."

43   *long since*] *The Posies* reads, "at first." Cf. note to ll. 17-21.

51   *Idoll*] Cf. note to ll. 4-5, p. 61.

58   *Walketh in a net*] Cf. note to ll. 22-23, p. 49.

Concl. Presumably the printer wrote this to supply an ending for the unfinished verses which he received from his author in Holland.

GLOSSARY

The glossary lists those words whose meanings seem obscure. (Naturally, a personal definition of "obscure" has to some extent been followed.) In general, frequently used words and those whose meanings do not require a lengthy explanation are here listed. Phrases and long explanations are to be found in the *Critical Notes*. The chief source of definition has been the *Oxford English Dictionary* with help from Skeat and Mayhew's *Tudor and Stuart Glossary*, and the same authors' *Concise Middle English Dictionary*.

If a noun appears in both singular and plural forms, only the singular is given. A verb occurring in various inflections is given as an infinitive. Variant spellings have been frequently noted in correct alphabetical order.

abjected, cast off, rejected.

affects, feelings, intentions, desires.

anoy, vexation, sadness.

apaide, satisfied, contented, pleased.

apeach, to impeach, accuse.

askances, as if saying.

assayes (at all—), at all events, in any case, always.

attones, at once.

bagges, stuffing for clothes.

bane (catch one's—), catch one's death.

bargynet, French dance.

bating, fluttering.

bear (—a note), to sustain, support (the burden or bass of a song).

begarded, variegated with colors.

behight, to promise.

bend, band across a shield (heraldic).

bend, border of a woman's cap.

bend, to incline.

bend (a sail), to extend or make it fast to its proper yard or stay.

bestow, to employ.

bet, past tense of beat.

bewray, to reveal, make known.

blinne, to remain.

bolstring, padding for clothes, puffing.

boorden, of boards, **i.e.** wooden.

borrell, unlearned, rude.

bost, boast.

bottom, clew or nucleus on which to wind thread.

bowne, boon.

braule (brake the—), left the dance.

braunce, branch.

braunfalne, thin, skinny.

brode (too—before), obvious.

browesse, mixture of broth and bread.

brute, to noise abroad.

brute, reputation, rumour.

bulbeefe, term of abuse.

bumbast(e), stuffing (for clothes). adj. stuffed.

by, (1) by.
    (2) concerning.

camerike, fine cloth from Kamerik in Flanders.

capacitie, active power or force of mind.

care, (1) regard.
    (2) grief, solicitude.

careful(l), sorrowful.

carefulnesse, anxiety, solicitude.

carelesse, lacking in consideration.

carke, distress, care.

carren, worthless, corrupt.

carrian, v. carren.

cartes, charts.

cast, (1) discarded.
    (2) condemned.
    (3) added up.

cast, to consider, ponder.

casting bottle, bottle for sprinkling perfume.

cates, bought provisions as distinguished from homemade, thus—choice viands, dainties.

caule, close-fitting woman's cap, often richly ornamented.

chaffayre, (1) traffic, trade.
    (2) goods for sale.

chancellour, secretary.

chase, haste, hurry.

cheare, (1) countenance.
    (2) frame of mind, cheerfulness.

cheere, v. cheare.

cheere (to make—), to make merry.

chere, v. cheare.

cherefull, of good cheer, gladsome.

chippe, worthless crust.

clappe, (1) abrupt explosive noise.
    (2) shock of misfortune, sudden mishap.

close (—conceit), hidden, secret.
clyves, cliffs.
collings, embracings.
commoditie, advantage, convenience.
compile, (1) to compose or collect an original work.
(2) to translate.
compyle, v. compile.
conceipt, (1) conception, thought, apprehension.
(2) device.
conceit, v. conceipt.
conceit (close—), hidden, secret.
concelebrate, celebrate together.
conceyte, v. conceipt.
congé, (1) bow on taking leave.
(2) departure.
congey, v. congé.
conject, to conjecture.
conster, to construe.
contentation, enjoyment, contentment, satisfaction.
cope, long cloak or cape, chiefly worn out of doors.
cordiall(e), medicine, food or beverage which invigorates the heart.
corosive, grief, annoyance.
corse, corpse, body.
coulored, feigned.
coumpt, to count, consider.
counterpoynt, counterpane.
coyfe, close-fitting cap.
crafte, (1) to attain, win.
(2) to make or devise skillfully.
(3) to exercise one's craft.
cubit, unit of length, 18-22 inches.
curtold, pointed.
cusshencloth, cushion case or covering.
despight(e), scorn, disdain.
despite, v. despight.
devise, (1) construction.
(2) action.
devise, (1) to construct, fashion.
(2) to resolve.
devoyre, dutiful act, courteous attention.
diet, (1) way of living.
(2) way of feeding.
dight, to prepare, make ready, as food.
discommend, to find fault with.
discypher, (1) to make out the meaning of.
(2) to discover, reveal.
disease, to deprive of ease.
disposition, (1) management.
(2) behaviour, mood.

distain, (1) to stain, to take away the color.
(2) to dishonor, defile.
disayne, v. distain.
distrein, to hold, constrain.
docke, rump, buttocks.
dolie, dolefull.
donne, down.
dragges, dregs.
drave, driven.

earst, at first.
eath, easy.
efte, a second time, again.
eftsones, soon afterwards, again.
eld, old age.
empeach, accusation.
enowe, enough.
ensignuate, to insinuate.
entre comoning, intercourse.
entreglancing, exchanging of glances.
entremeete, to meet together, mingle.
entronised, enthroned.
everychone, every one, each one.
expresse, to press out, squeeze out.
extremitie, unrestrained expression of emotion.
eyen, eyes.

fadome, fathom.
fantasie, fancy.
fare, appearance, condition.
faye, faith.
fearefull, full of fear, awe, reverence.
fearly, v. ferly.
fearse, fierce.
feere, companion, peer.
fend, fiend.
ferly, wonderful, strange.
firce, fierce.
fitte, experience.
flakes, sparks.
flittering, fluttering.
foist, light galley.
fond, to make foolish.
fond, foolish.
foyld, defiled.
fret, a gnawing away.
frette, to gnaw away.
front, forehead.
furniture, equipment, trappings.

gald (p.p. gald or galded), variant spelling of gaul, q.v.
gate, way, water-track.
gaul (p.p. gauled), to harass, oppress, annoy.

geare, affair, business.
geason, uncommon, scarce.
geast(e), guest.
gentils, gentlefolk.
gest, guest.
ginne, trap.
gite, gown.
glose, explanation. interpretation.
gondalaes, gondolas
goonshot, gunshot.
graffes, shoots, sprouts.
gramercy, thanks.
grappes, grapes.
grease (—a sheep), in order to preserve it from insects in hot weather.
gree, favor.
grote, silver coin worth 4d.
grutch, complaining, grumbling.
grutch, to grudge, murmur.
guerdone, reward.
guerison, good health.
gyglot, wanton girl.

hagger, wild, strange.
hallontyde, season of All Saints, first week in November.
handkerchewes, handkerchiefs.
hap, (1) chance, luck.
　(2) happening, occurrence.
hardely, boldly.
hardly, v. hardely.
hault, high.
heares, hairs.
hearne, heron.
heast, command.
hent, to catch.
hooches, chests.
humorall, of the humours.
humour, any one of the fluids which controlled health and temperament.

impe, young person.
inexprimable, inexpressible.
invention, literary composition.

jape, to play, to jest, jeer.
jet, to strut.

kite, scavenging hawk.
kyte, v. kite.

lap, loose or overlapping part of a garment.
lash, to drive.
lash (to leave in the—), to leave in the lurch.
leese, to lose.
lemman, unlawful lover.

lettes, hindrances.
lips (to lay on the—), to kiss.
list, (1) to desire, wish.
　(2) to be willing.
lode, load.
lust, pleasure.
lustless, listless.

make, mate.
manling, little man.
mannor, (1) manner.
　　(2) manor.
maystries, masteries.
mazor, large drinking bowl.
measne, land held from an over-lord.
meede, reward.
mell, honey.
merely, merrily.
minion, (1) lover.
　　(2) servile creature.
mought, might.
mould, bodily form.
mowldiwarpe, mole.
moyling, defiling itself.
muckte, manured.

nam, am not.
ne, not, neither—nor.
neate, cattle.
nill, will not.
noddye, simpleton, fool.
nonce (for the—), (1) for the occasion.
　　　(2) on the spur of the moment.
nouryture, nourishment.
nousled, brought up, educated.

pale, pallor.
pallad, pallet.
paradventure, by chance, perhaps.
paragon, (1) consort, mate.
　　(2) rival.
parchase, purchase.
pardie, by God!
parlee, conference for debating points in dispute.
parsonage, personage.
parties, parts.
pastaunce, recreation, pastime.
peare, pier.
peares, peers.
peason, peas.
pelter, paltry, peddling person.
pent(e), enclosed, confined.
percase, perhaps.

perdie, v. pardie.

perstande, understand, perceive.

pestred, thickly crowded.

pheare, companion, mate.

phip, imitation of the chip of a sparrow.

phippe, v. phip.

pickethankes, (1) tale-bearers.
　　　　　　　(2) flatterers.

pight, pitched, arrayed.

pile, large building.

pill, to pillage.

pilles, piles.

pillowbere, pillow-case.

pinfolde, place of confinement.

placket, slit in the seam of a skirt or petticoat.

playne, to complain, lament.

playster, plaster.

plight, to plot.

polshorne, tonsured.

porpentine, porcupine.

port coulez, portcullis.

porte, carriage, mien.

ports, gates.

poticare, apothecary.

pound, place of confinement.

povert, poverty.

pranke, to sport, caper, dance.

pray, prey.

prease, (n) press.
　　　　 (v) to press.

preasse, v. prease.

prest, ready.

pretence, purpose.

prety, ingenious, artful.

prime, spring.

prink, to set off, show off.

proyned, preened.

puttock, bird of prey of the kite family.

quest, body of men summoned to hold an inquiry.

quick (touch at—), to touch a tender spot.

quit, to requite, relieve, acquit.

quite, v. quit.

quyer, choir.

race, erase.

rathe, speedy, vehement.

reacht, retched.

reakes, pranks, wanton or riotous tricks.

reave, to plunder, deprive.

rechate, series of notes to call the hounds together.

recompt, to consider, reflect upon.

recule, to retire, go back.

recure, recovery.

remediles, without remedy.

repreefe, reproof.

resiaunce, residence.

reve, to plunder, deprive.

ripes, ripens.

roome, position, rank, station.

roon, to run.

rounding, whispering.

roundly, readily.

rueth, v. ruth.

russet, coarse homespun fabric.

ruth, sorrow, repentance.

sakeles, innocent, guiltless.

salve, to salvage.

sarcenet, silk material.

sarsenet, v. sarcenet.

sauce, to dress, flavor.

saufer, safer.

scout, scouting, guarding.

scute, shield (heraldic).

sect, class, kind.

seely, wretched, hapless.

seelly, v. seely.

selde, seldom.

semblant, demeanour.

semblant (to make—), to make a pretence.

shadow(es), (1) portrait.
　　　　　　 (2) unreal appearance.
　　　　　　 (3) reflection.

shente, put to shame.

shooen, shoes.

shoon, to shun.

shrich owle, screech owl.

shriking, shrieking.

shrowd, to take shelter.

sinderlyke, cinder-like.

sit, to be fitting.

sithens, since.

skamble, to struggle wildly.

skathe, harm, misfortune.

skowred, cleaned.

sleast, slayest.

slippe, twig, shoot (botanical).

slipper, slippery.

slipt, (1) lost one's footing.
　　　 (2) cut off, as a twig or shoot of a plant or tree.

sloppe, wide baggy breeches.

smoogskind, sleek- or smooth-skinned.

solle, sun.

some deale, somewhat.

sonder, one who measures the depth of water by means of a sounding lead.

sortes, fates.

soust, drenched.

sowst, v. soust.

soyle, sail.

spryte, spirit.

staine, to excell, surpass.

stayne, v. staine.

steed (in—of), instead of.

steine, v. staine.

steinch, to staunch.

stench, v. steinch.

stewes, brothels.

steyne, v. staine.

stocks, stockings.

stonde, barrel.

strange, alien, foreign.

streking, stretching.

strykes, springs (the trap).

suppose, supposition, conjecture.

swadde, clown, rustic.

swage, to assuage.

swelt, to faint, swoon.

tallents, talons.

tane, taken.

tare, tore.

tewed, brought into a proper state.

tewne, tune.

thewes, good qualities. But see Critical Note on poem 8, Intro.

thristie, thirsty.

throughly, thoroughly.

tickle, unstable, uncertain.

tikes, base fellows.

tilth, cultivation of the soil.

toome, tomb.

touche, to use, deal with.

toye, trifle, pl. trifling ornaments or things.

trace, course of action.

traine, to allure, entice.

traynes, artifices, stratagems.

trewant, truant.

tronchman, interpreter.

trull, strumpet.

twist, (1) thread of life.
(2) wick of a candle.

tyse (pp. tysed, tyste), entice.

unwares, unawares, suddenly.

unethes, scarcely, with difficulty.

unkouth, unknown, alien.

uttred, offered for sale.

veale, veil or covering.

violands, violins.

vytayle, victuals.

wale, the ridge in cloth, the warp.

waltering, weltering, rolling.

wanhope, dejection.

ware, aware.

warrantise, warranties.

waymenting, lamenting.

weale, prosperity.

weare, were.

wear(e), to wear away.

wearishe, listless.

weld, to endure.

whilome (whillome), formerly.

whipstockes, handles of whips.

white, center circle of an archer's target.

whitled, drunk.

whoary, hoary.

whot, hot.

whottely, hotly.

whylome, v. whilome.

wight, person.

wile, (1) will.
(2) v. wyle.

wond, (1) extricated.
(2) (naut.) to hoist sail.

wot(e), knowest.

wracke, destruction.

wrighte, to write.

writhled, wrinkled.

wroong, vexed, racked.

wroth, vexation, sorrow.

wyle, stratagem.

wynde, to blow (a horn).

yerks, jerks.

yfeere, together.

yfret, eaten, worn away.

younker, gay or fashionable young man.

ywis, certainly.

ywrapt, wrapped.

INDEX OF POEMS BY FIRST LINES

INDEX OF POEMS BY NUMBER